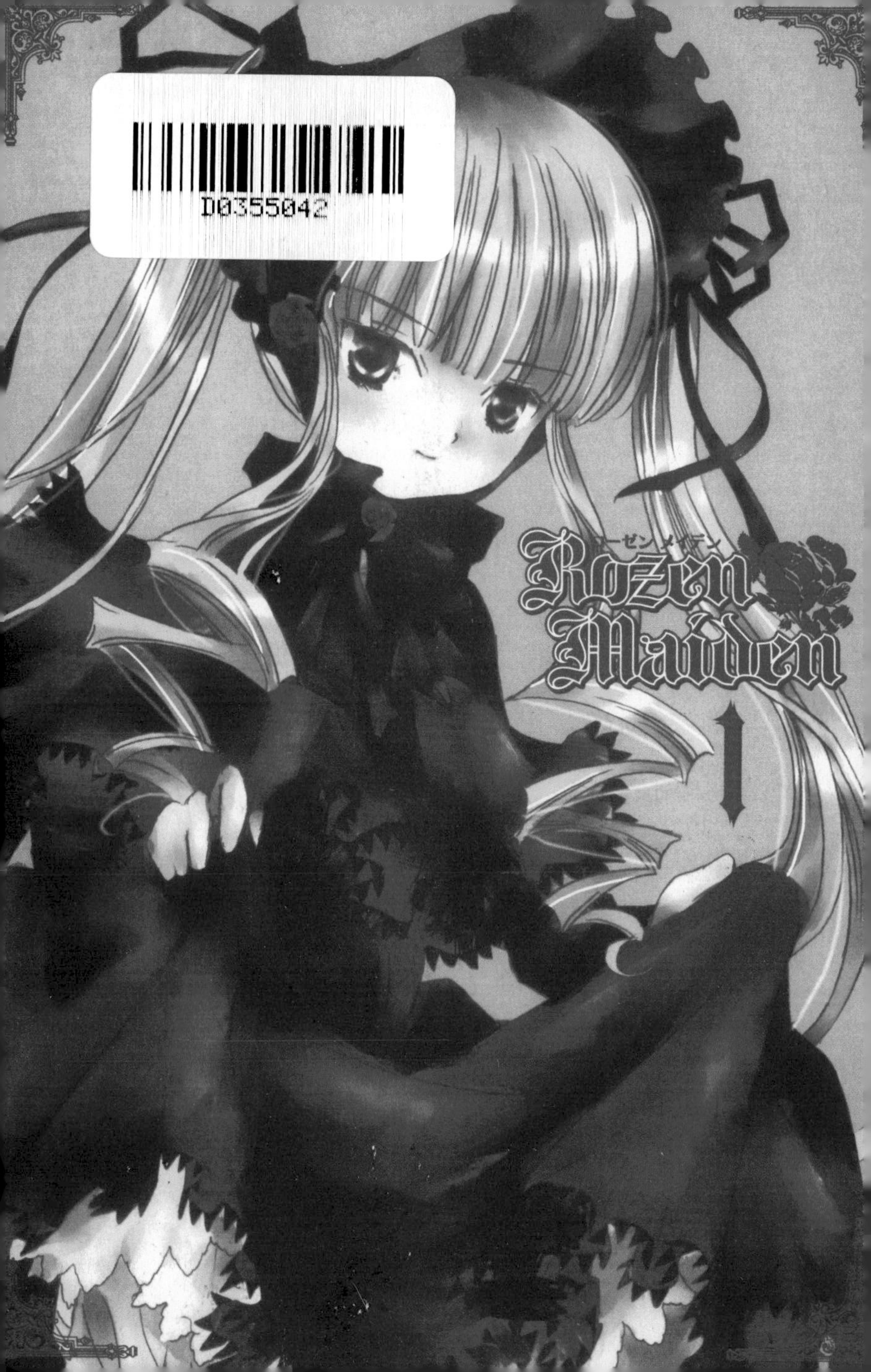
ローゼンメイデン
Rozen Maiden
1

Rozen Maiden Vol.1
Created by Peach Pit

Translation - Yuko Fukami
English Adaptation - Jerome Halligan
Copy Editor - Peter Ahlstro
Retouch and Lettering - Jennifer Carbajal
Production Artist - Jennifer Carbajal
Cover Design - Al-Insan Lashley

Editor - Luis Reyes
Digital Imaging Manager - Chris Buford
Managing Editor - Lindsey Johnston
Editor in Chief - Rob Tokar
VP of Production - Ron Klamert
Publisher - Mike Kiley
President and C.O.O. - John Parker
C.E.O. and Chief Creative Officer - Stuart Levy

A  Manga

TOKYOPOP Inc.
5900 Wilshire Blvd. Suite 2000
Los Angeles, CA 90036

E-mail: info@TOKYOPOP.com
Come visit us online at www.TOKYOPOP.com

ISBN: 1-59816-312-4

First TOKYOPOP printing: May 2006
10 9 8 7 6 5 4 3
Printed in the USA

PEACH-PIT

1

HAMBURG // LONDON // LOS ANGELES // TOKYO

Rozen Maiden

1

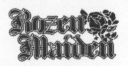

Table of Contents

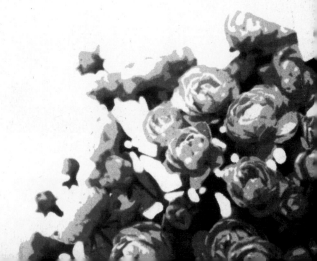

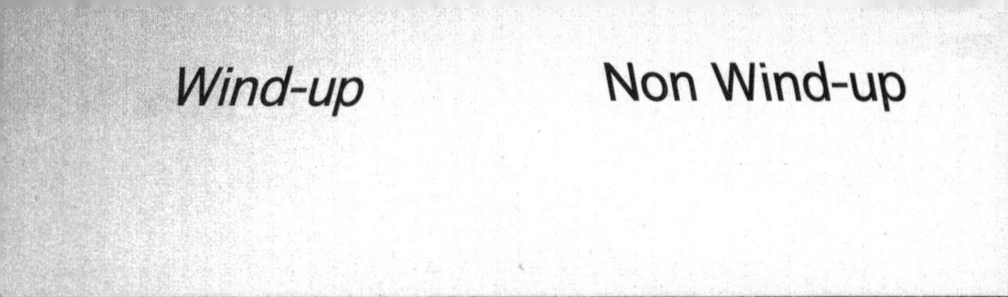
Non Wind-up
Wind-up

Prologue Part I

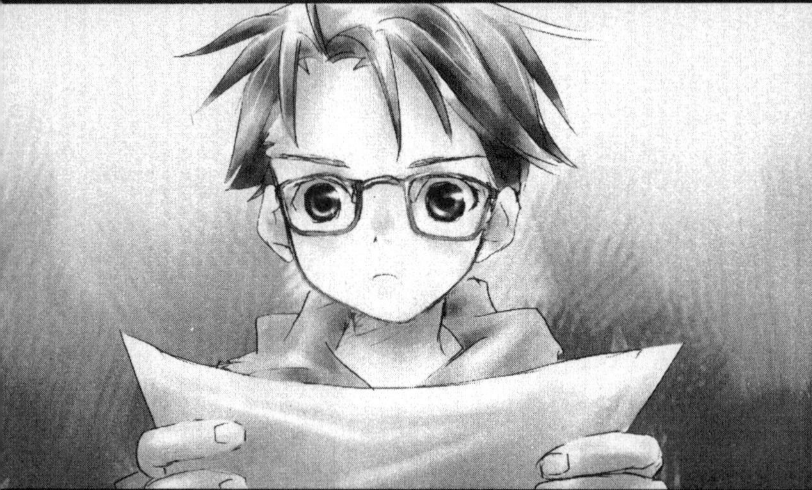

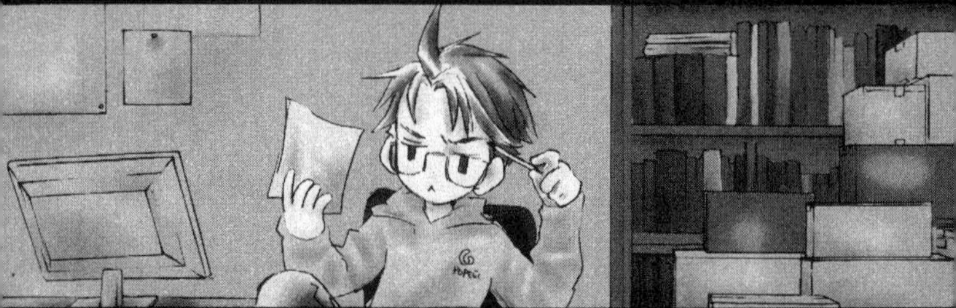

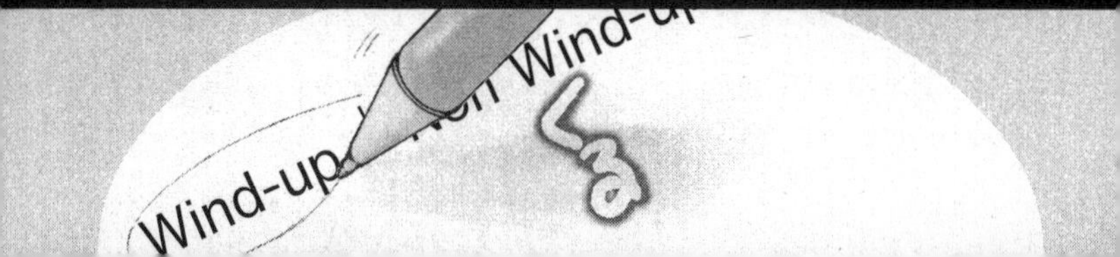
Non Wind-u
Wind-up

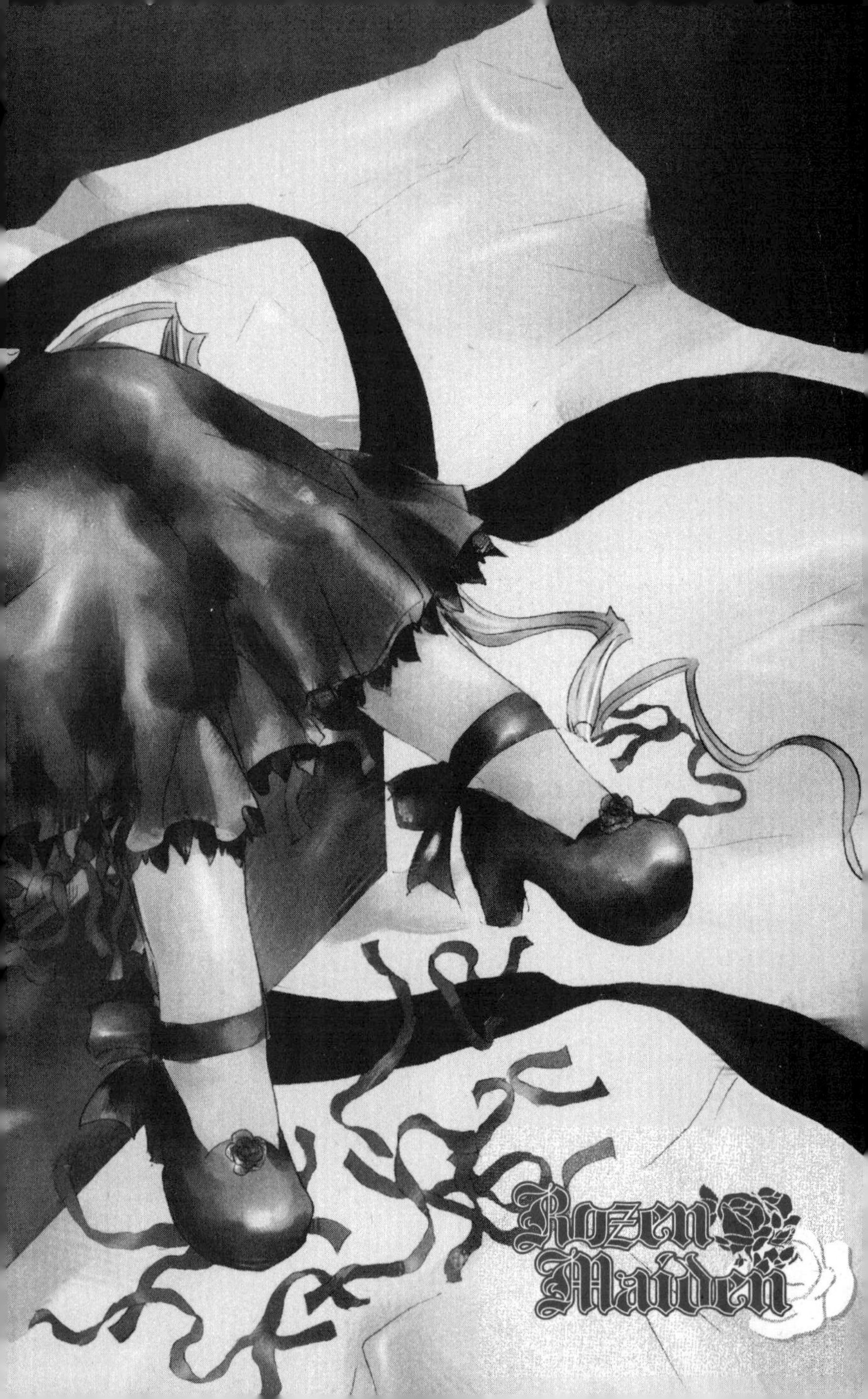
Rozen Maiden

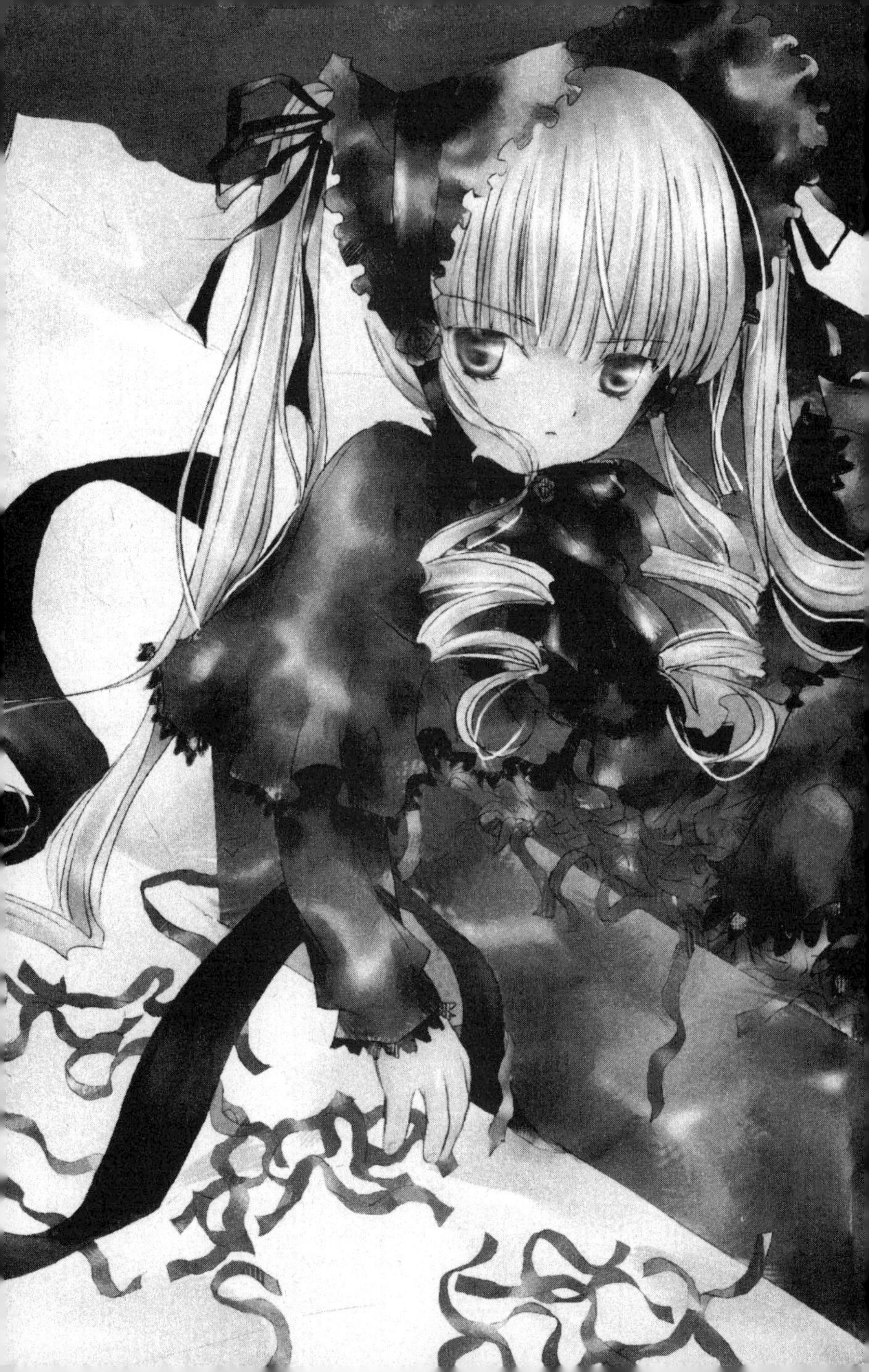

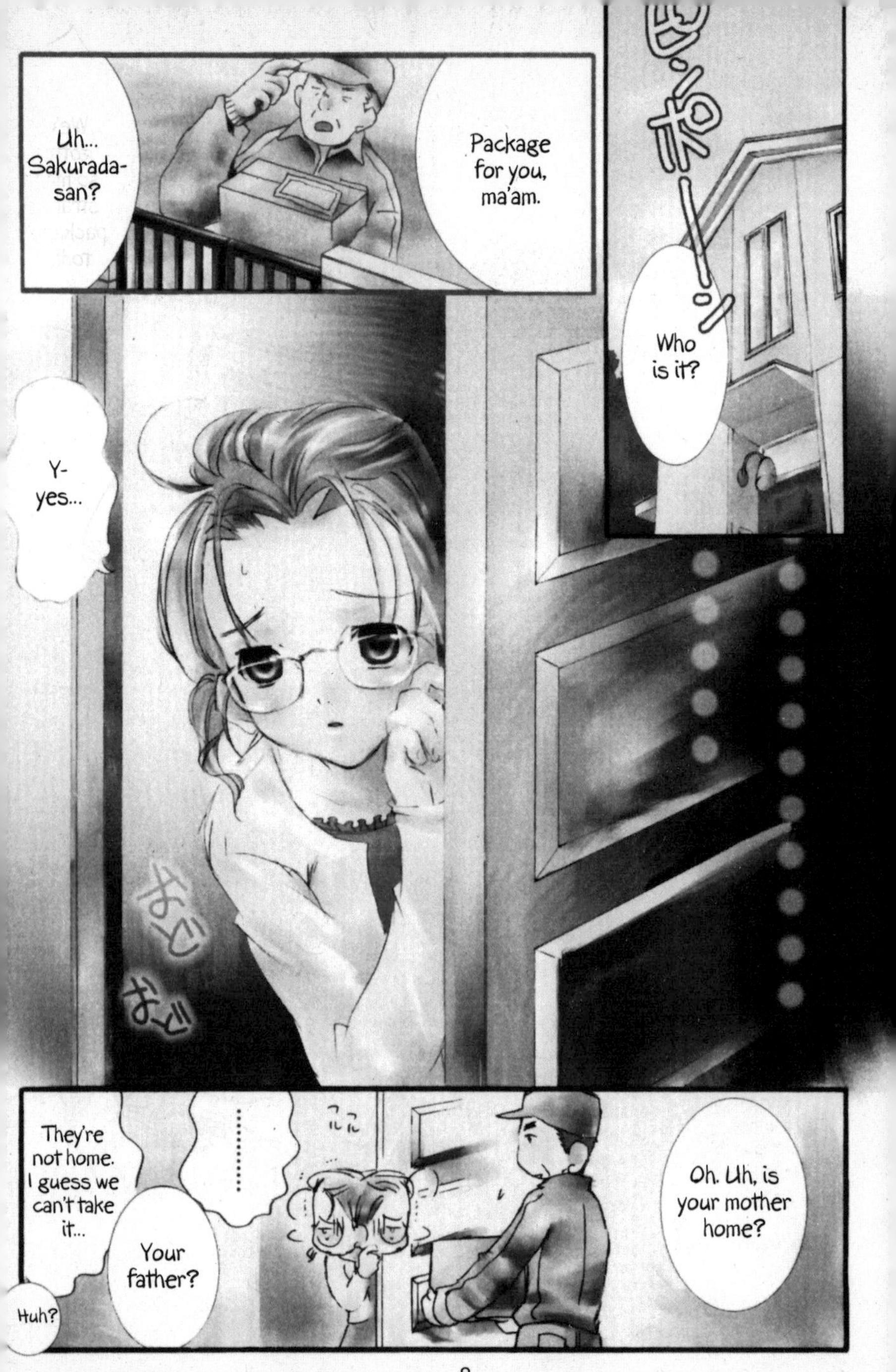
Who is it?
Package for you, ma'am.
Uh... Sakurada-san?
Y- yes...
おど おど
Oh. Uh, is your mother home?
....
Your father?
They're not home. I guess we can't take it...
Huh?

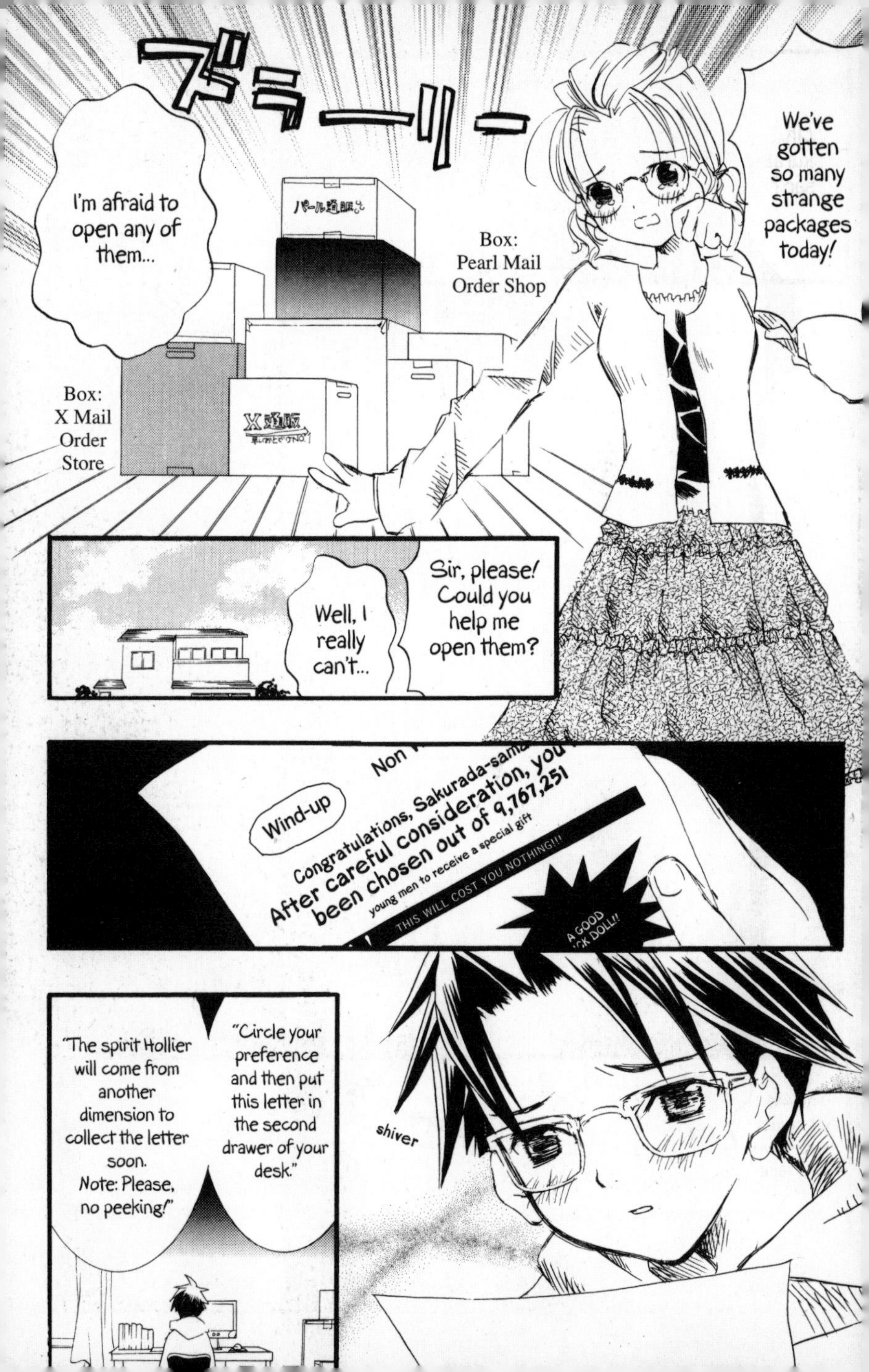

ズラーリー
We've gotten so many strange packages today!
パール通販
Box: Pearl Mail Order Shop
I'm afraid to open any of them...
X通販
Box: X Mail Order Store
Sir, please! Could you help me open them?
Well, I really can't...
Non
Wind-up
Congratulations, Sakurada-sama
After careful consideration, you
been chosen out of 9,767,251
young men to receive a special gift
THIS WILL COST YOU NOTHING!!!
A GOOD
shiver
"Circle your preference and then put this letter in the second drawer of your desk."
"The spirit Hollier will come from another dimension to collect the letter soon. Note: Please, no peeking!"

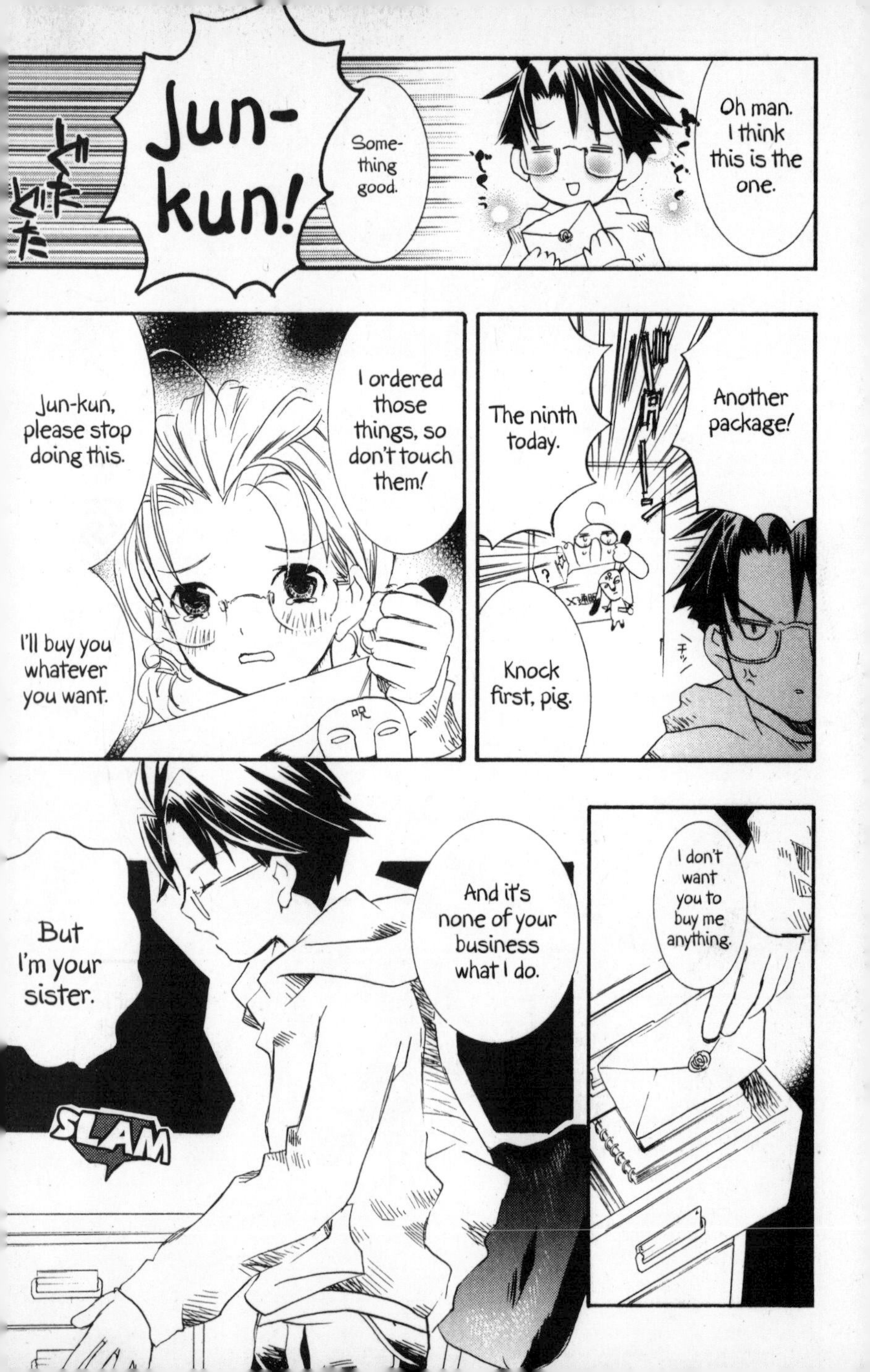
Oh man. I think this is the one.
Something good.
Jun-kun!
Another package!
The ninth today.
Knock first, pig.
I ordered those things, so don't touch them!
Jun-kun, please stop doing this.
I'll buy you whatever you want.
I don't want you to buy me anything.
And it's none of your business what I do.
But I'm your sister.
SLAM

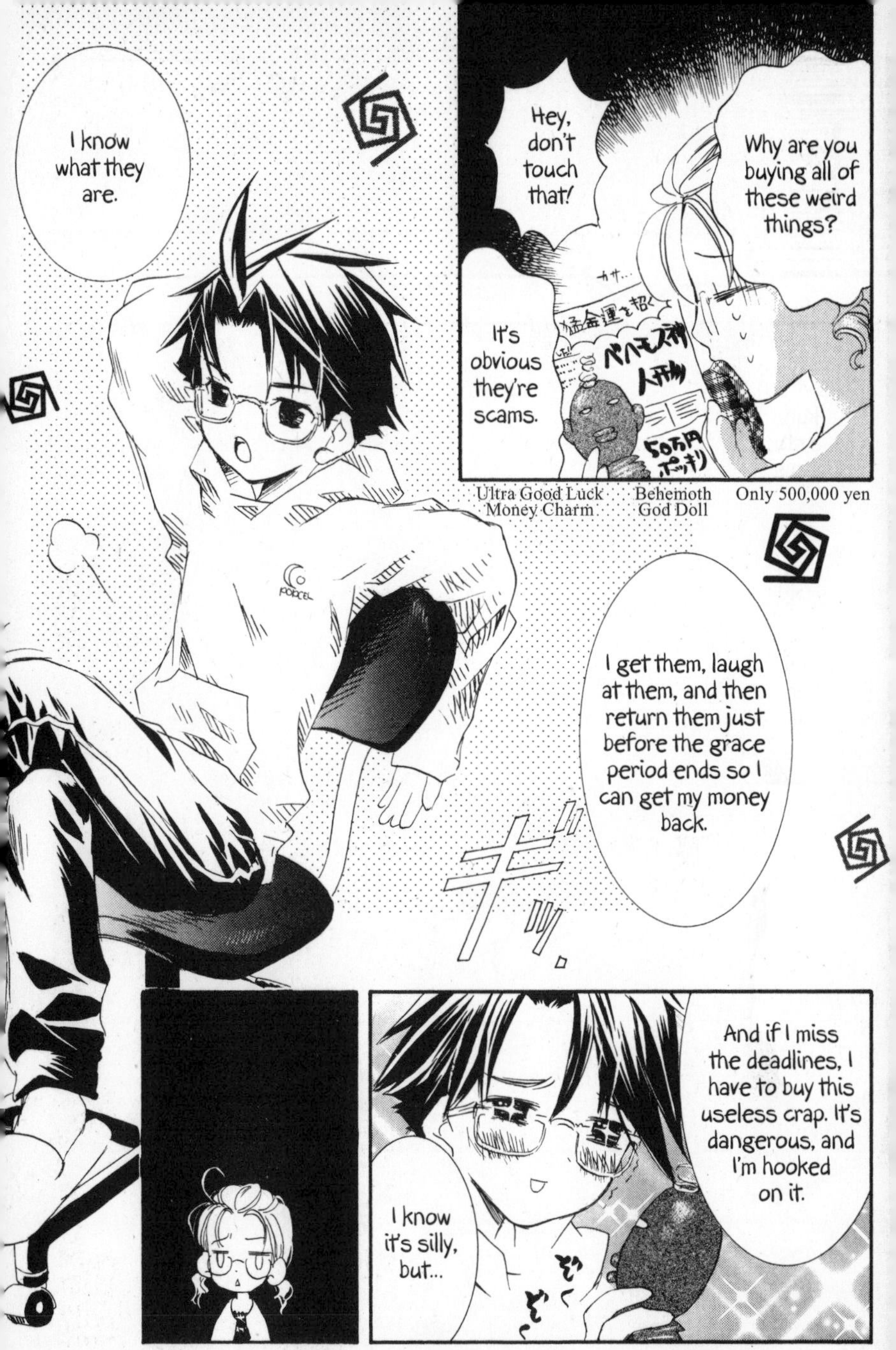
Why are you buying all of these weird things?
Hey, don't touch that!
カサ…
ベヘモス神人形
50万円ポッキリ
It's obvious they're scams.
Ultra Good Luck Money Charm
Behemoth God Doll
Only 500,000 yen
I know what they are.
I get them, laugh at them, and then return them just before the grace period ends so I can get my money back.
ギッ
And if I miss the deadlines, I have to buy this useless crap. It's dangerous, and I'm hooked on it.
I know it's silly, but...
どくどく

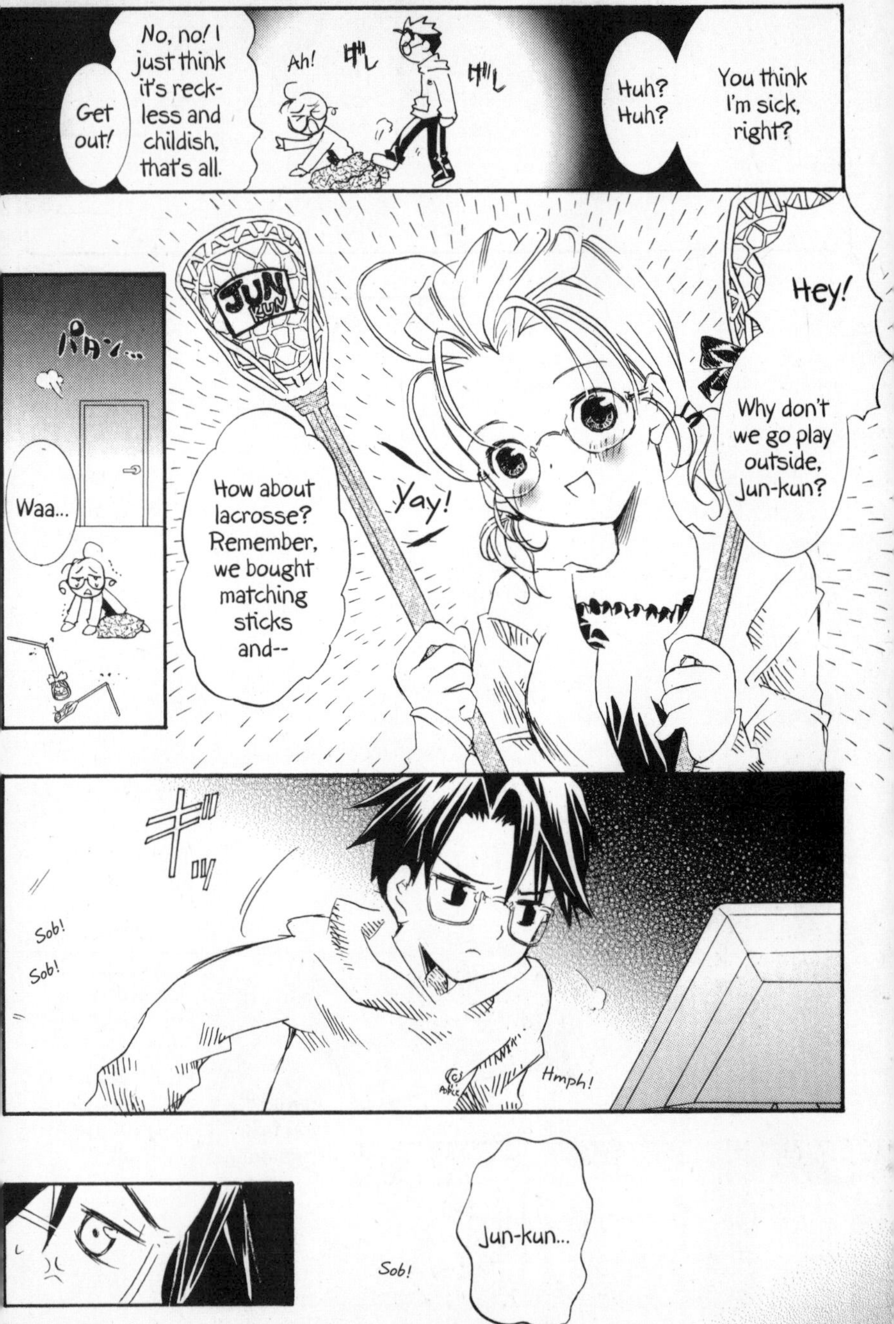
You think I'm sick, right?
Huh? Huh?
Ah!
No, no! I just think it's reckless and childish, that's all.
Get out!
Hey!
Why don't we go play outside, Jun-kun?
JUN KUN
Yay!
How about lacrosse? Remember, we bought matching sticks and--
Waa...
Sob!
Sob!
Hmph!
Jun-kun...
Sob!

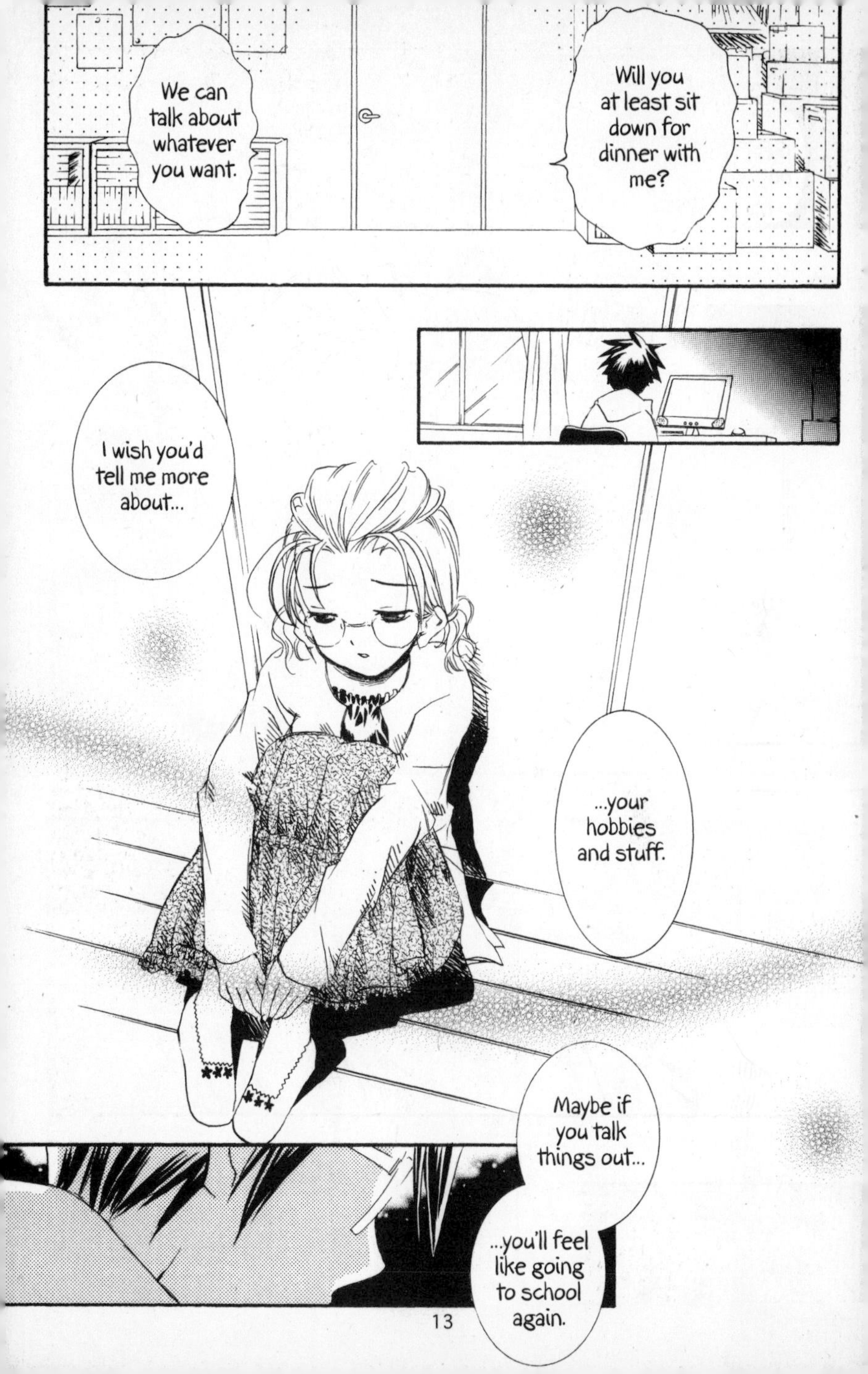
Will you at least sit down for dinner with me?
We can talk about whatever you want.
I wish you'd tell me more about...
...your hobbies and stuff.
Maybe if you talk things out...
...you'll feel like going to school again.

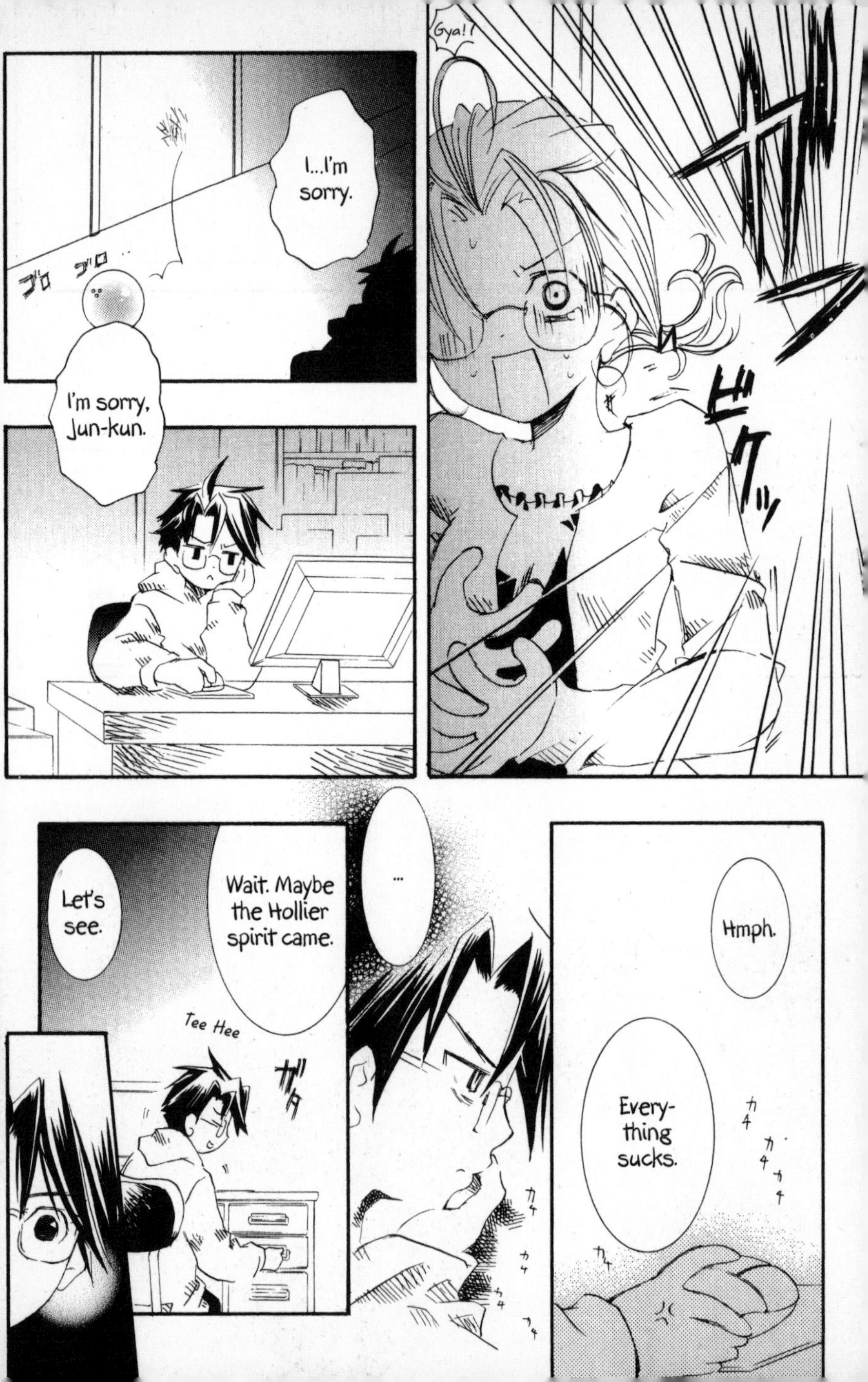
Gya!?
ビクッ
I...I'm sorry.
ゴロ ゴロ..
I'm sorry, Jun-kun.
Hmph.
Everything sucks.
...
Wait. Maybe the Hollier spirit came.
Let's see.
Tee Hee
ガタ

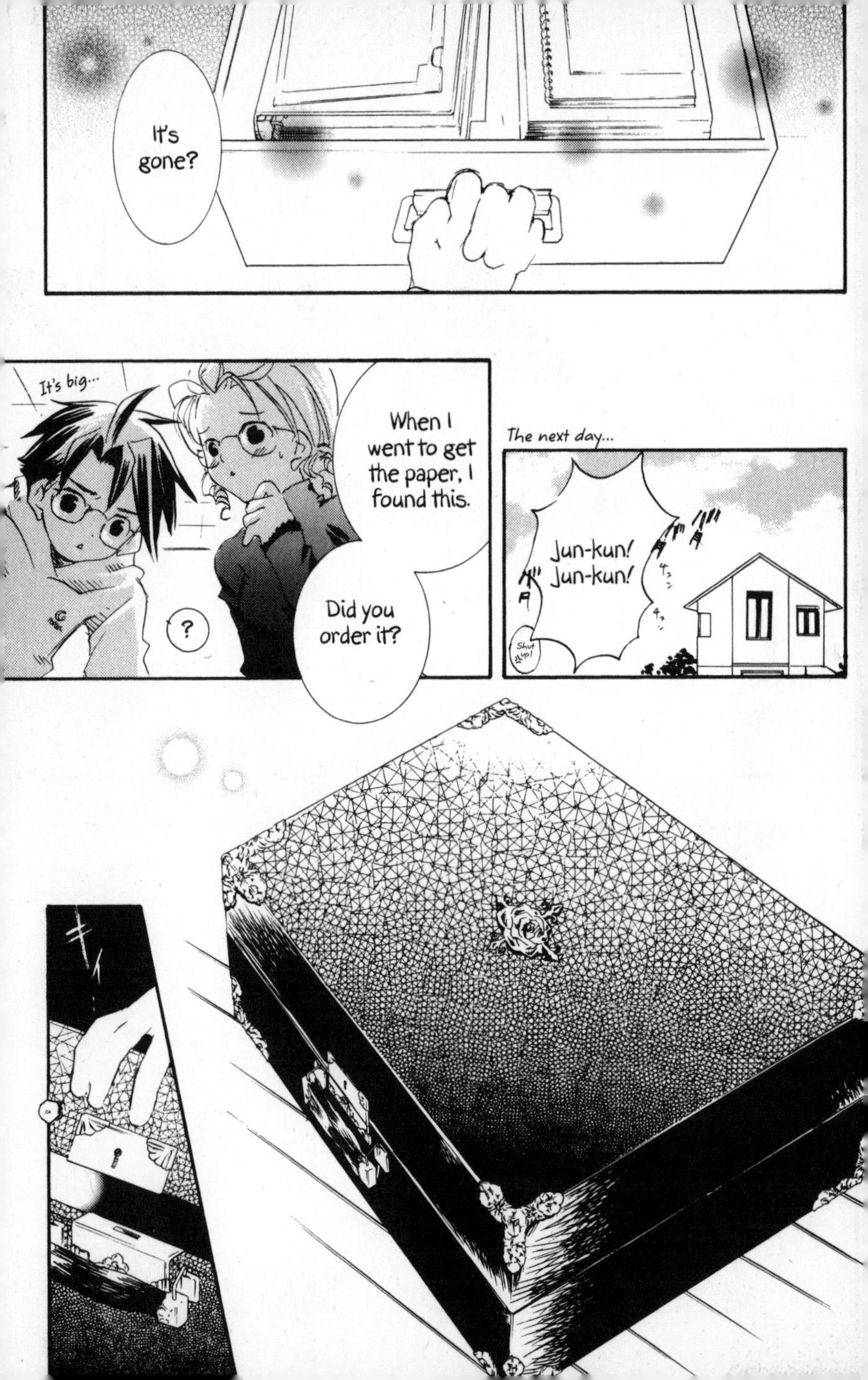
It's gone?
The next day...
Jun-kun! Jun-kun!
Shut up!
When I went to get the paper, I found this.
Did you order it?
It's big...
?

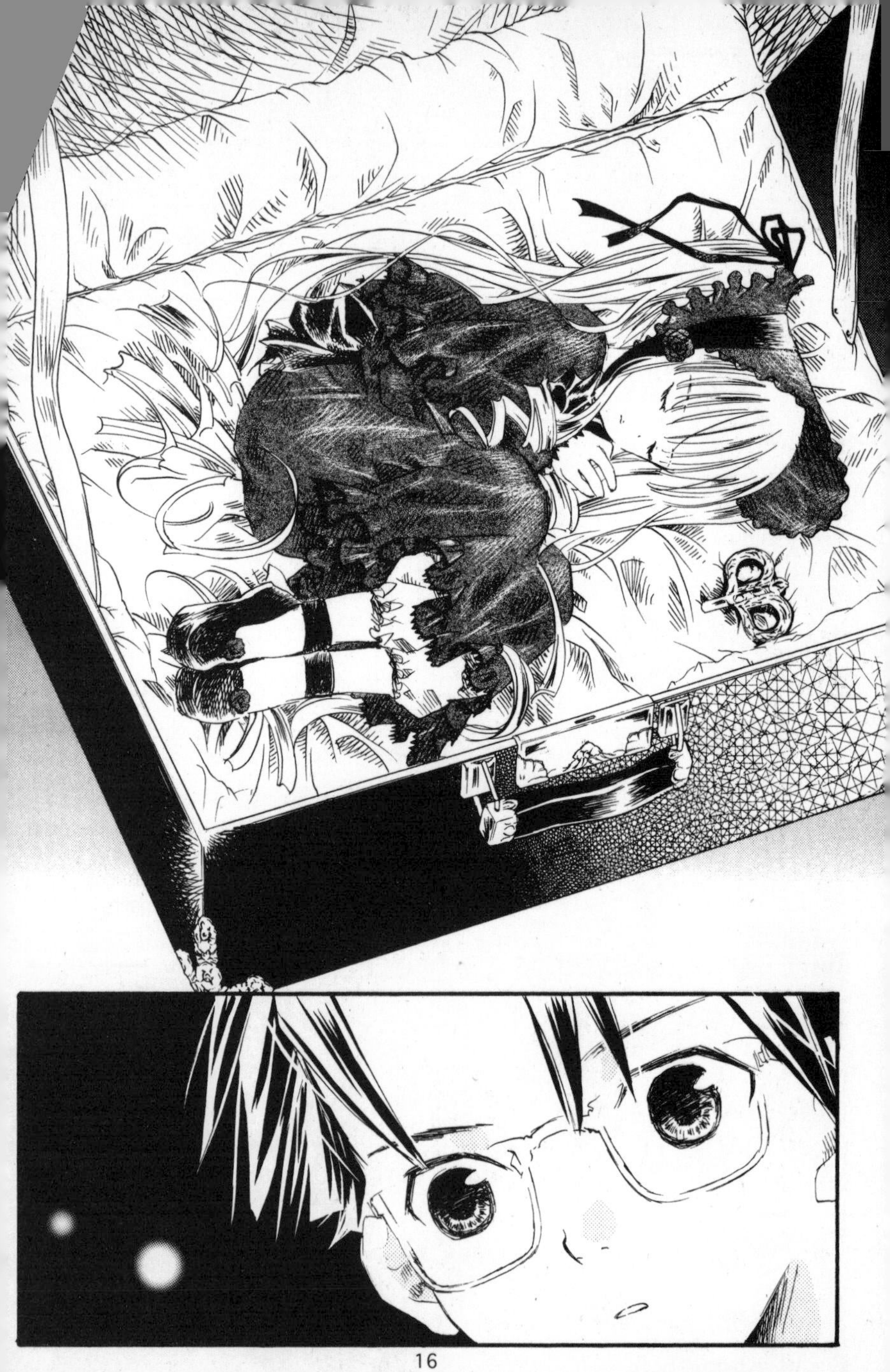

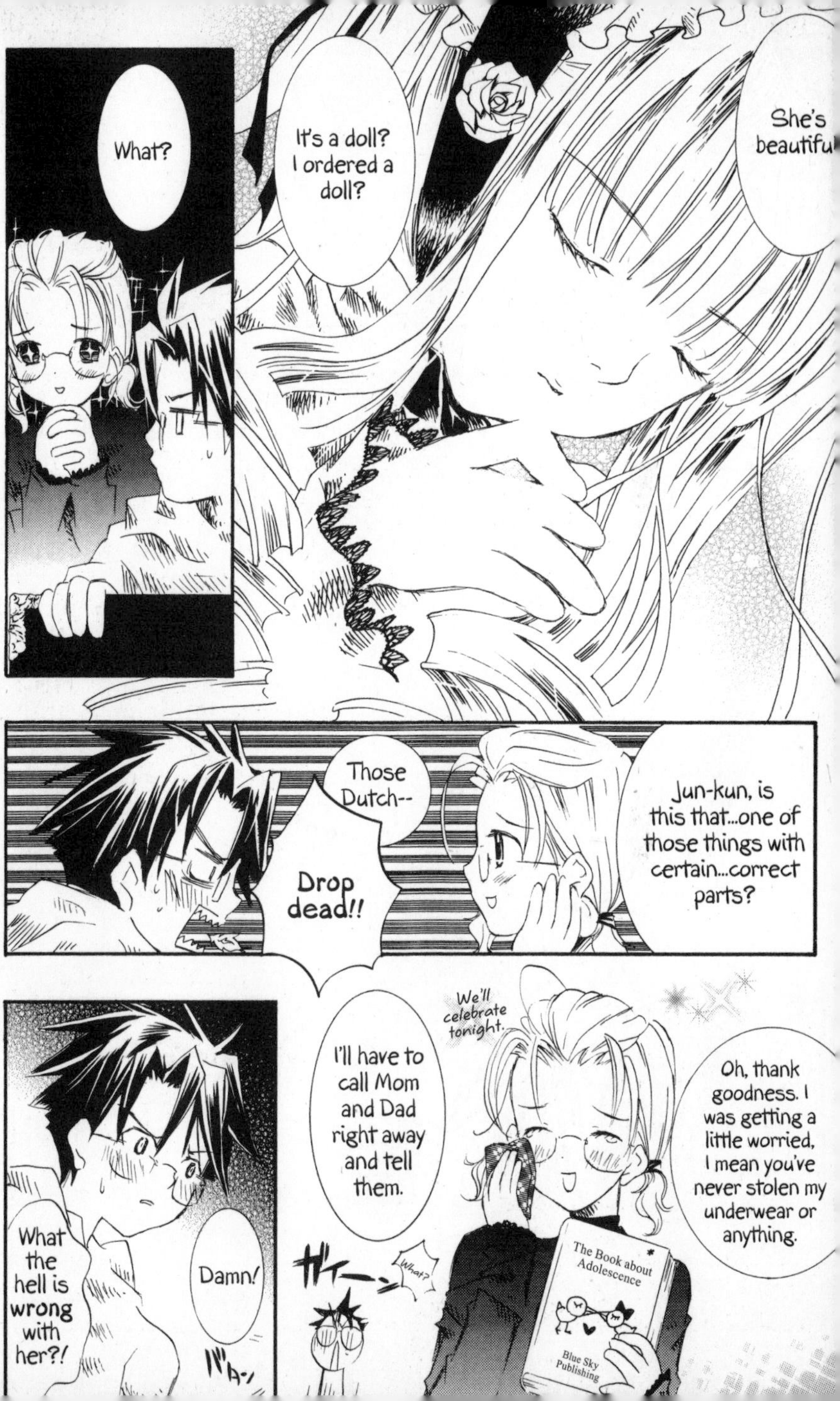
She's beautifu
It's a doll? I ordered a doll?
What?
Jun-kun, is this that...one of those things with certain...correct parts?
Those Dutch--
Drop dead!!
Oh, thank goodness. I was getting a little worried, I mean you've never stolen my underwear or anything.
We'll celebrate tonight.
I'll have to call Mom and Dad right away and tell them.
The Book about Adolescence
Blue Sky Publishing
What?
Damn!
What the hell is wrong with her?!

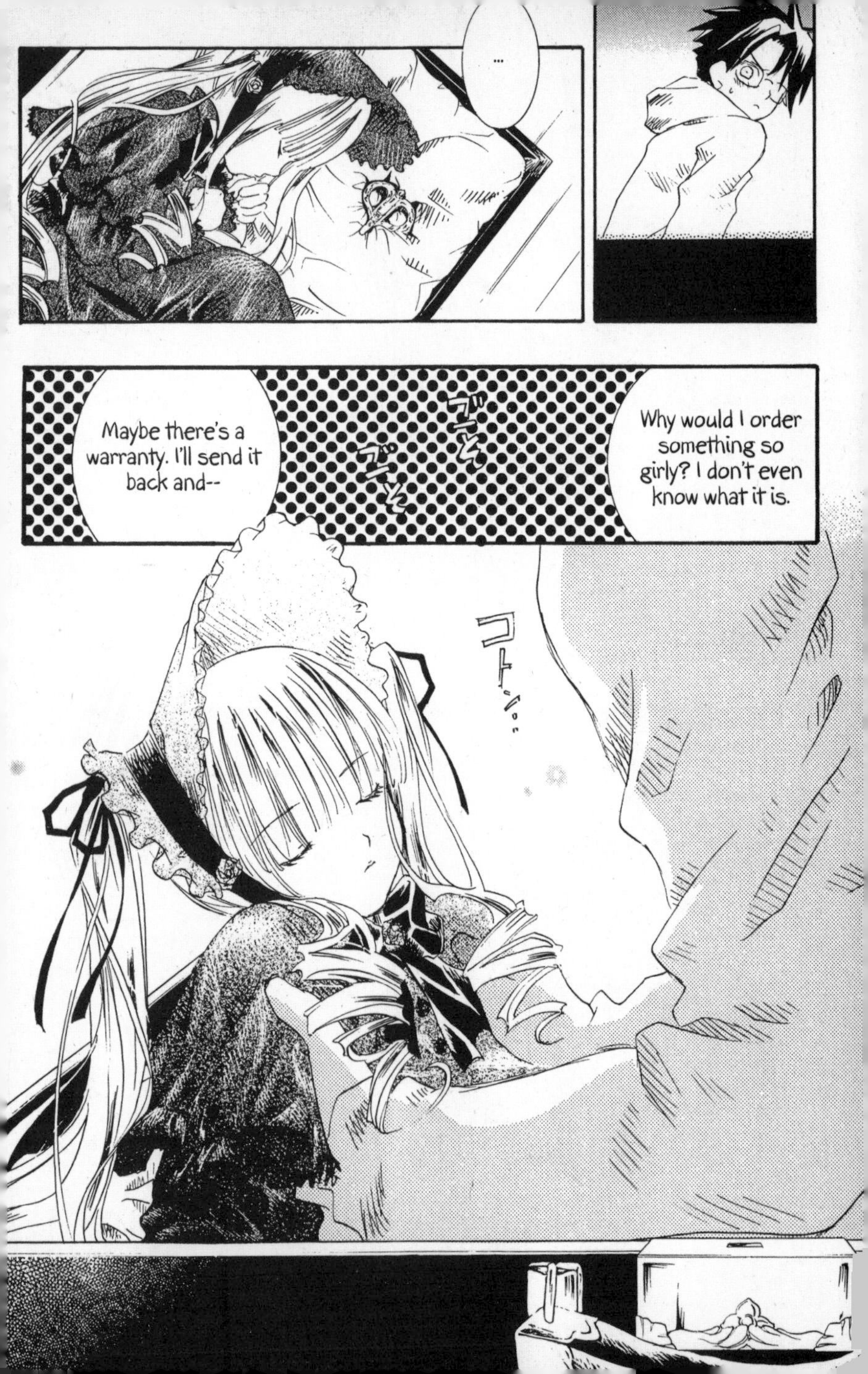
...
Why would I order something so girly? I don't even know what it is.
ゴーと
ゴーと
Maybe there's a warranty. I'll send it back and--
コト

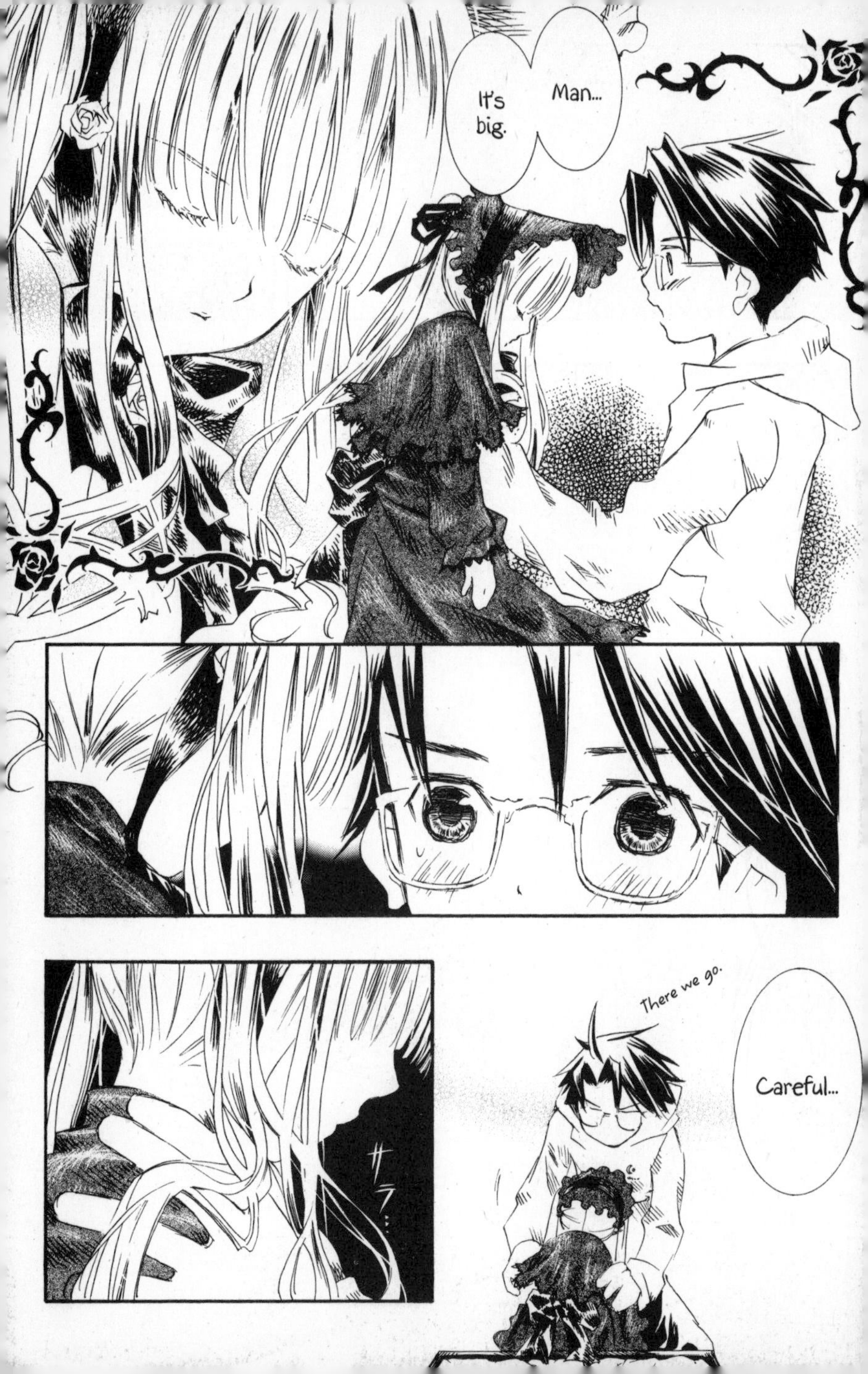
Man...
It's big.
Careful...
There we go.
サラ…

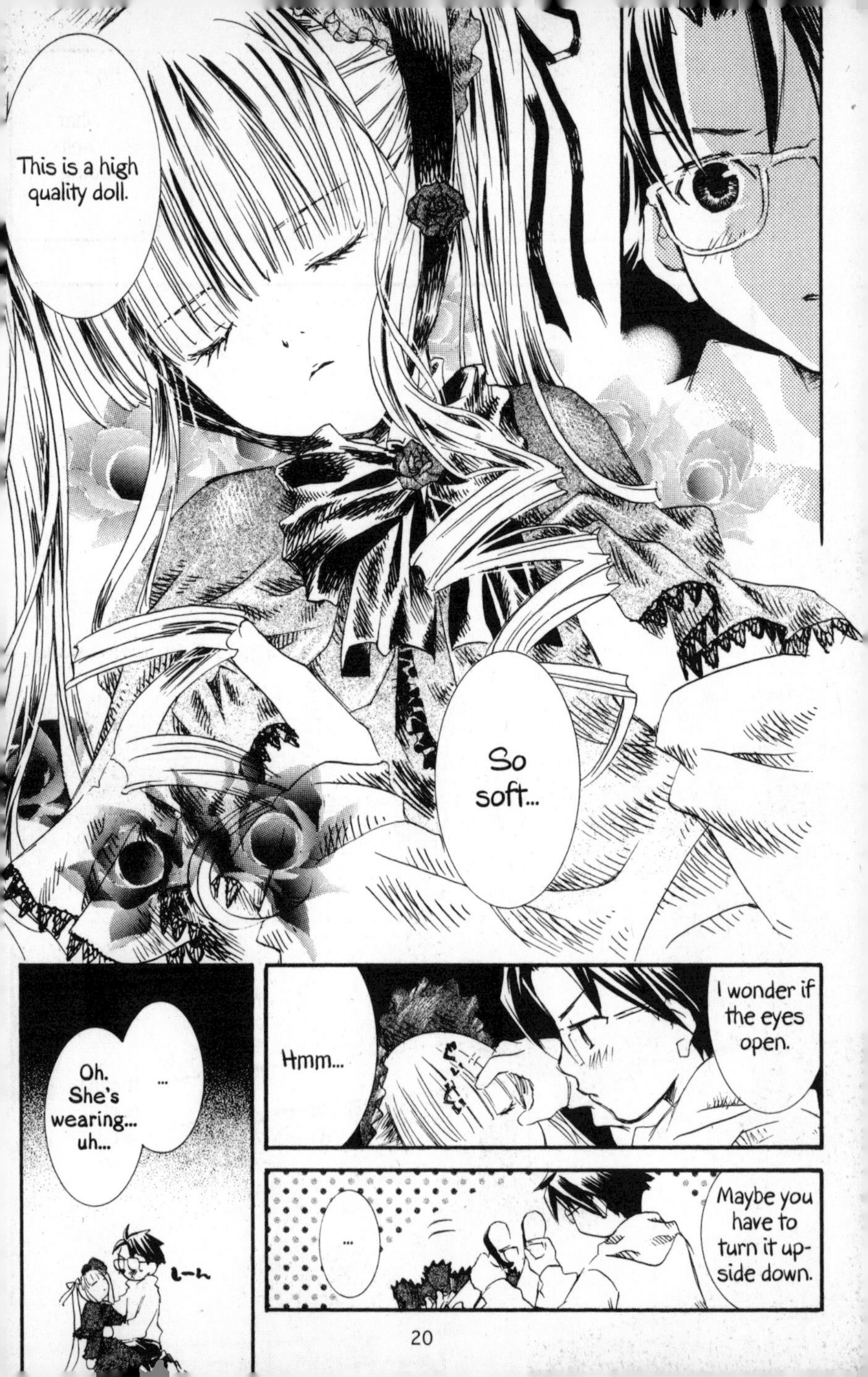
So soft...
This is a high quality doll.
I wonder if the eyes open.
Hmm...
Maybe you have to turn it upside down.
...
...
Oh. She's wearing... uh...
しーん

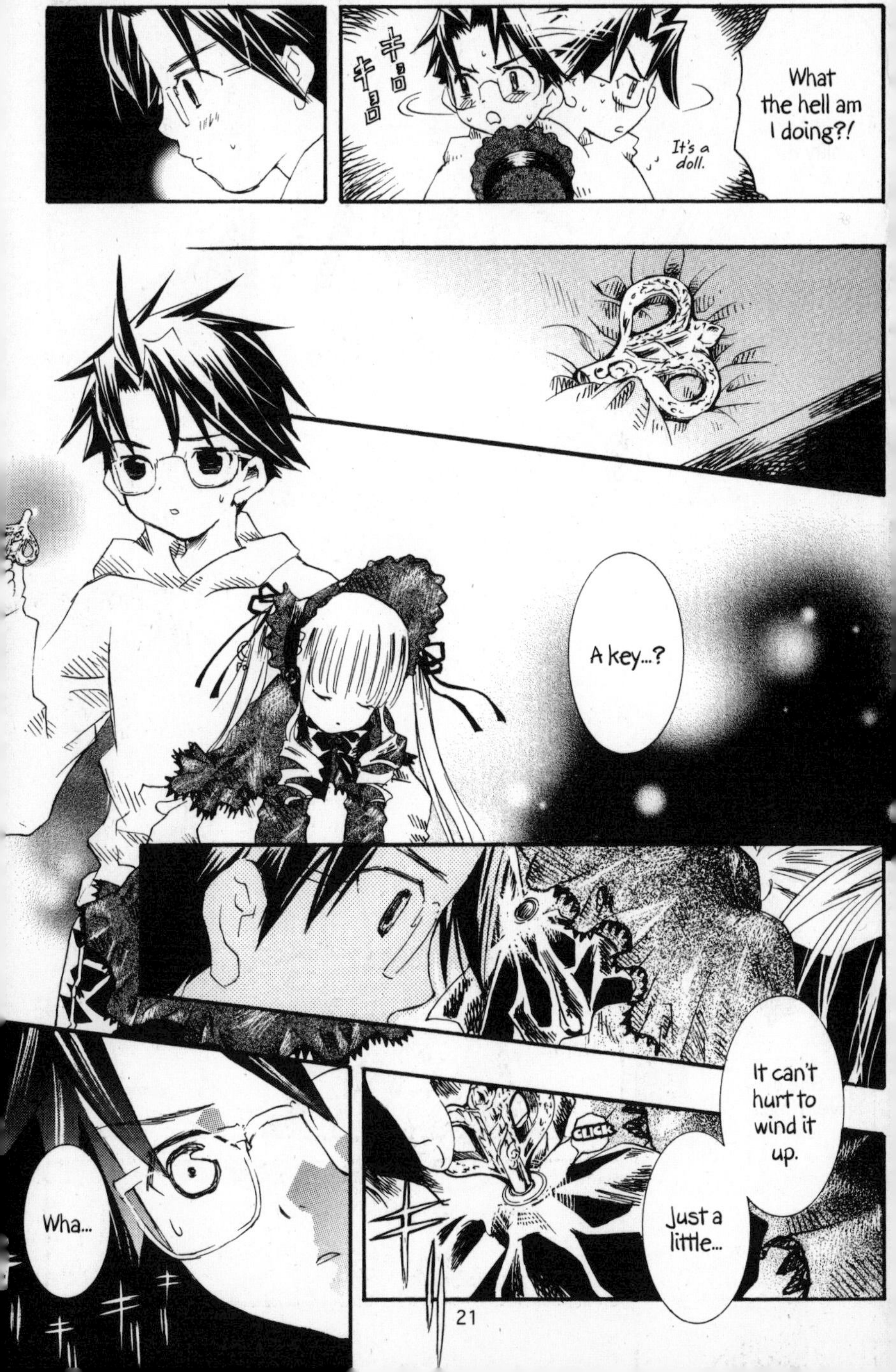
What the hell am I doing?!
It's a doll.
キョロキョロ
A key...?
It can't hurt to wind it up.
CLICK
Just a little...
Wha...

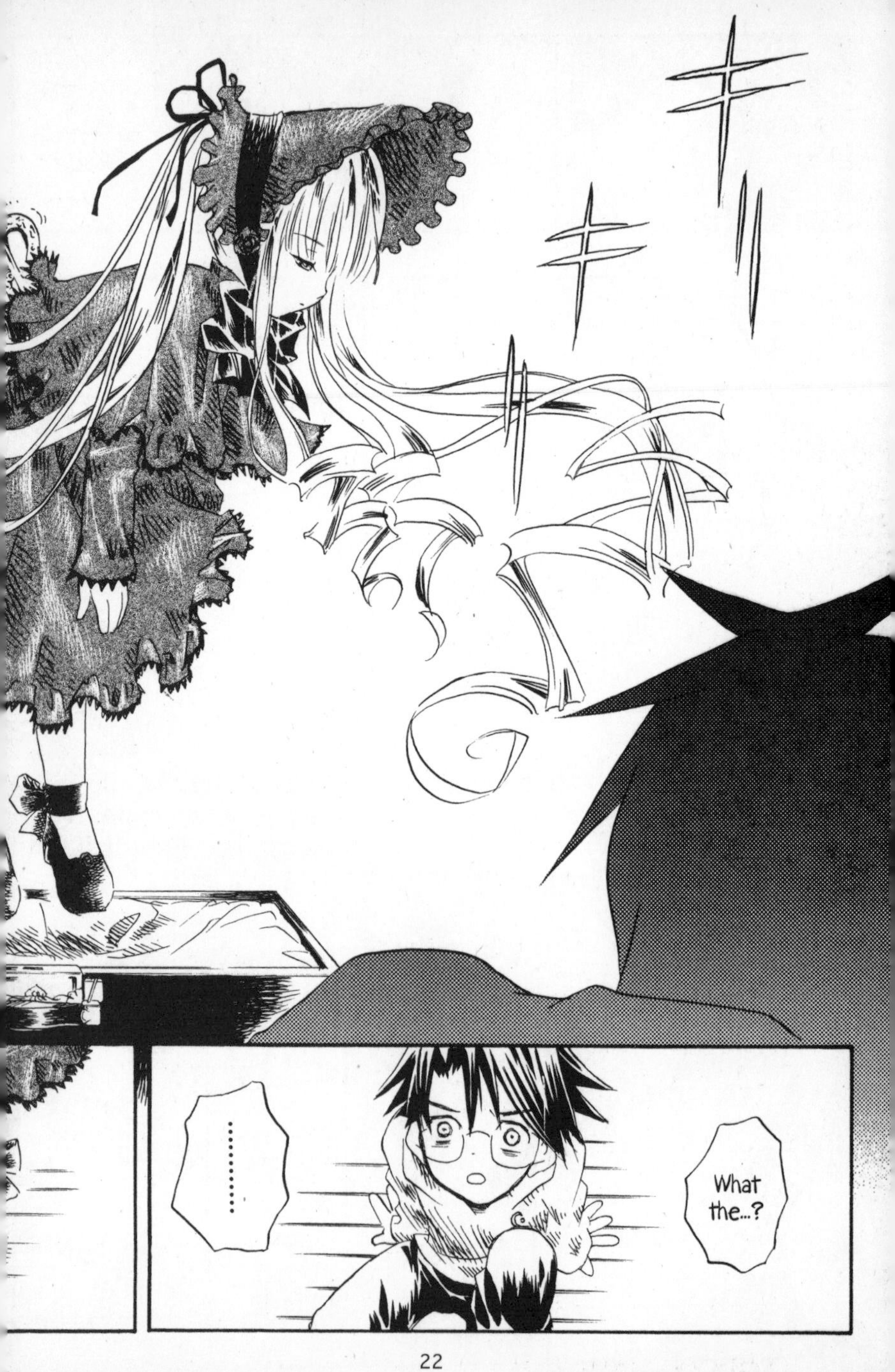
What the...?
....

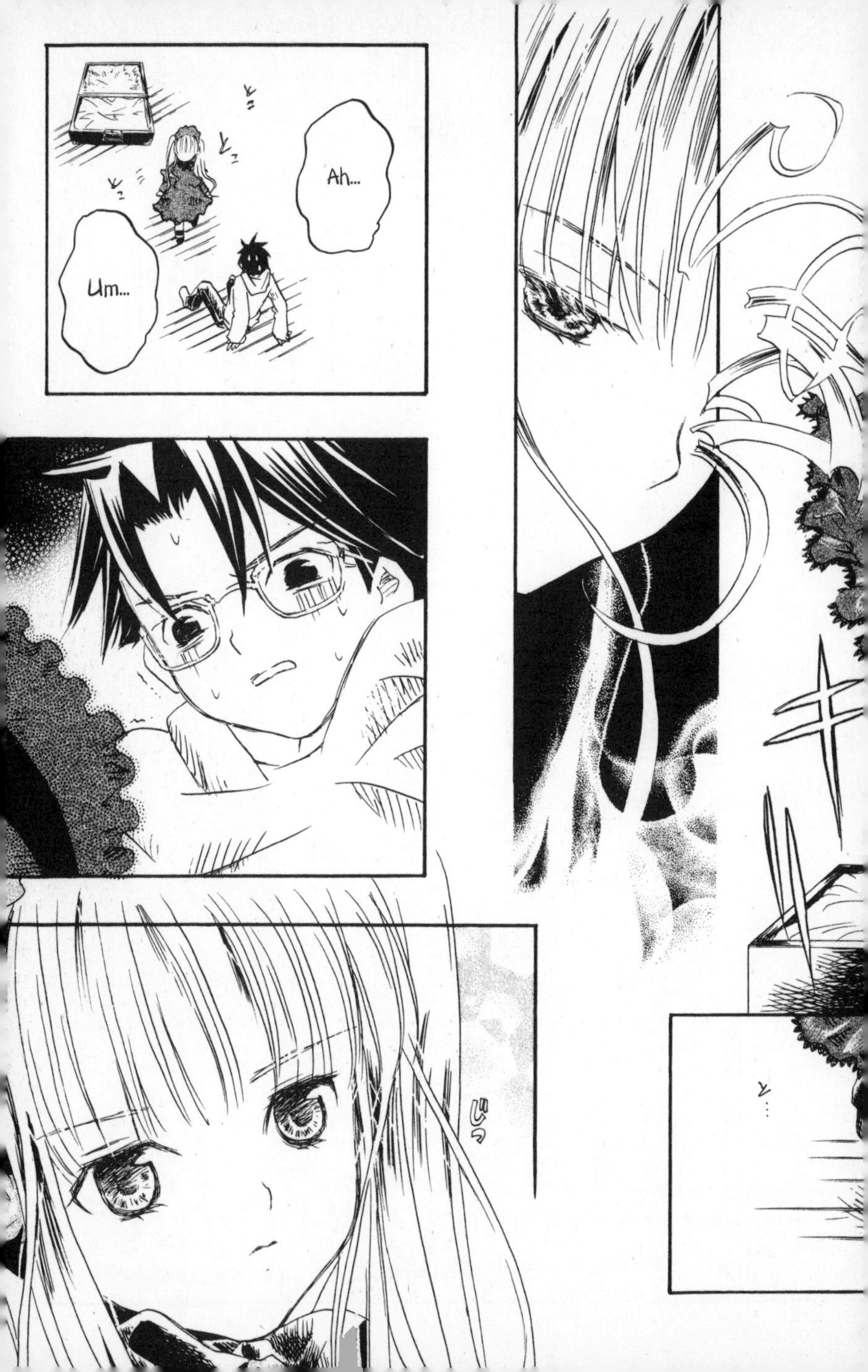

と…
Ah...
とこ
とこ
とこ
Um...
じっ

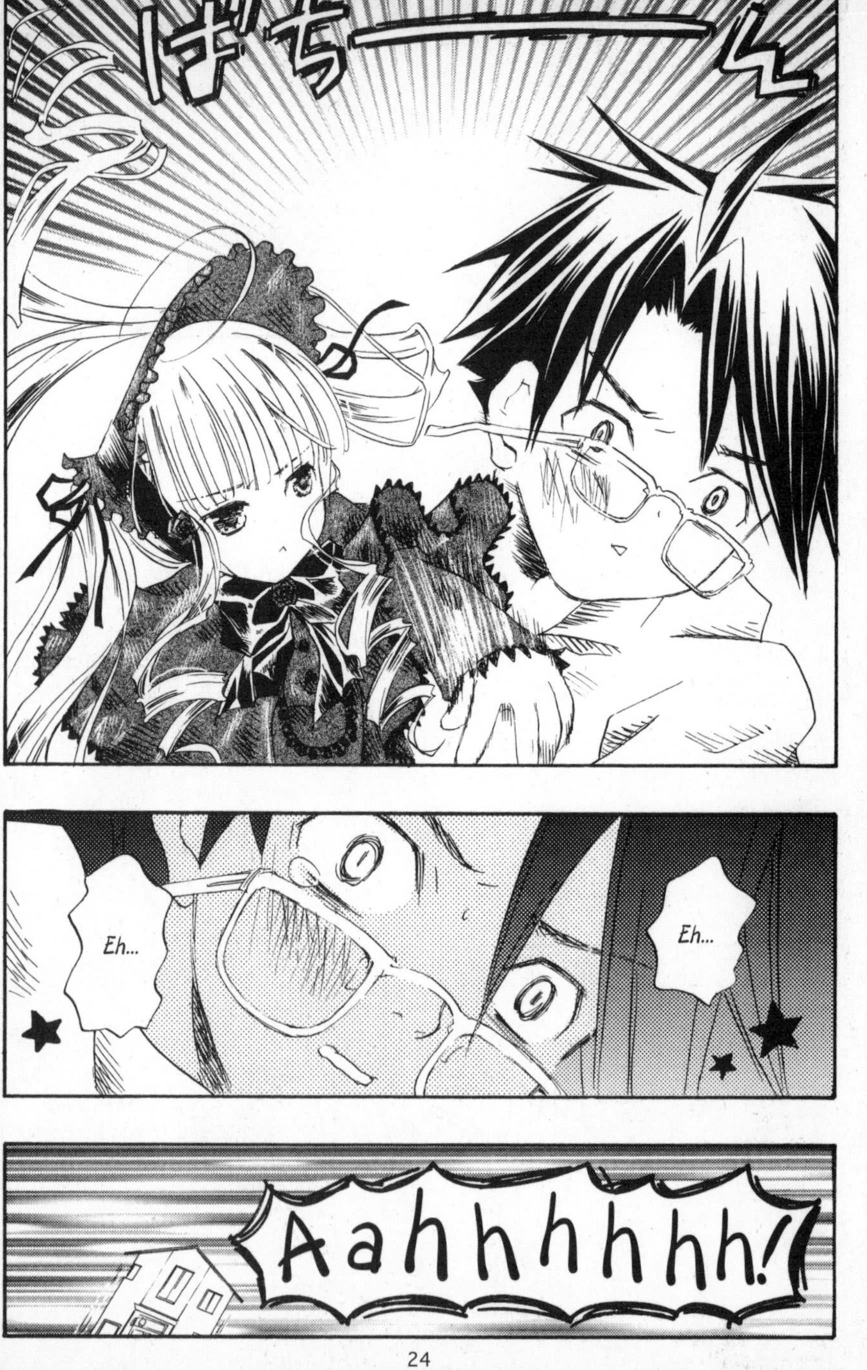
ばちーーーん
Eh...
Eh...
Aahhhhhh!

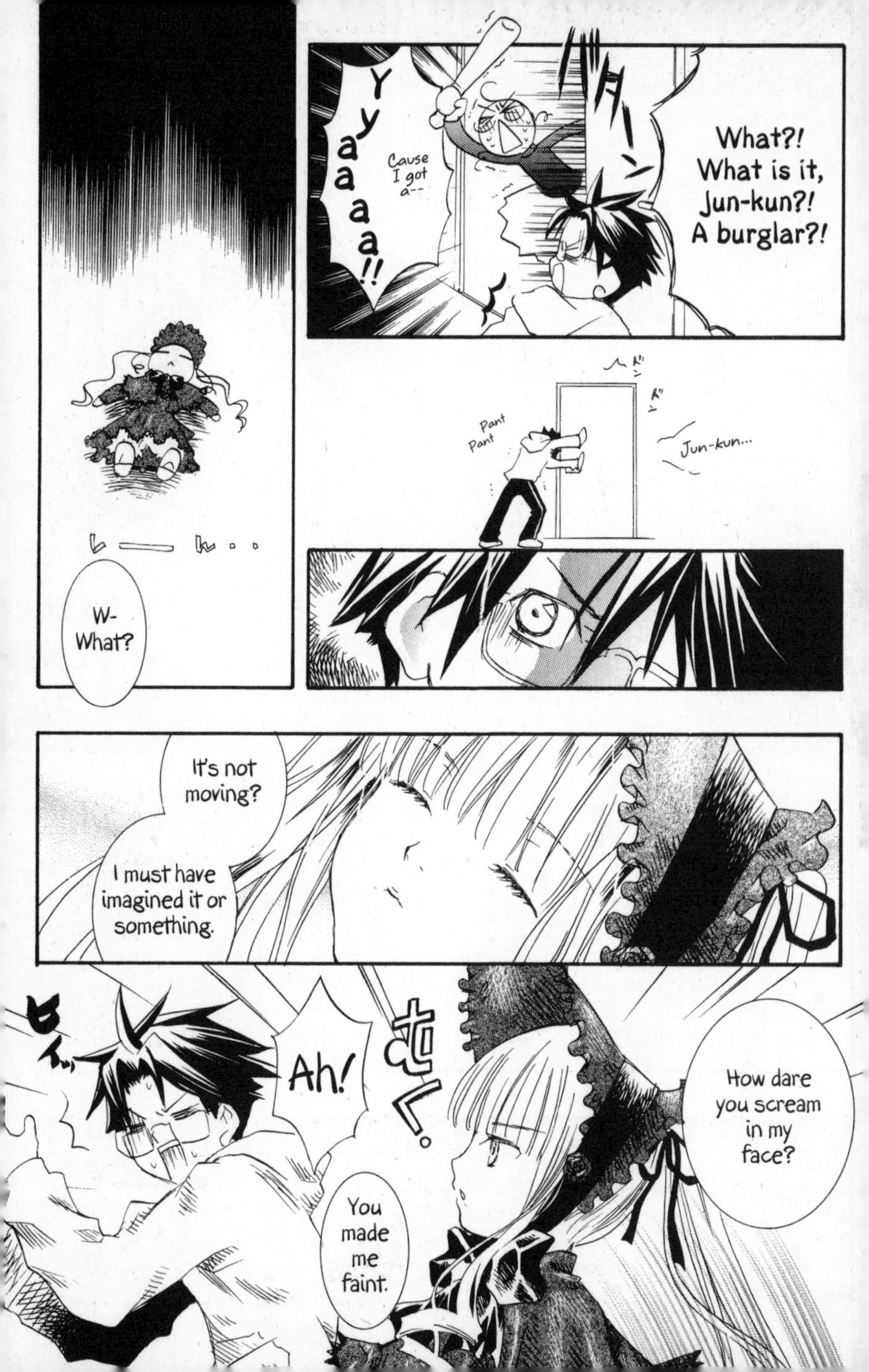
What?! What is it, Jun-kun?! A burglar?!
Yyaaaaa!!
Cause I got a--
Pant Pant
Jun-kun...
W- What?
It's not moving?
I must have imagined it or something.
How dare you scream in my face?
You made me faint.
Ah!

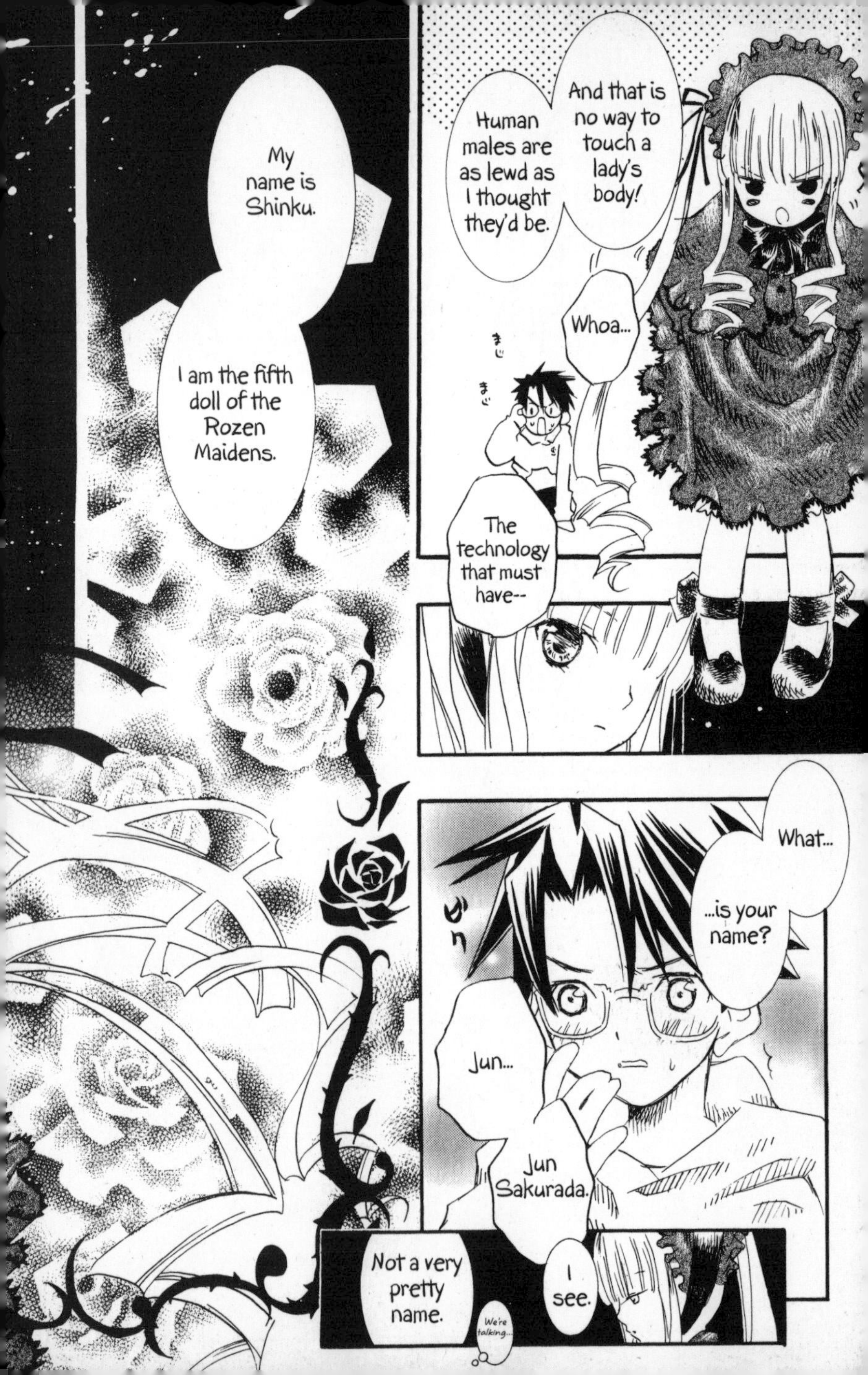
And that is no way to touch a lady's body!
Human males are as lewd as I thought they'd be.
Whoa...
まじ
まじ
The technology that must have--
What...
...is your name?
ピク
Jun...
Jun Sakurada.
I see.
Not a very pretty name.
We're talking...
My name is Shinku.
I am the fifth doll of the Rozen Maidens.

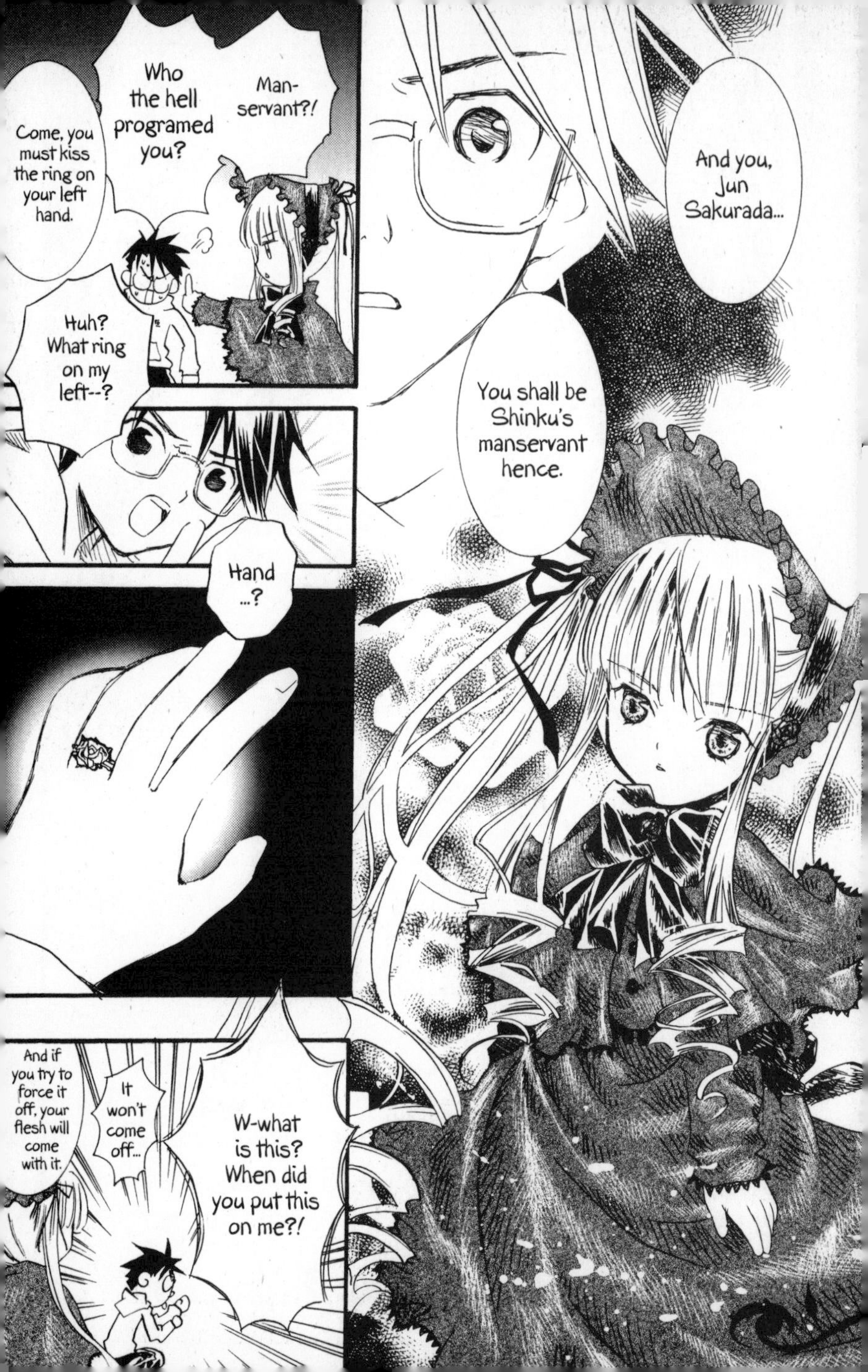
And you, Jun Sakurada...
You shall be Shinku's manservant hence.
Man-servant?!
Who the hell programed you?
Come, you must kiss the ring on your left hand.
Huh? What ring on my left--?
Hand ...?
W-what is this? When did you put this on me?!
It won't come off...
And if you try to force it off, your flesh will come with it.

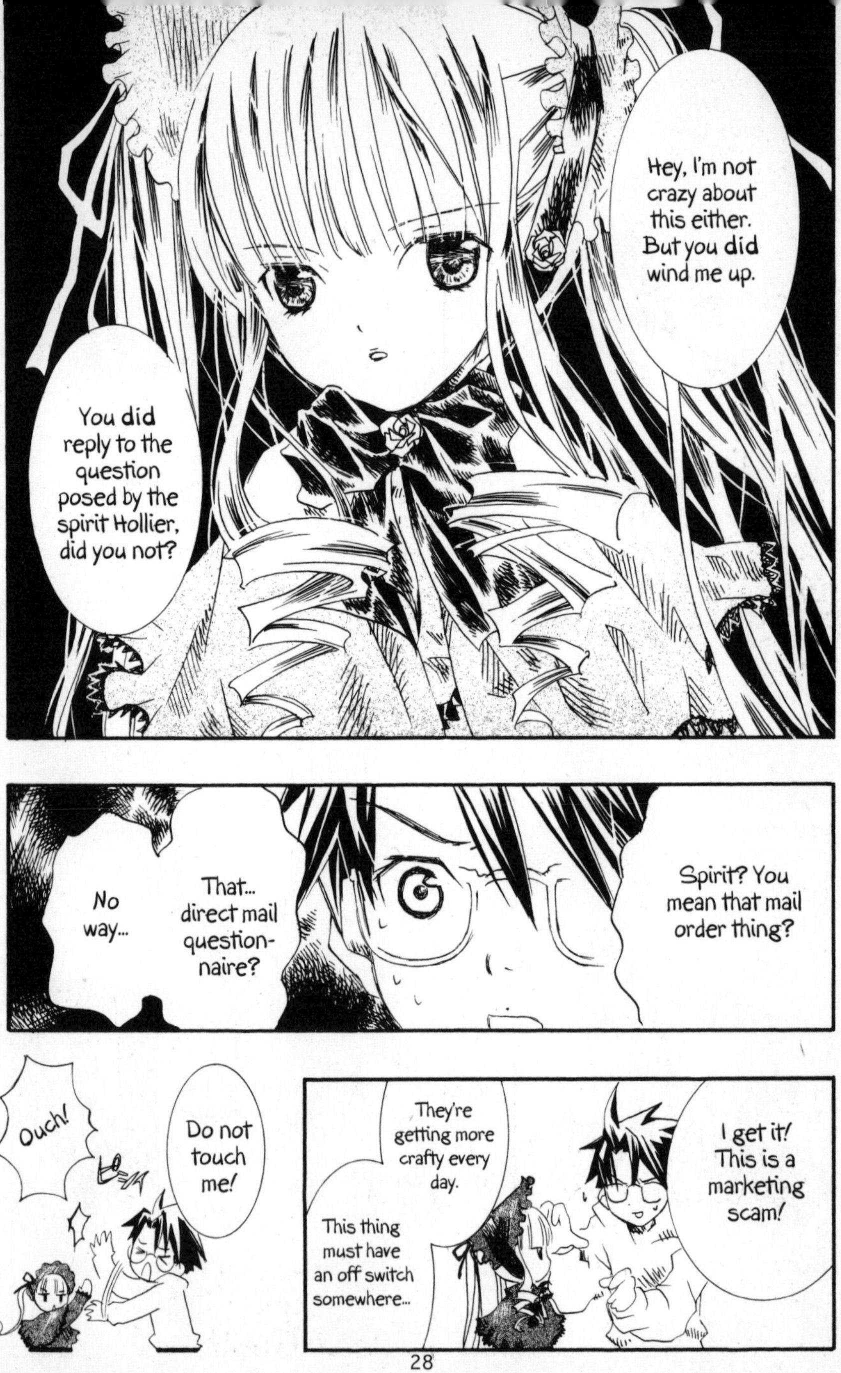
Hey, I'm not crazy about this either. But you did wind me up.
You did reply to the question posed by the spirit Hollier, did you not?
Spirit? You mean that mail order thing?
That... direct mail question-naire?
No way...
I get it! This is a marketing scam!
They're getting more crafty every day.
This thing must have an off switch somewhere...
Do not touch me!
Ouch!

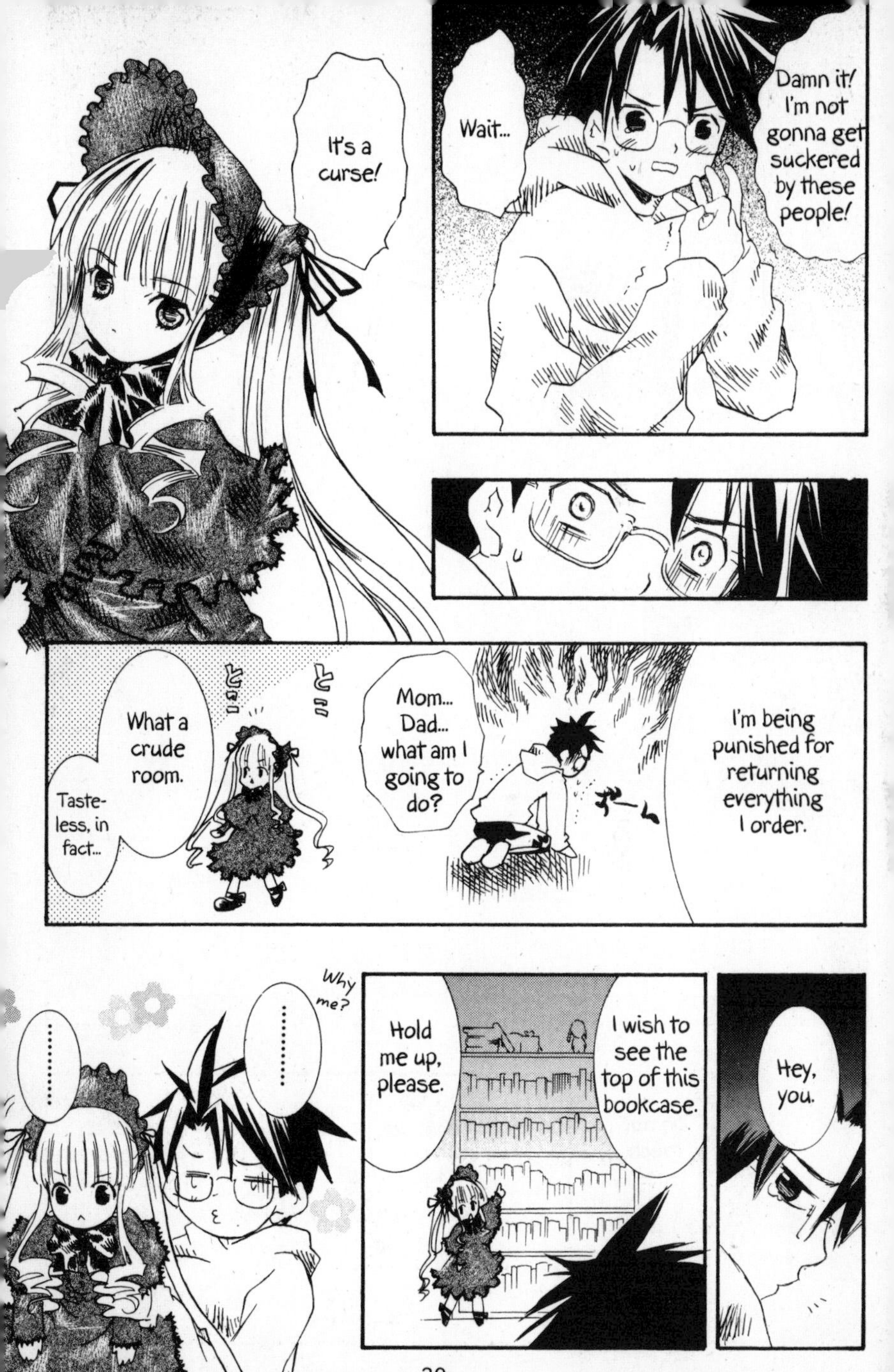

Damn it! I'm not gonna get suckered by these people!
Wait...
It's a curse!
I'm being punished for returning everything I order.
Mom... Dad... what am I going to do?
What a crude room.
Taste-less, in fact...
Hey, you.
I wish to see the top of this bookcase.
Hold me up, please.
Why me?
....
....

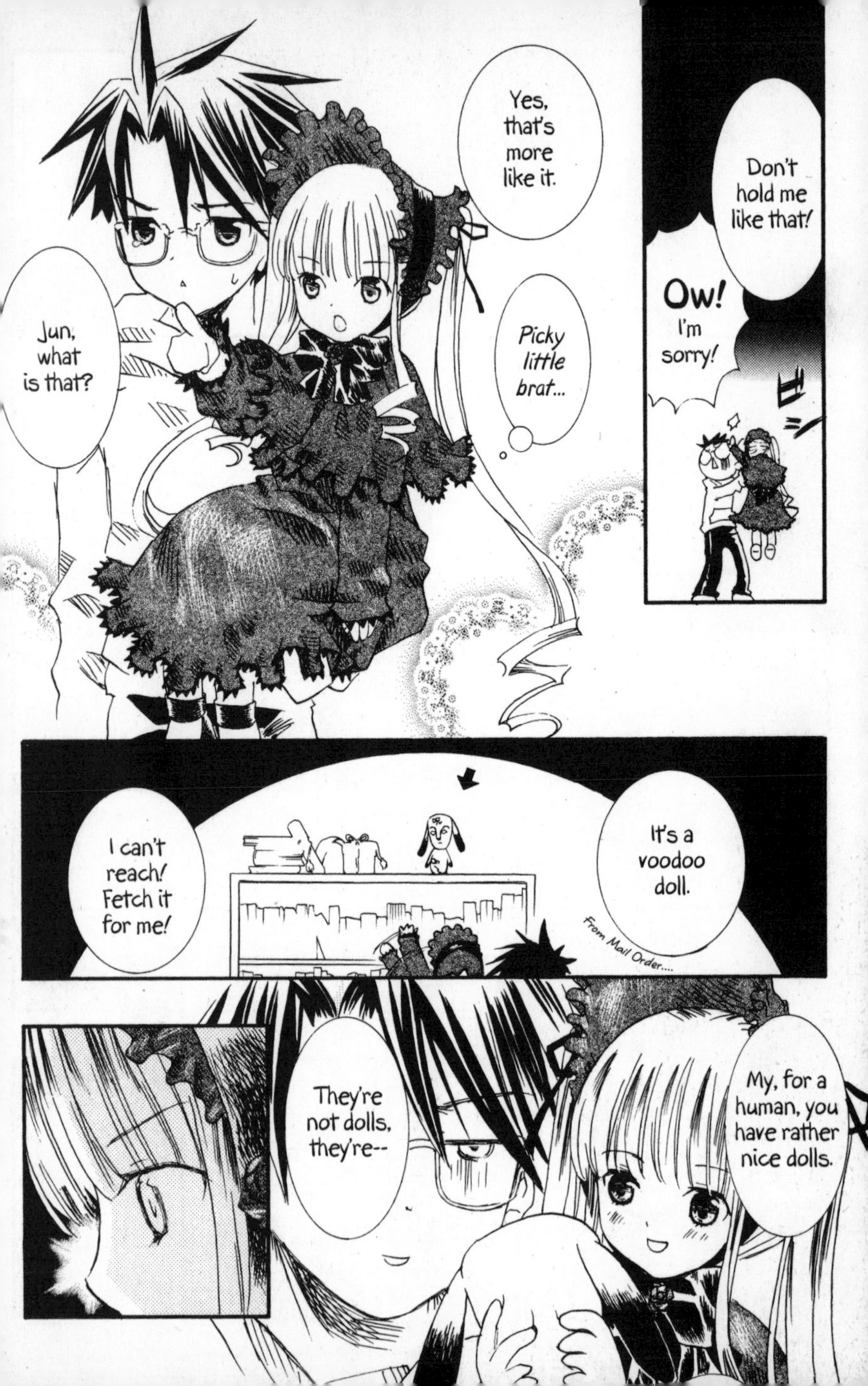
Don't hold me like that!
Ow! I'm sorry!
Yes, that's more like it.
Picky little brat...
Jun, what is that?
It's a voodoo doll.
From Mail Order....
I can't reach! Fetch it for me!
My, for a human, you have rather nice dolls.
They're not dolls, they're--

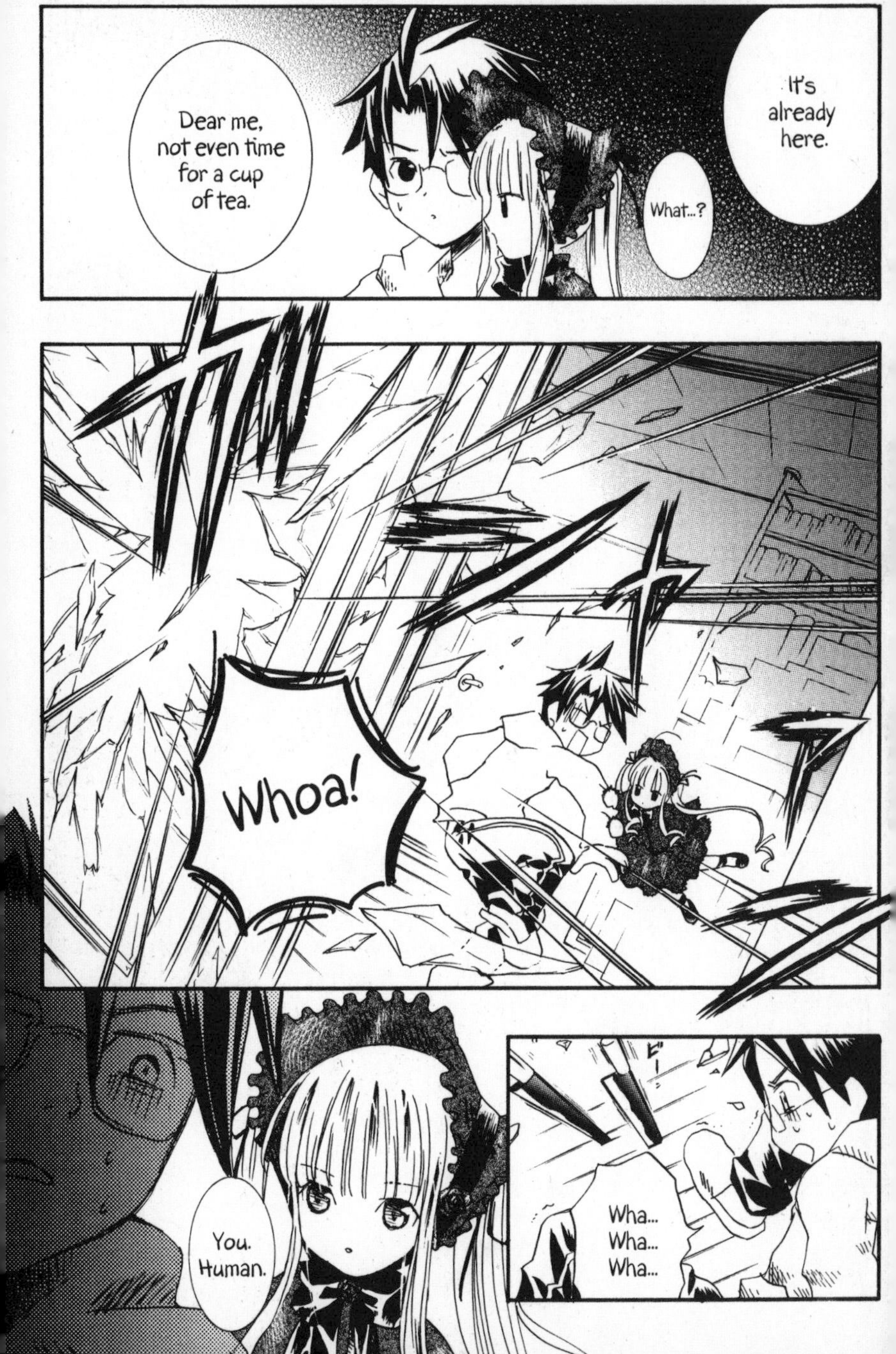
It's already here.
What...?
Dear me, not even time for a cup of tea.
Whoa!
Wha... Wha... Wha...
You. Human.

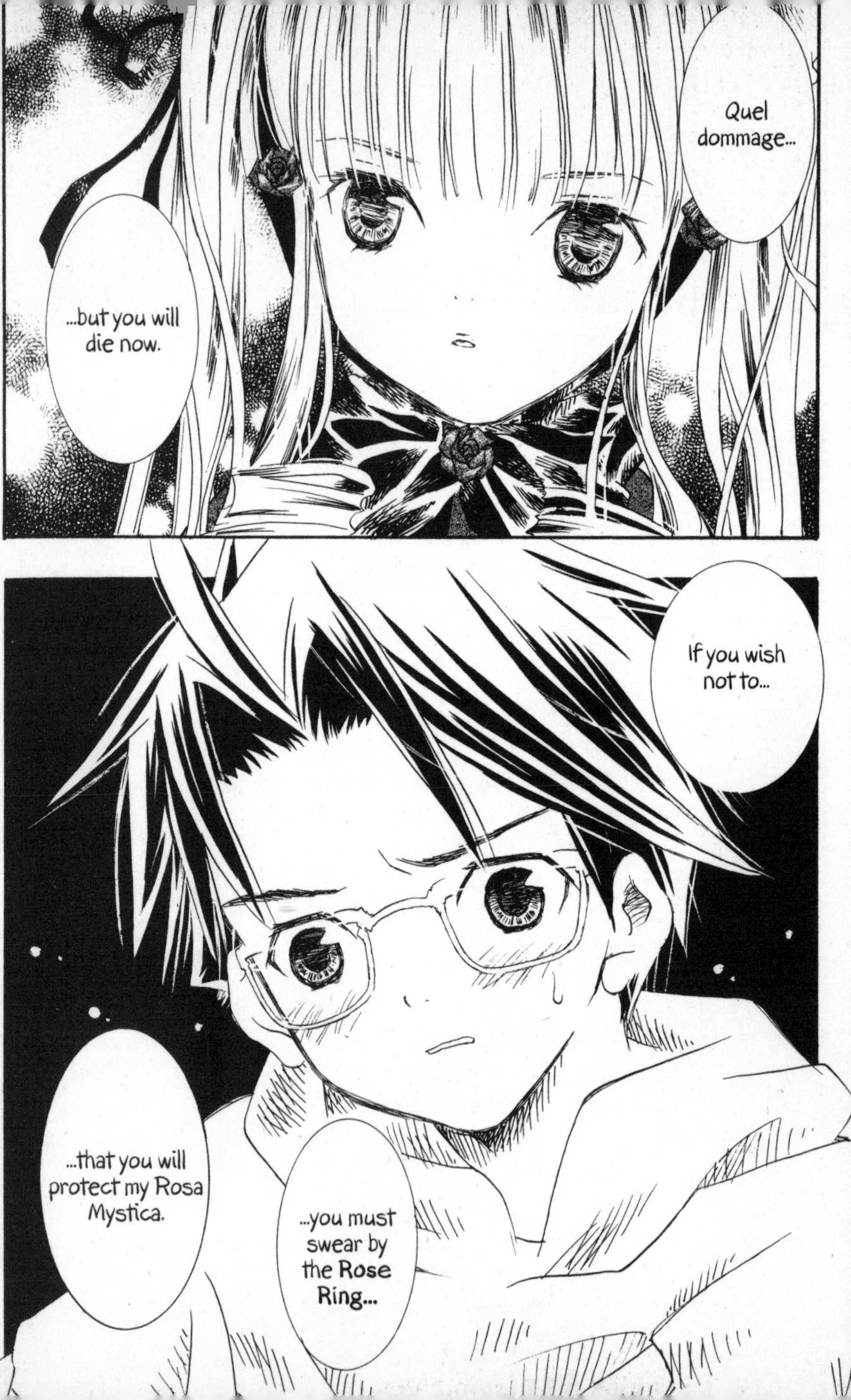
Quel dommage...
...but you will die now.
If you wish not to...
...you must swear by the Rose Ring...
...that you will protect my Rosa Mystica.

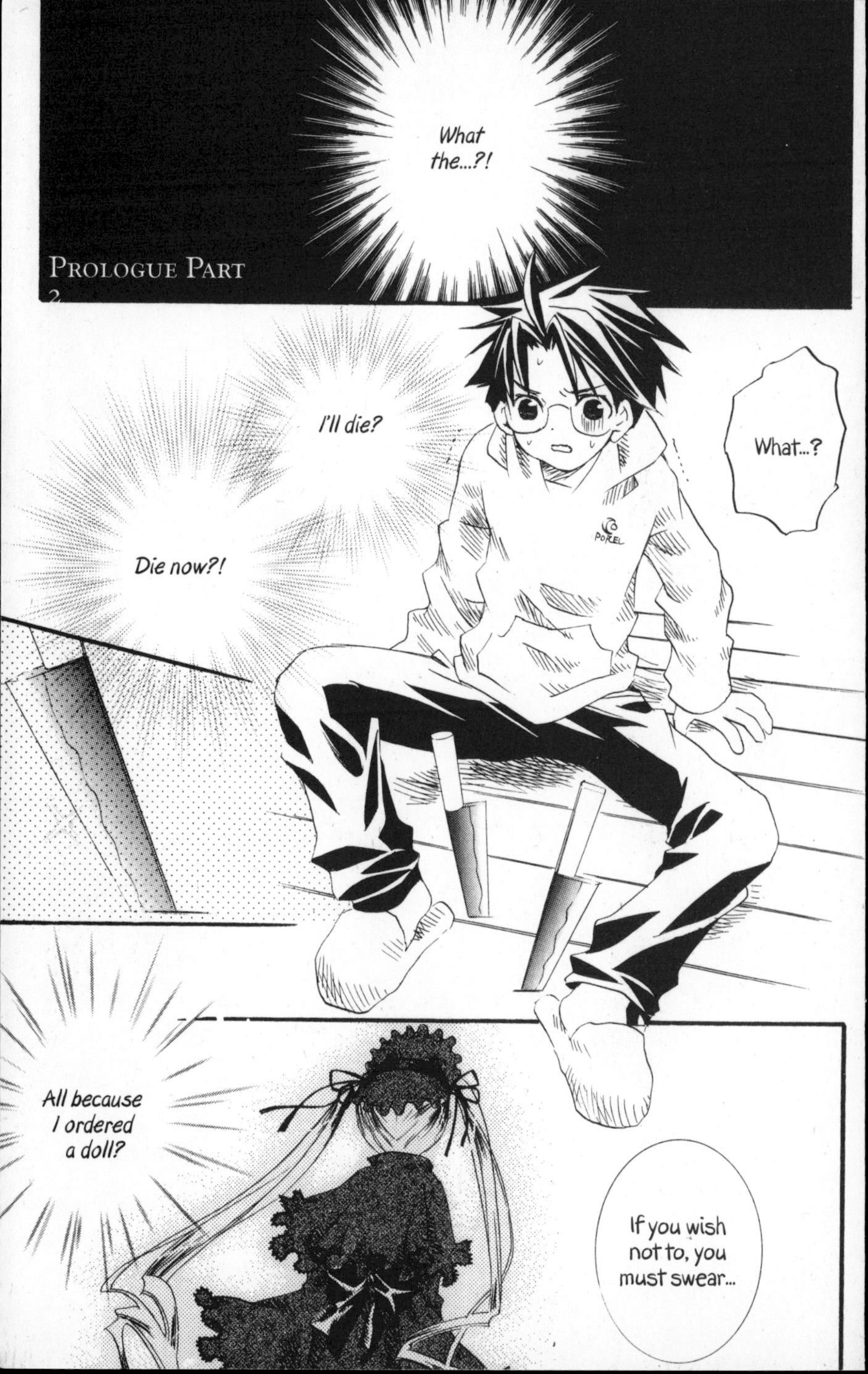
PROLOGUE PART 2
What the...?!
What...?
I'll die?
Die now?!
If you wish not to, you must swear...
All because I ordered a doll?

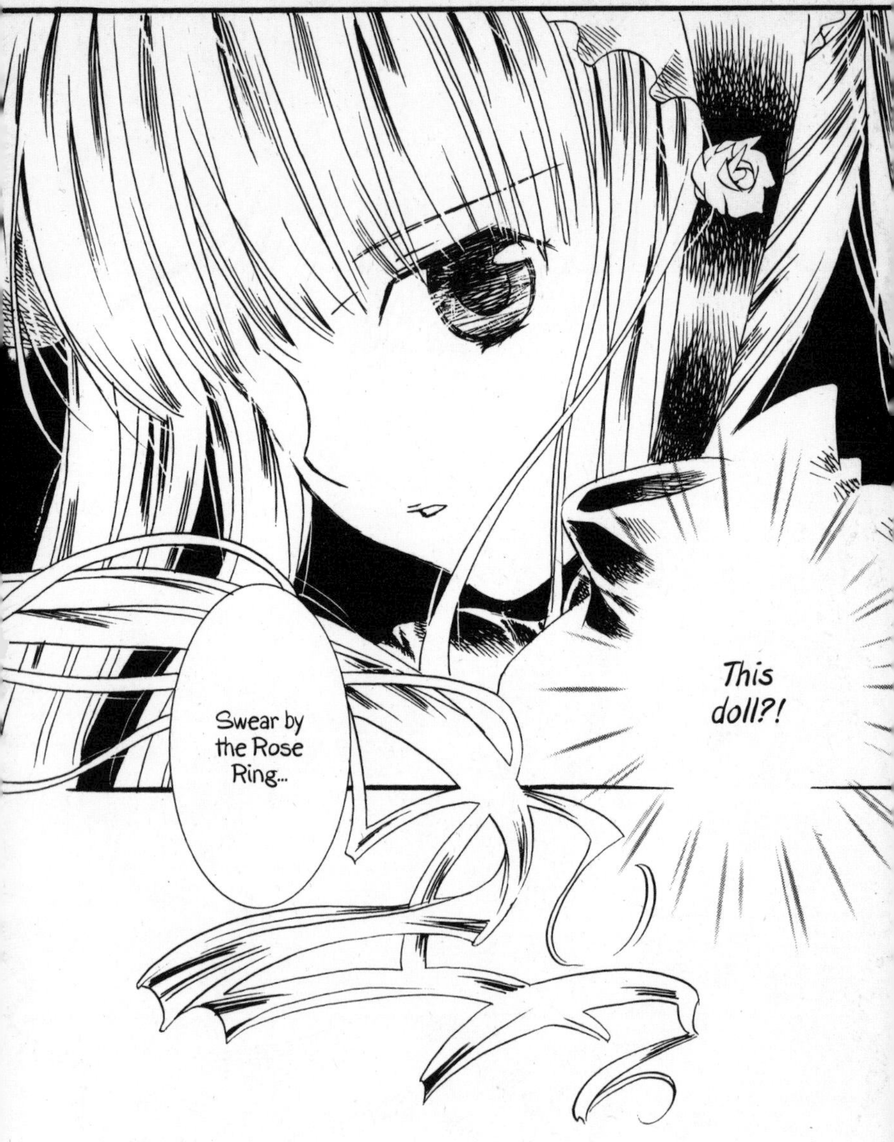
This doll?!
Swear by the Rose Ring...

PROLOGUE PART II

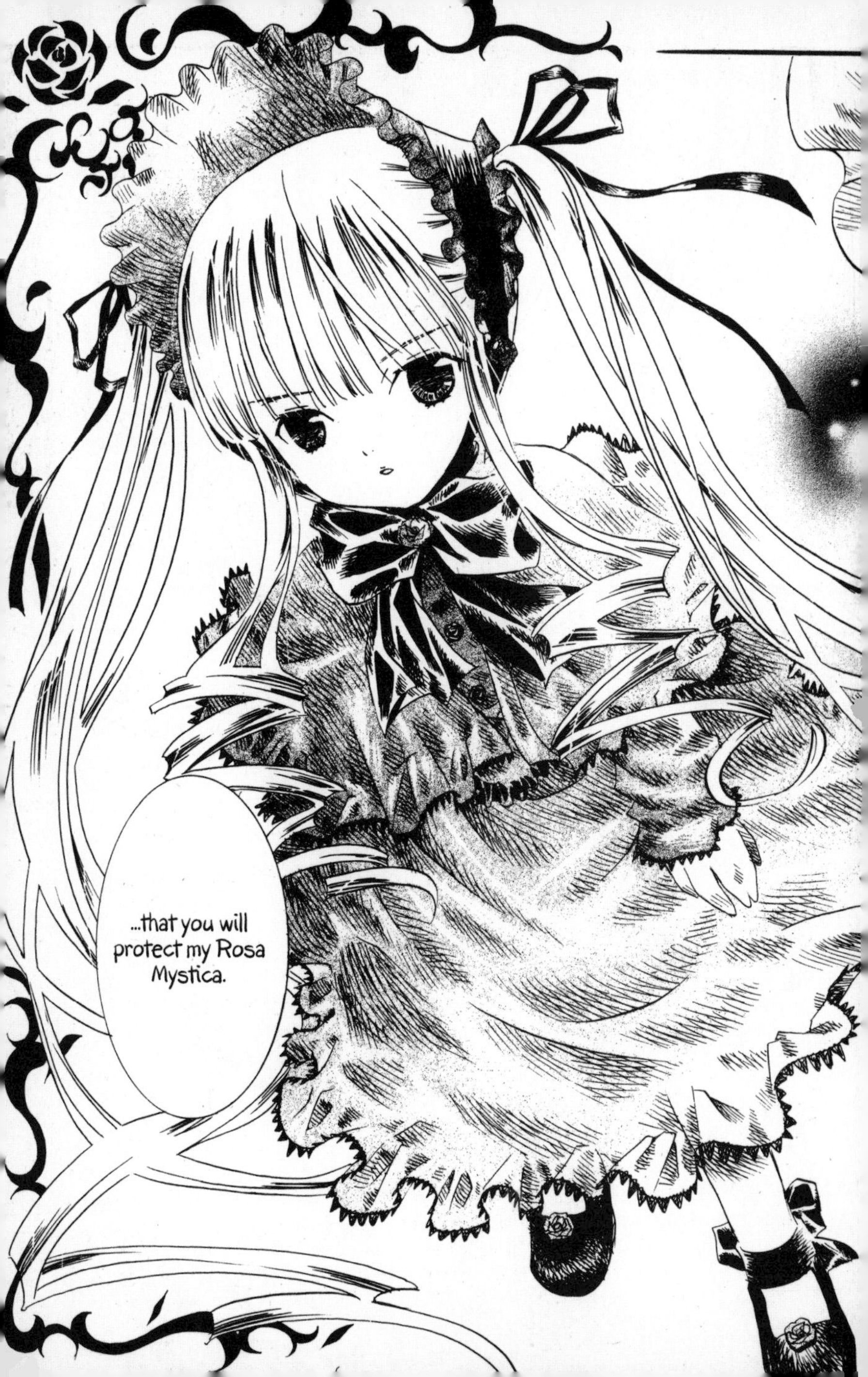
...that you will protect my Rosa Mystica.

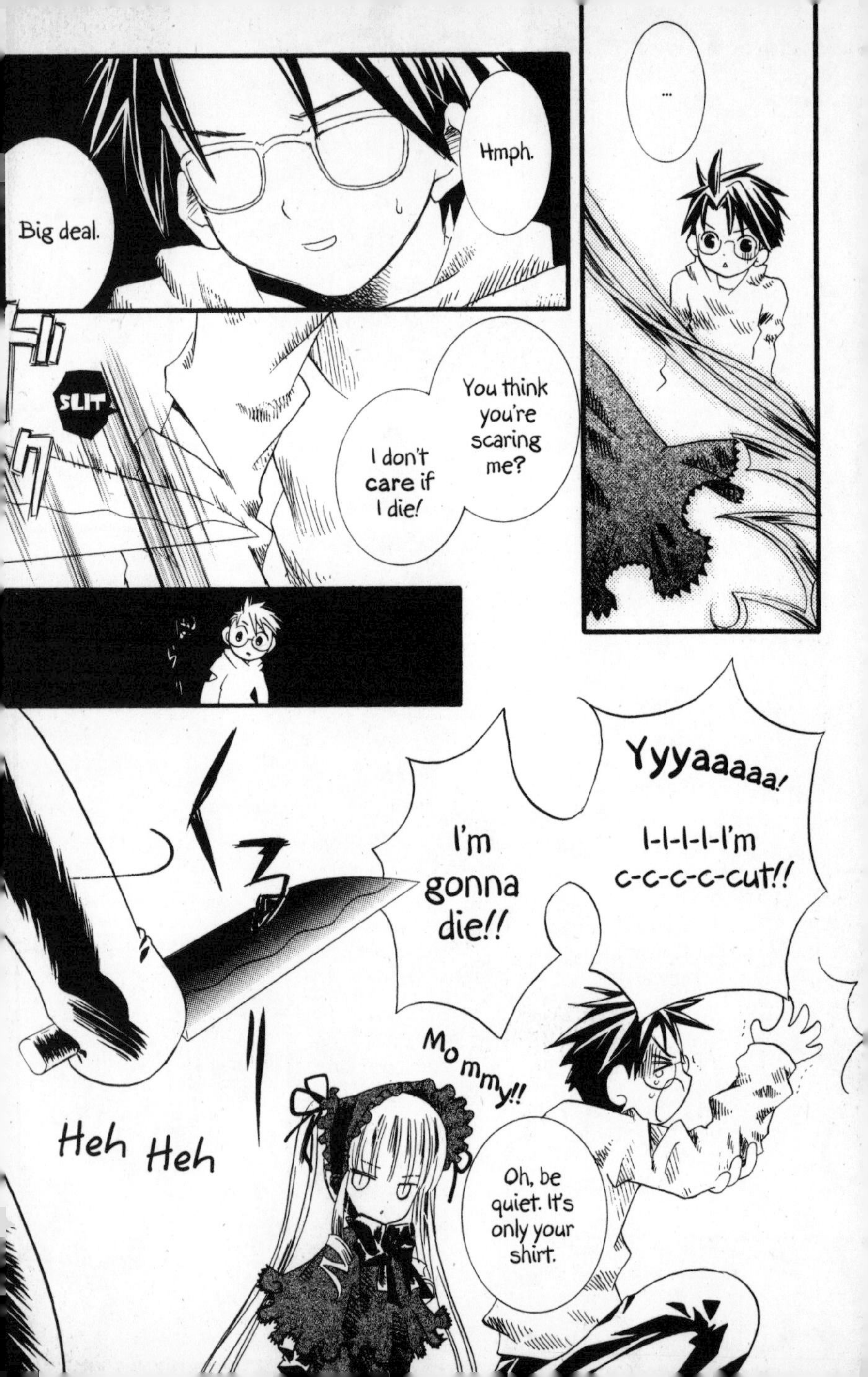
...
Hmph.
Big deal.
You think you're scaring me?
I don't care if I die!
SLIT
Yyyaaaaa!
I-I-I-I-I'm c-c-c-c-cut!!
I'm gonna die!!
Mommy!!
Oh, be quiet. It's only your shirt.
Heh Heh

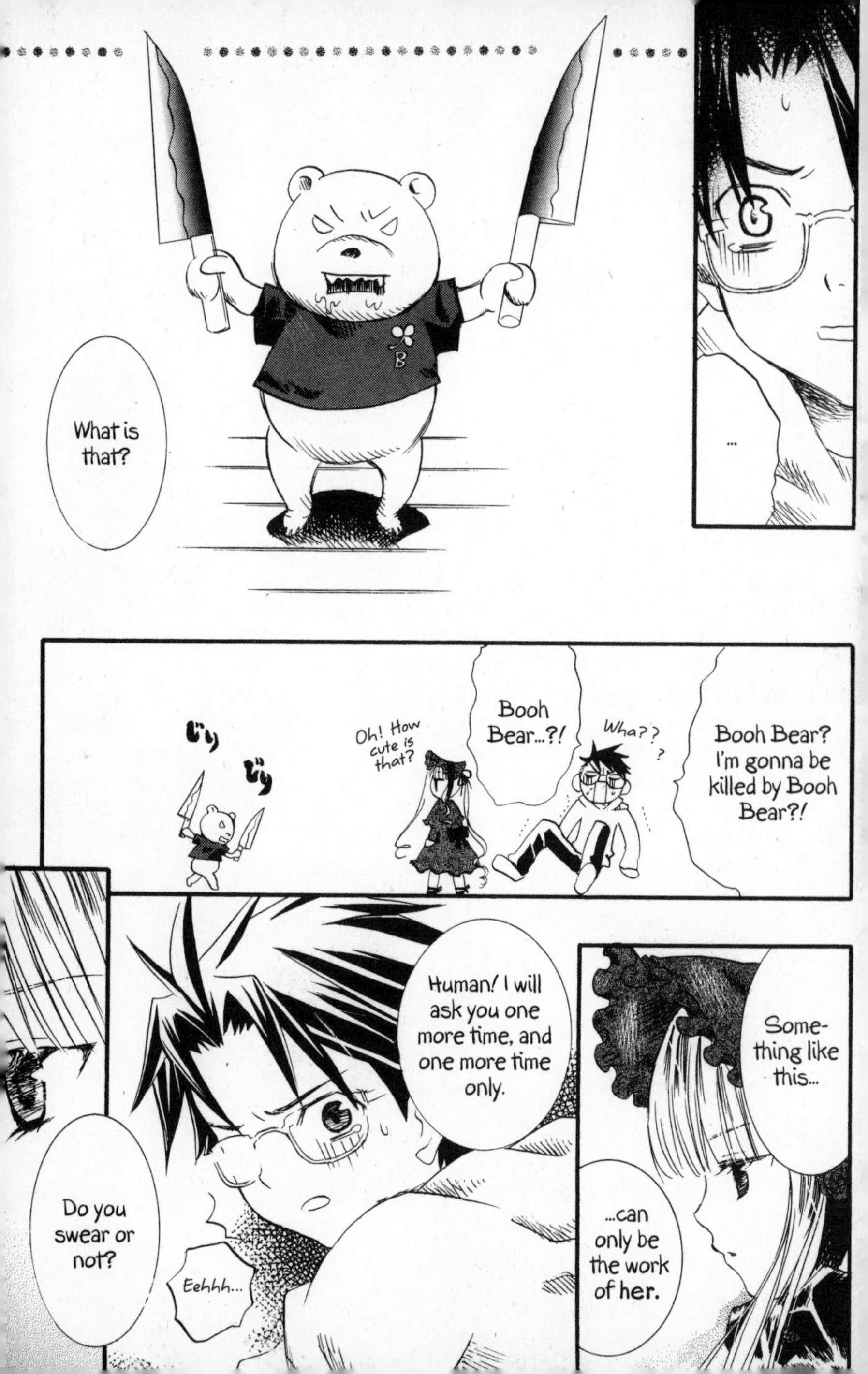
...
What is that?
Booh Bear? I'm gonna be killed by Booh Bear?!
Wha?? ?
Booh Bear...?!
Oh! How cute is that?
じり
じり
Some-thing like this...
...can only be the work of her.
Human! I will ask you one more time, and one more time only.
Do you swear or not?
Eehhh...

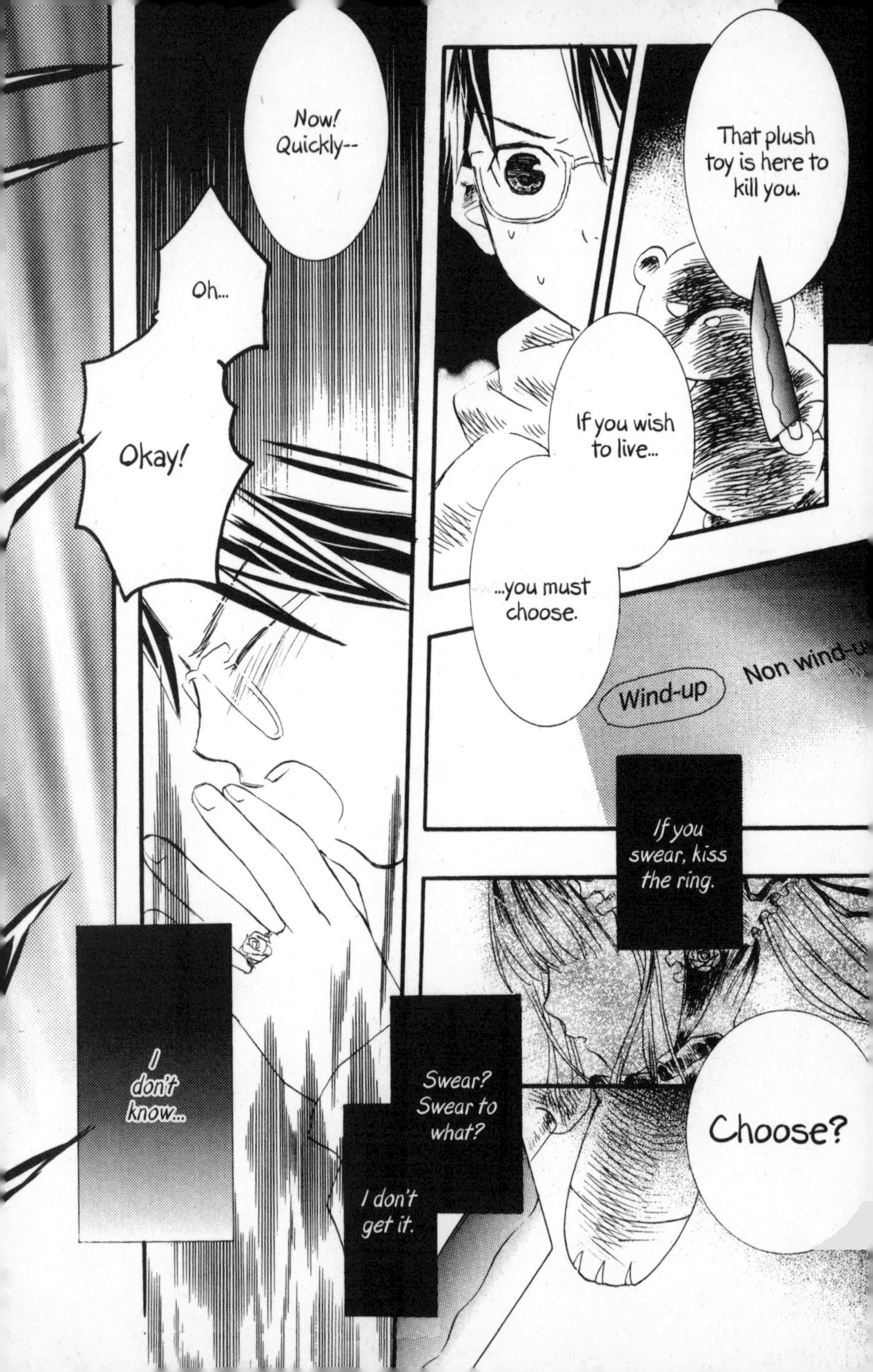
That plush toy is here to kill you.
If you wish to live...
...you must choose.
Wind-up
Non wind-u
If you swear, kiss the ring.
Choose?
Now! Quickly--
Oh...
Okay!
Swear? Swear to what?
I don't get it.
I don't know...

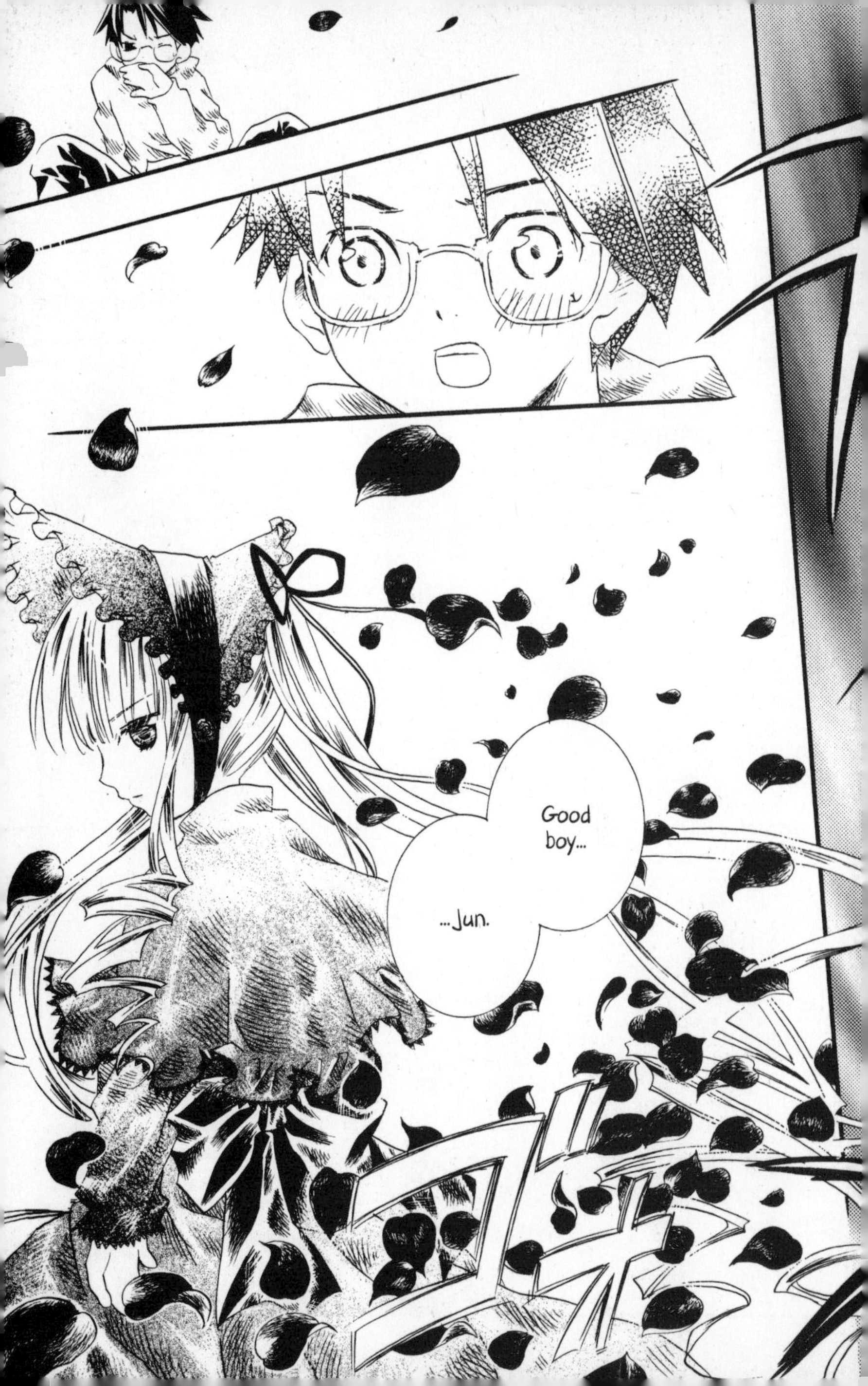
Good boy...
...Jun.

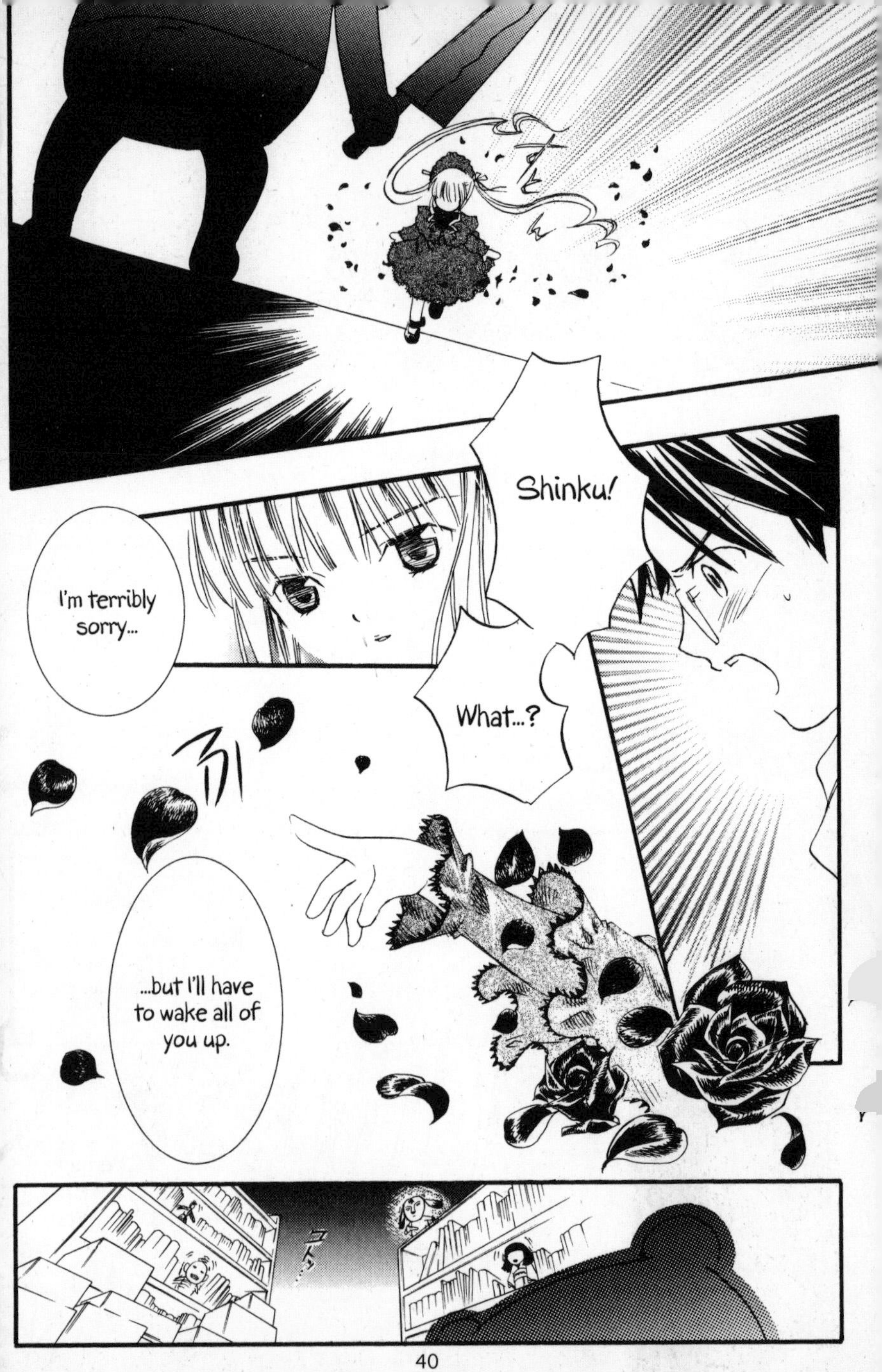
Shinku!
I'm terribly sorry...
What...?
...but I'll have to wake all of you up.

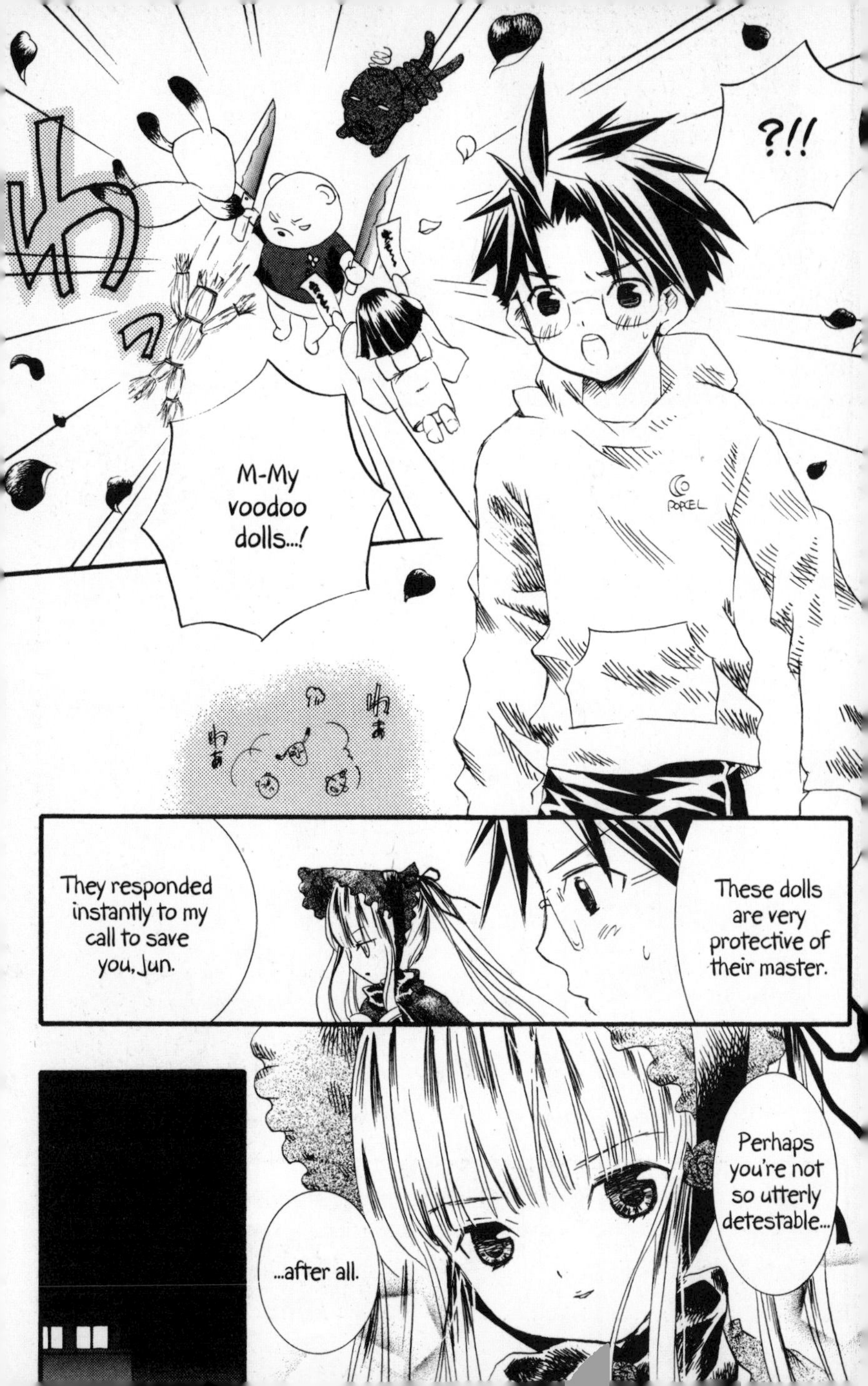
?!!
M-My voodoo dolls...!
These dolls are very protective of their master.
They responded instantly to my call to save you, Jun.
Perhaps you're not so utterly detestable...
...after all.

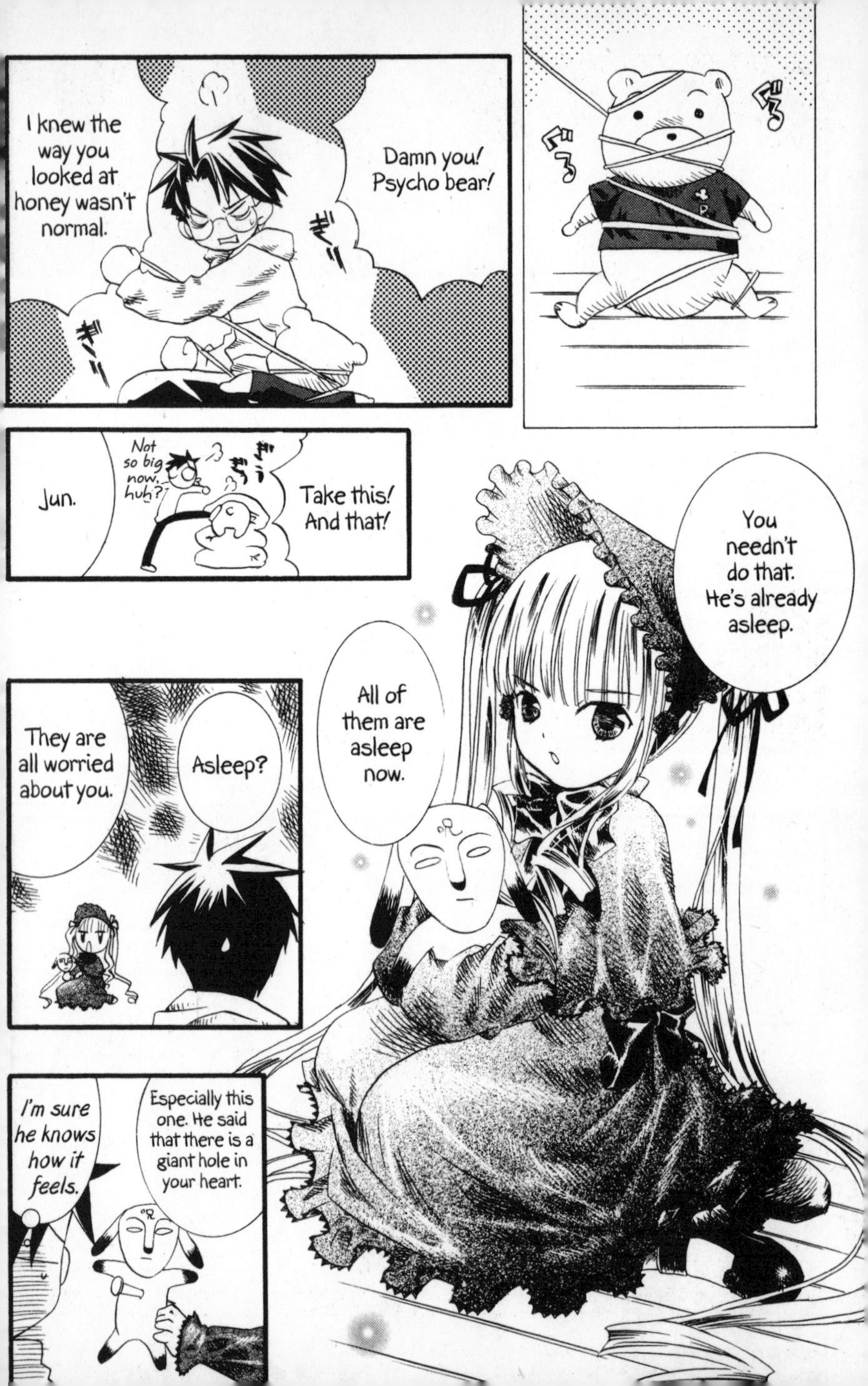
Damn you! Psycho bear!
I knew the way you looked at honey wasn't normal.
You needn't do that. He's already asleep.
All of them are asleep now.
Take this! And that!
Not so big now, huh?
Jun.
Asleep?
They are all worried about you.
Especially this one. He said that there is a giant hole in your heart.
I'm sure he knows how it feels.

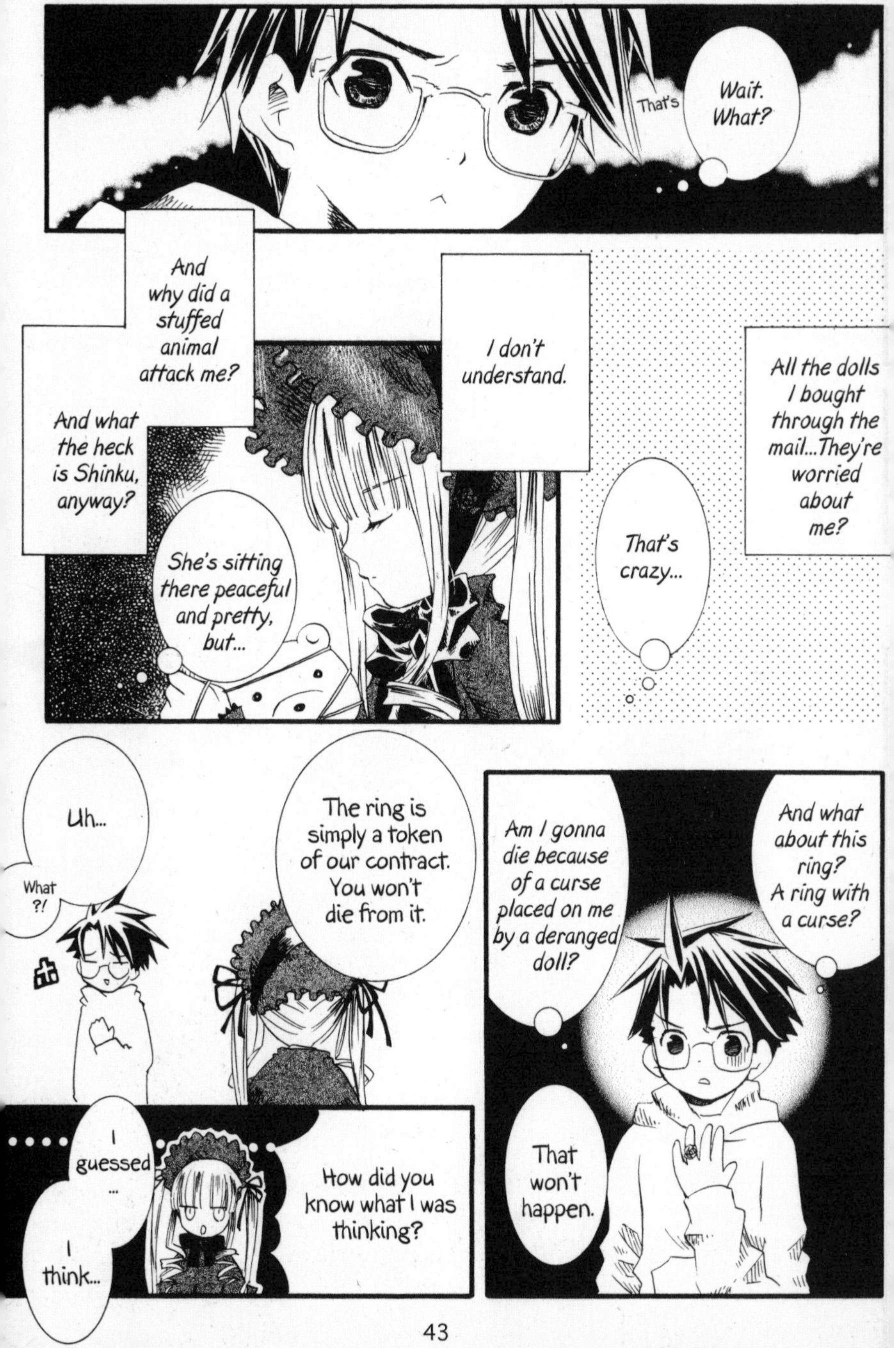

Wait. What?
That's
All the dolls I bought through the mail...They're worried about me?
That's crazy...
I don't understand.
And why did a stuffed animal attack me?
And what the heck is Shinku, anyway?
She's sitting there peaceful and pretty, but...
And what about this ring? A ring with a curse?
Am I gonna die because of a curse placed on me by a deranged doll?
That won't happen.
The ring is simply a token of our contract. You won't die from it.
Uh...
What ?!
How did you know what I was thinking?
.....
I guessed ...
I think...

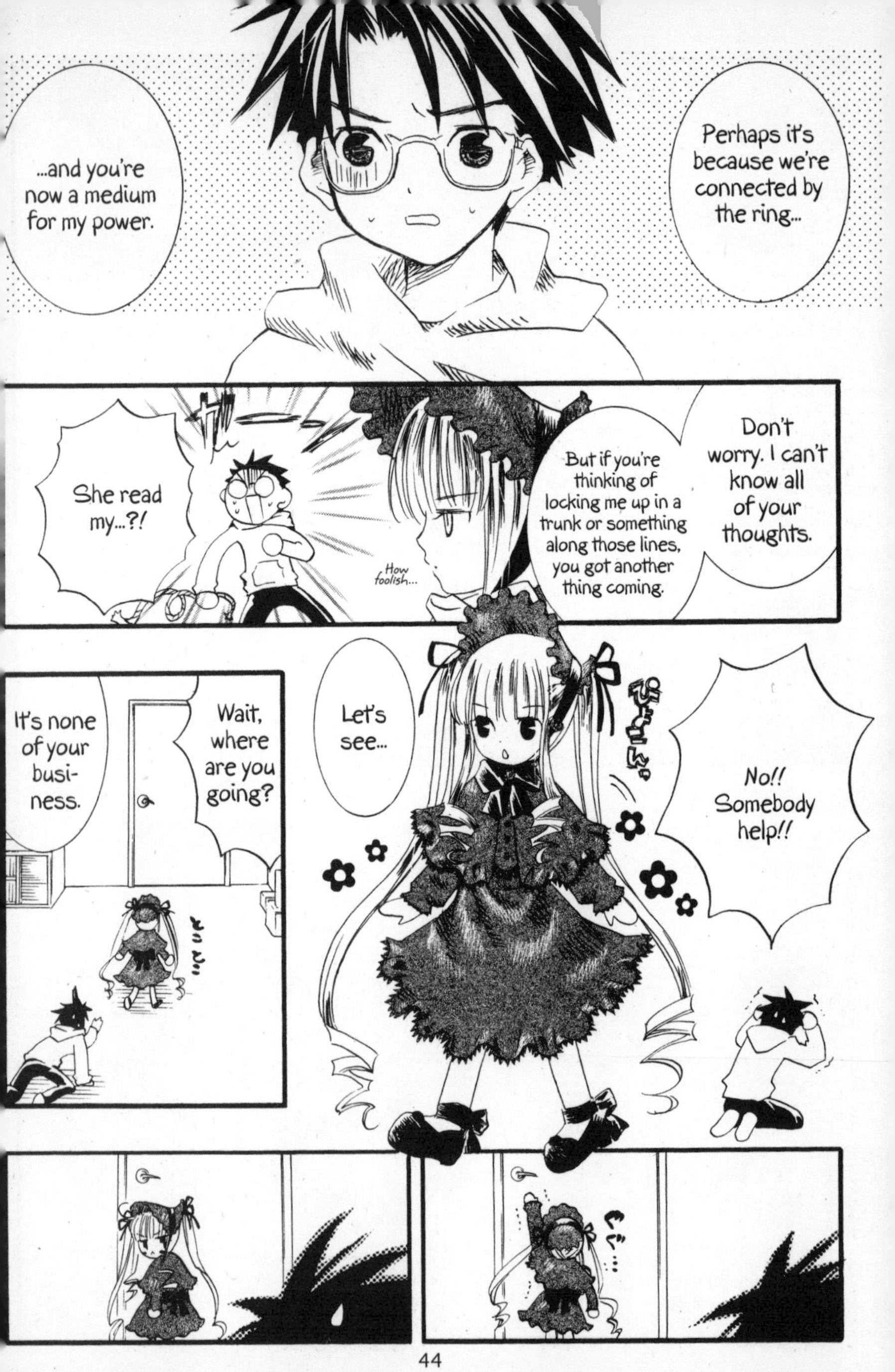
Perhaps it's because we're connected by the ring...
...and you're now a medium for my power.
Don't worry. I can't know all of your thoughts.
But if you're thinking of locking me up in a trunk or something along those lines, you got another thing coming.
How foolish...
She read my...?!
No!! Somebody help!!
Let's see...
Wait, where are you going?
It's none of your business.

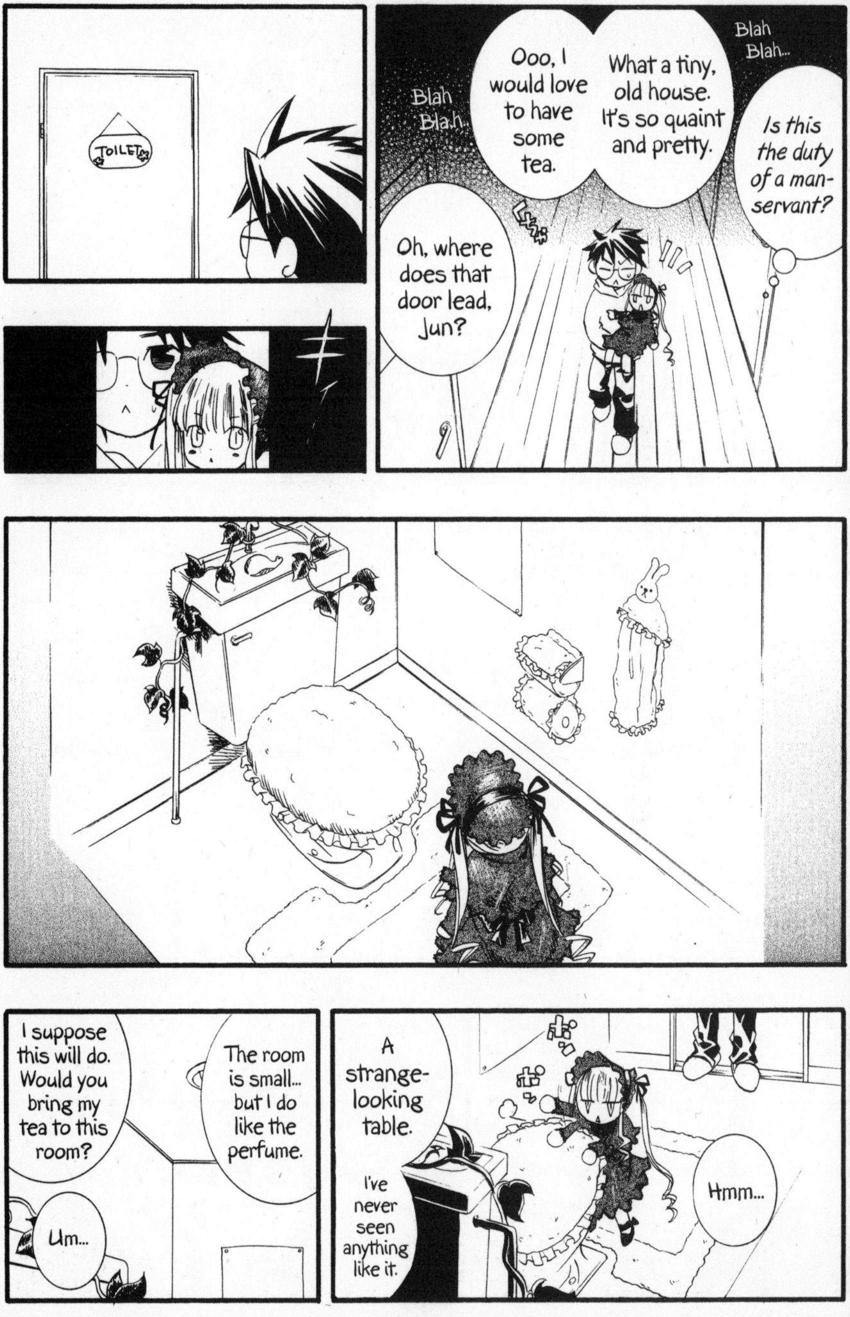
Blah Blah...
Is this the duty of a man-servant?
What a tiny, old house. It's so quaint and pretty.
Ooo, I would love to have some tea.
Blah Blah...
Oh, where does that door lead, Jun?
TOILET
Hmm...
A strange-looking table.
I've never seen anything like it.
The room is small... but I do like the perfume.
I suppose this will do. Would you bring my tea to this room?
Um...

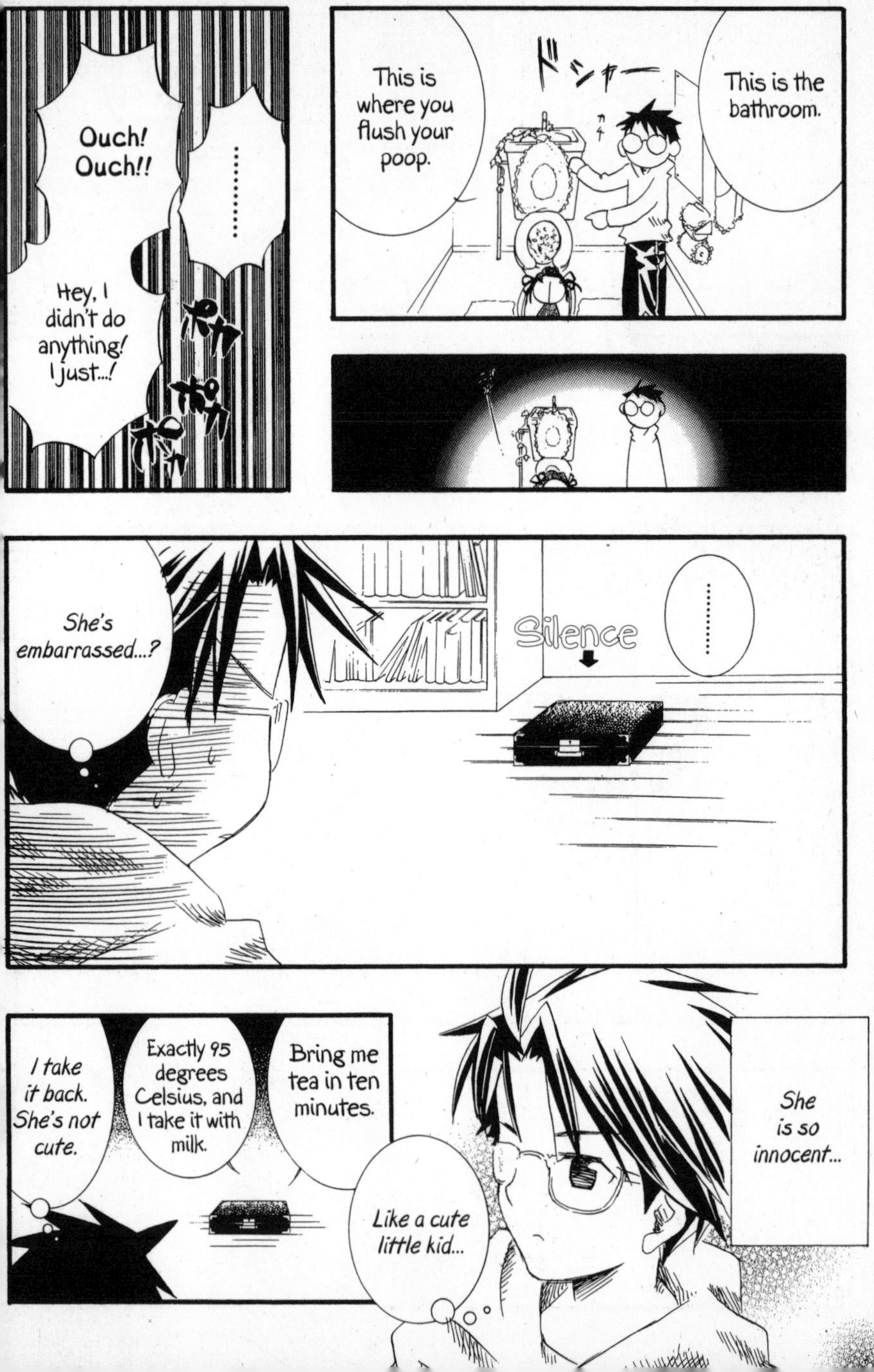
ドシャー
This is the bathroom.
This is where you flush your poop.
……
Ouch! Ouch!!
Hey, I didn't do anything! I just...!
ポカ ポカ ポカ
……
Silence
She's embarrassed...?
She is so innocent...
Like a cute little kid...
Bring me tea in ten minutes.
Exactly 95 degrees Celsius, and I take it with milk.
I take it back. She's not cute.

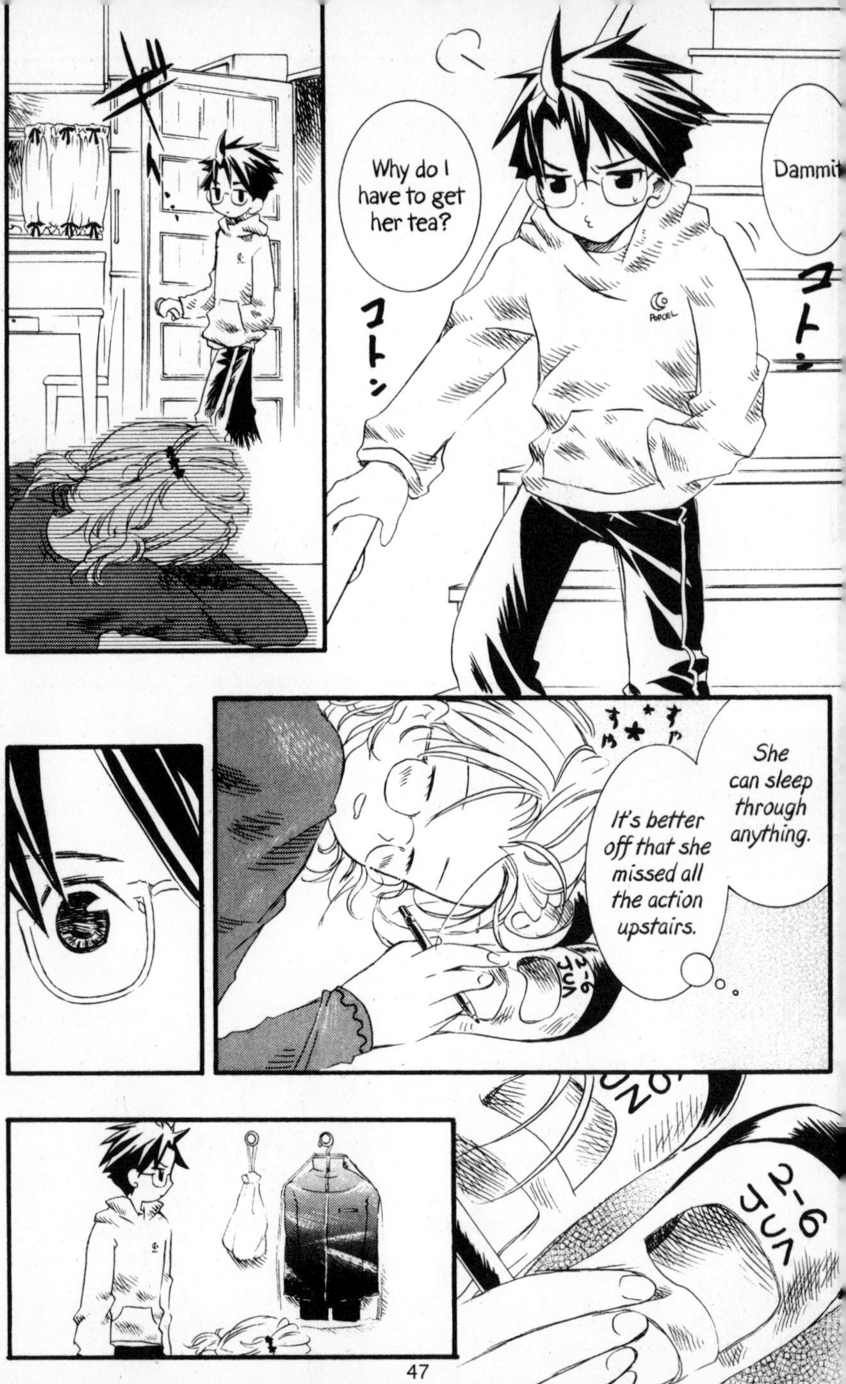
Dammit
コトン
Why do I have to get her tea?
コトン
すやすや
She can sleep through anything.
It's better off that she missed all the action upstairs.
2-6 JUN
2-6 JUN

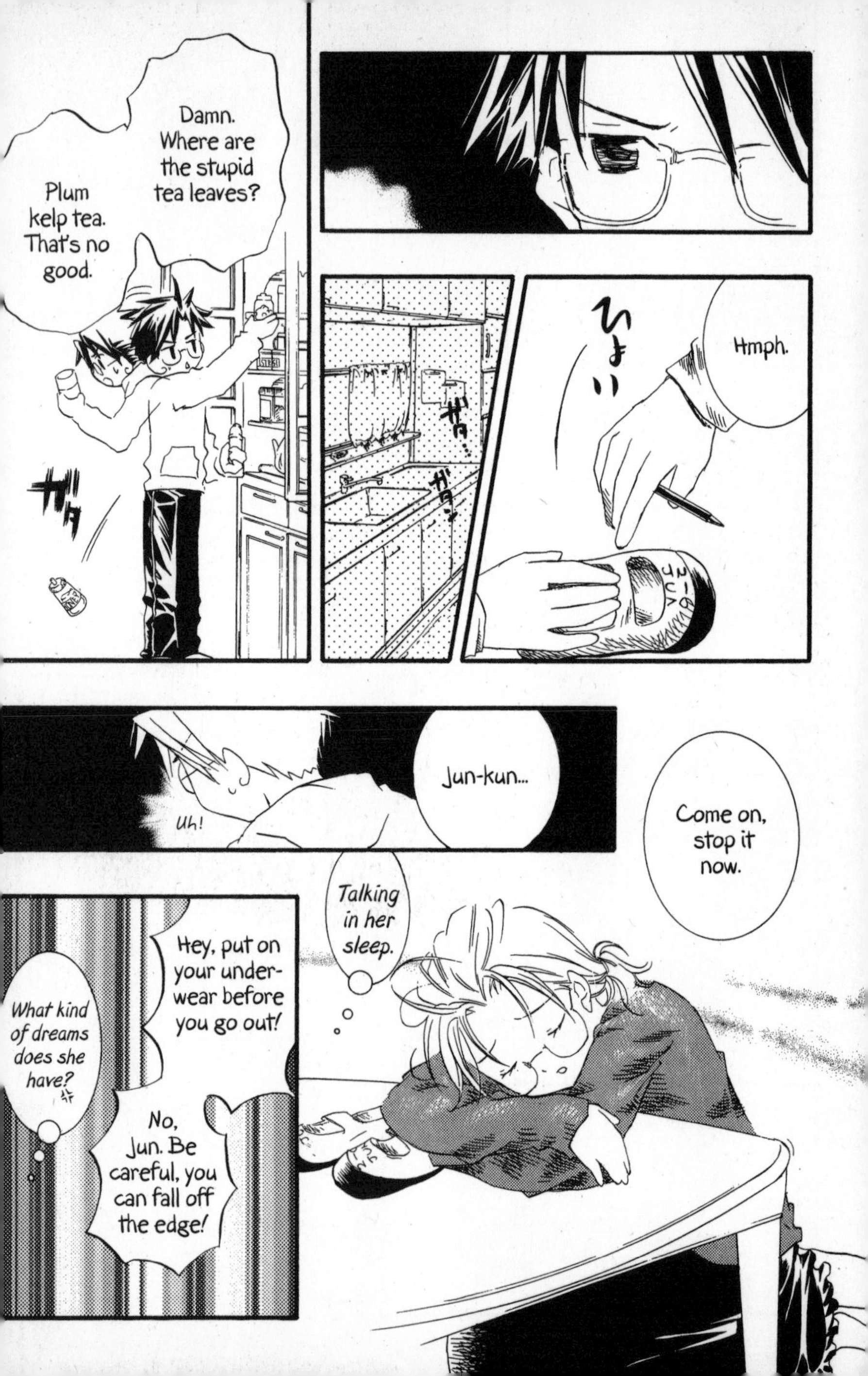

ひょい
Hmph.
ガタ…
ガタッ
Damn. Where are the stupid tea leaves?
Plum kelp tea. That's no good.
ガタ
Jun-kun...
Uh!
Come on, stop it now.
Talking in her sleep.
Hey, put on your under-wear before you go out!
No, Jun. Be careful, you can fall off the edge!
What kind of dreams does she have?

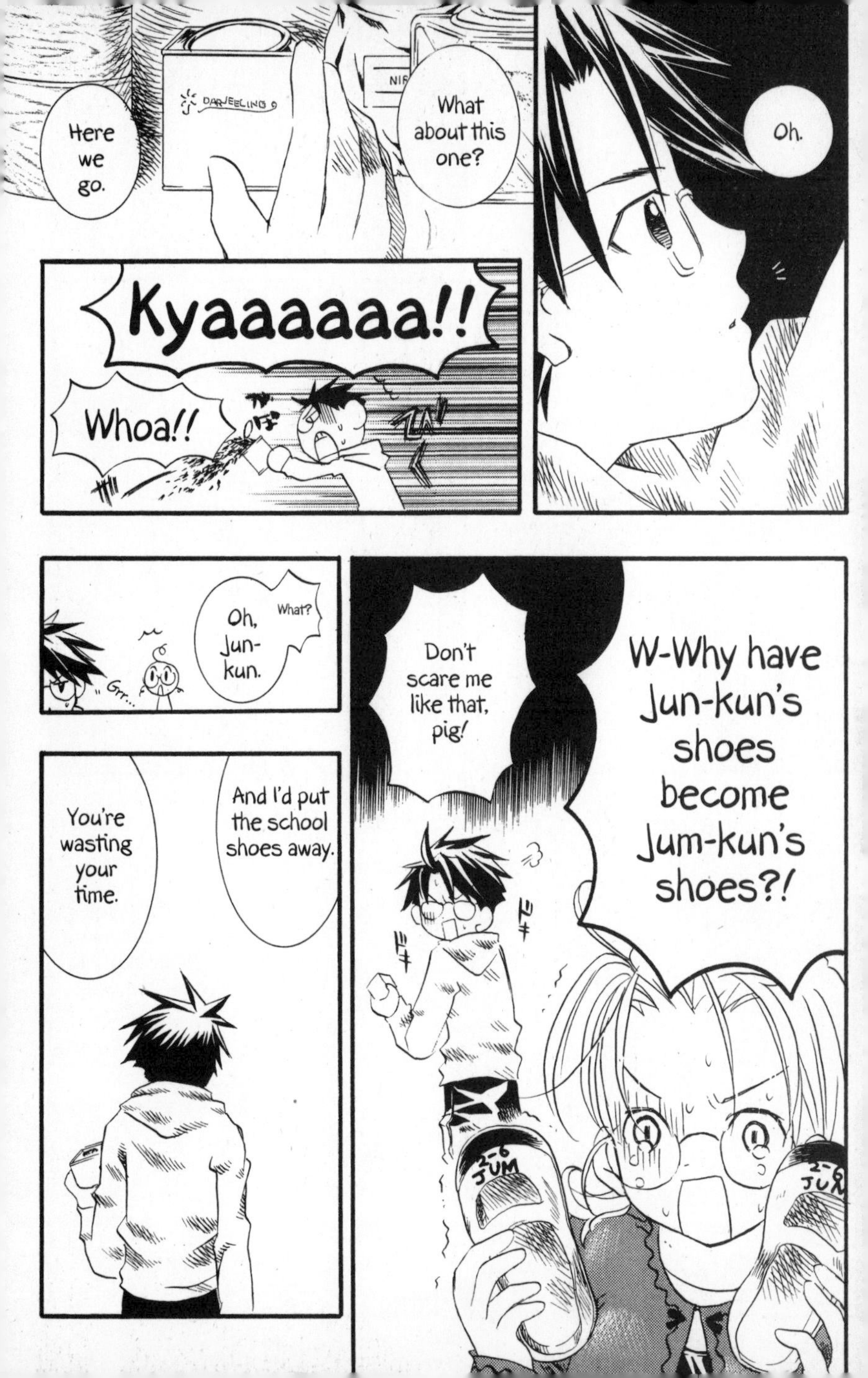
Oh.
What about this one?
DARJEELING
Here we go.
Kyaaaaaaa!!
Whoa!!
W-Why have Jun-kun's shoes become Jum-kun's shoes?!
Don't scare me like that, pig!
2-6 JUM
What?
Oh, Jun-kun.
Grrr...
And I'd put the school shoes away.
You're wasting your time.

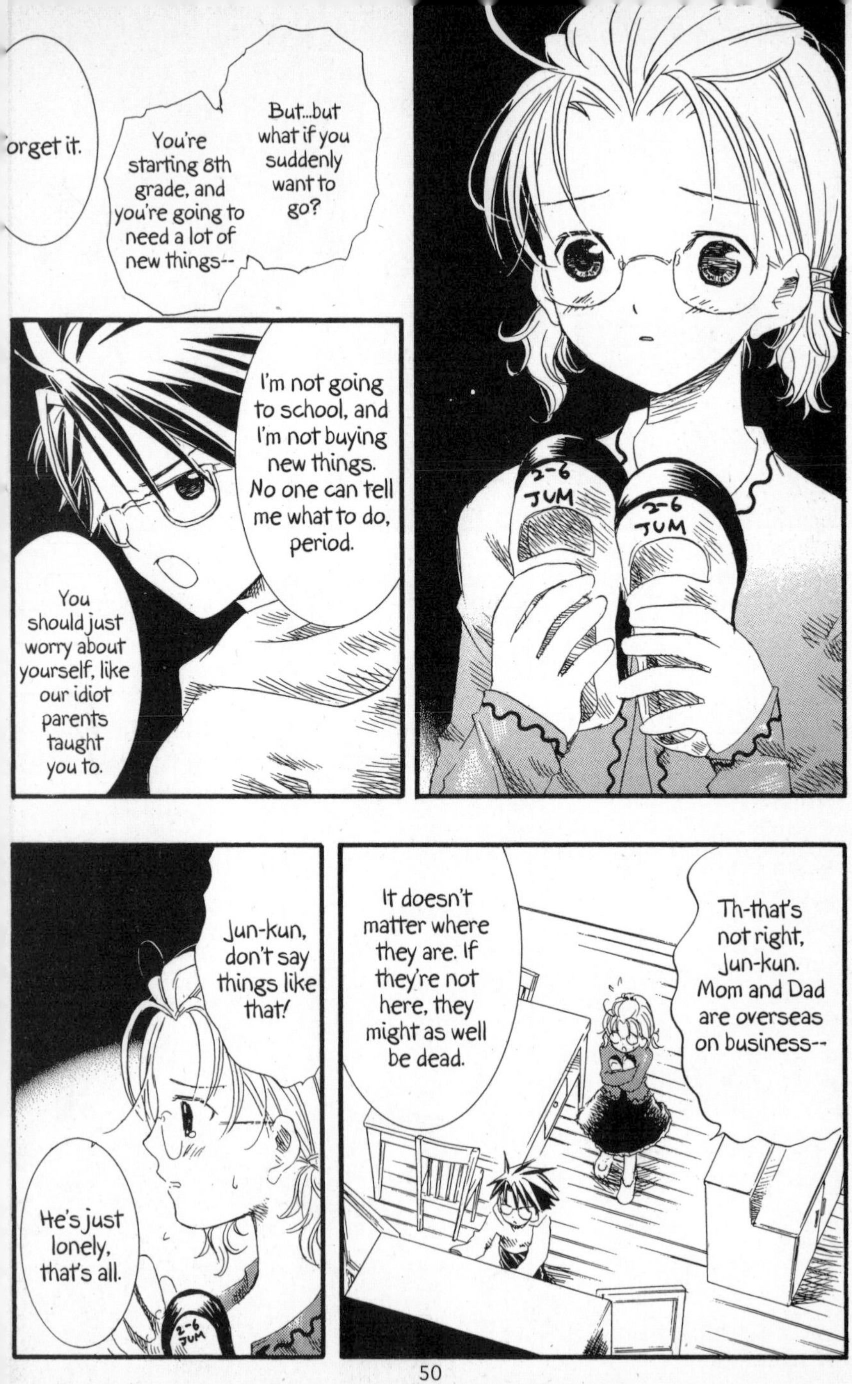
2-6 JUM
2-6 JUM
But...but what if you suddenly want to go?
You're starting 8th grade, and you're going to need a lot of new things--
orget it.
I'm not going to school, and I'm not buying new things. No one can tell me what to do, period.
You should just worry about yourself, like our idiot parents taught you to.
Th-that's not right, Jun-kun. Mom and Dad are overseas on business--
It doesn't matter where they are. If they're not here, they might as well be dead.
Jun-kun, don't say things like that!
He's just lonely, that's all.
2-6 JUM

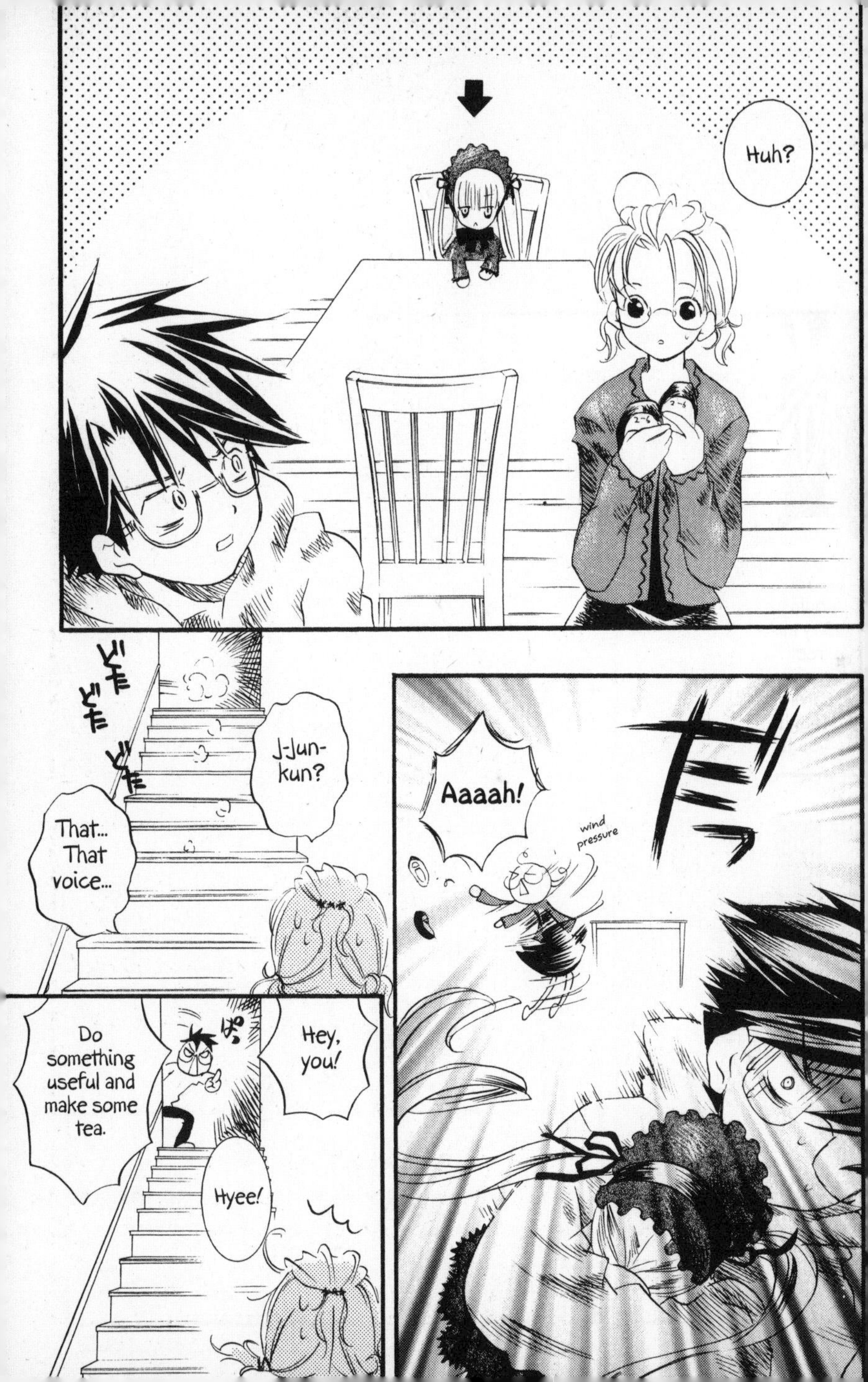
Huh?
Aaaah!
wind pressure
J-Jun-kun?
That... That voice...
Hey, you!
Do something useful and make some tea.
Hyee!

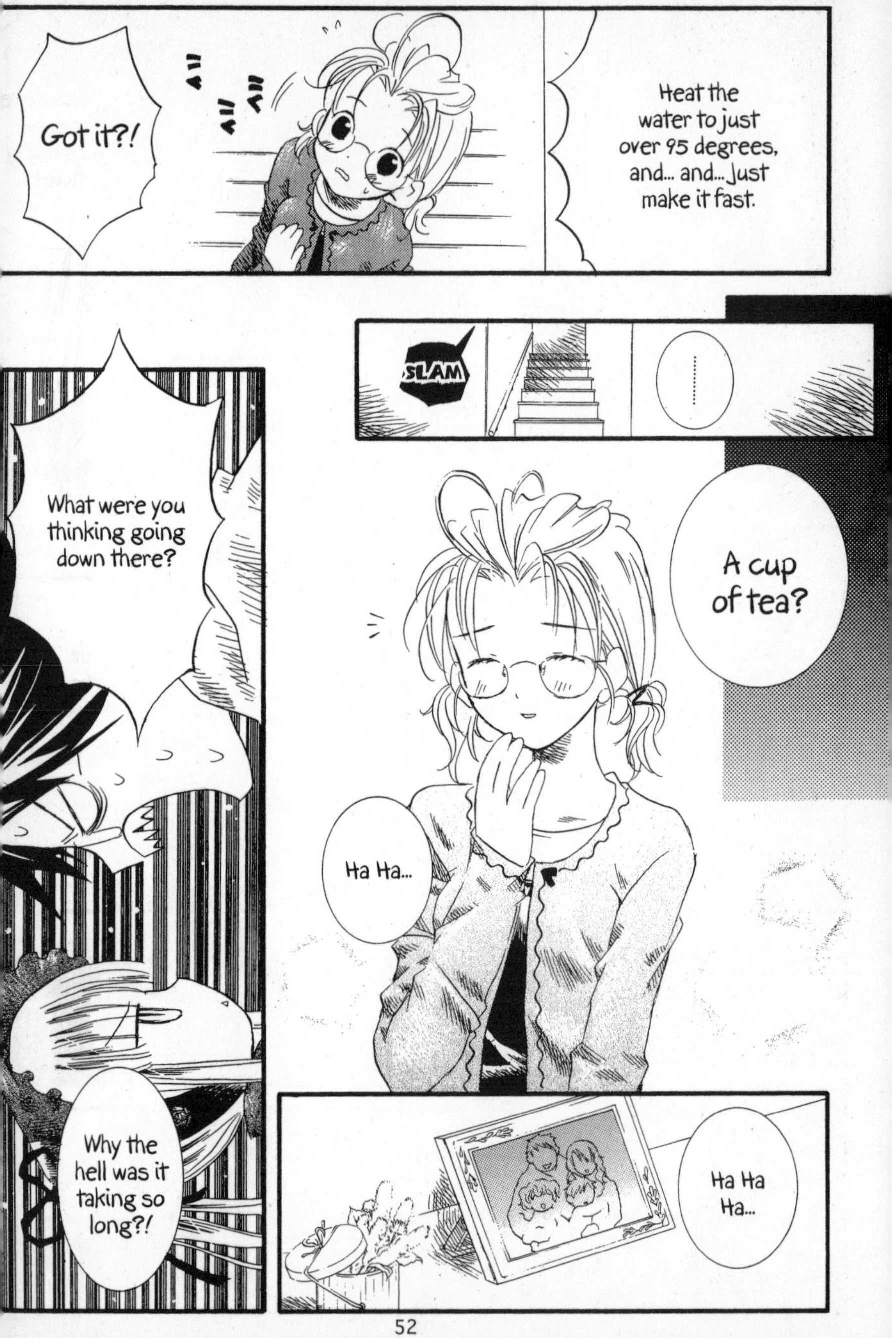
Heat the water to just over 95 degrees, and... and... Just make it fast.
Got it?!
......
SLAM
A cup of tea?
Ha Ha...
Ha Ha Ha...
What were you thinking going down there?
Why the hell was it taking so long?!

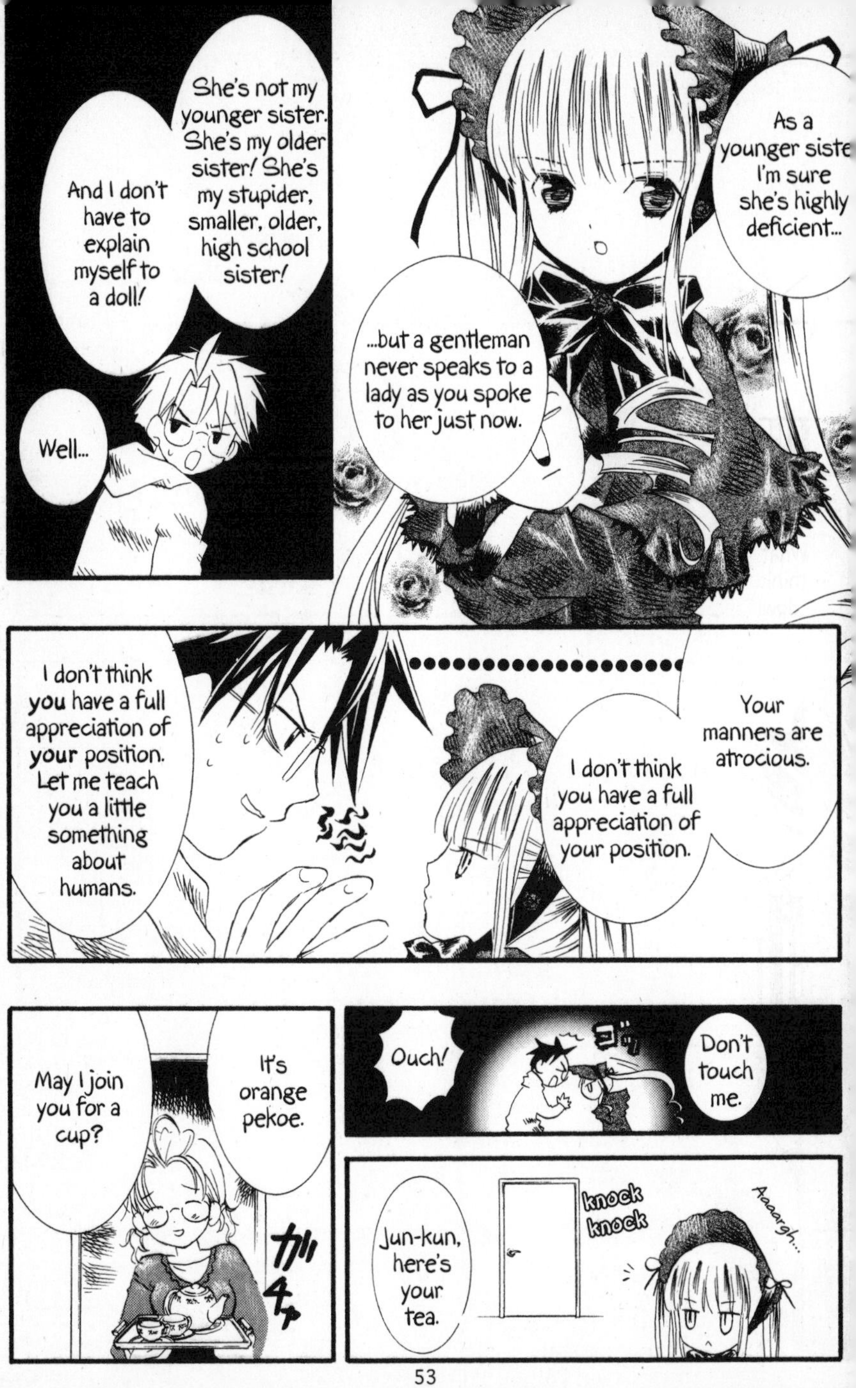
As a younger siste I'm sure she's highly deficient...
...but a gentleman never speaks to a lady as you spoke to her just now.
She's not my younger sister. She's my older sister! She's my stupider, smaller, older, high school sister!
And I don't have to explain myself to a doll!
Well...
Your manners are atrocious.
I don't think you have a full appreciation of your position.
I don't think **you** have a full appreciation of **your** position. Let me teach you a little something about humans.
Don't touch me.
Ouch!
Aaaargh...
knock knock
Jun-kun, here's your tea.
It's orange pekoe.
May I join you for a cup?

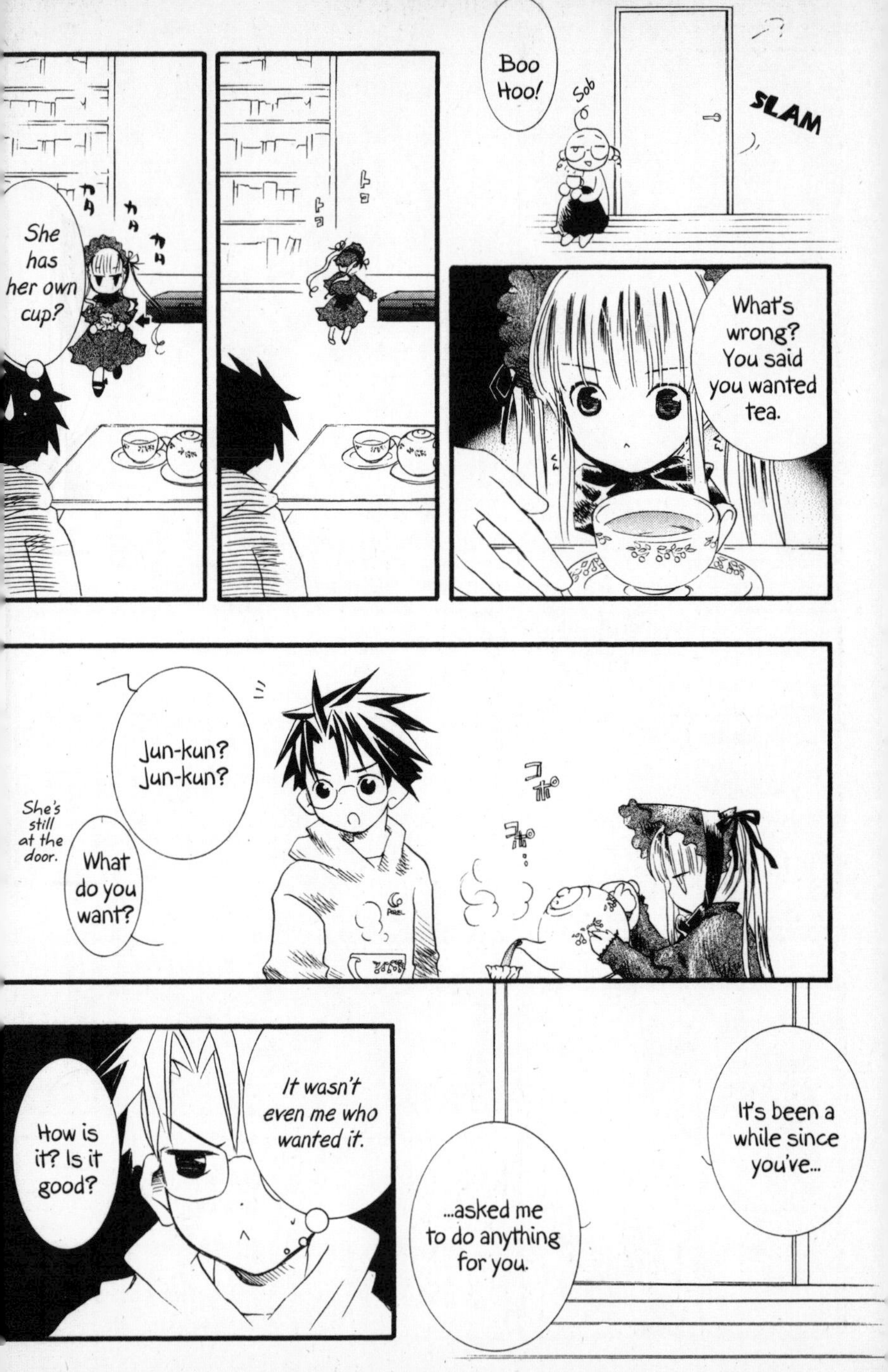
Boo Hoo!
Sob
SLAM
What's wrong? You said you wanted tea.
She has her own cup?
Jun-kun? Jun-kun?
She's still at the door.
What do you want?
It's been a while since you've...
...asked me to do anything for you.
It wasn't even me who wanted it.
How is it? Is it good?

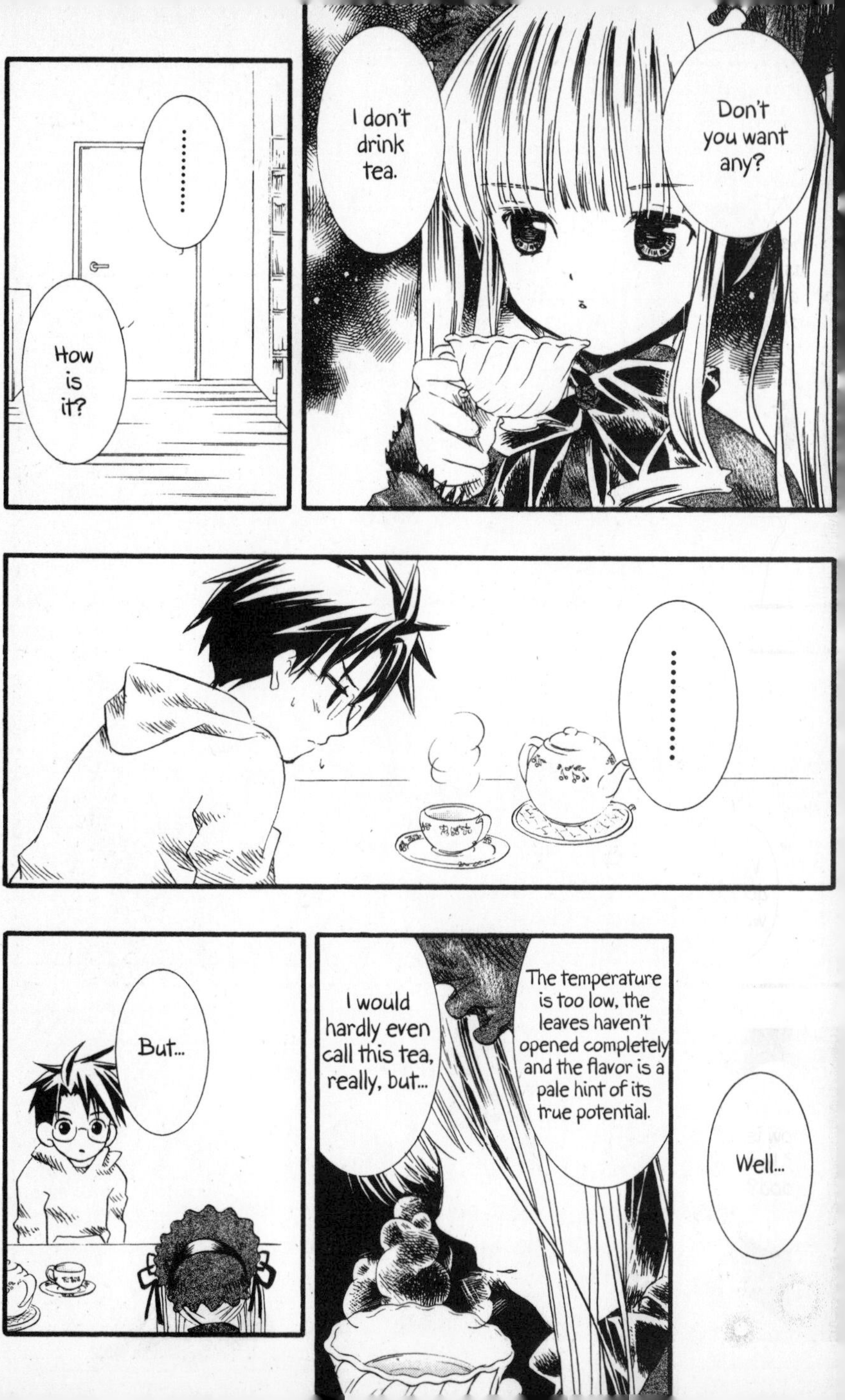
Don't you want any?
I don't drink tea.
....
How is it?
....
Well...
The temperature is too low, the leaves haven't opened completely and the flavor is a pale hint of its true potential.
I would hardly even call this tea, really, but...
But...

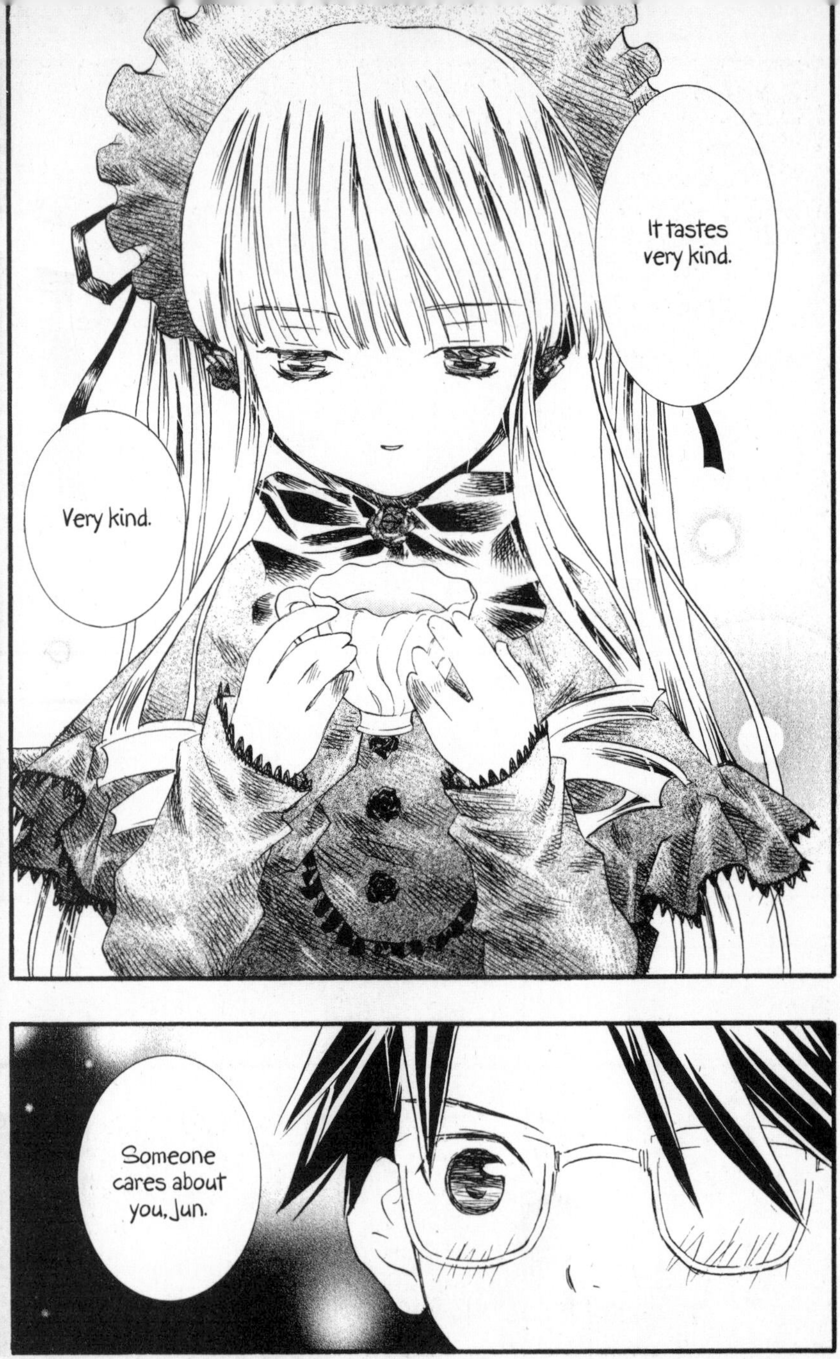
It tastes very kind.
Very kind.
Someone cares about you, Jun.

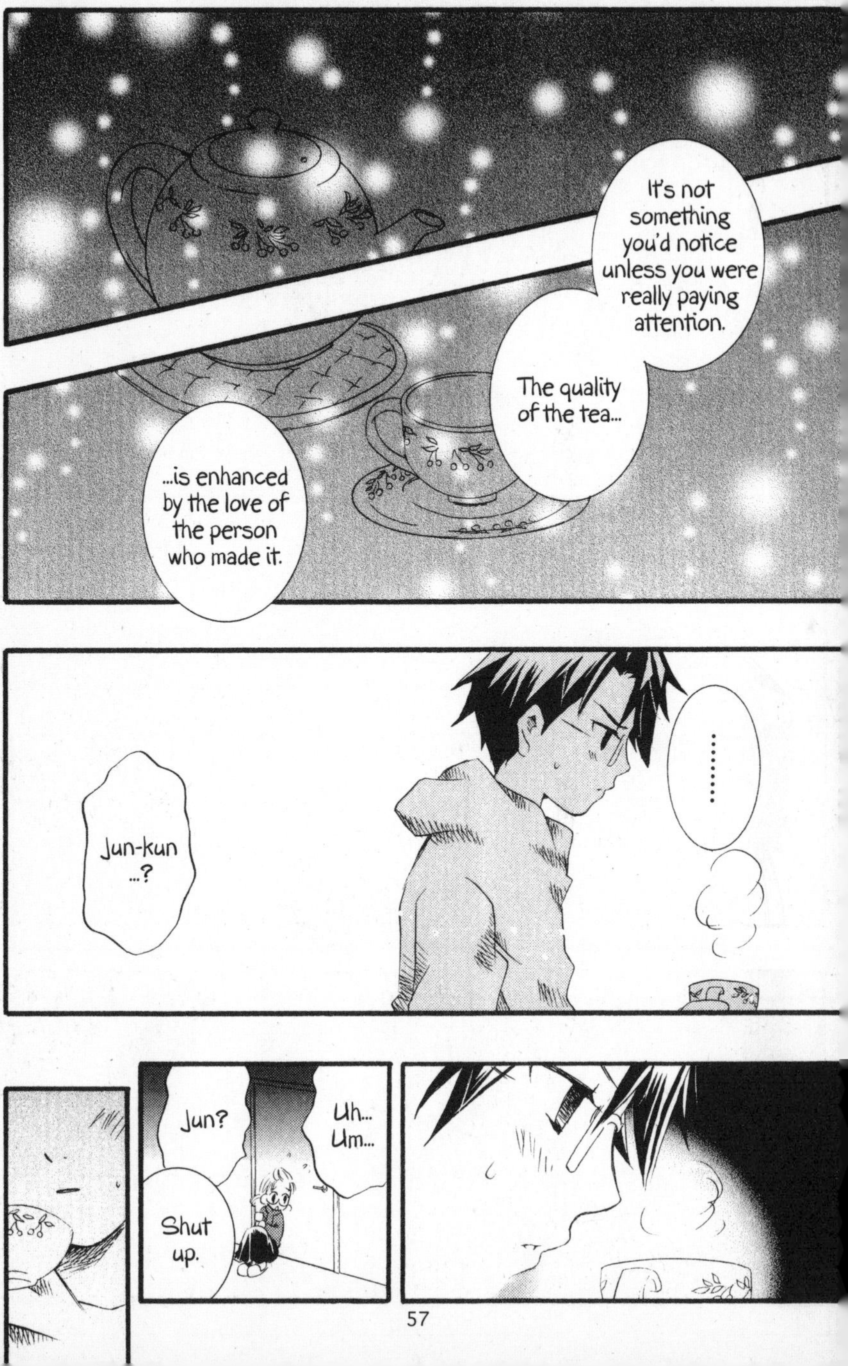
It's not something you'd notice unless you were really paying attention.
The quality of the tea...
...is enhanced by the love of the person who made it.
....
Jun-kun ...?
Uh... Um...
Jun?
Shut up.

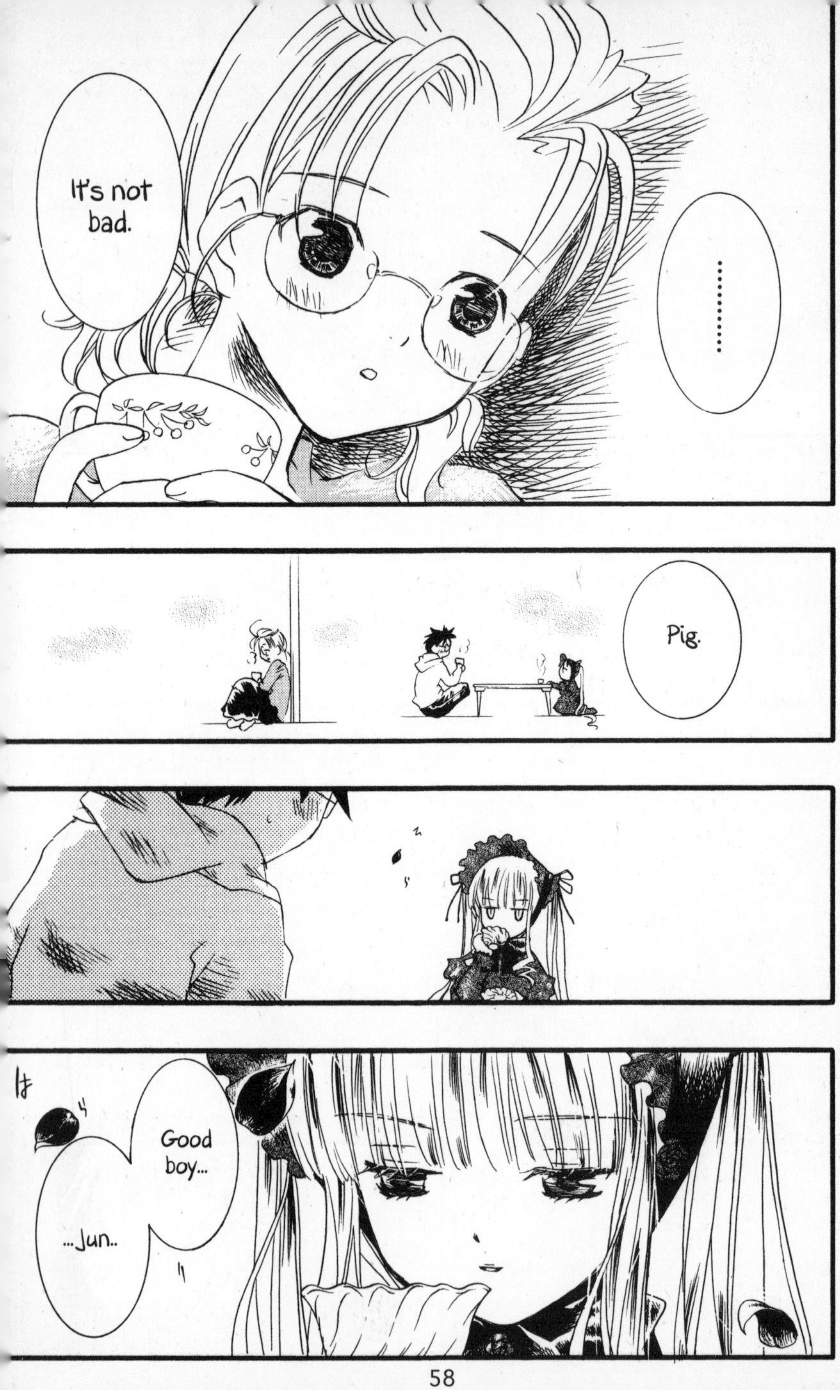
......
It's not bad.
Pig.
Good boy...
...Jun..
は

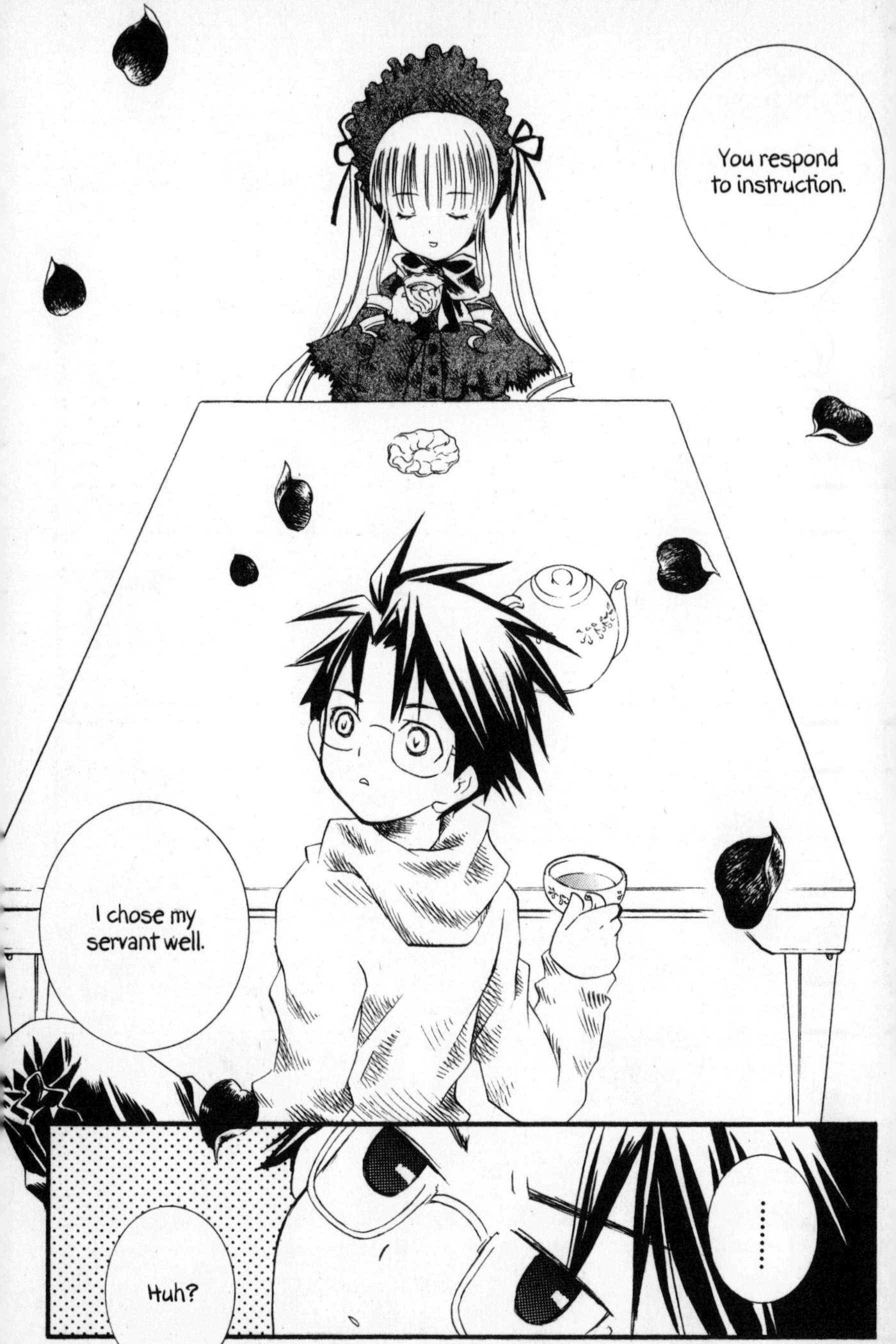
You respond to instruction.
I chose my servant well.
......
Huh?

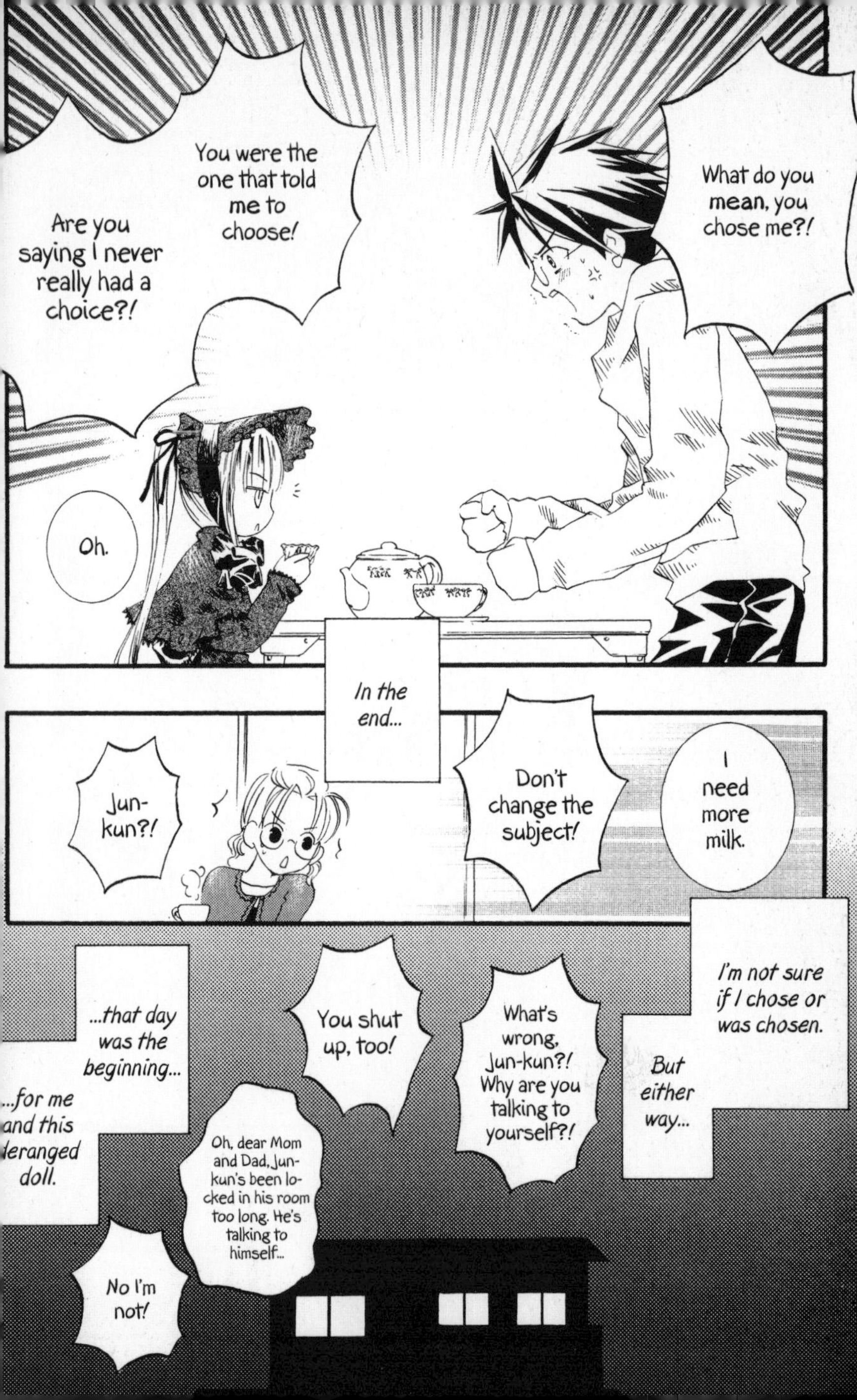
What do you mean, you chose me?!
You were the one that told me to choose!
Are you saying I never really had a choice?!
Oh.
In the end...
I need more milk.
Don't change the subject!
Jun-kun?!
I'm not sure if I chose or was chosen.
But either way...
What's wrong, Jun-kun?! Why are you talking to yourself?!
You shut up, too!
...that day was the beginning...
...for me and this deranged doll.
Oh, dear Mom and Dad, Jun-kun's been locked in his room too long. He's talking to himself...
No I'm not!

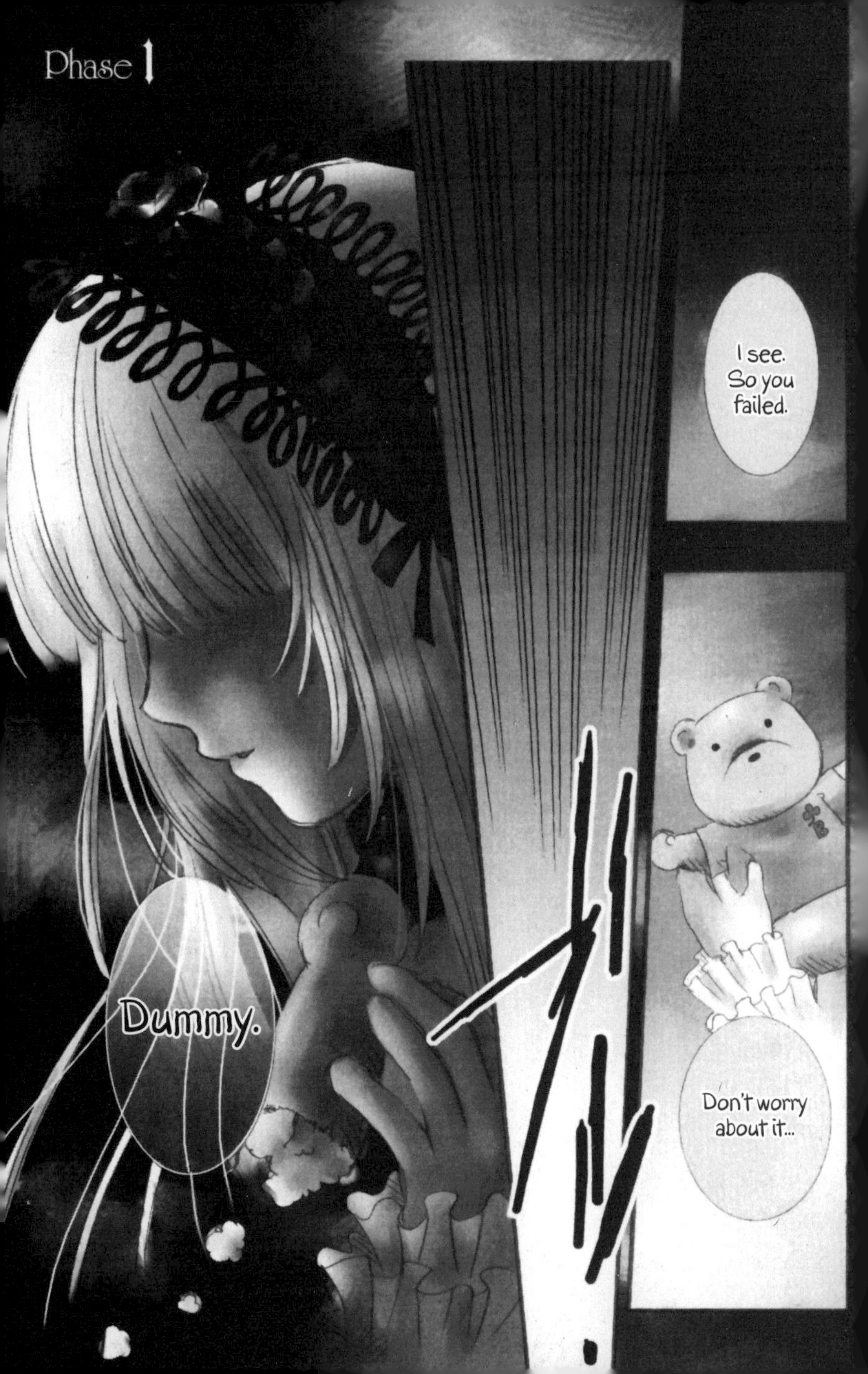
Phase 1
I see. So you failed.
Don't worry about it...
Dummy.

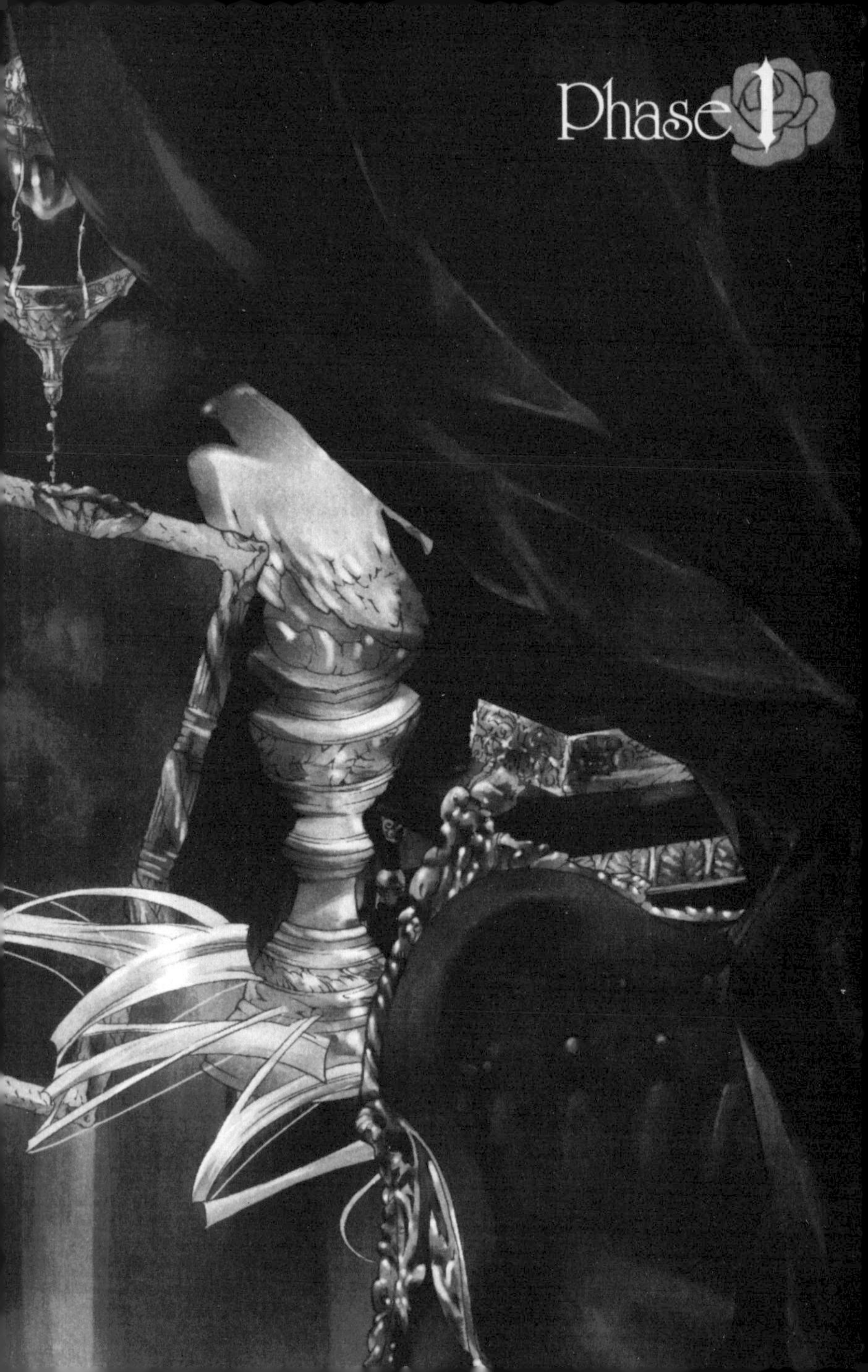
Phase 1

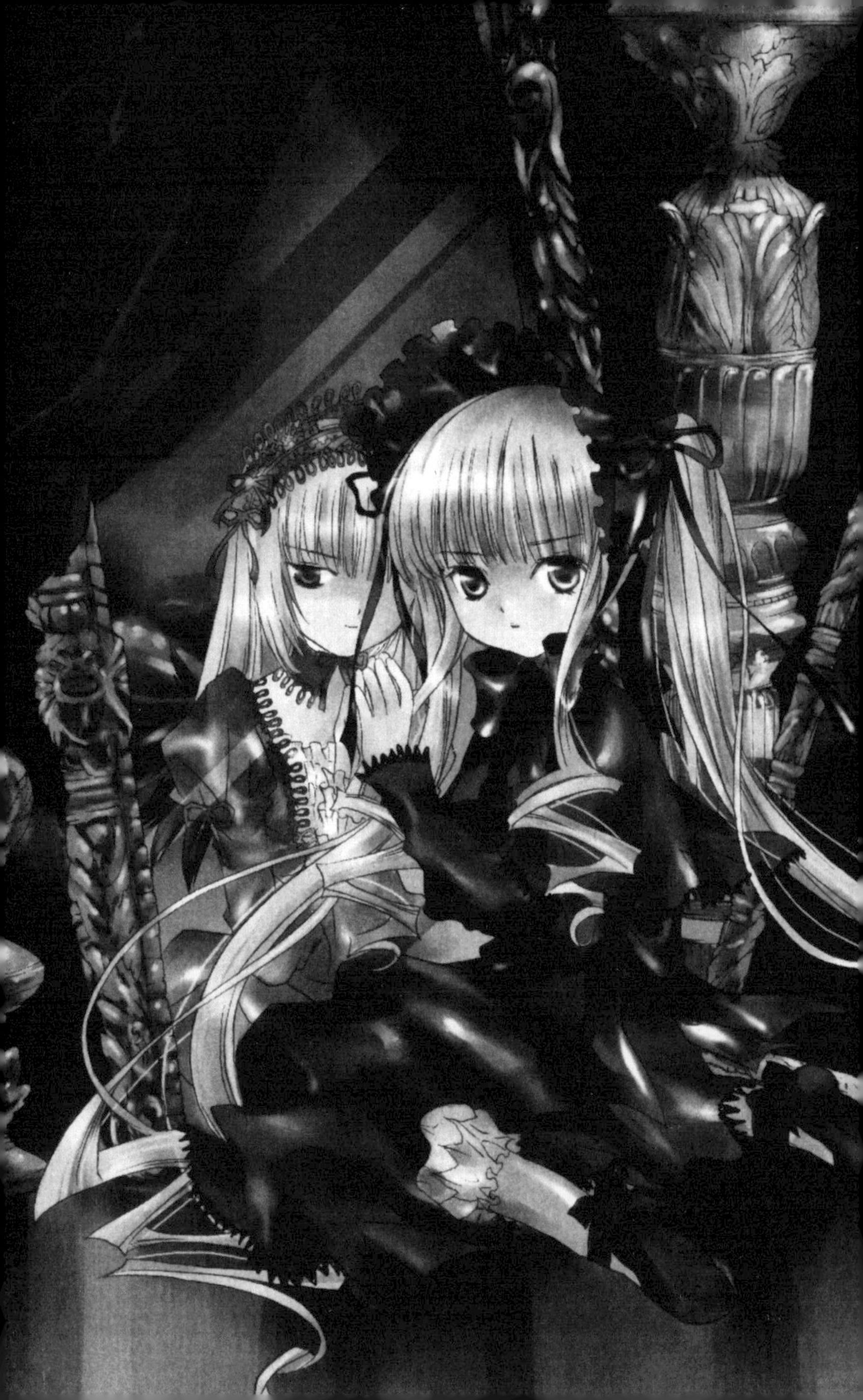

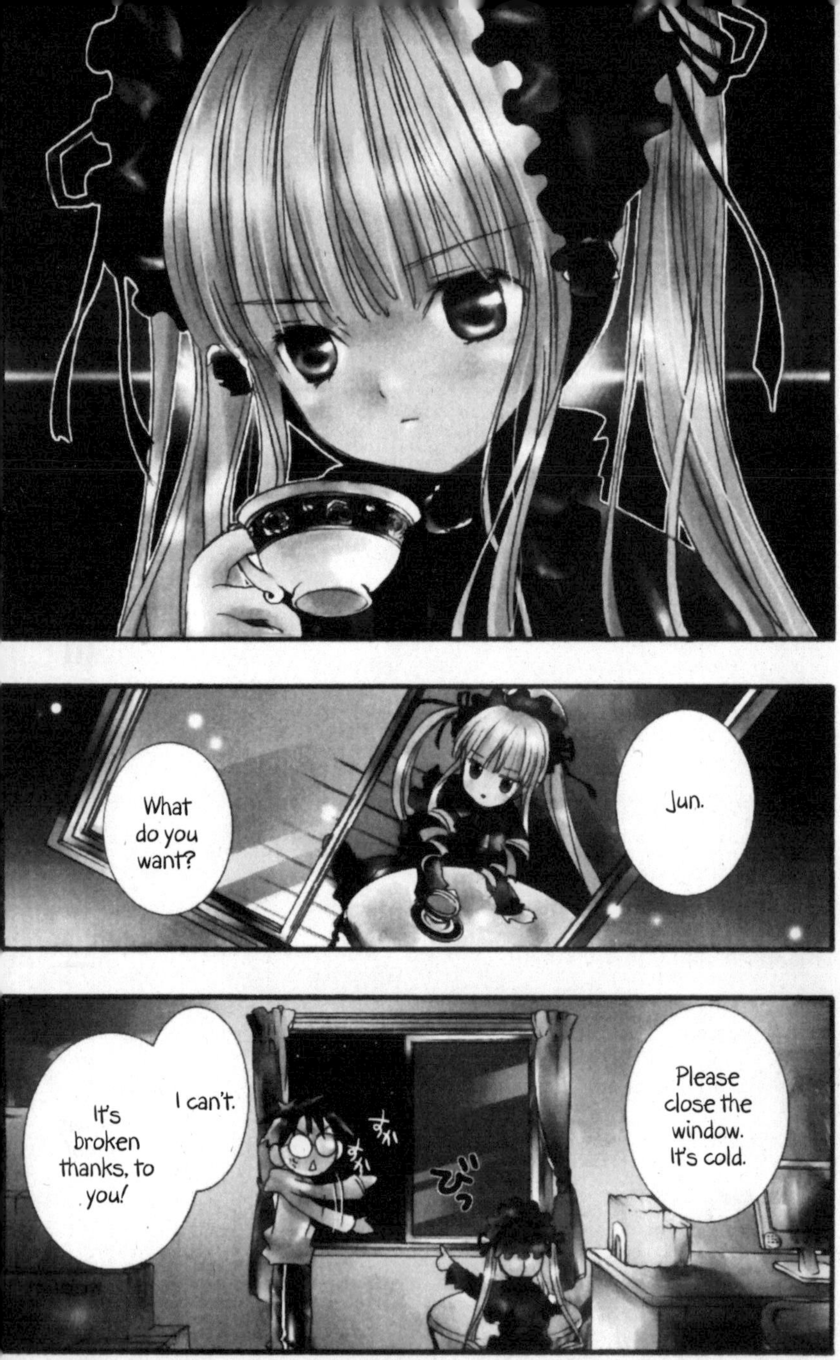
Jun.
What do you want?
Please close the window. It's cold.
I can't.
It's broken thanks, to you!

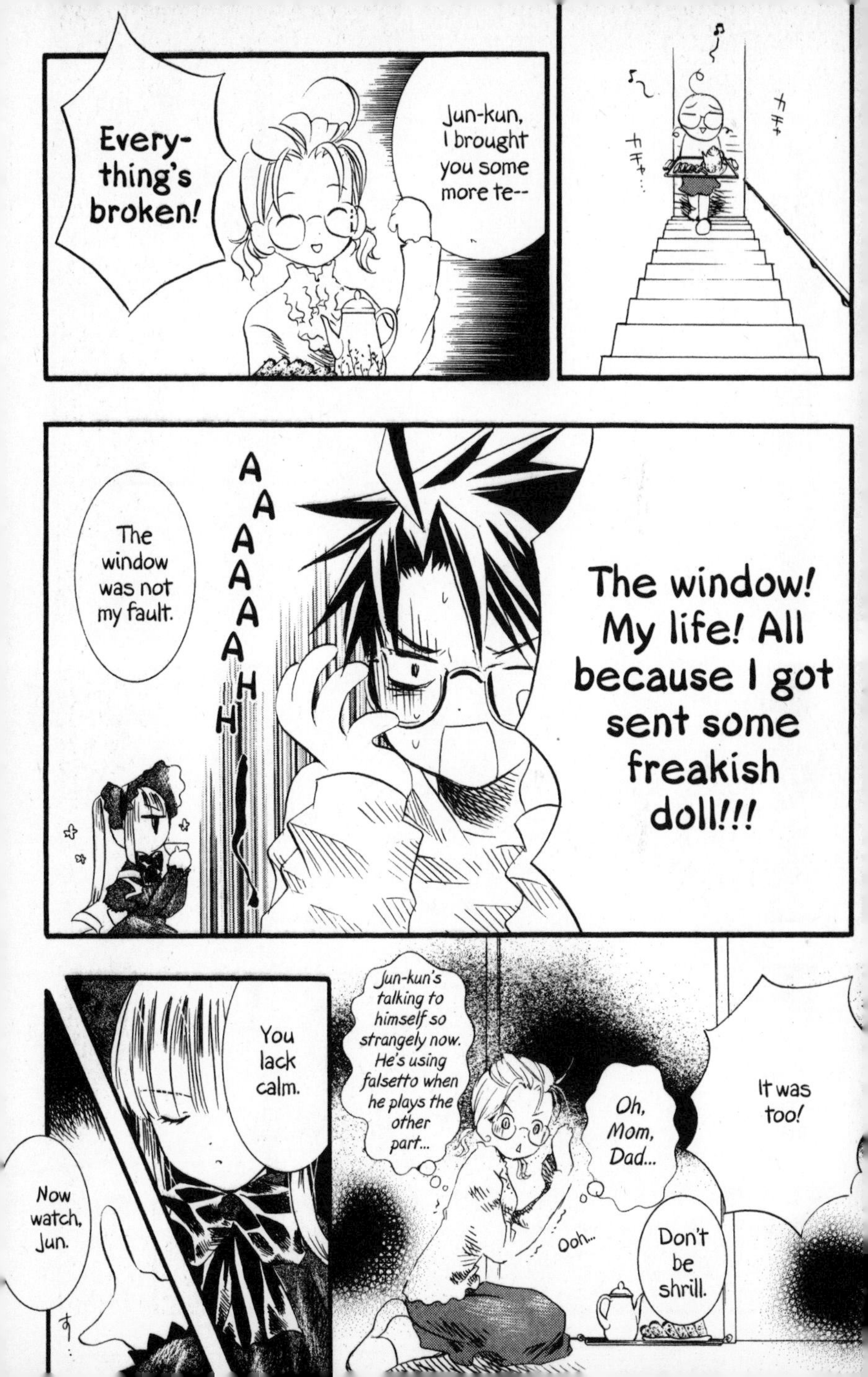
Jun-kun, I brought you some more te--
Every-thing's broken!
The window! My life! All because I got sent some freakish doll!!!
AAAAAAAHH
The window was not my fault.
It was too!
Jun-kun's talking to himself so strangely now. He's using falsetto when he plays the other part...
Oh, Mom, Dad...
Don't be shrill.
Ooh...
You lack calm.
Now watch, Jun.

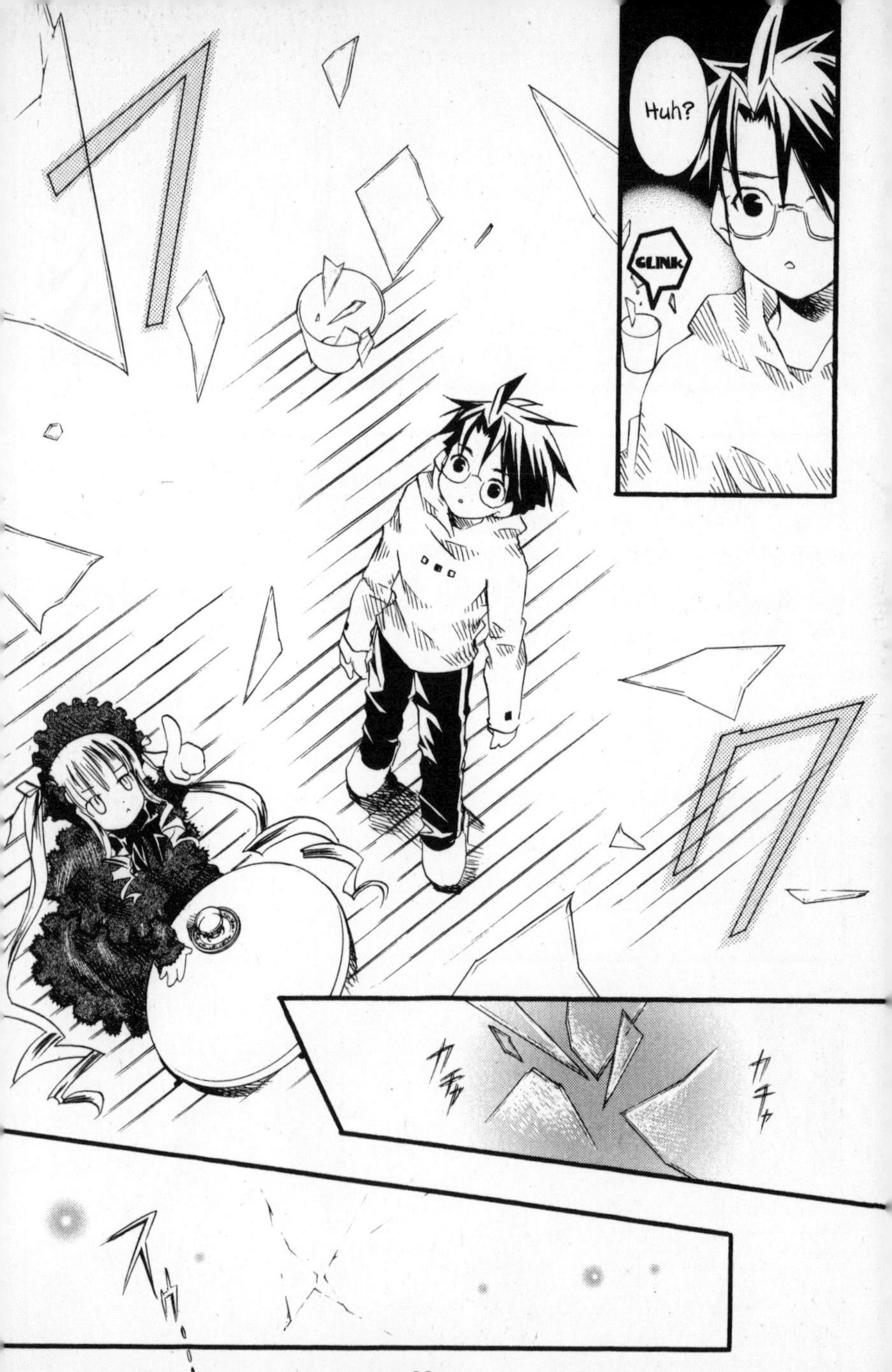
Huh?
GLINK
カチャ
カチャ
スッ…

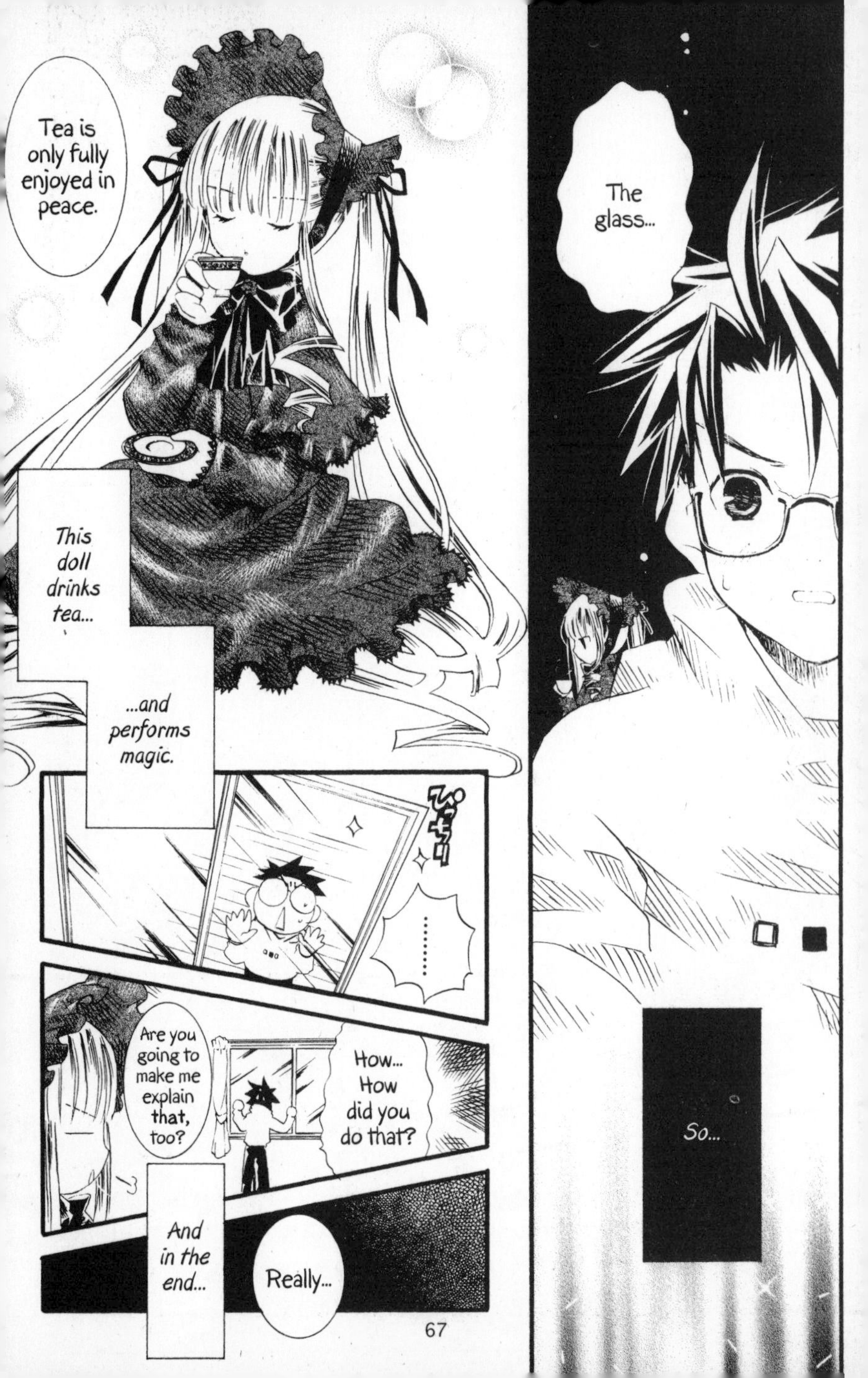
The glass...
So...
Tea is only fully enjoyed in peace.
This doll drinks tea...
...and performs magic.
....
How... How did you do that?
Are you going to make me explain that, too?
Really...
And in the end...

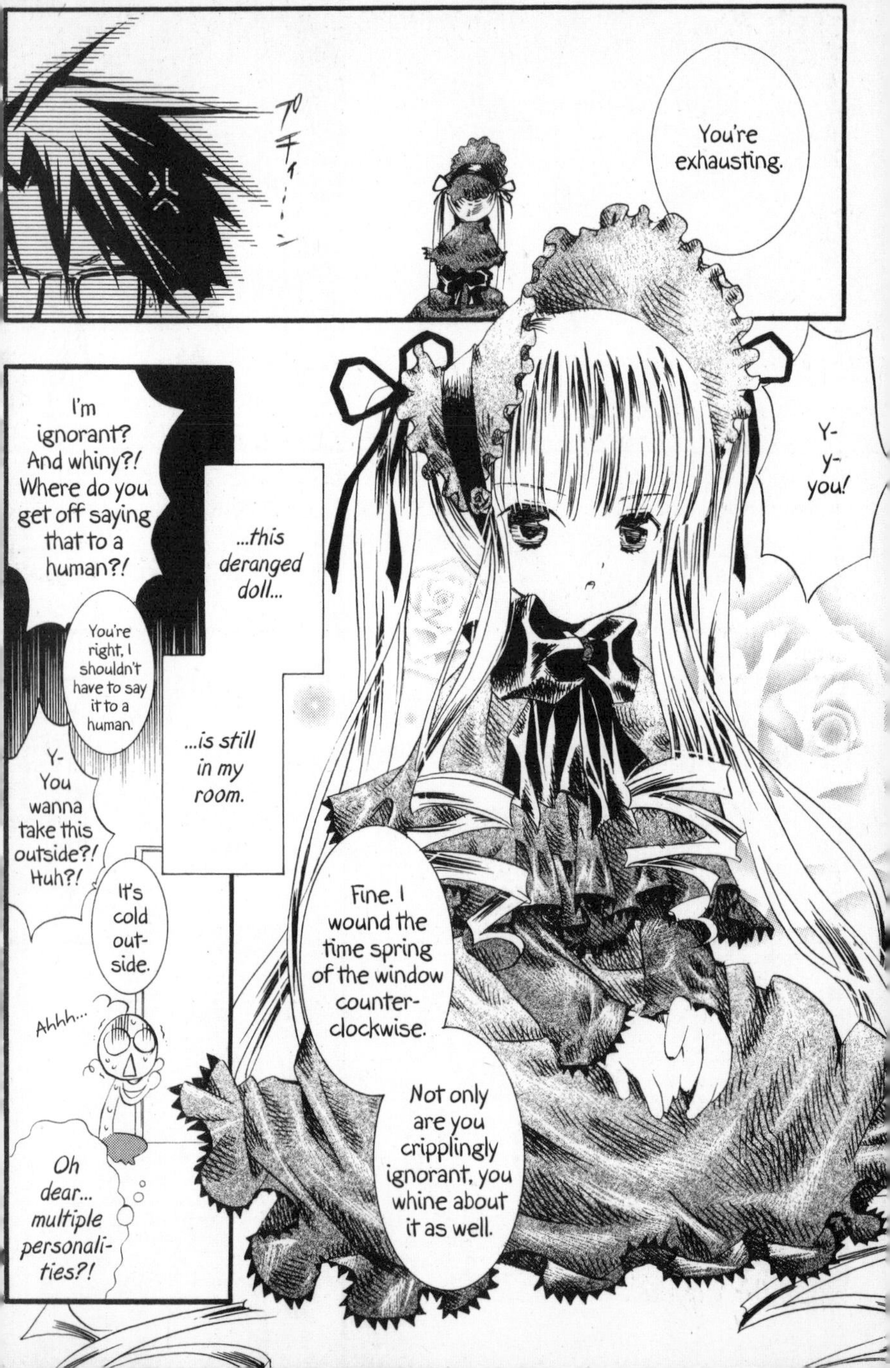
You're exhausting.
Y- y- you!
Fine. I wound the time spring of the window counter-clockwise.
Not only are you cripplingly ignorant, you whine about it as well.
I'm ignorant? And whiny?! Where do you get off saying that to a human?!
...this deranged doll...
...is still in my room.
You're right, I shouldn't have to say it to a human.
Y- You wanna take this outside?! Huh?!
It's cold out- side.
Ahhh...
Oh dear... multiple personali- ties?!

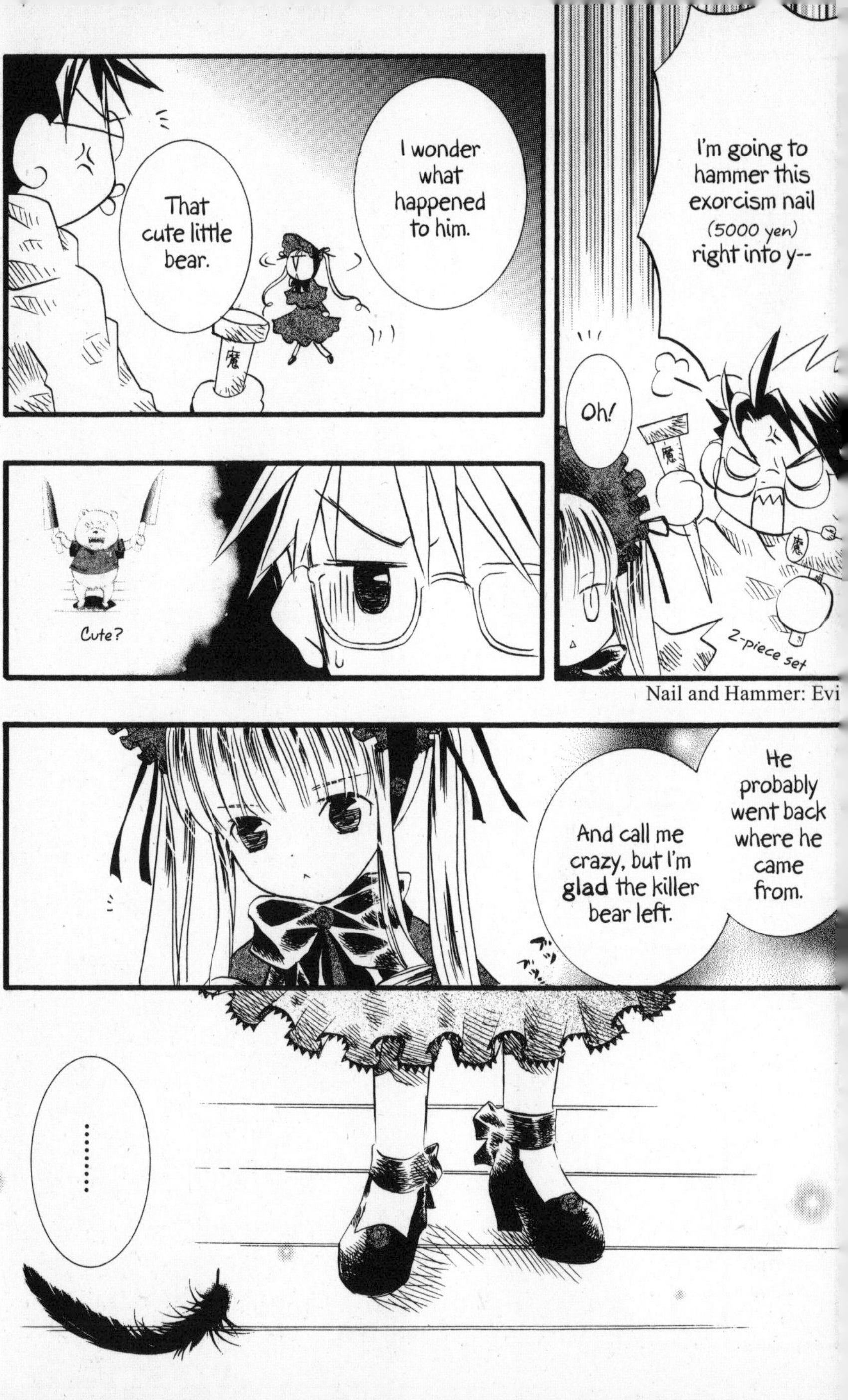
I'm going to hammer this exorcism nail (5000 yen) right into y--
Oh!
2-piece set
Nail and Hammer: Evi
I wonder what happened to him.
That cute little bear.
Cute?
He probably went back where he came from.
And call me crazy, but I'm glad the killer bear left.
……

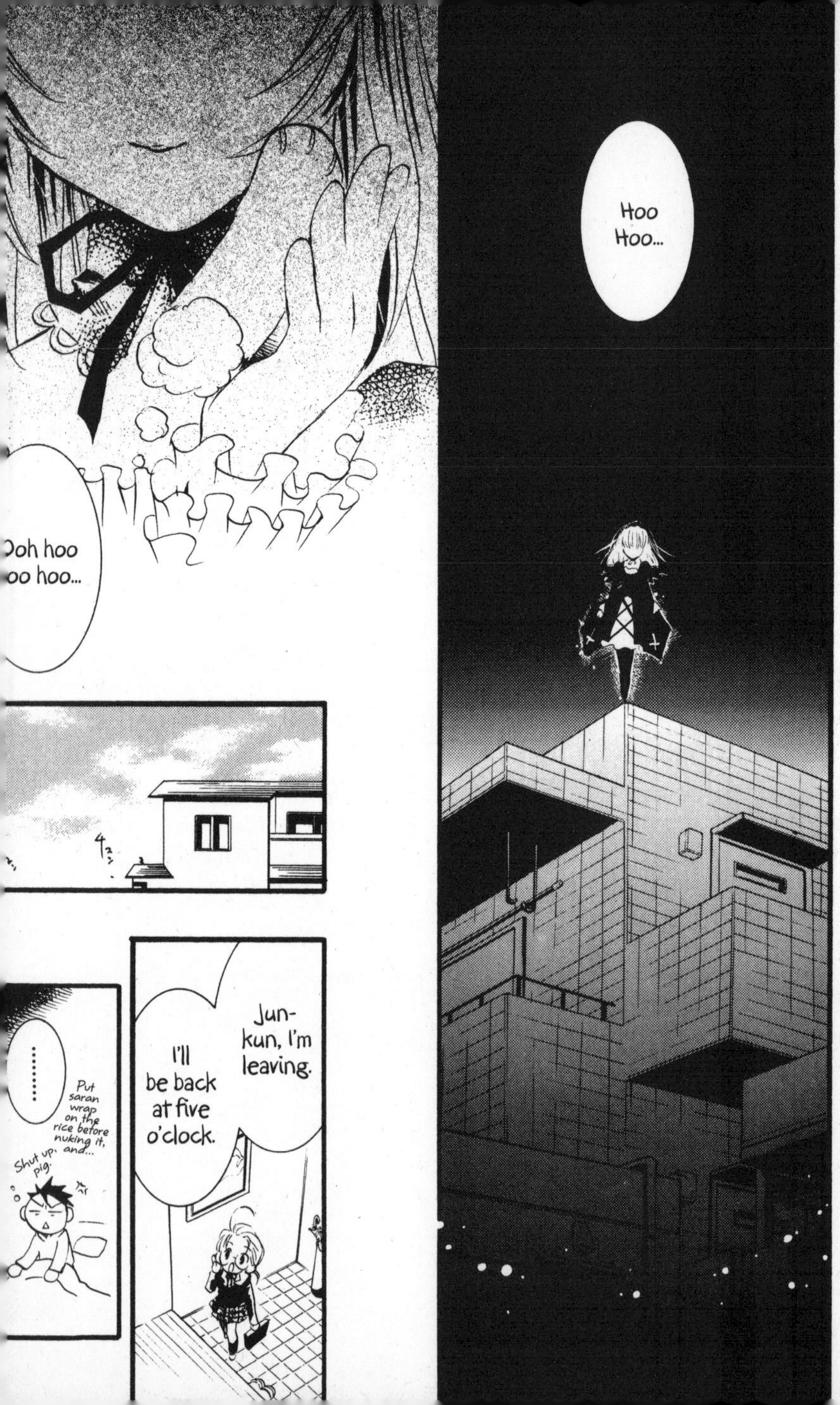

Hoo Hoo...
Ooh hoo oo hoo...
Jun-kun, I'm leaving.
I'll be back at five o'clock.
....
Put saran wrap on the rice before nuking it, and...
Shut up, pig.

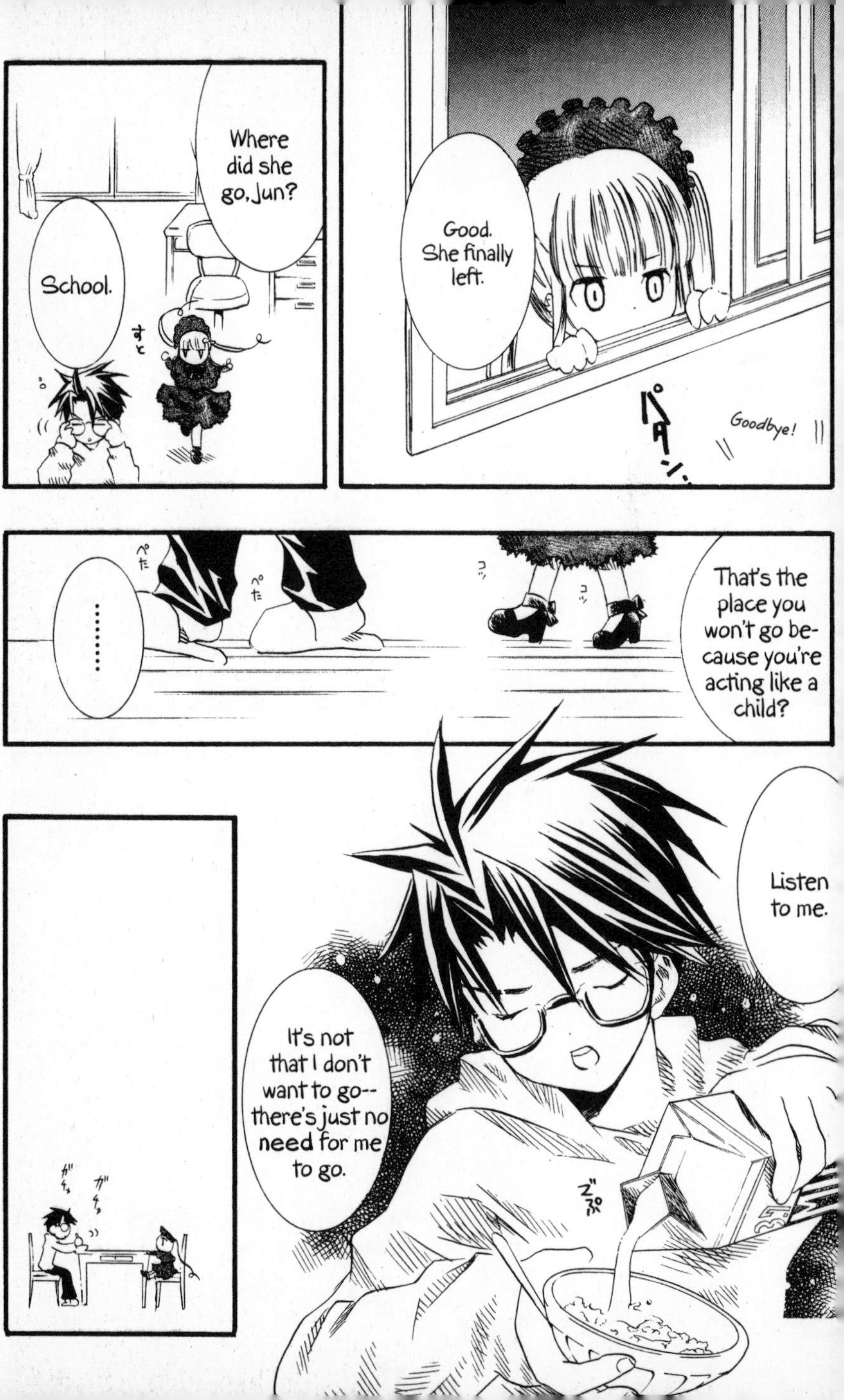
Good. She finally left.
Goodbye!
Where did she go, Jun?
School.
That's the place you won't go be-cause you're acting like a child?
......
Listen to me.
It's not that I don't want to go-- there's just no need for me to go.

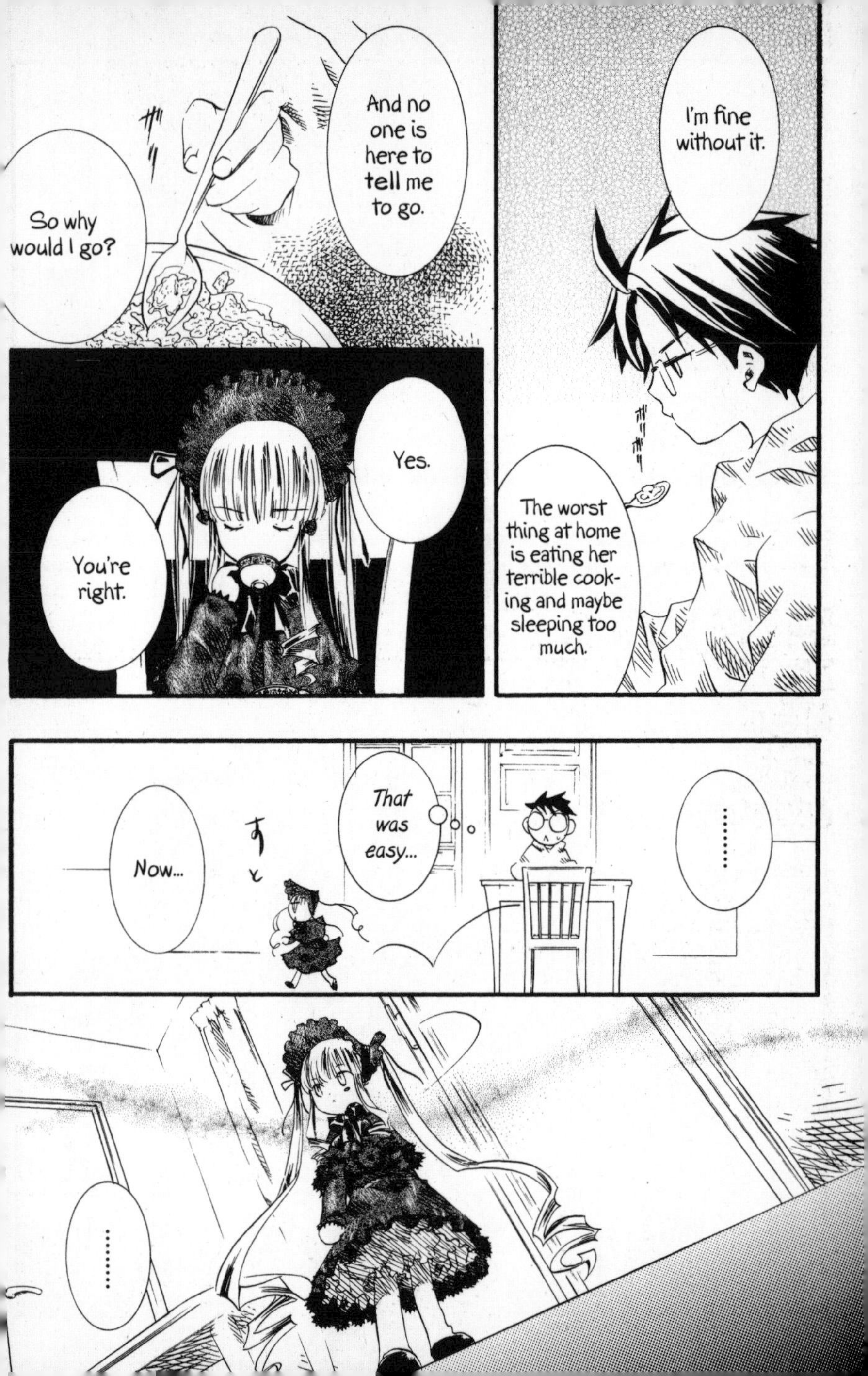
I'm fine without it.
The worst thing at home is eating her terrible cooking and maybe sleeping too much.
And no one is here to tell me to go.
So why would I go?
Yes.
You're right.
……
That was easy…
すと
Now…
……

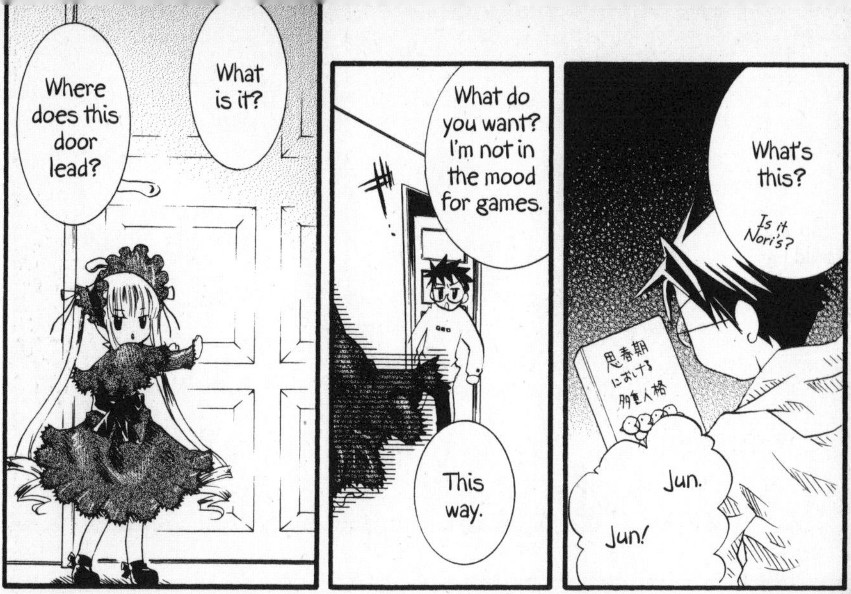
What's this?
Is it Nori's?
思春期における多重人格
Jun.
Jun!
What do you want? I'm not in the mood for games.
This way.
What is it?
Where does this door lead?

Book: Multiple Personalities Among Adolescents

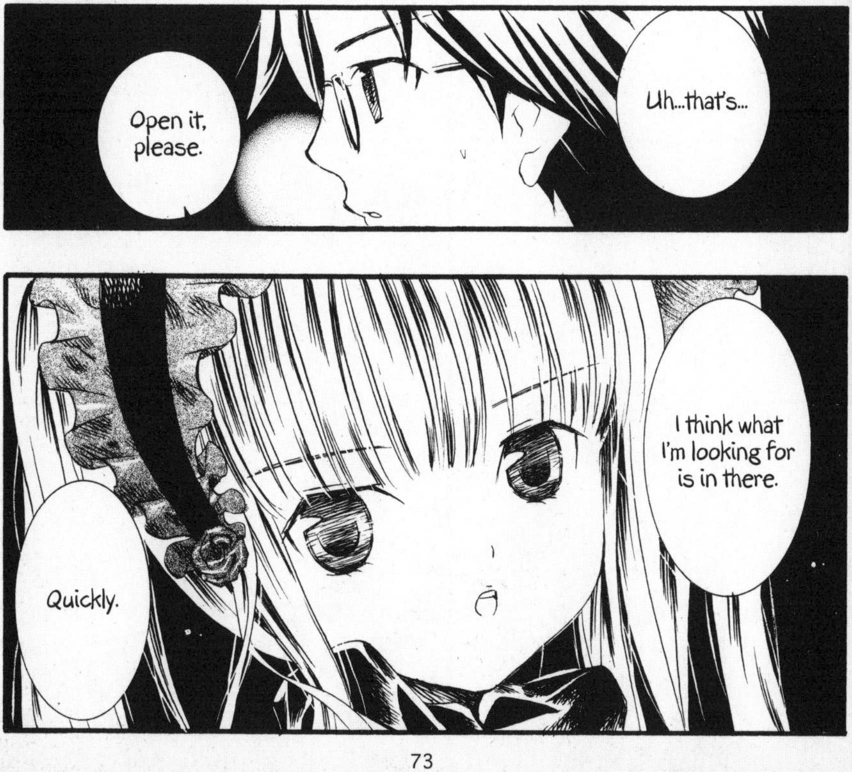
Uh...that's...
Open it, please.
I think what I'm looking for is in there.
Quickly.

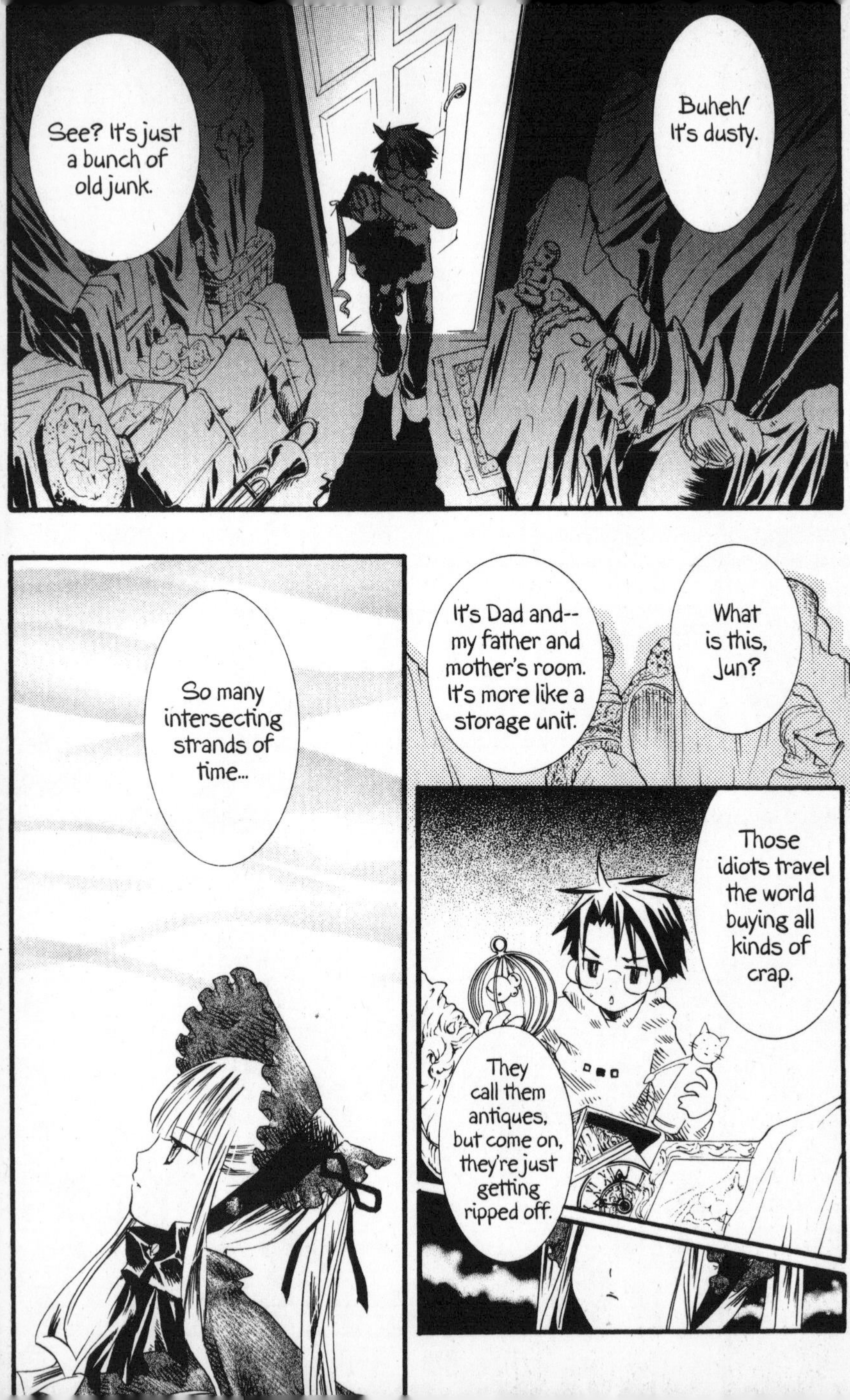
Buheh! It's dusty.
See? It's just a bunch of old junk.
What is this, Jun?
It's Dad and-- my father and mother's room. It's more like a storage unit.
Those idiots travel the world buying all kinds of crap.
They call them antiques, but come on, they're just getting ripped off.
So many intersecting strands of time...

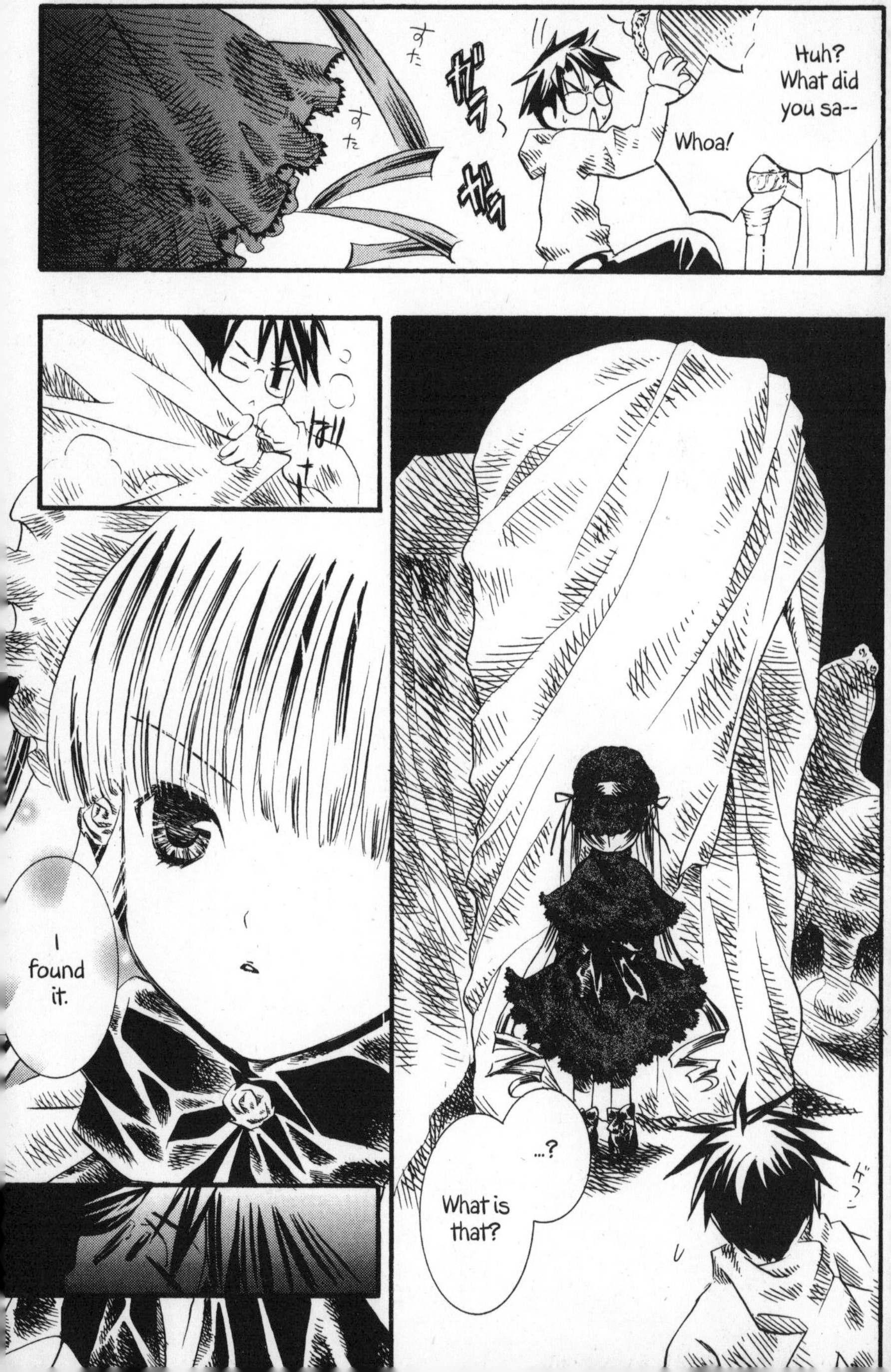
Huh? What did you sa--
Whoa!
すた
すた
...?
What is that?
I found it.

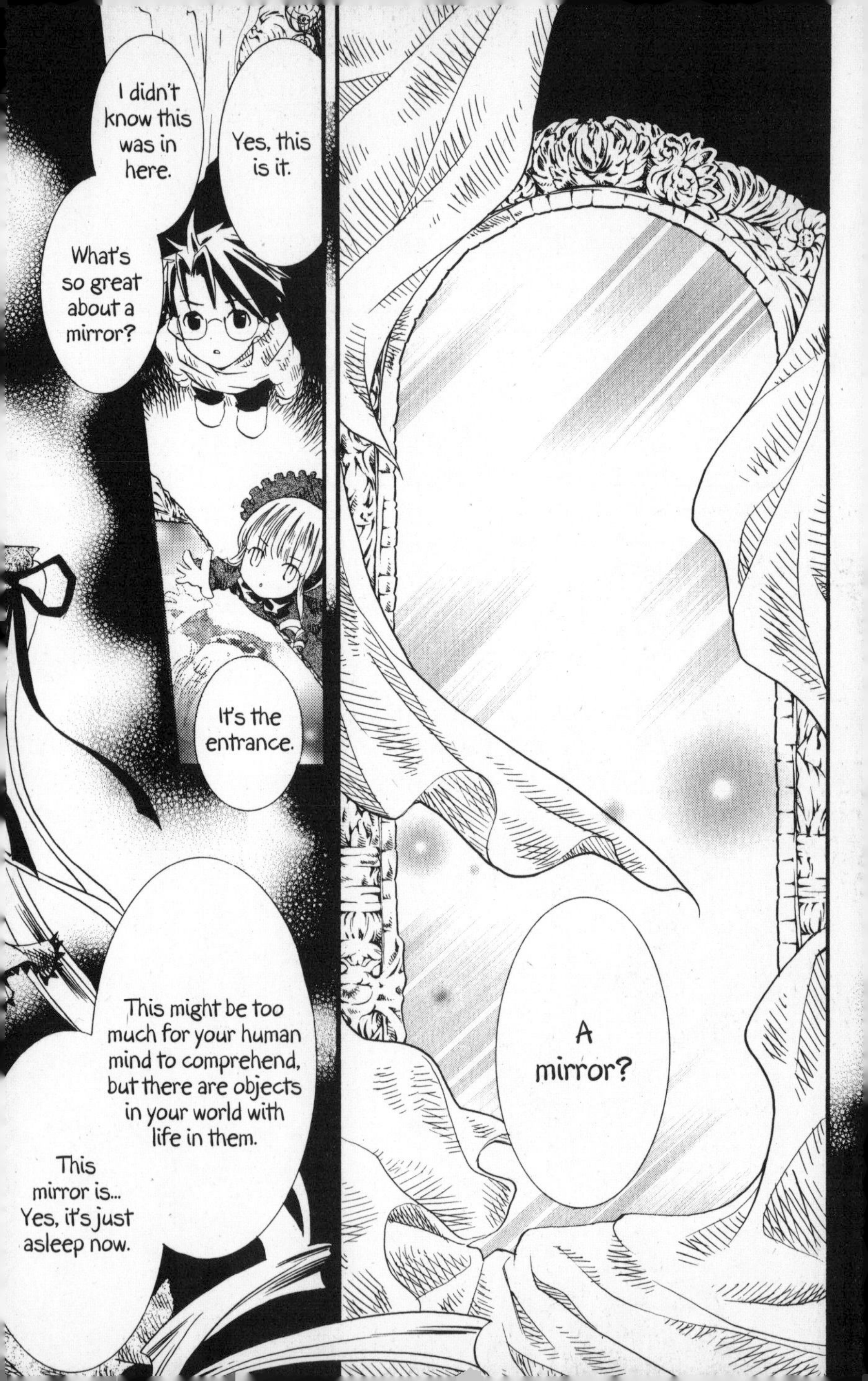
A mirror?
Yes, this is it.
I didn't know this was in here.
What's so great about a mirror?
It's the entrance.
This might be too much for your human mind to comprehend, but there are objects in your world with life in them.
This mirror is... Yes, it's just asleep now.

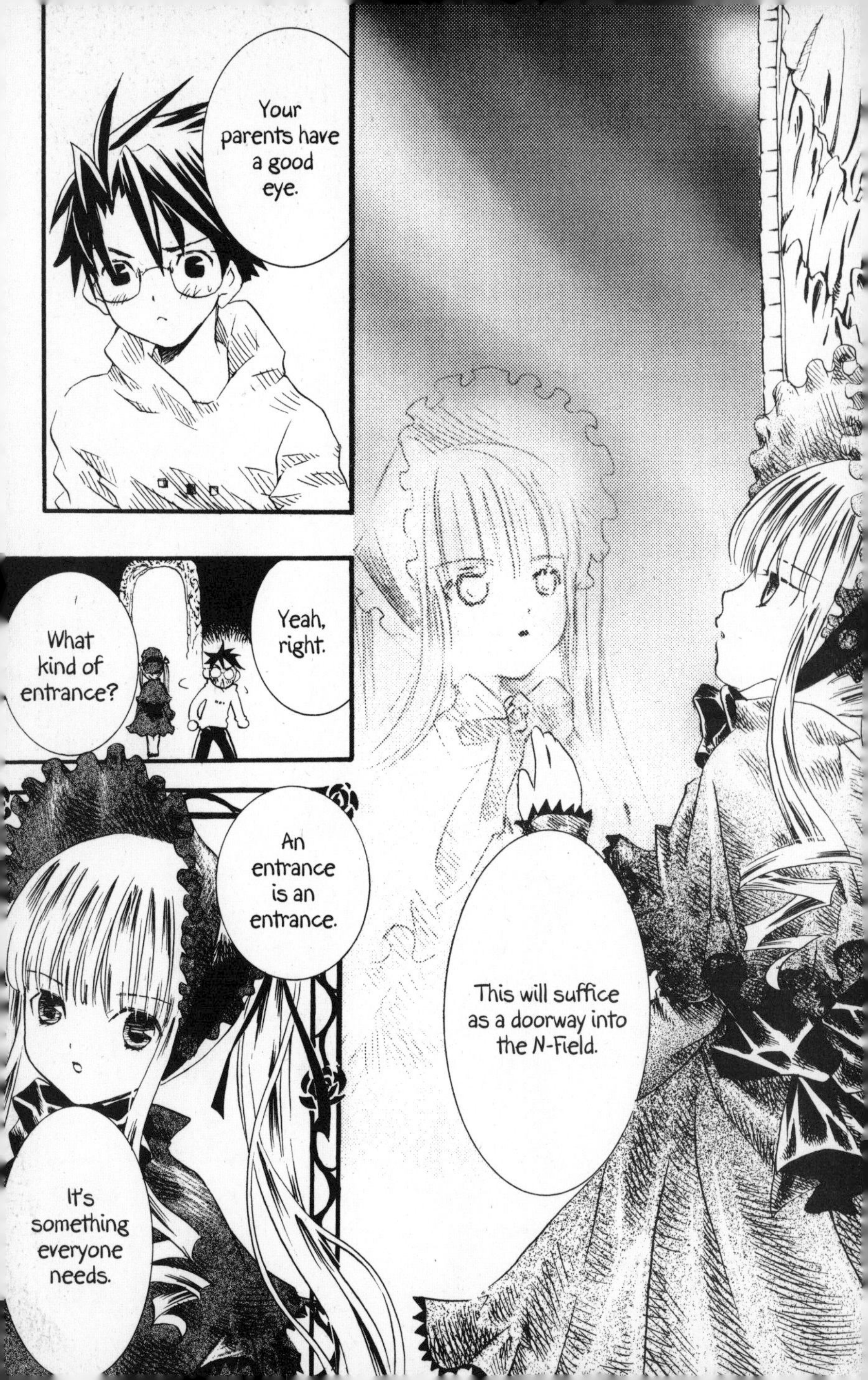
This will suffice as a doorway into the N-Field.
Your parents have a good eye.
Yeah, right.
What kind of entrance?
An entrance is an entrance.
It's something everyone needs.

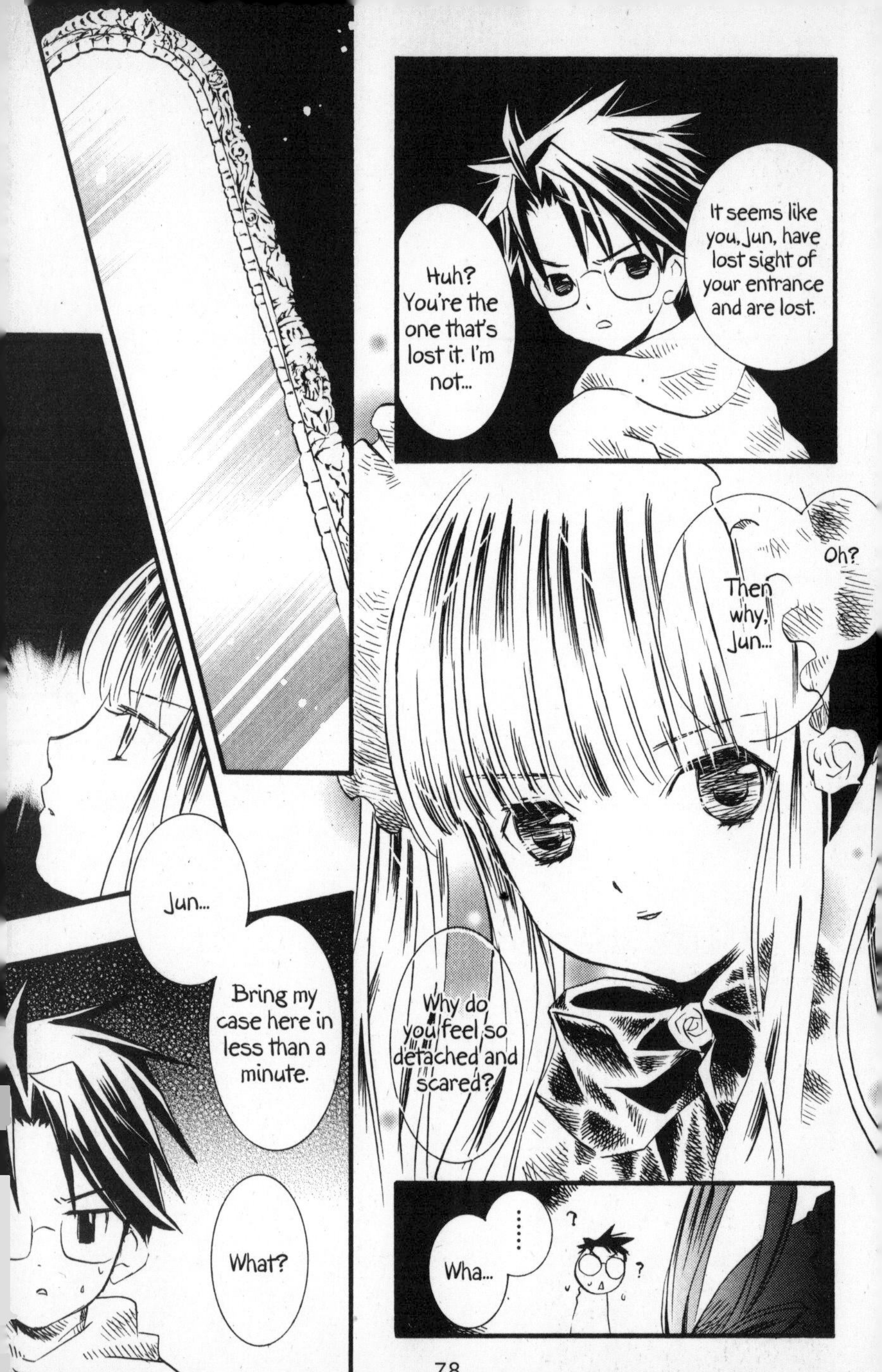
It seems like you, Jun, have lost sight of your entrance and are lost.
Huh? You're the one that's lost it. I'm not...
Oh?
Then why, Jun...
Why do you feel so detached and scared?
......
Wha...
Jun...
Bring my case here in less than a minute.
What?

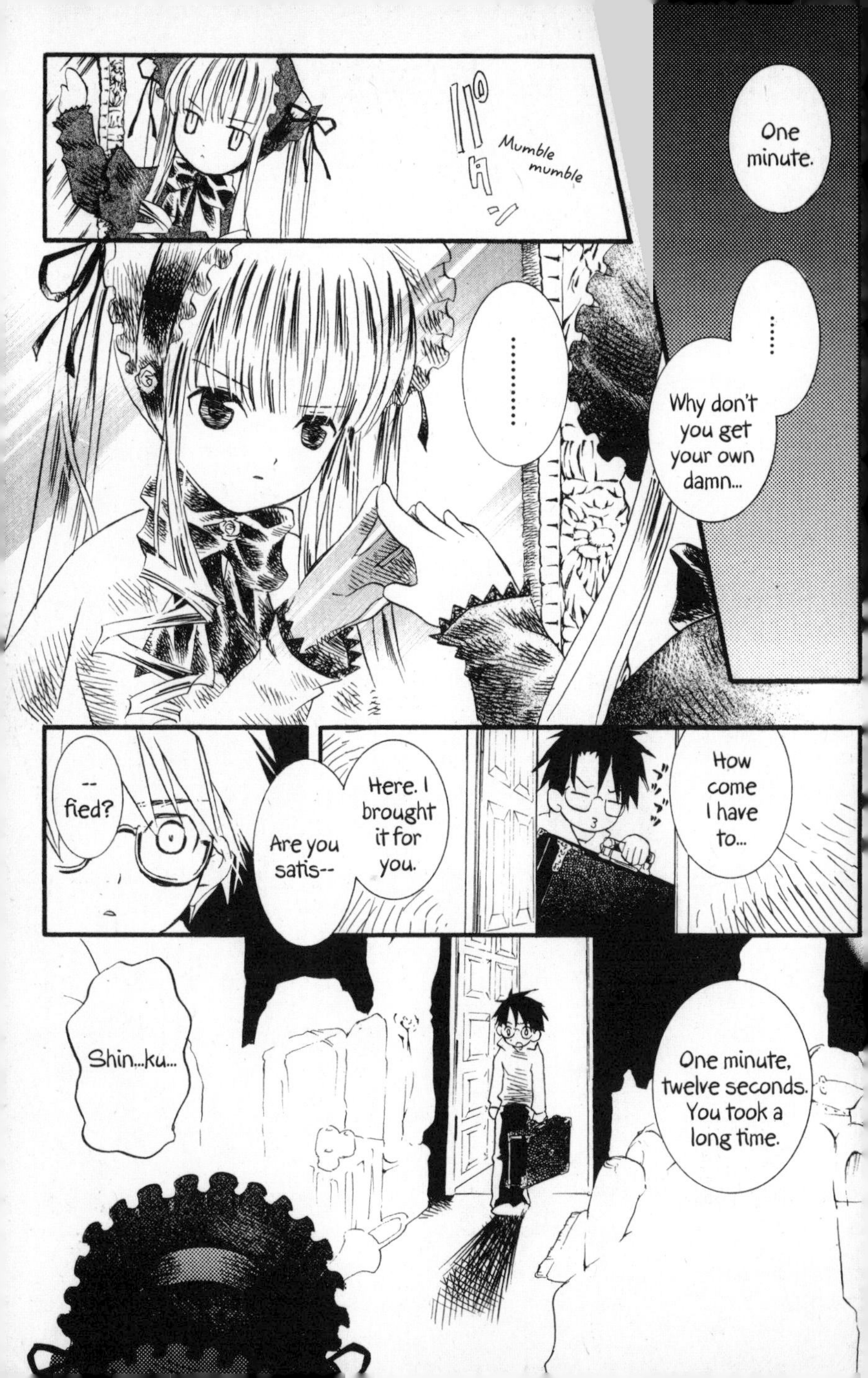
One minute.
......
Why don't you get your own damn...
Mumble mumble
....
How come I have to...
Here. I brought it for you.
Are you satis--
--fied?
One minute, twelve seconds. You took a long time.
Shin...ku...

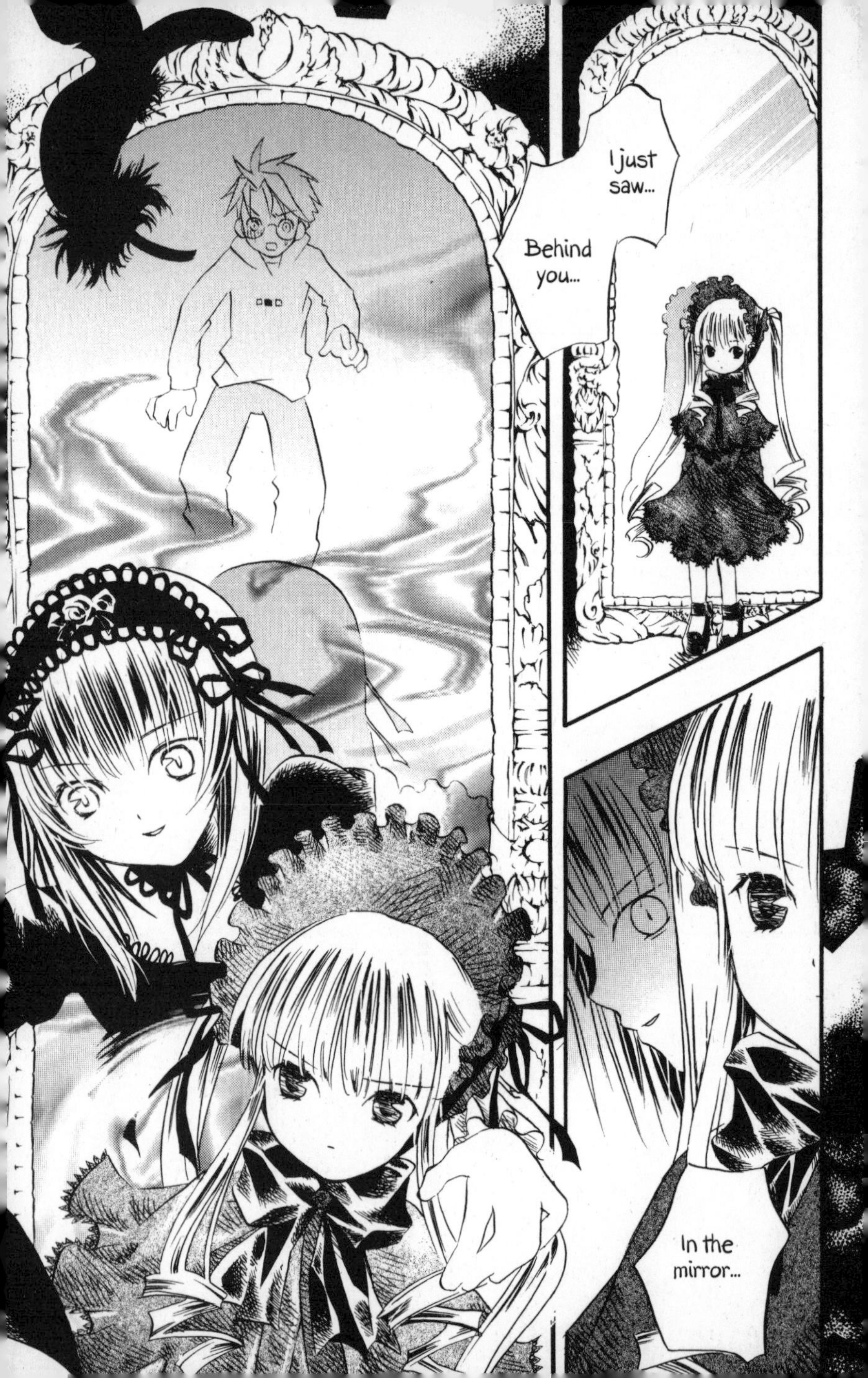
I just saw...
Behind you...
In the mirror...

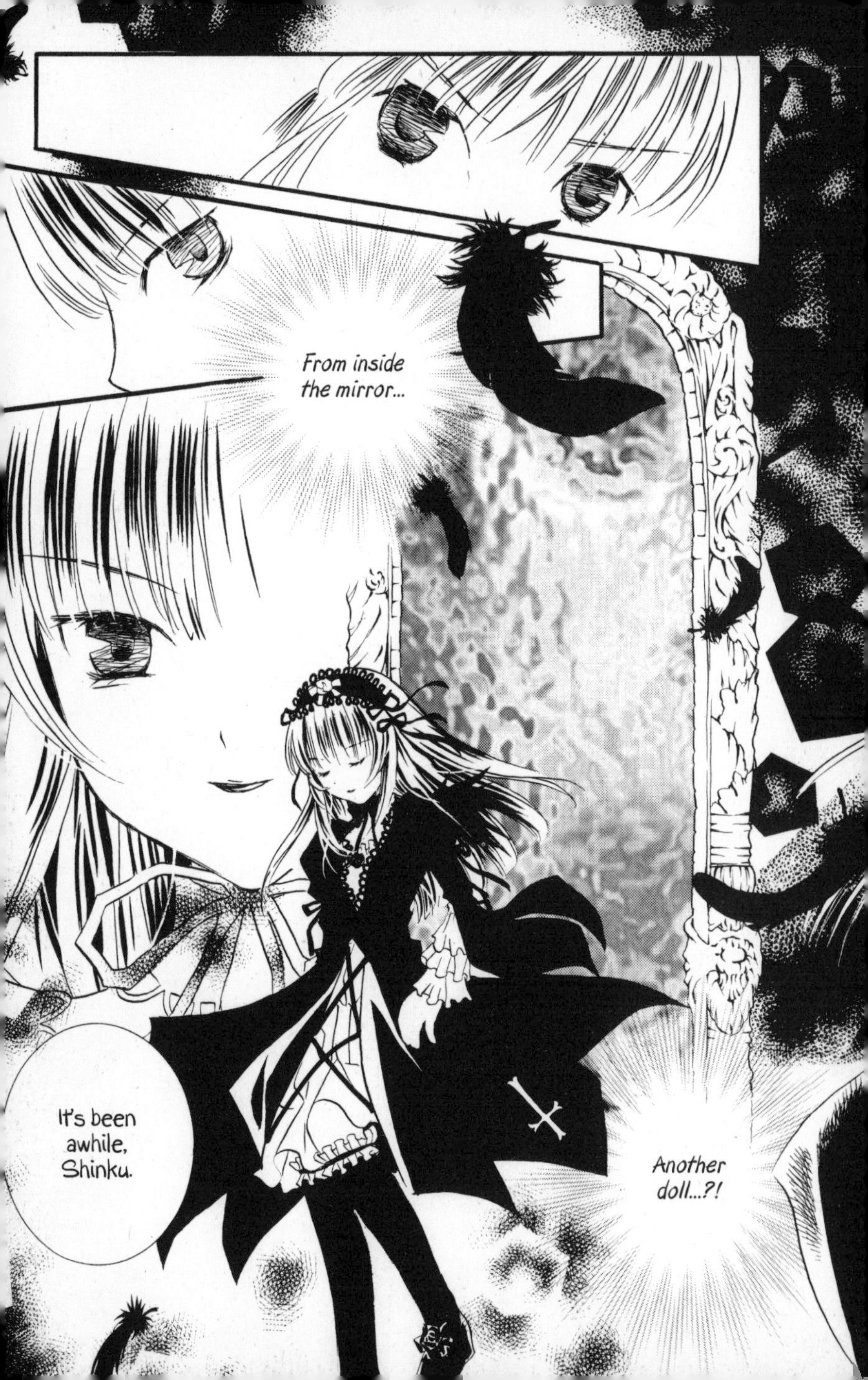
From inside the mirror...
Another doll...?!
It's been awhile, Shinku.

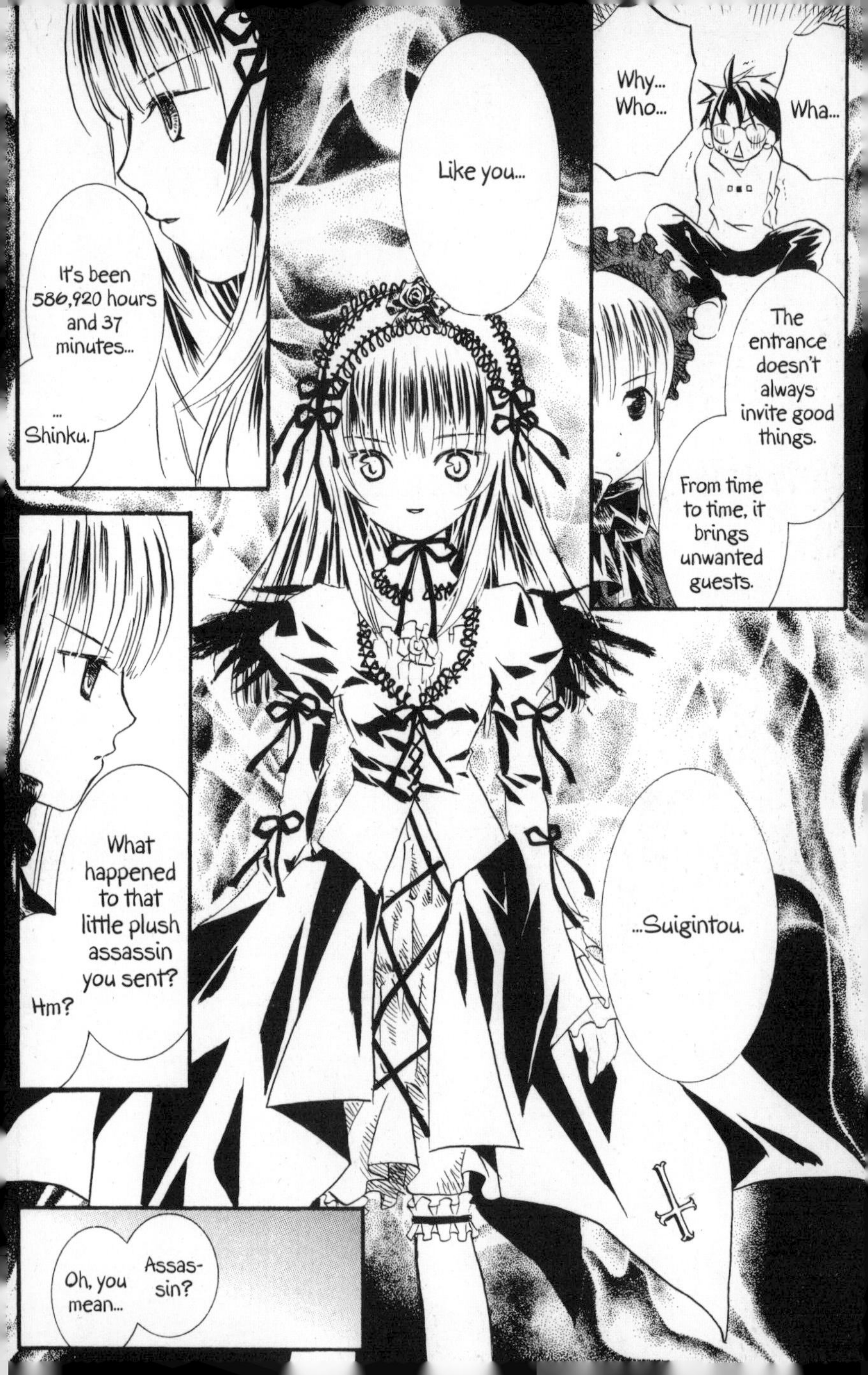
Wha...
Why... Who...
The entrance doesn't always invite good things.
From time to time, it brings unwanted guests.
Like you...
...Suigintou.
It's been 586,920 hours and 37 minutes...
... Shinku.
What happened to that little plush assassin you sent?
Hm?
Assas-sin?
Oh, you mean...

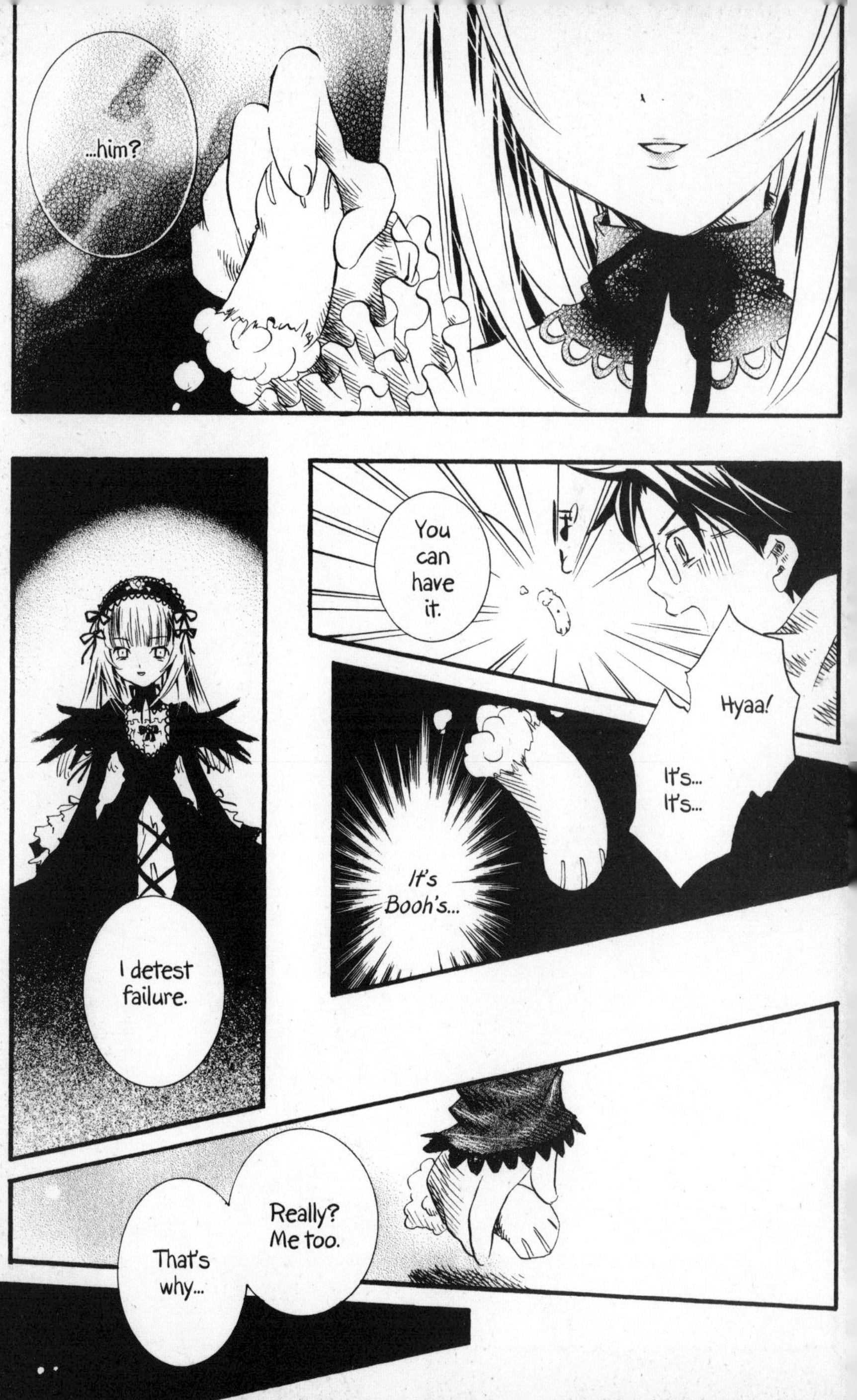
...him?
You can have it.
Hyaa!
It's... It's...
It's Booh's...
I detest failure.
Really? Me too.
That's why...

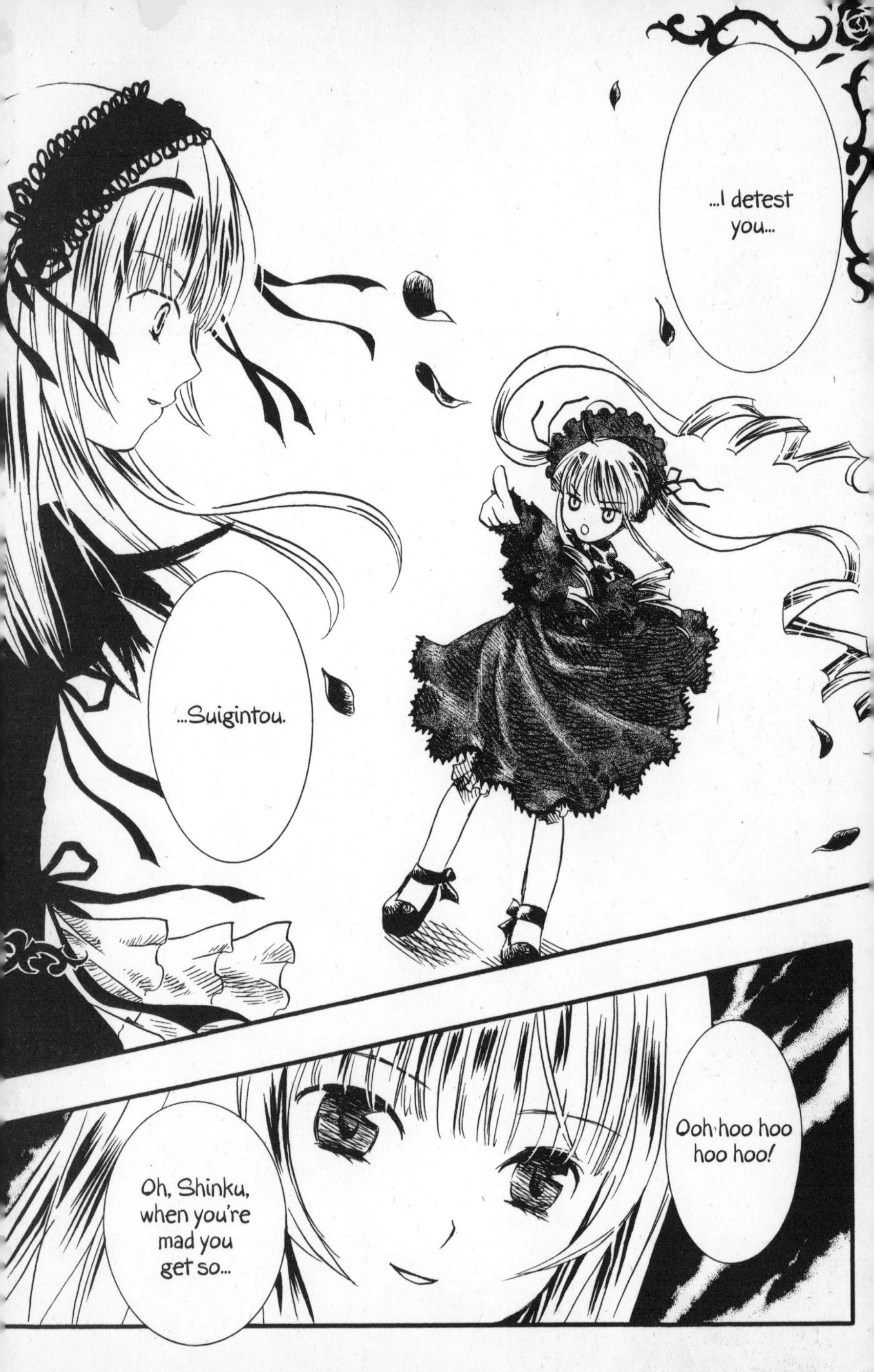
...I detest you...
...Suigintou.
Ooh-hoo hoo hoo hoo!
Oh, Shinku, when you're mad you get so...

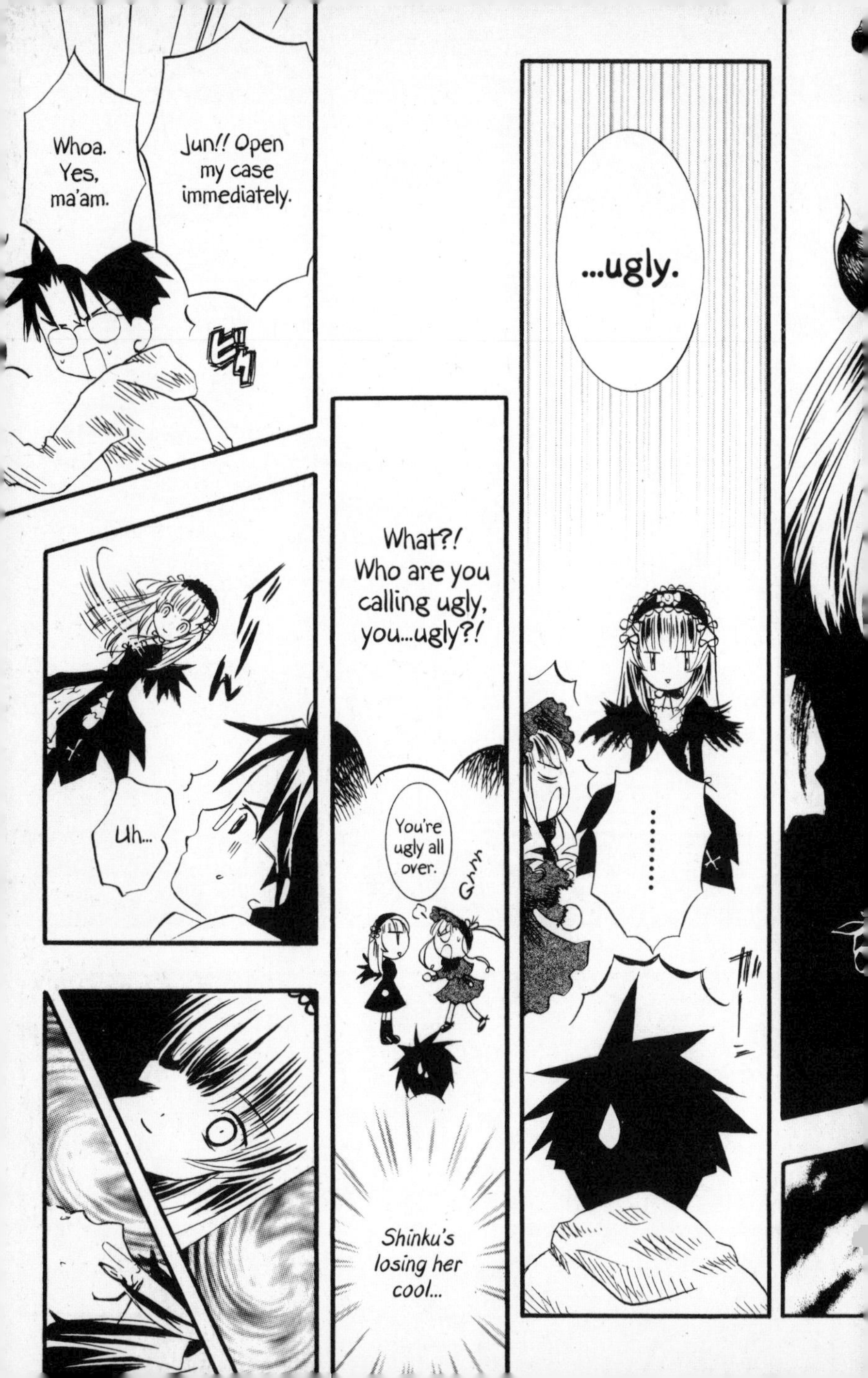
...ugly.
......
What?! Who are you calling ugly, you...ugly?!
You're ugly all over.
Grrr
Shinku's losing her cool...
Jun!! Open my case immediately.
Whoa. Yes, ma'am.
Uh...

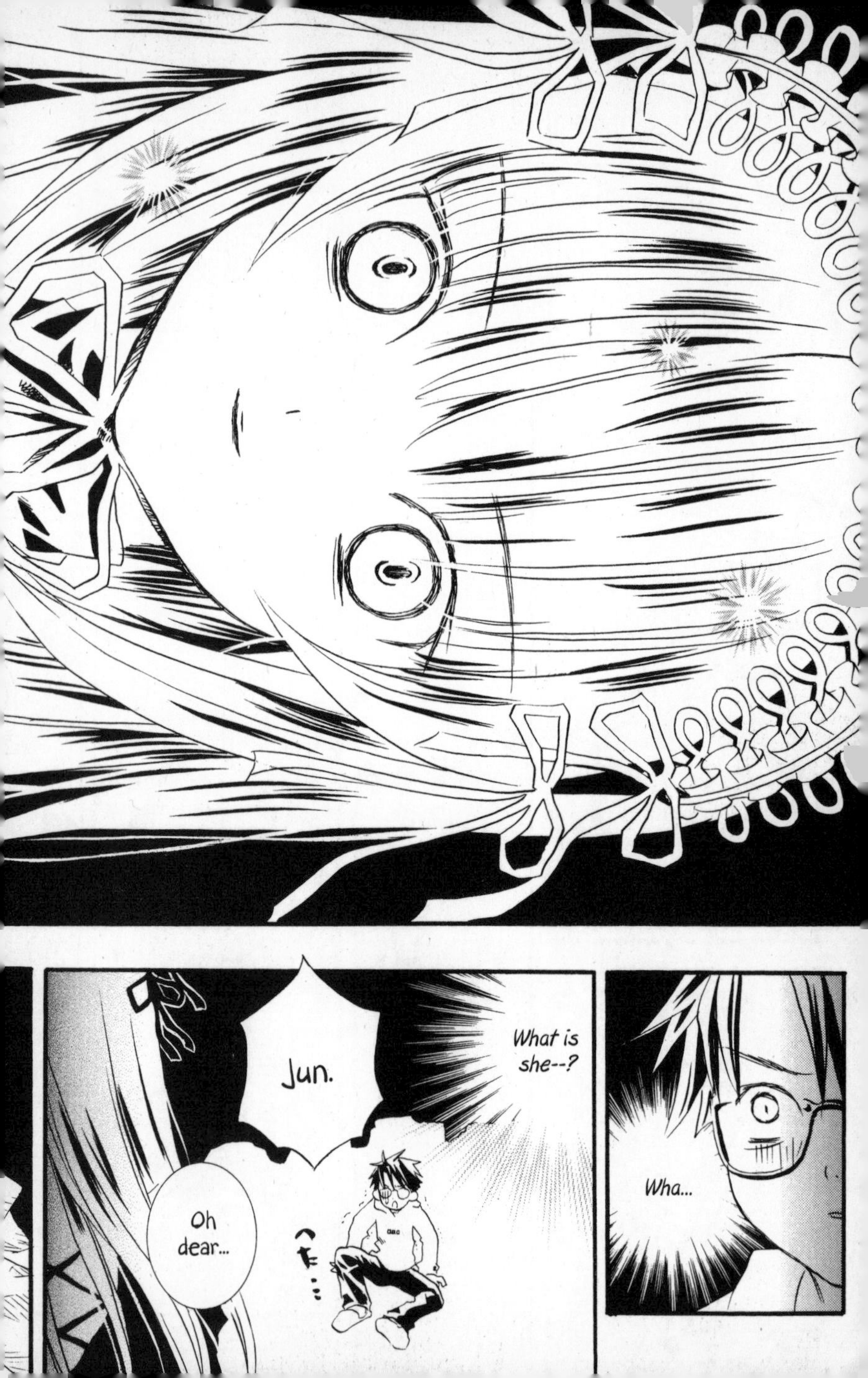
Wha...
What is she--?
Jun.
Oh dear...
へた...

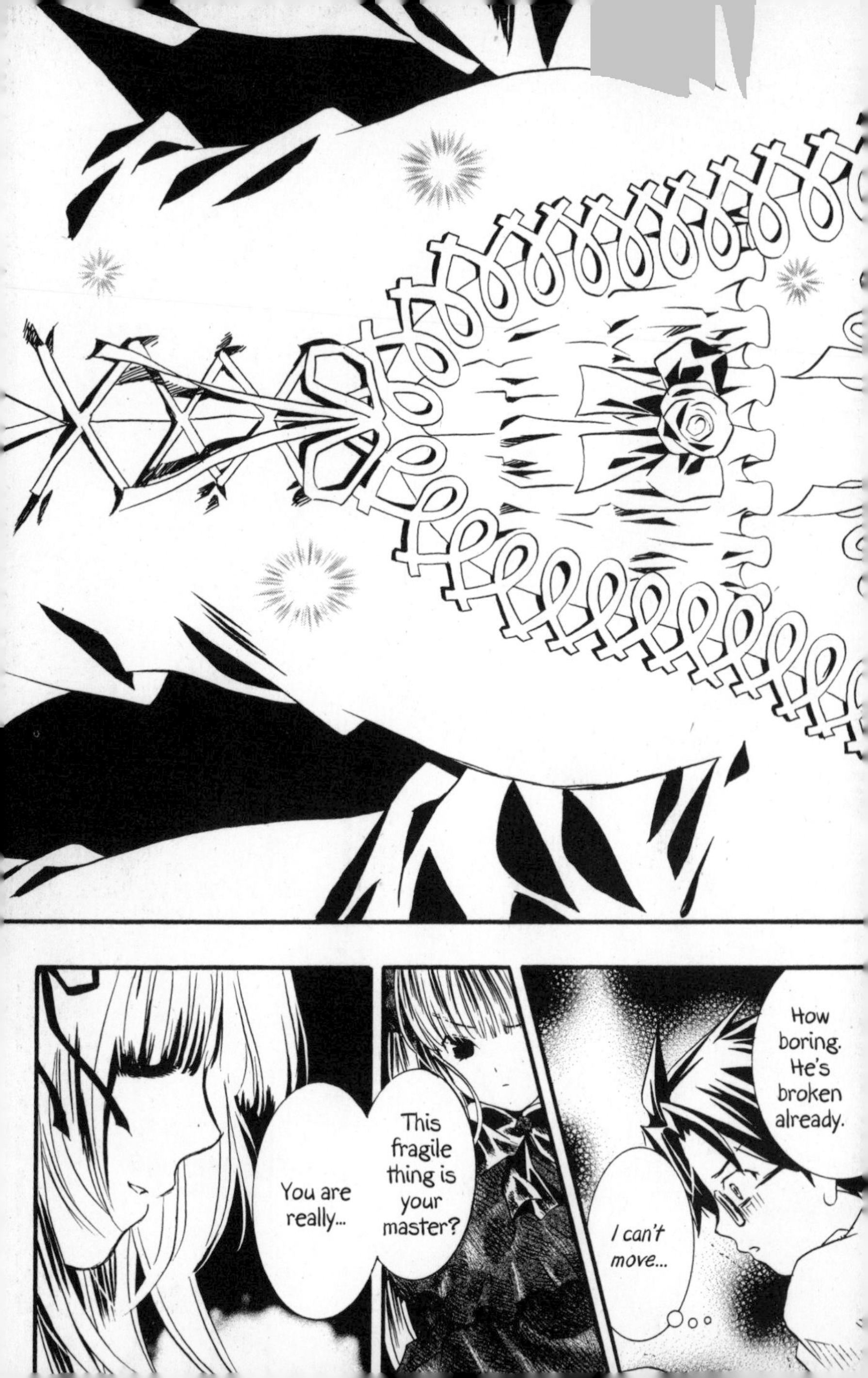
How boring. He's broken already.
I can't move...
This fragile thing is your master?
You are really...

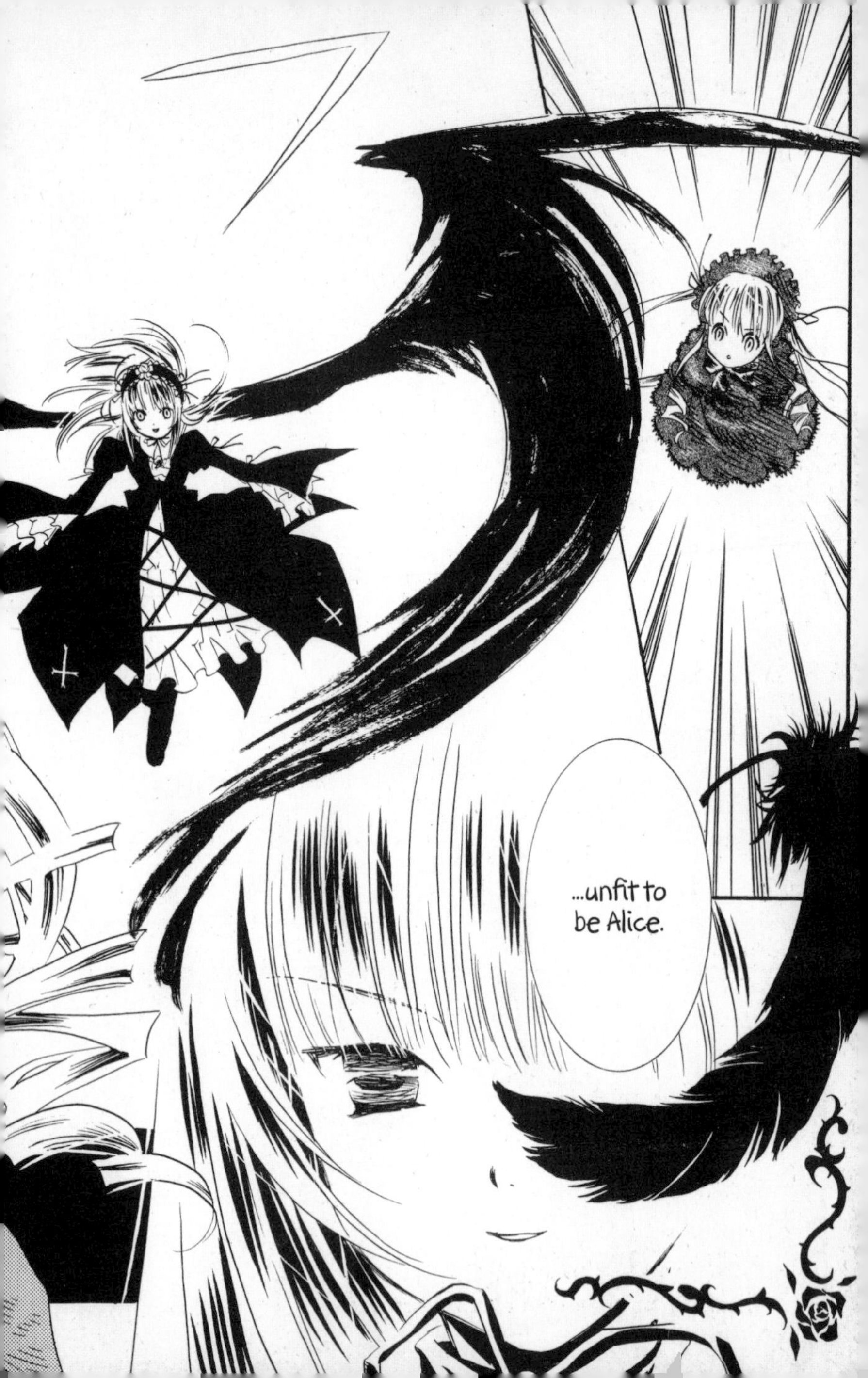
...unfit to be Alice.

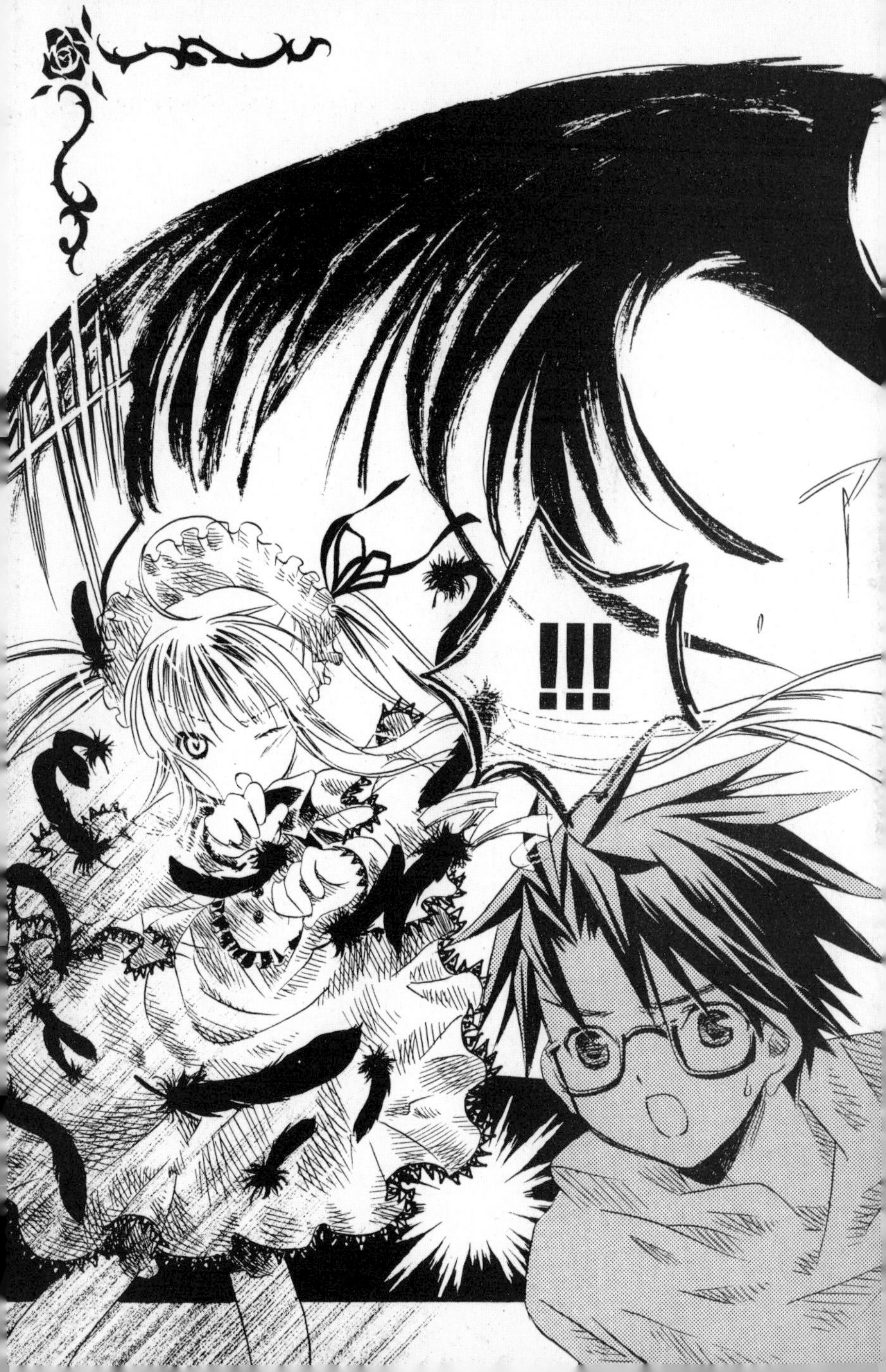
!!!

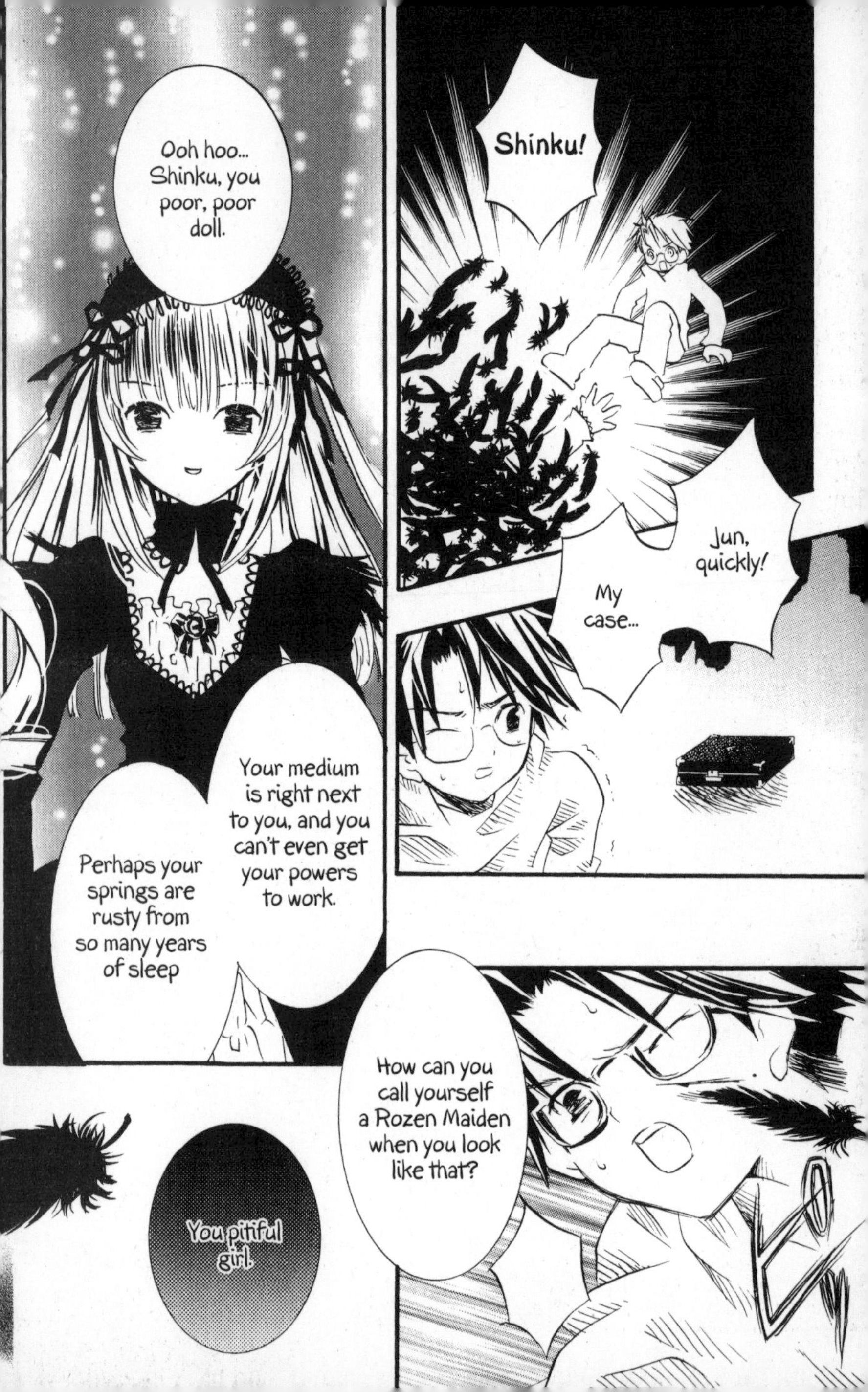
Shinku!
Jun, quickly!
My case...
Ooh hoo... Shinku, you poor, poor doll.
Your medium is right next to you, and you can't even get your powers to work.
Perhaps your springs are rusty from so many years of sleep
How can you call yourself a Rozen Maiden when you look like that?
You pitiful girl.

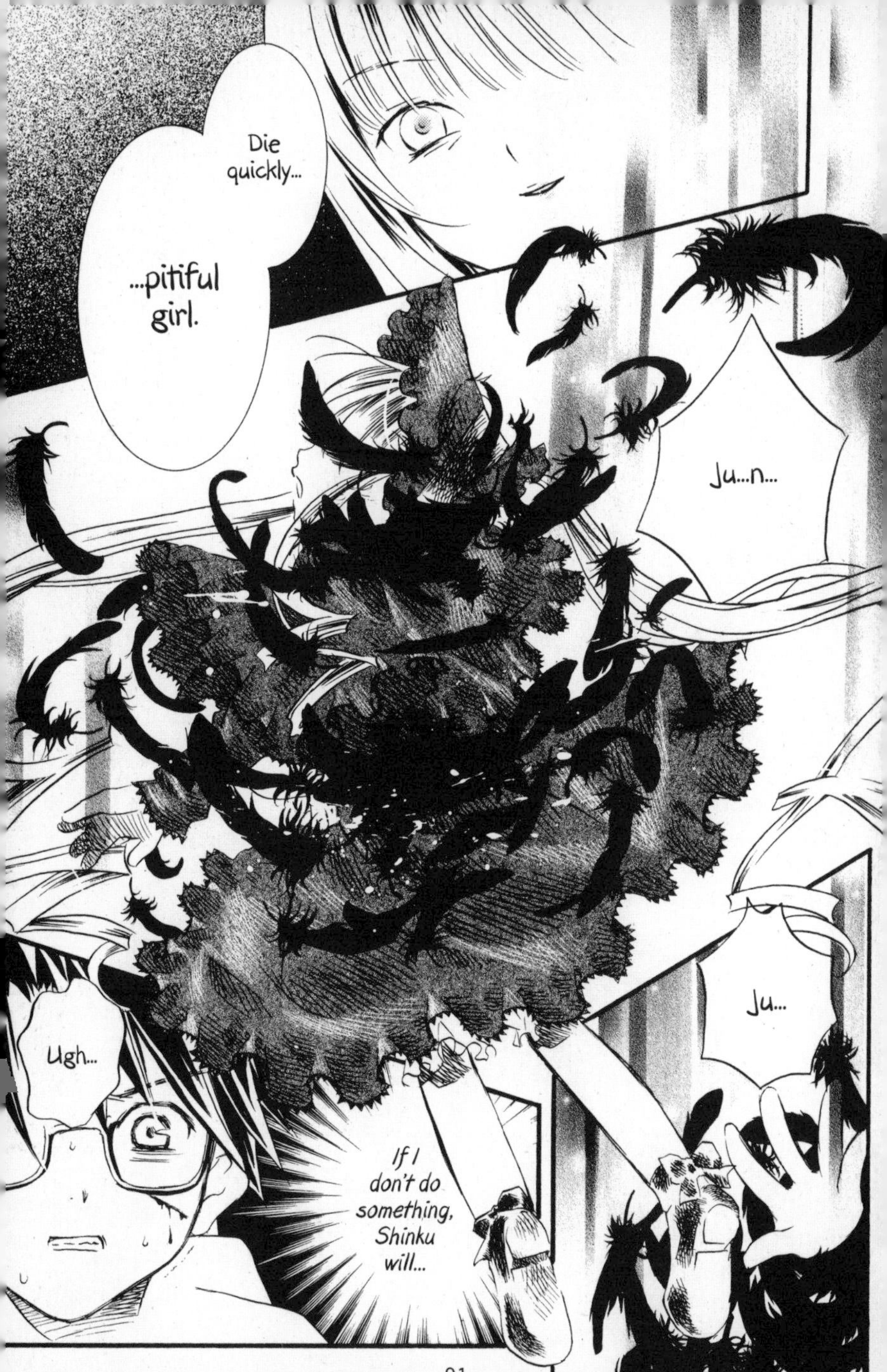
Die quickly...
...pitiful girl.
Ju...n...
Ju...
Ugh...
If I don't do something, Shinku will...

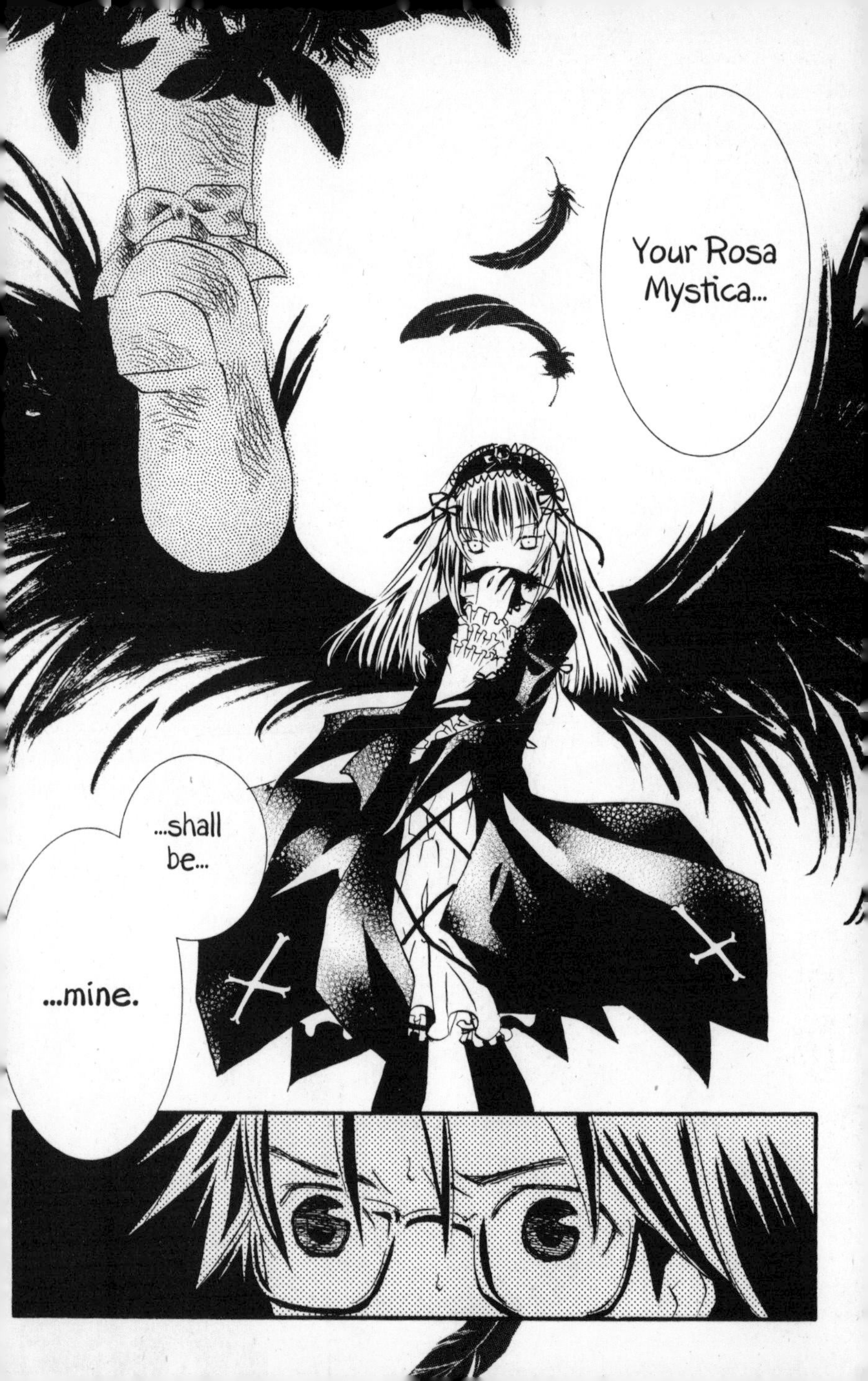
Your Rosa Mystica...
...shall be...
...mine.

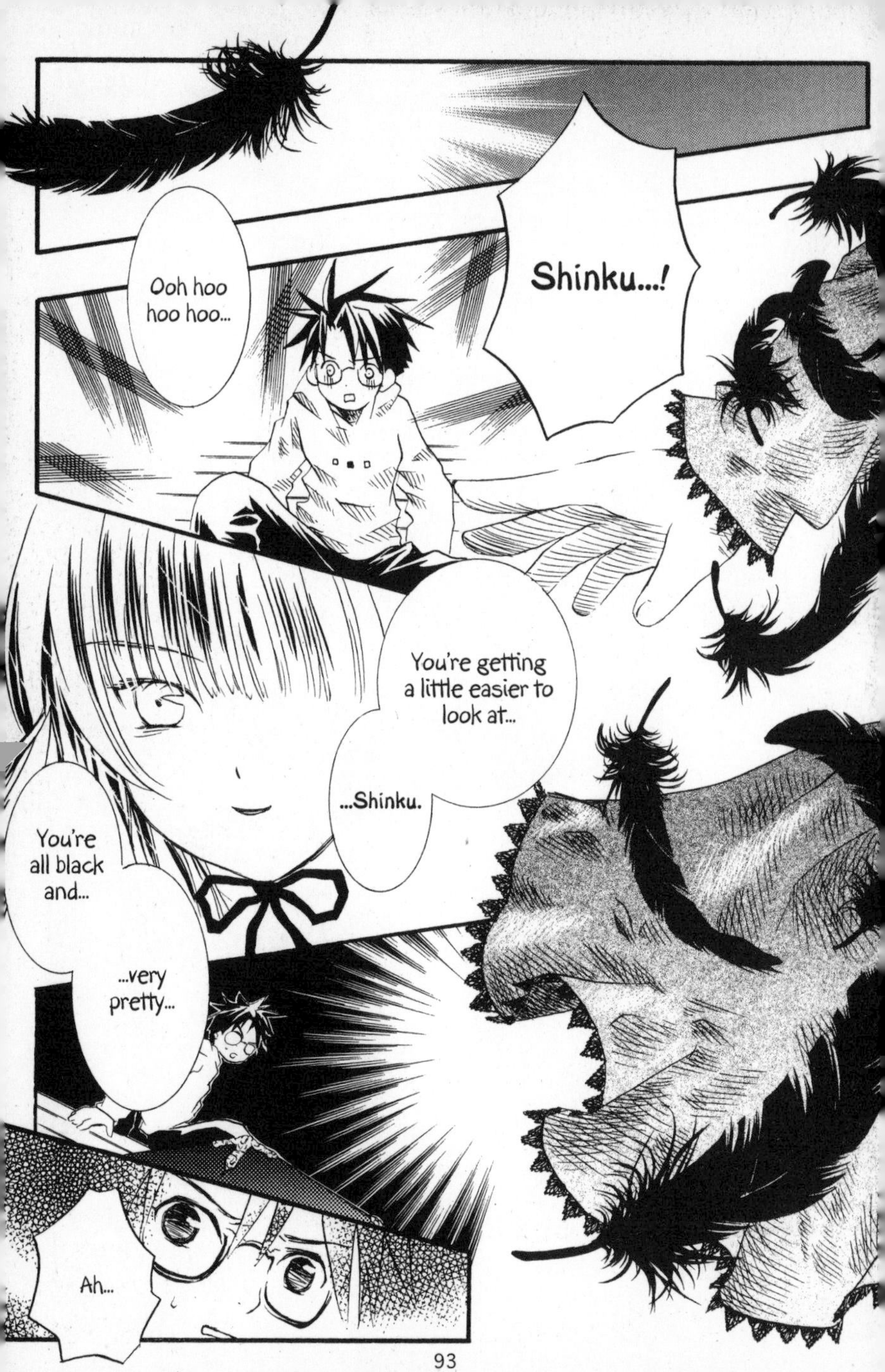
Shinku...!
Ooh hoo hoo hoo...
You're getting a little easier to look at...
...Shinku.
You're all black and...
...very pretty...
Ah...

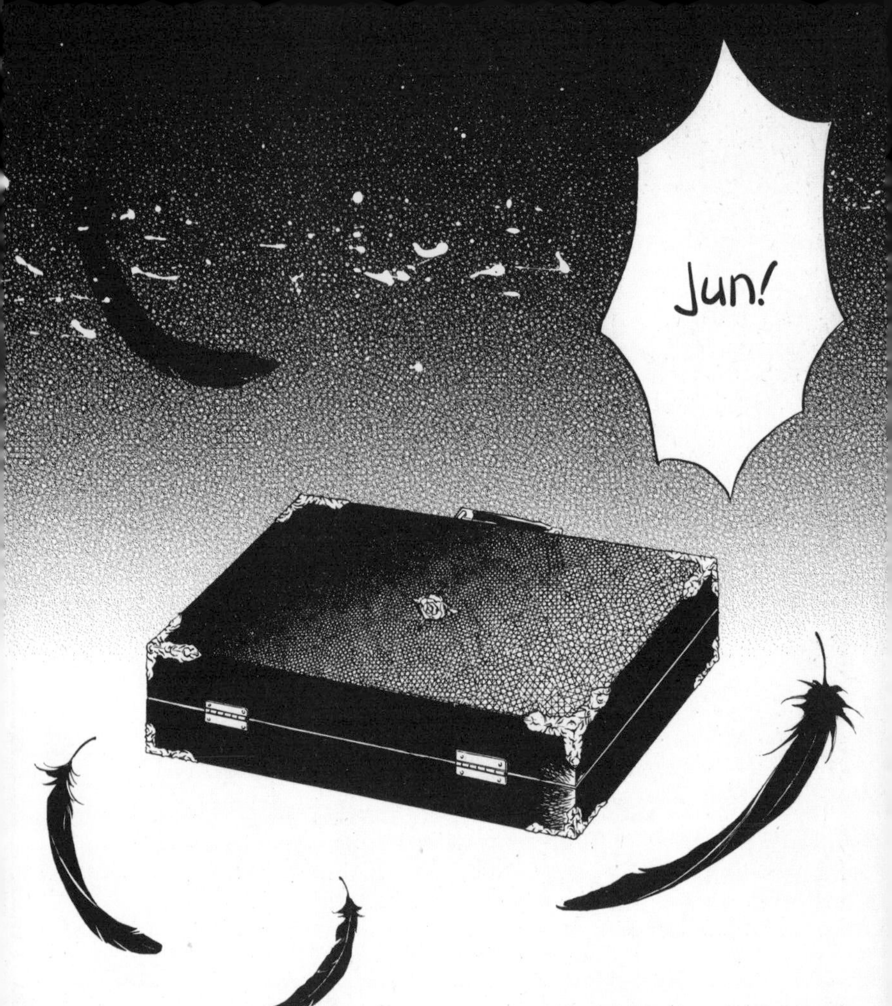
Jun!

Phase 2

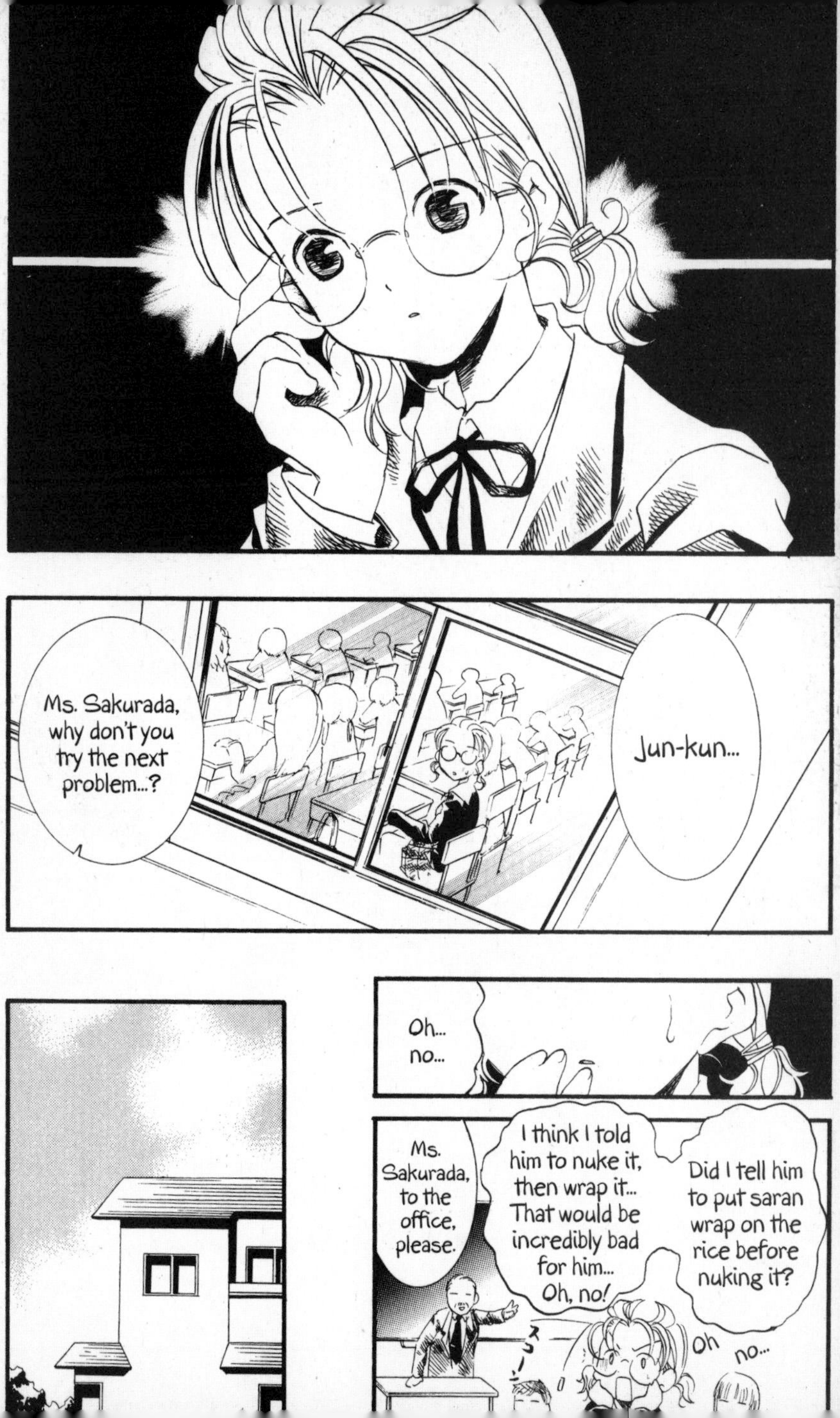
Jun-kun...
Ms. Sakurada, why don't you try the next problem...?
Oh... no...
Did I tell him to put saran wrap on the rice before nuking it?
I think I told him to nuke it, then wrap it... That would be incredibly bad for him... Oh, no!
Ms. Sakurada, to the office, please.
Oh no...

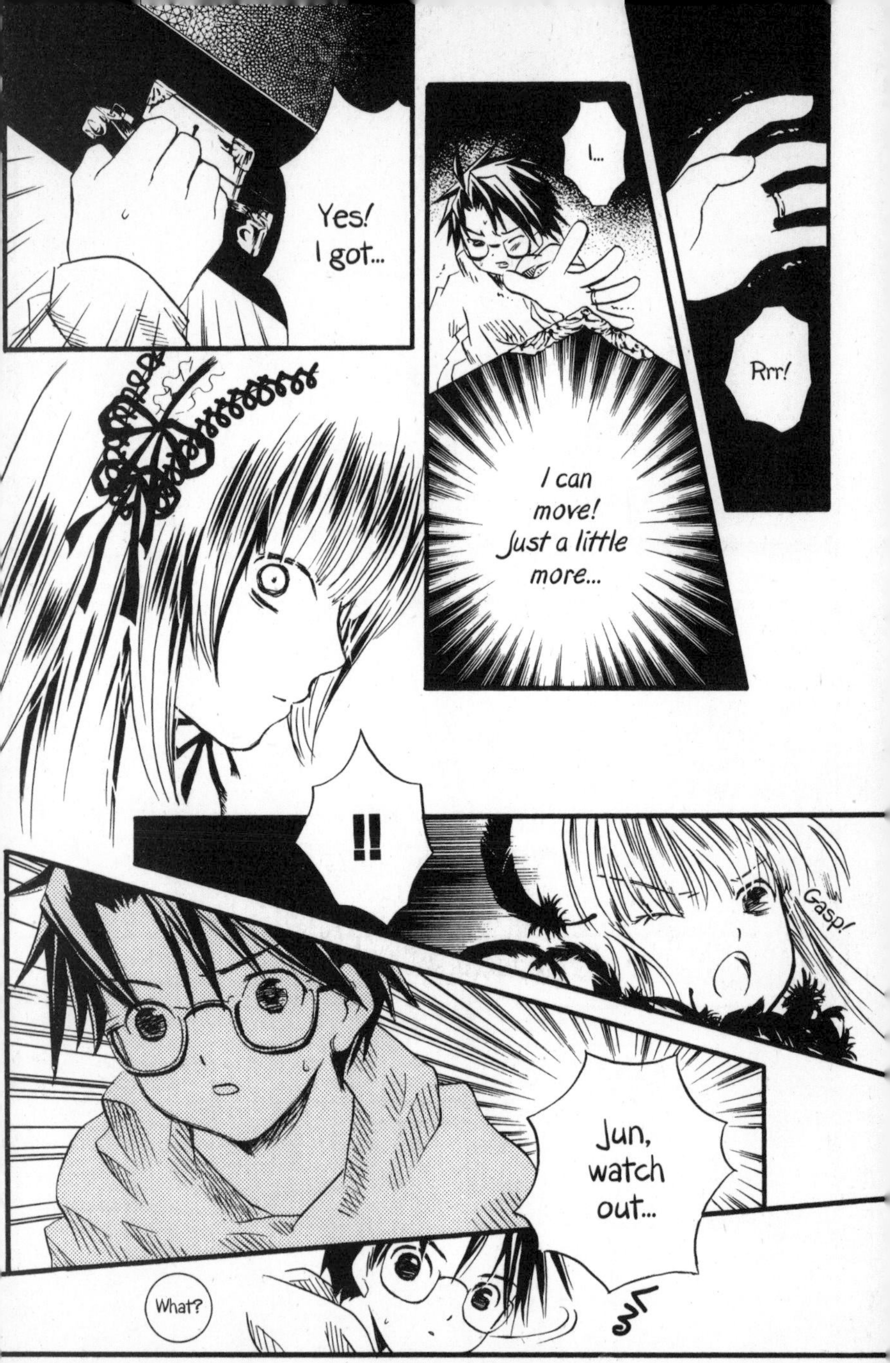
Rrr!
I...
I can move! Just a little more...
Yes! I got...
!!
Gasp!
Jun, watch out...
What?

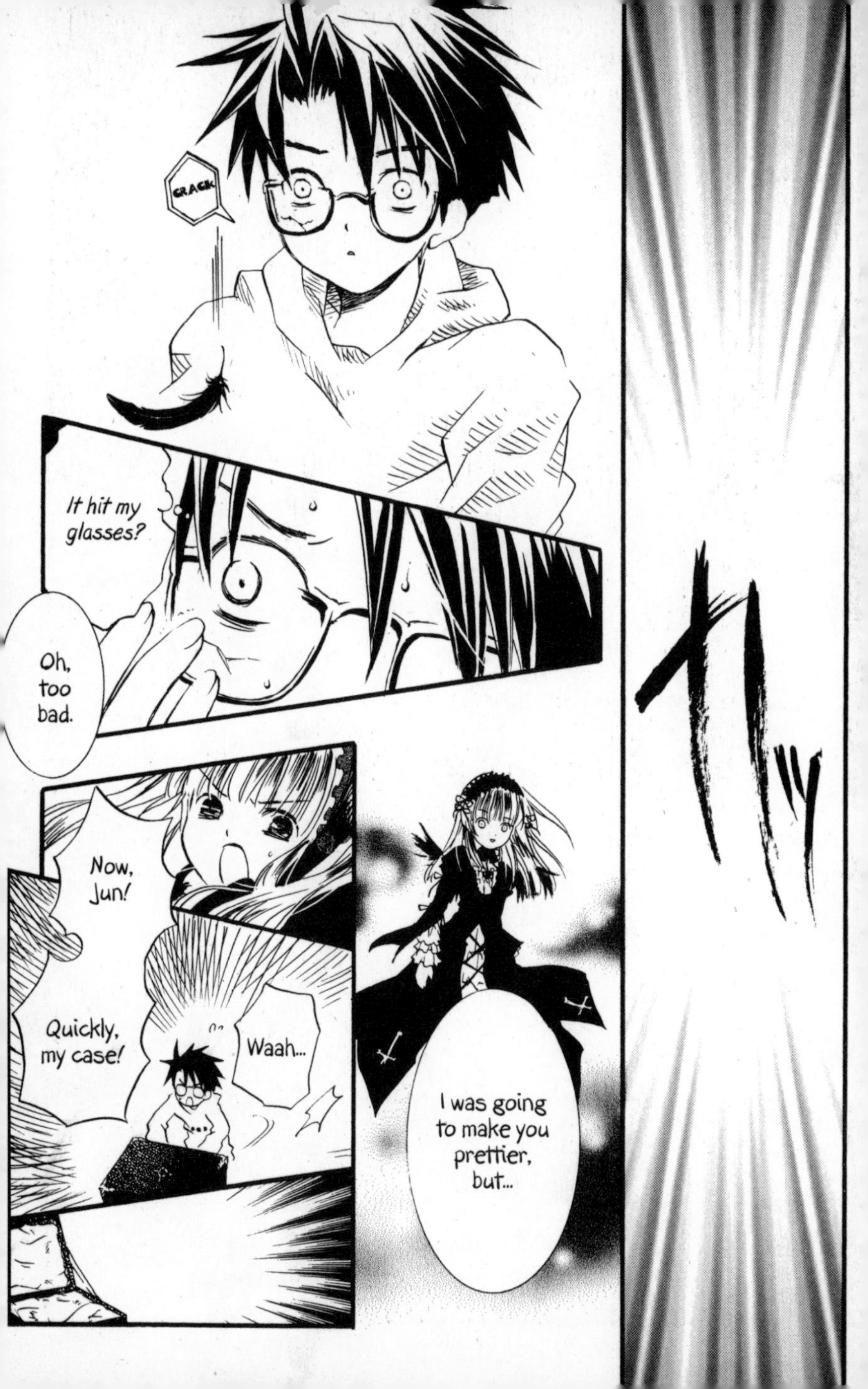
CRACK
It hit my glasses?
Oh, too bad.
I was going to make you prettier, but...
Now, Jun!
Quickly, my case!
Waah...

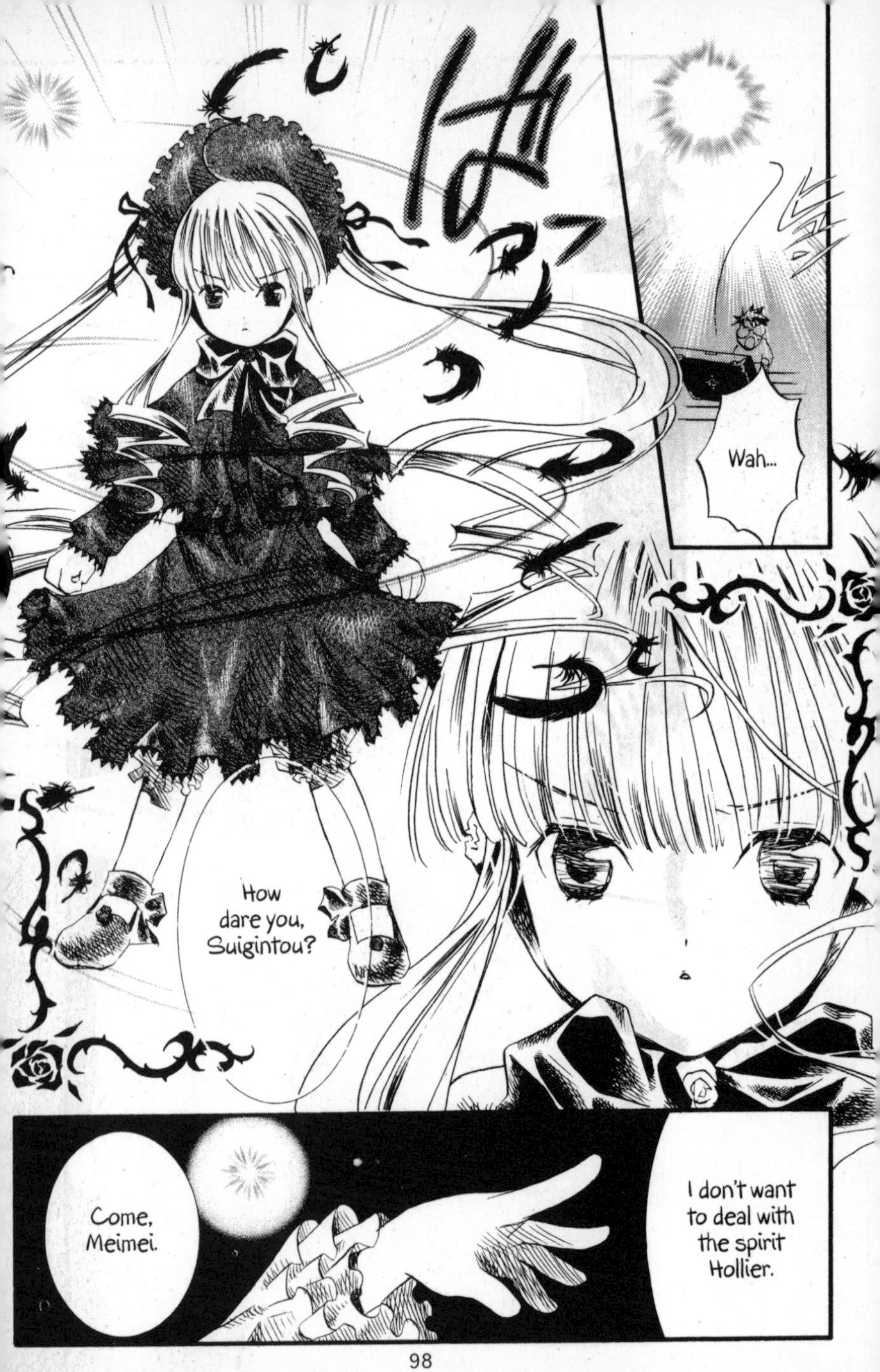
Wah...
How dare you, Suigintou?
I don't want to deal with the spirit Hollier.
Come, Meimei.

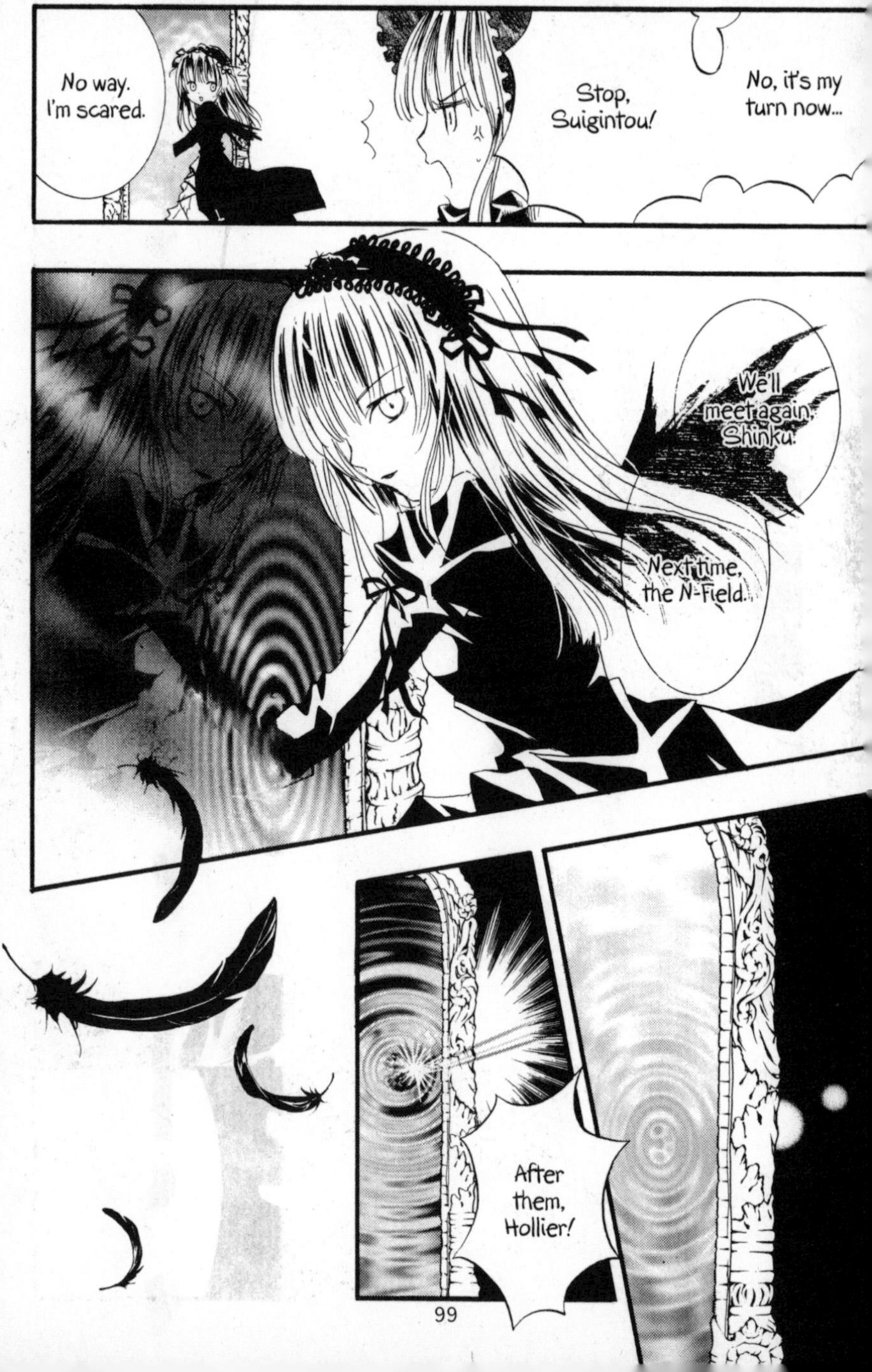
No, it's my turn now...
Stop, Suigintou!
No way. I'm scared.
We'll meet again, Shinku.
Next time, the N-Field.
After them, Hollier!

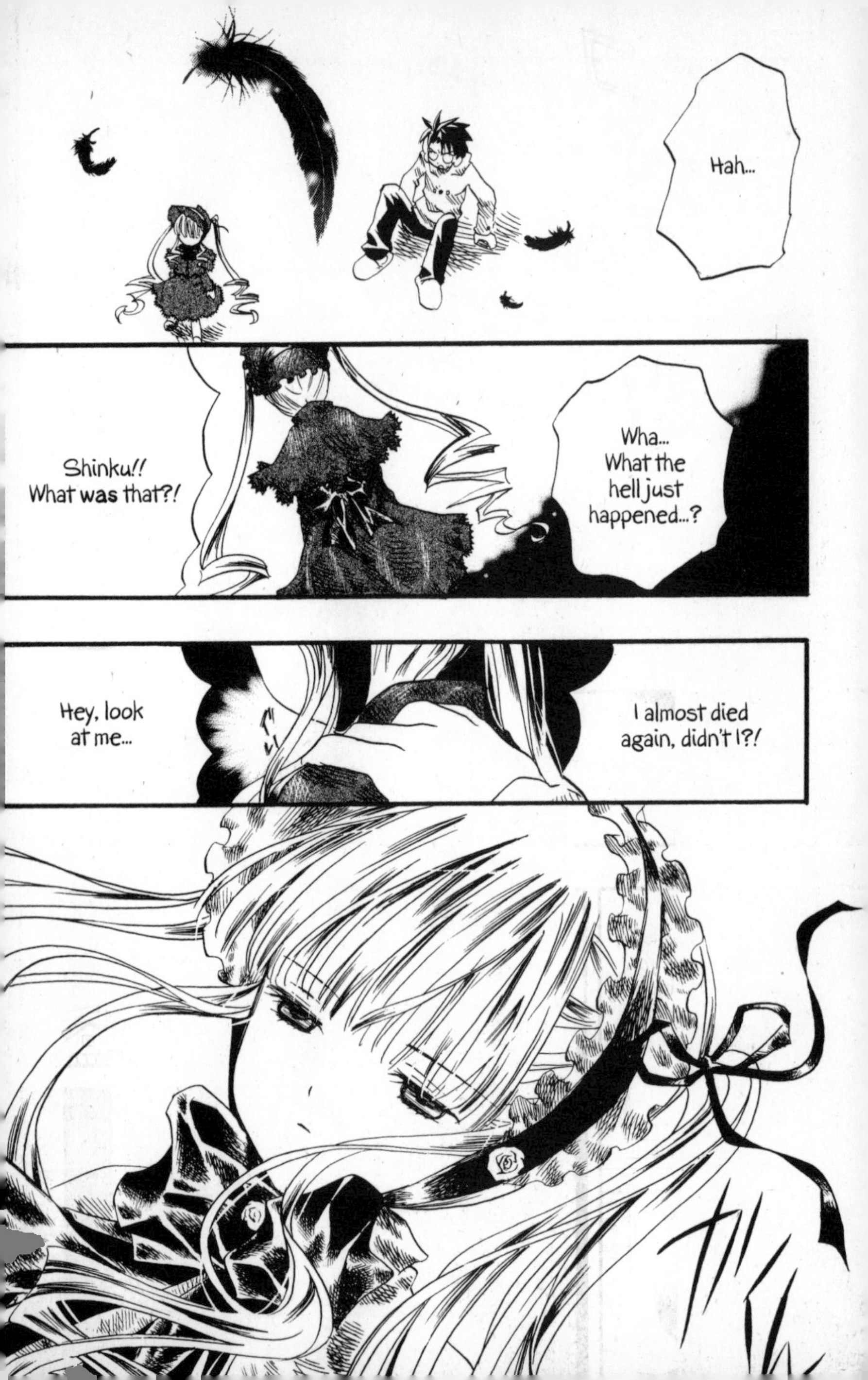
Hah...
Wha... What the hell just happened...?
Shinku!! What was that?!
I almost died again, didn't I?!
Hey, look at me...

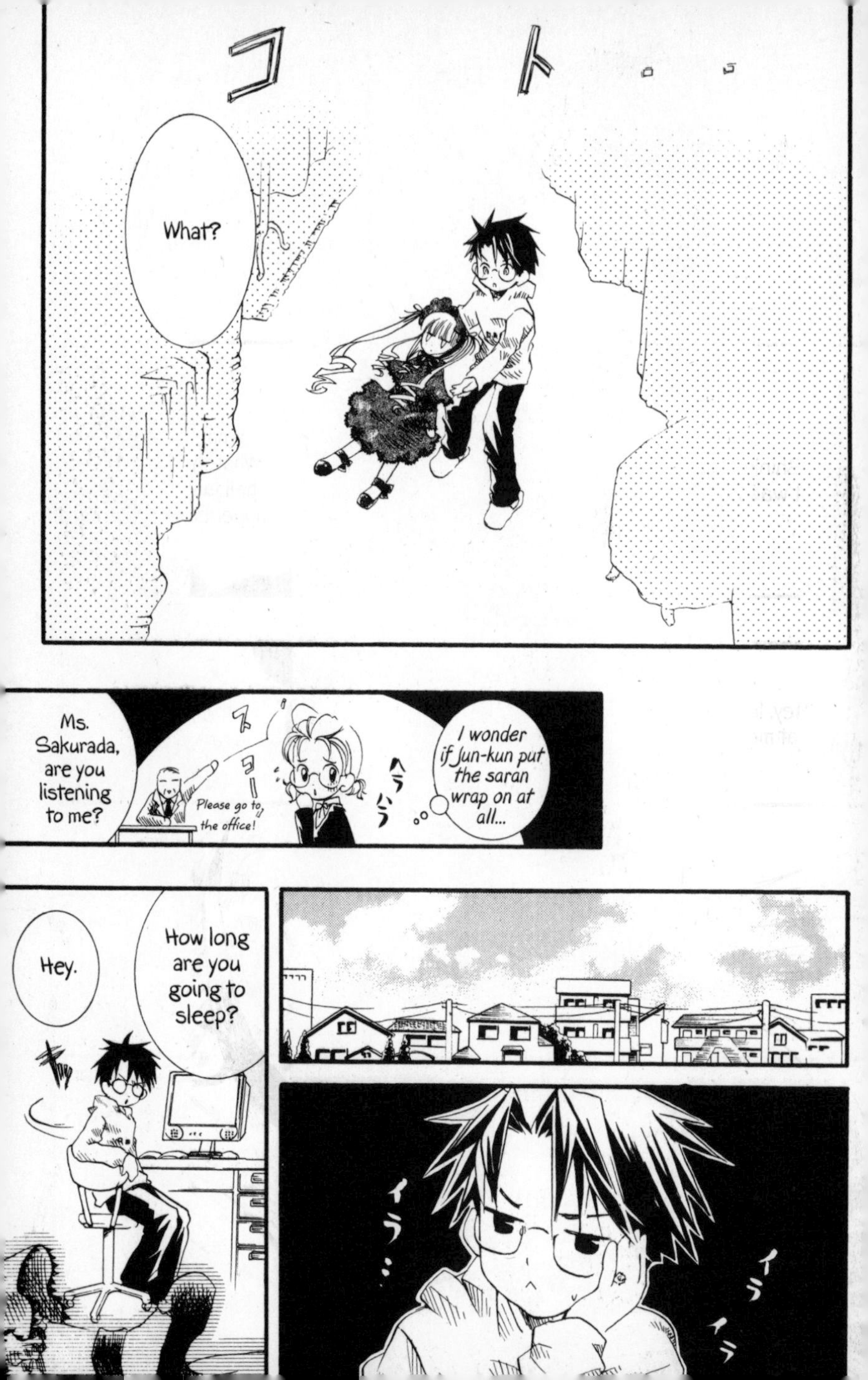
コト
What?
I wonder if Jun-kun put the saran wrap on at all...
Please go to the office!
Ms. Sakurada, are you listening to me?
イラ…
イラ イラ
How long are you going to sleep?
Hey.

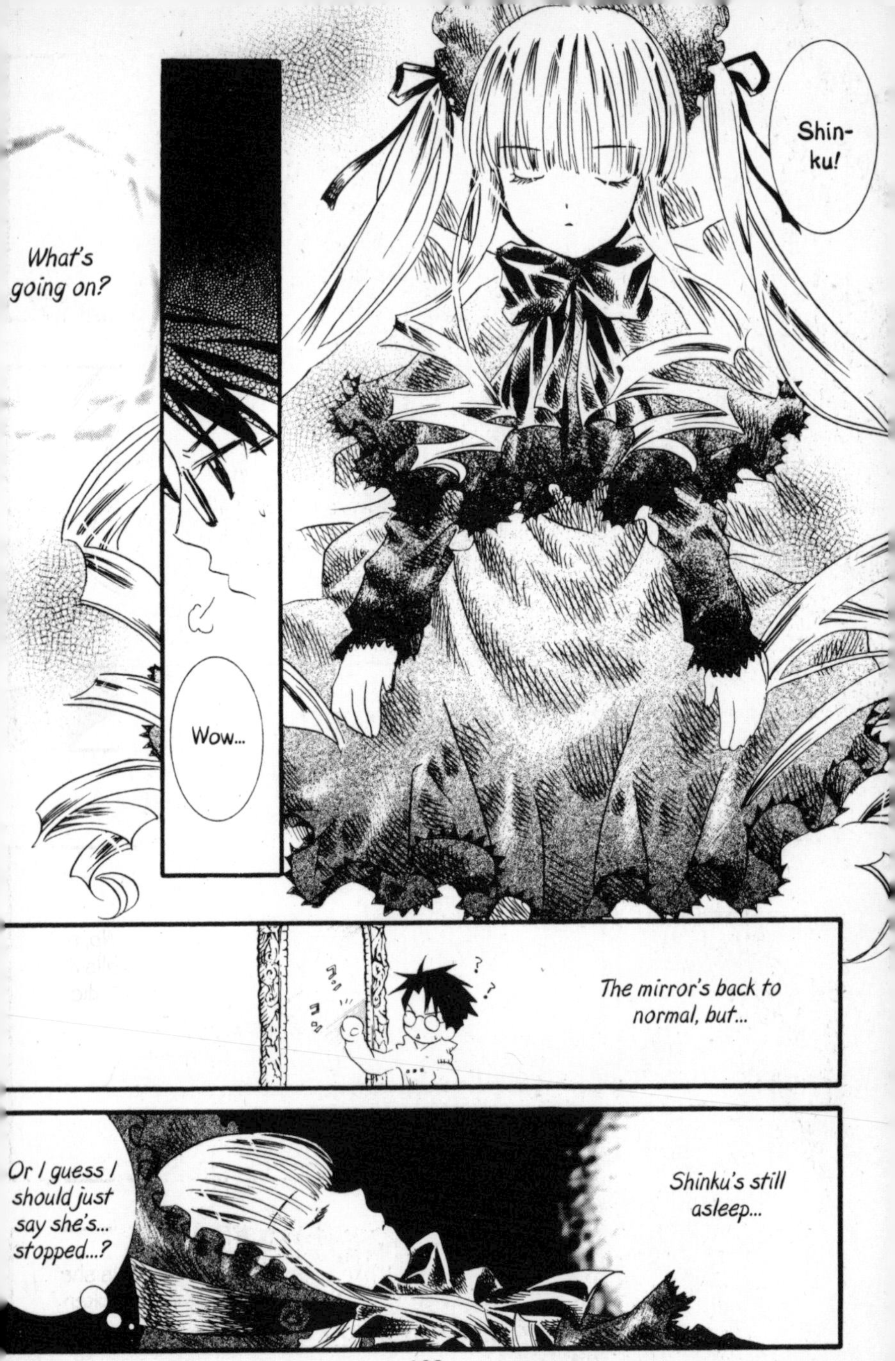
Shin-ku!
Wow...
What's going on?
The mirror's back to normal, but...
Shinku's still asleep...
Or I guess I should just say she's... stopped...?

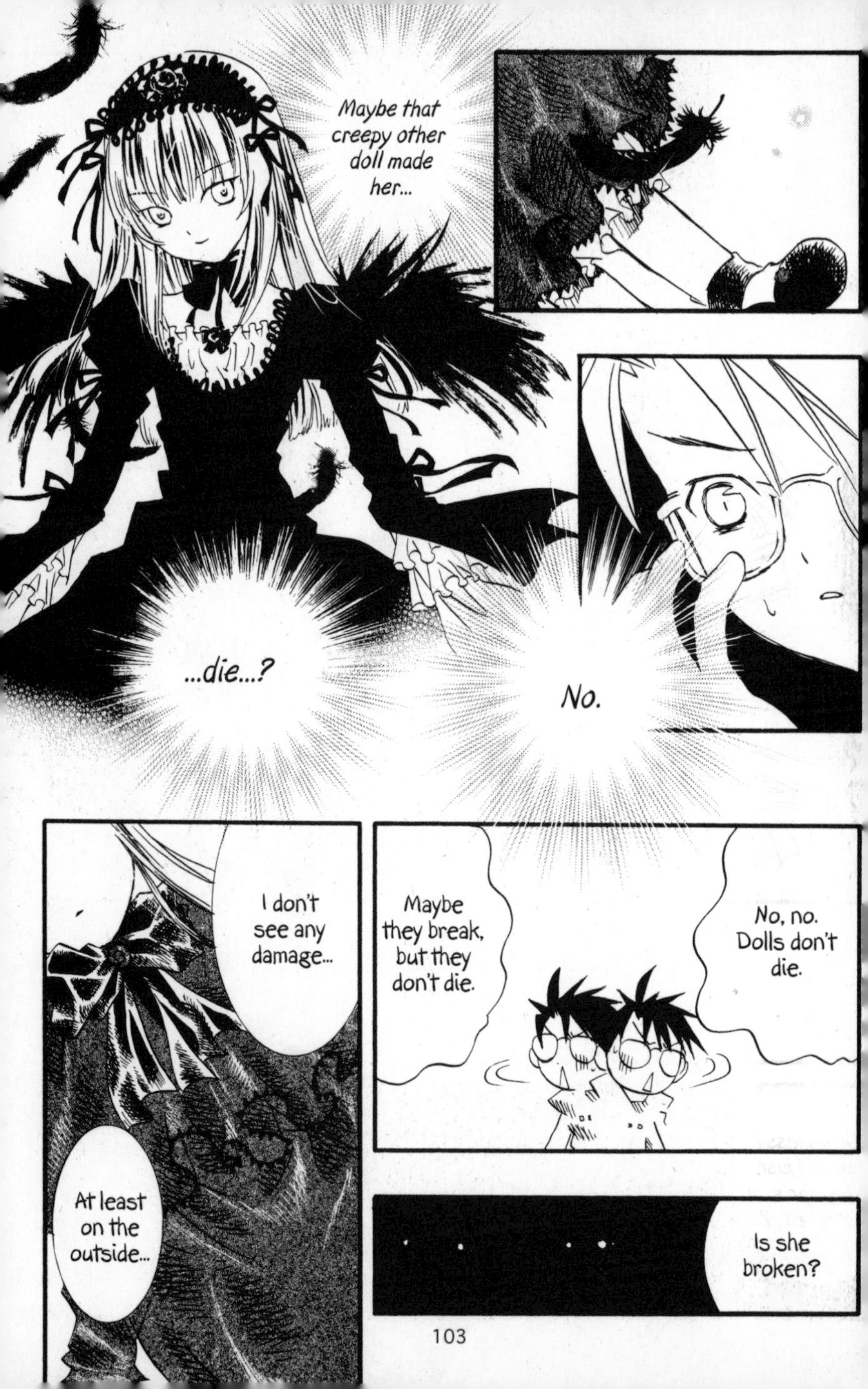
Maybe that creepy other doll made her...
...die...?
No.
No, no. Dolls don't die.
Maybe they break, but they don't die.
Is she broken?
I don't see any damage...
At least on the outside...

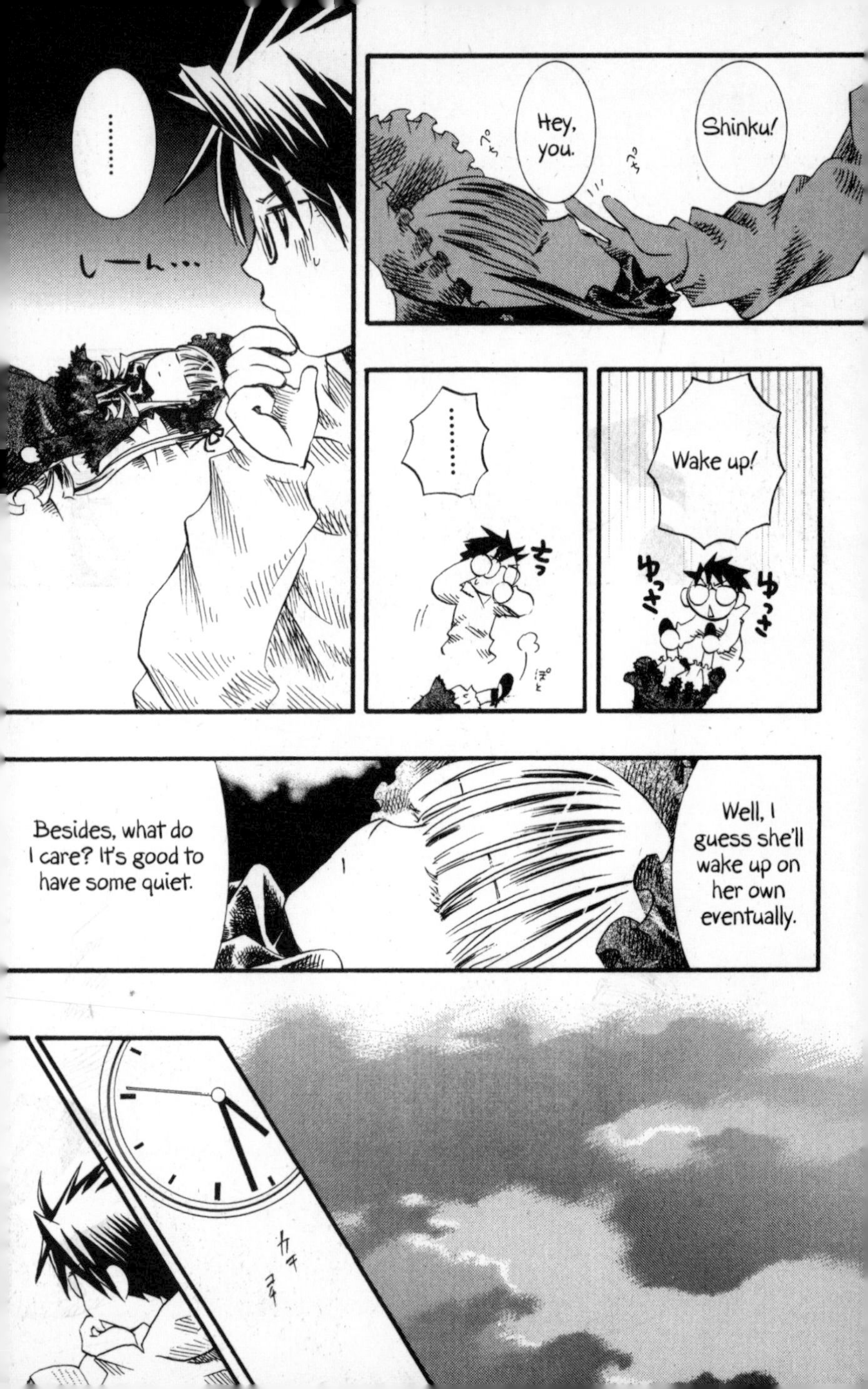
Shinku!
Hey, you.
Wake up!
ゆっさ
ゆっさ
……
……
しーん…
Well, I guess she'll wake up on her own eventually.
Besides, what do I care? It's good to have some quiet.
カチ
コチ

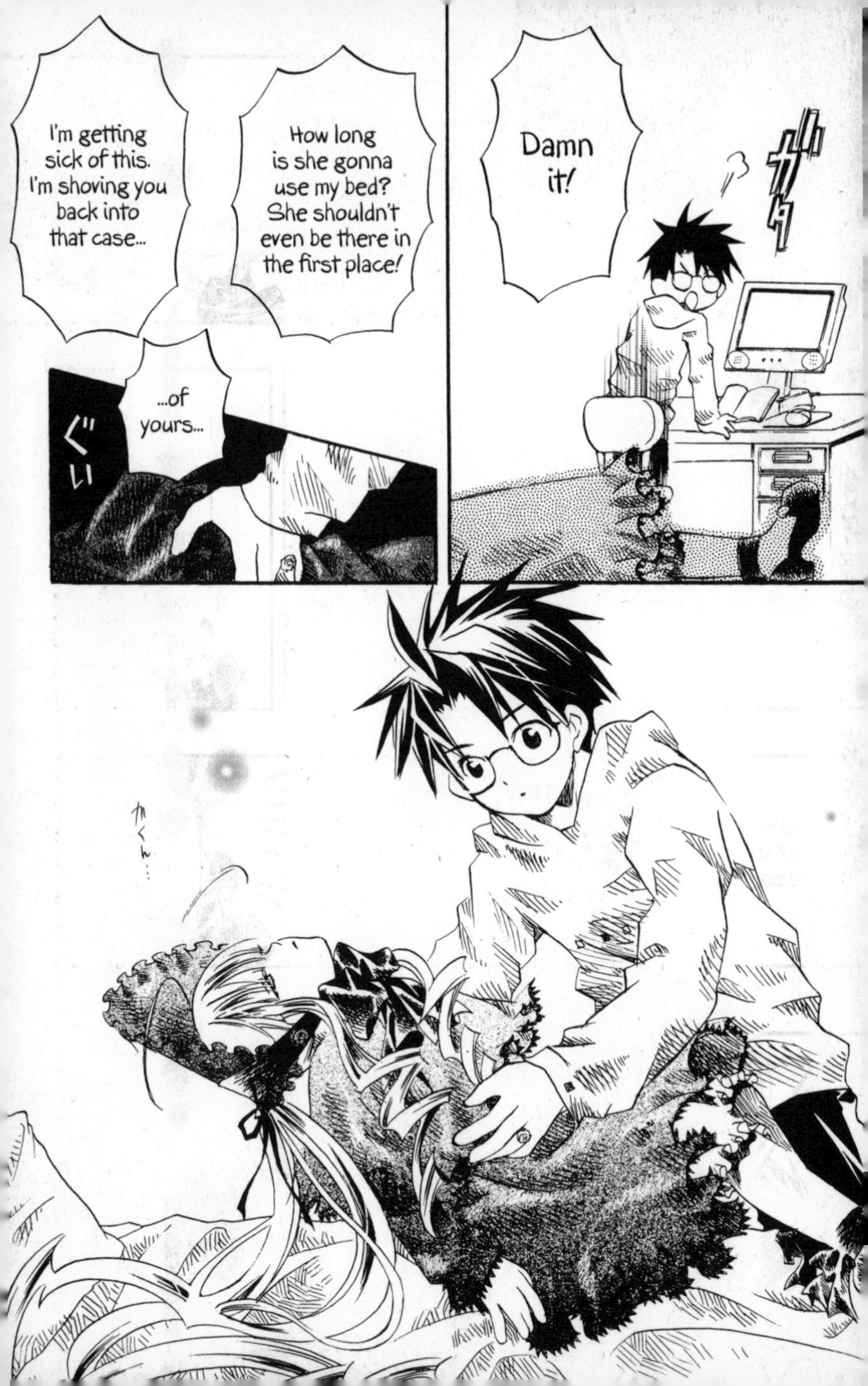
ガタ
Damn it!
How long is she gonna use my bed? She shouldn't even be there in the first place!
I'm getting sick of this. I'm shoving you back into that case...
...of yours...
ぐい
かくん…

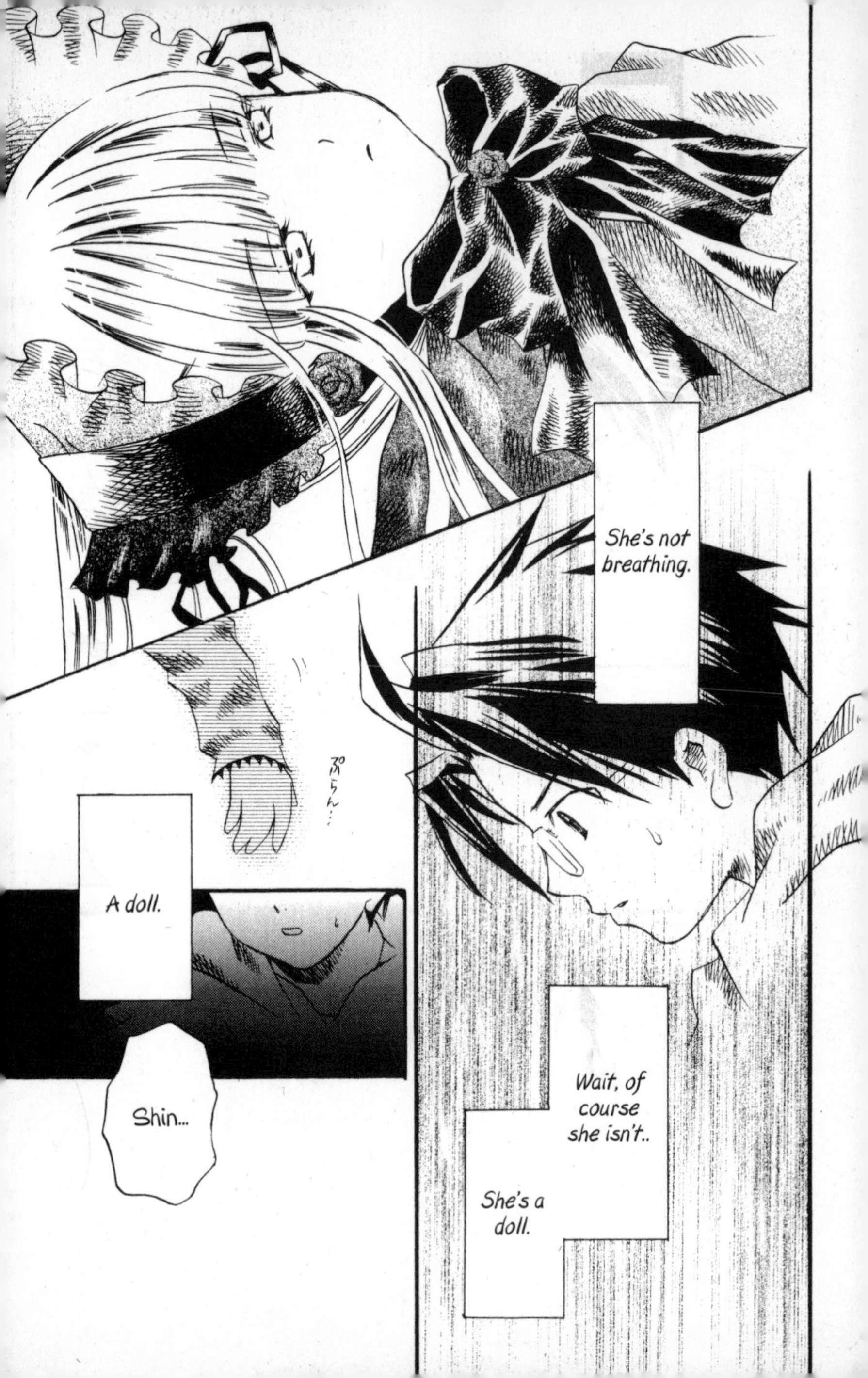
She's not breathing.
Wait, of course she isn't..
She's a doll.
ぷらん…
A doll.
Shin...

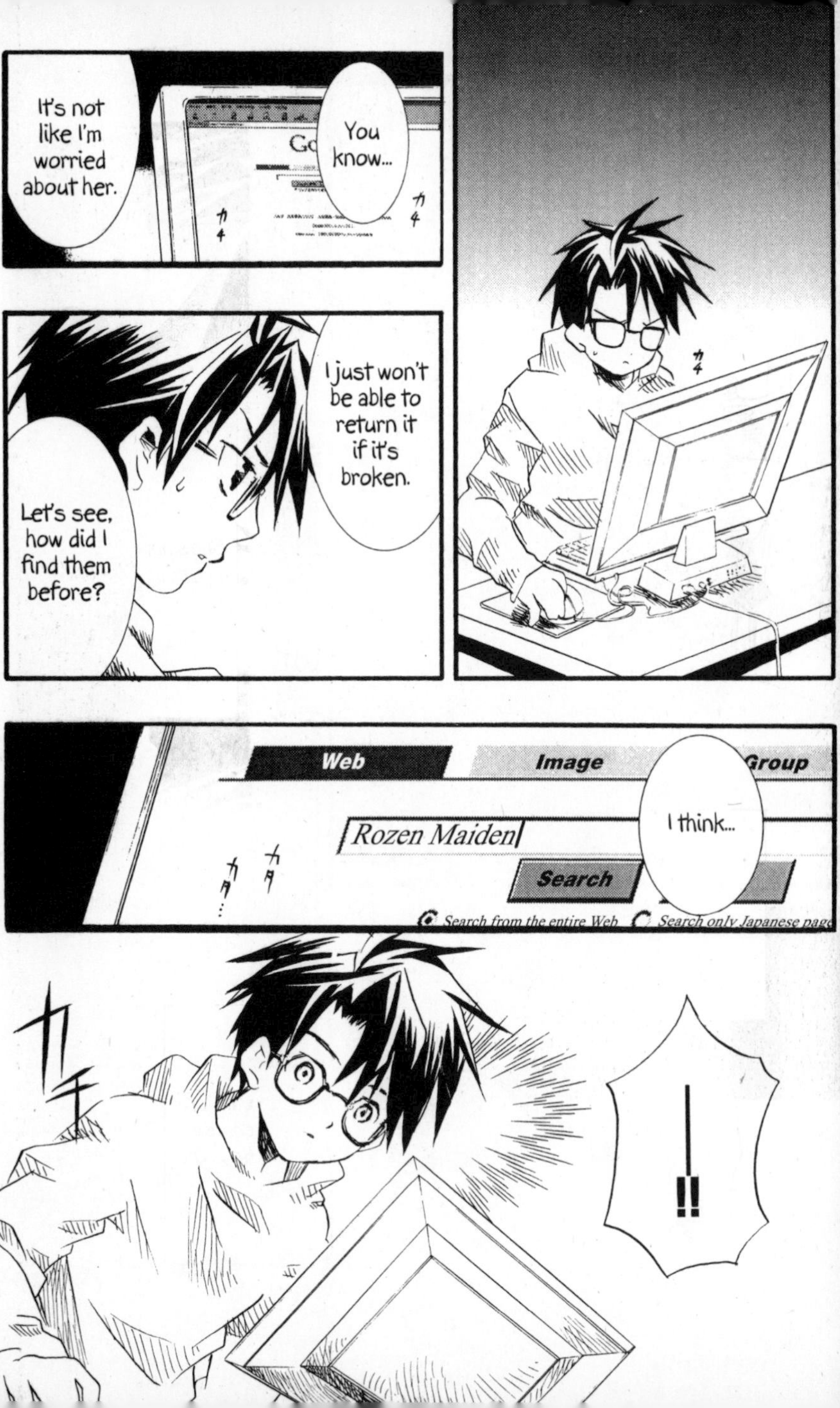
You know...
It's not like I'm worried about her.
I just won't be able to return it if it's broken.
Let's see, how did I find them before?
Web
Image
Group
I think...
Rozen Maiden
Search
カタ
カタ...
Search from the entire Web
Search only Japanese page
!!
カチ

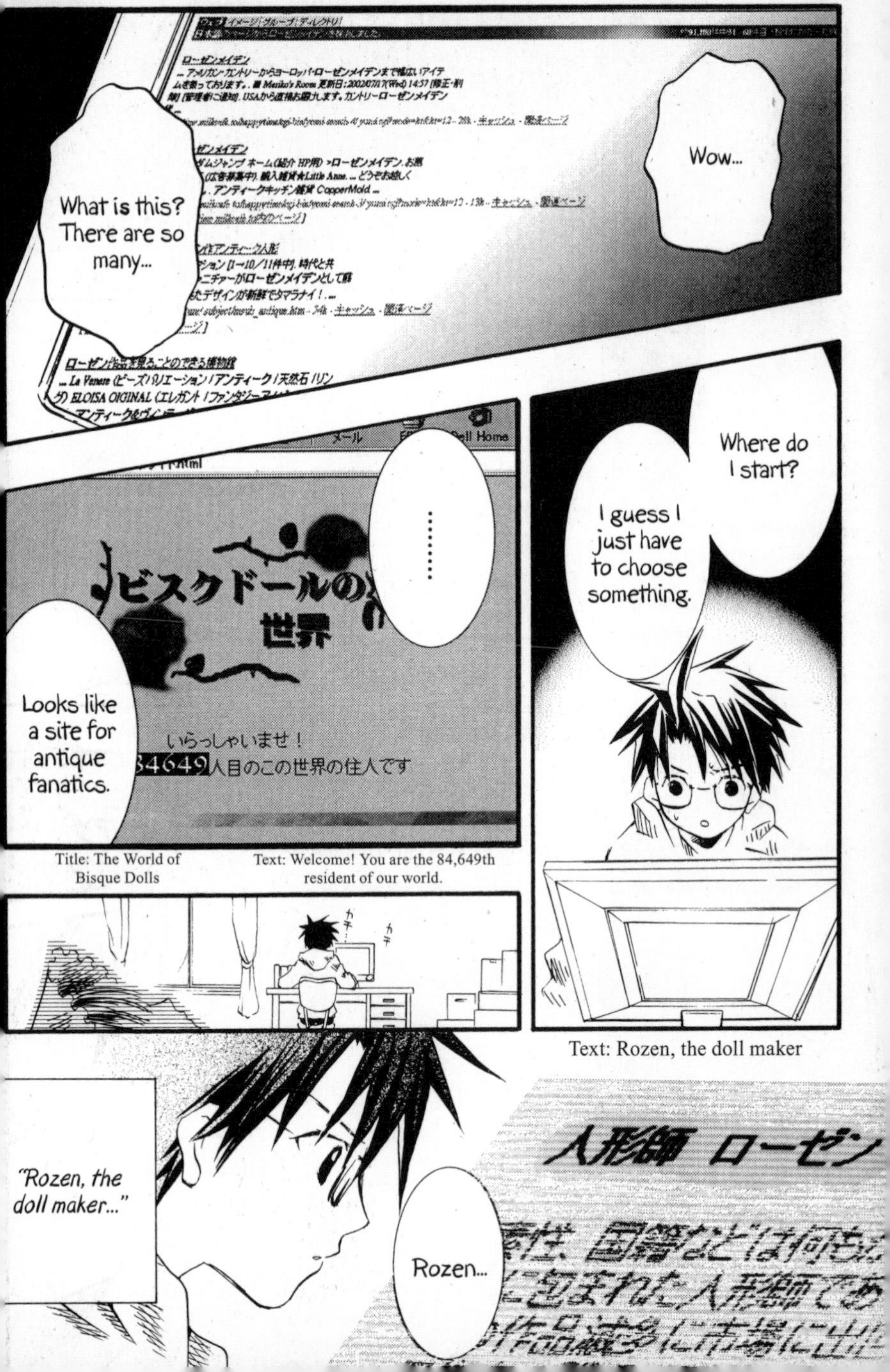
Wow...
What is this? There are so many...
Where do I start?
I guess I just have to choose something.
......
ビスクドールの世界
いらっしゃいませ！
人目のこの世界の住人です
Looks like a site for antique fanatics.
Title: The World of Bisque Dolls
Text: Welcome! You are the 84,649th resident of our world.
カチ
カチ
Text: Rozen, the doll maker
人形師 ローゼン
Rozen...
"Rozen, the doll maker..."

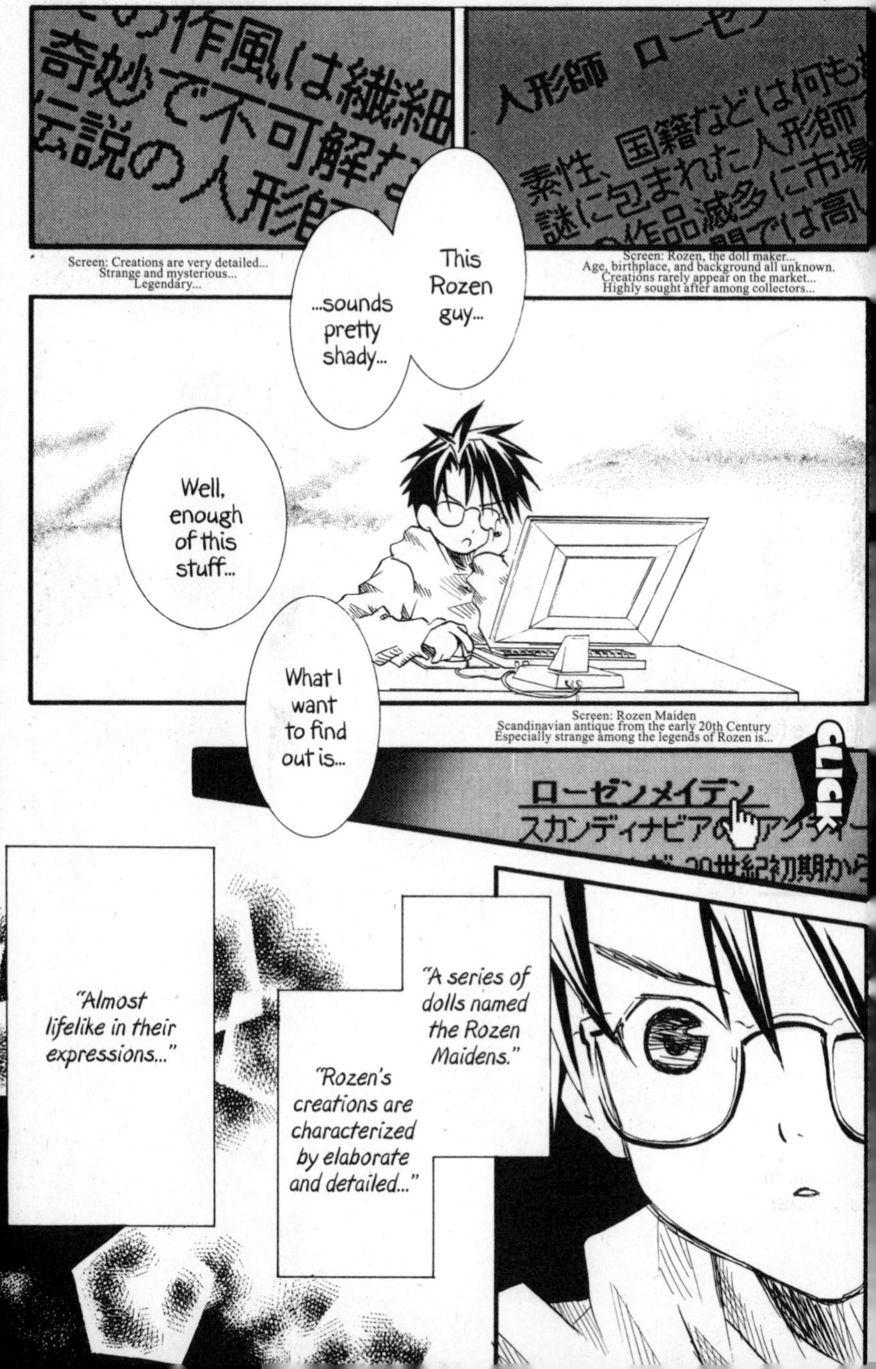
Screen: Rozen, the doll maker...
Age, birthplace, and background all unknown.
Creations rarely appear on the market...
Highly sought after among collectors...
Screen: Creations are very detailed...
Strange and mysterious...
Legendary...
This Rozen guy...
...sounds pretty shady...
Well, enough of this stuff...
What I want to find out is...
Screen: Rozen Maiden
Scandinavian antique from the early 20th Century
Especially strange among the legends of Rozen is...
CLICK
"A series of dolls named the Rozen Maidens."
"Rozen's creations are characterized by elaborate and detailed..."
"Almost lifelike in their expressions..."

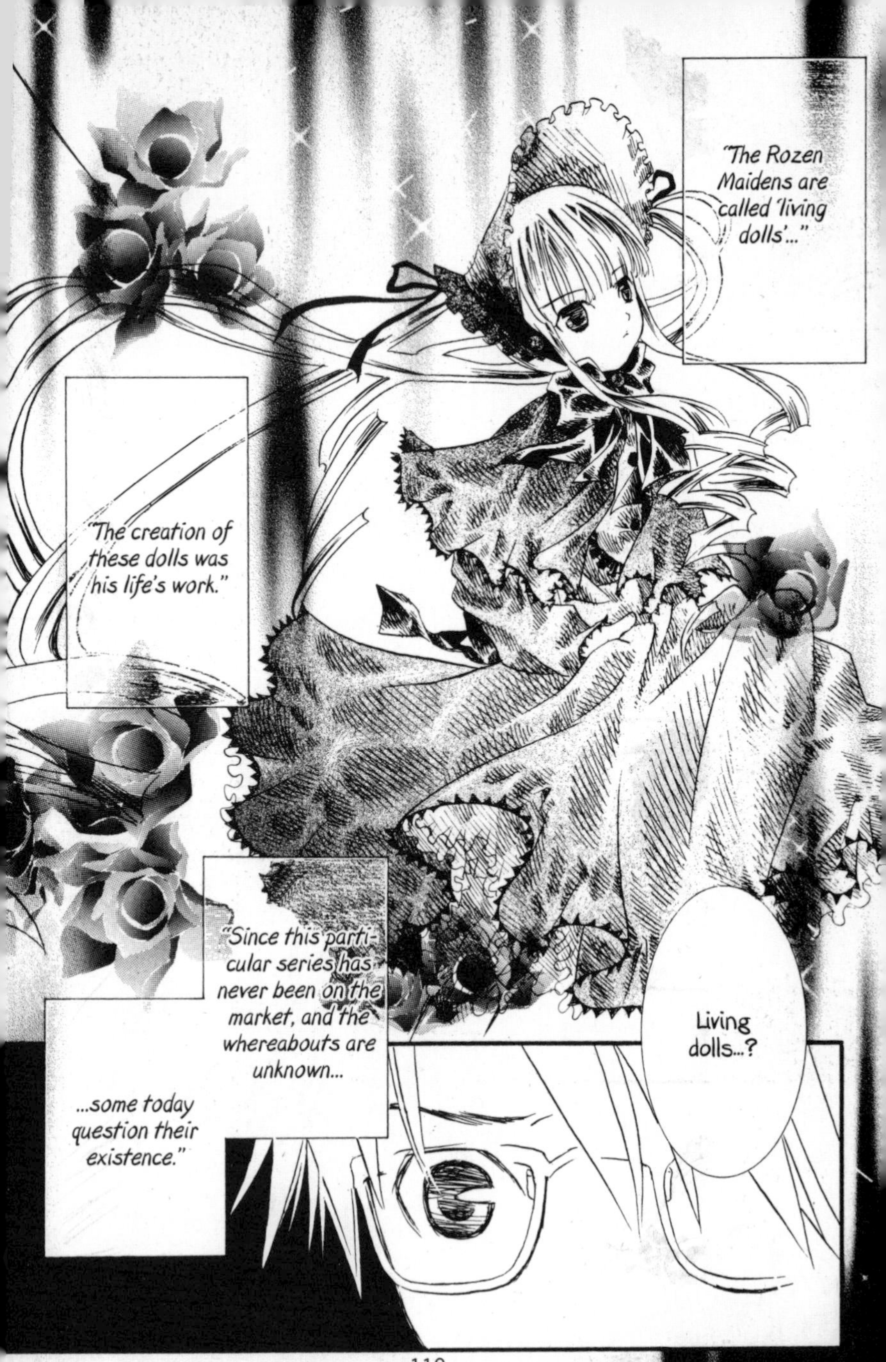
"The Rozen Maidens are called 'living dolls'..."
"The creation of these dolls was his life's work."
"Since this particular series has never been on the market, and the whereabouts are unknown...
...some today question their existence."
Living dolls...?

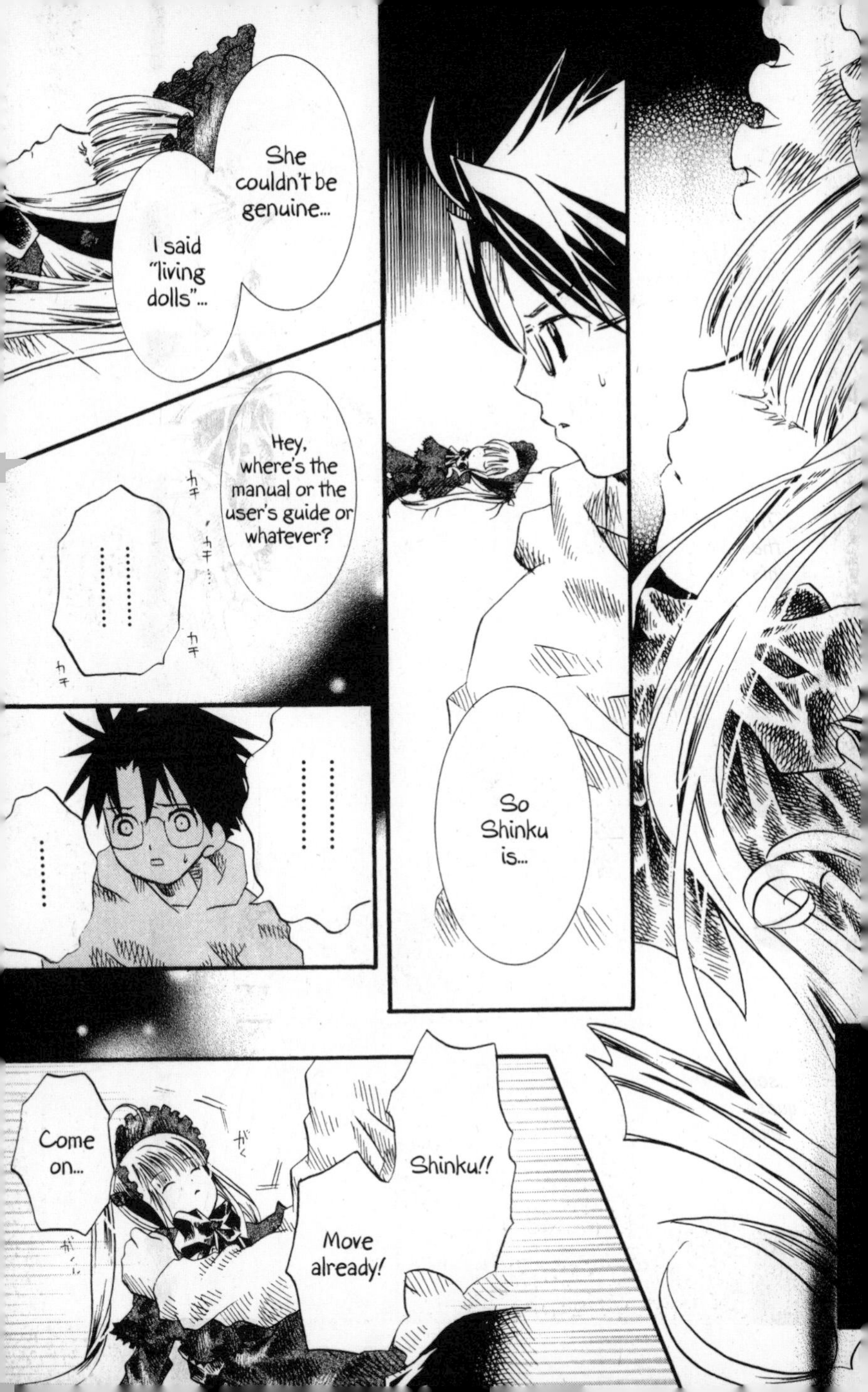
So Shinku is...
She couldn't be genuine...
I said "living dolls"...
Hey, where's the manual or the user's guide or whatever?
......
カチ
カチ
カチ
カチ
......
......
Shinku!!
Move already!
Come on...
がく

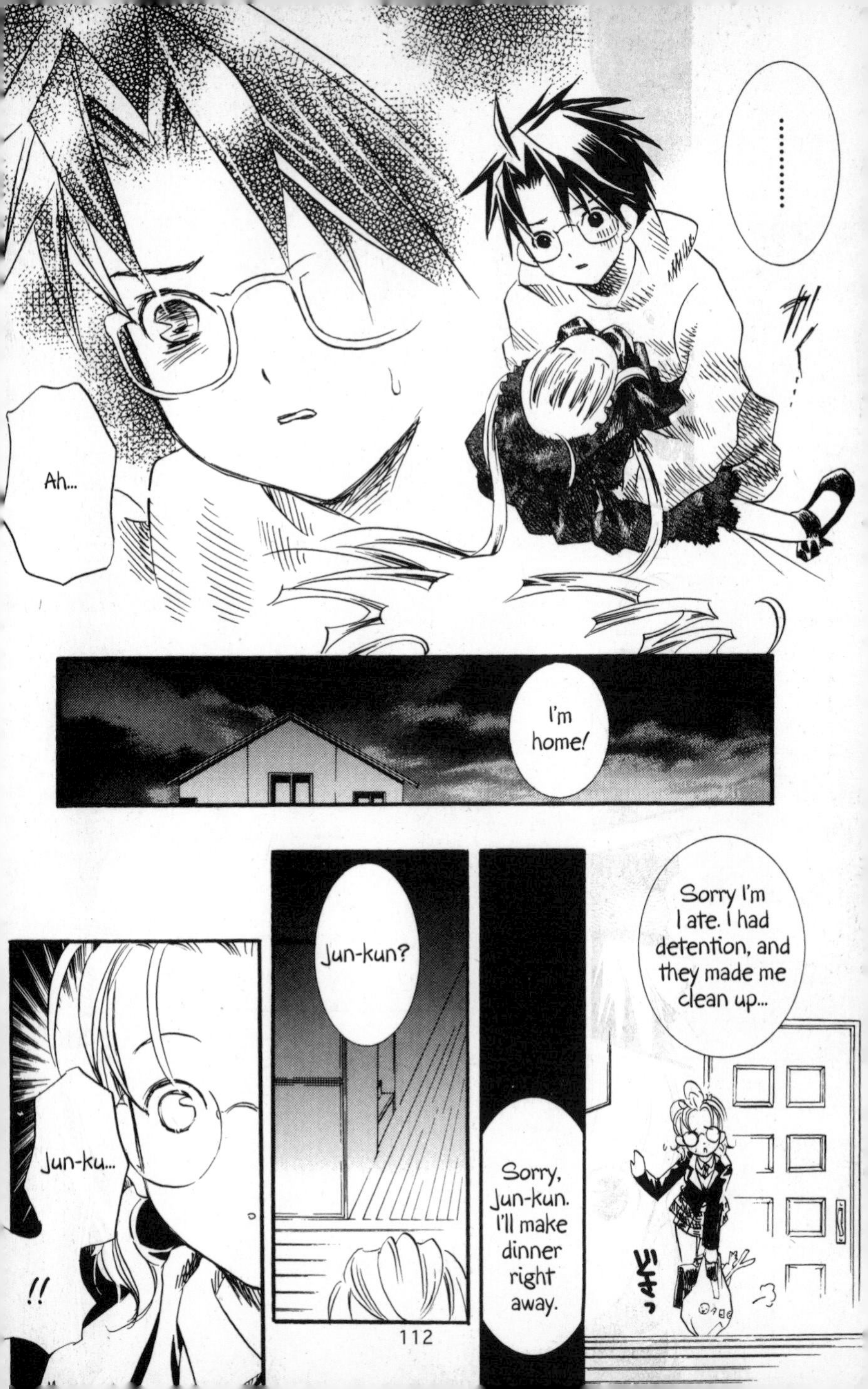
......
Ah...
I'm home!
Sorry I'm late. I had detention, and they made me clean up...
Sorry, Jun-kun. I'll make dinner right away.
Jun-kun?
Jun-ku...
!!

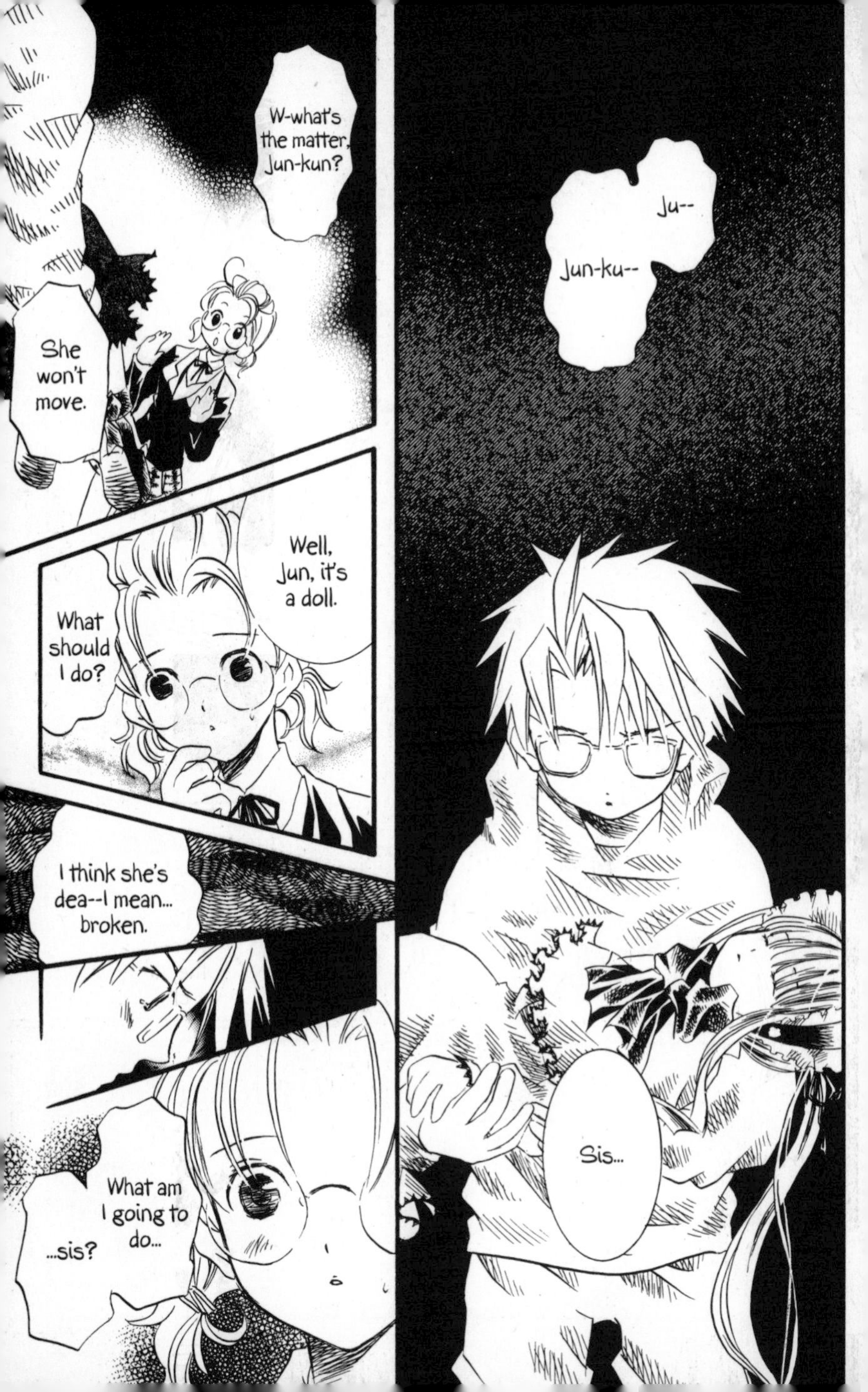
Ju--
Jun-ku--
Sis...
W-what's the matter, Jun-kun?
She won't move.
Well, Jun, it's a doll.
What should I do?
I think she's dea--I mean... broken.
What am I going to do...
...sis?

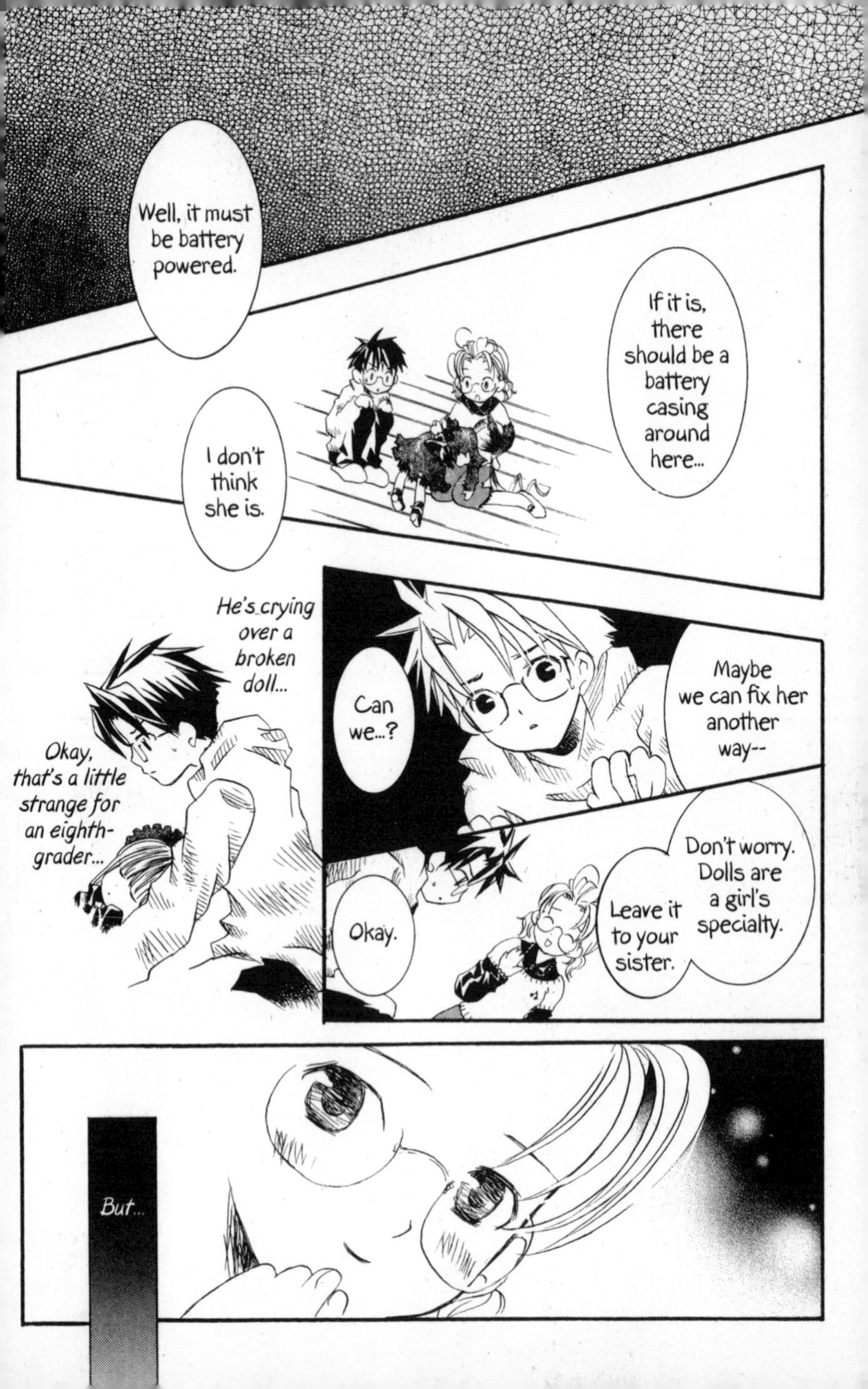

Well, it must be battery powered.
If it is, there should be a battery casing around here...
I don't think she is.
Maybe we can fix her another way--
Can we...?
Don't worry. Dolls are a girl's specialty.
Leave it to your sister.
Okay.
He's crying over a broken doll...
Okay, that's a little strange for an eighth-grader...
But...

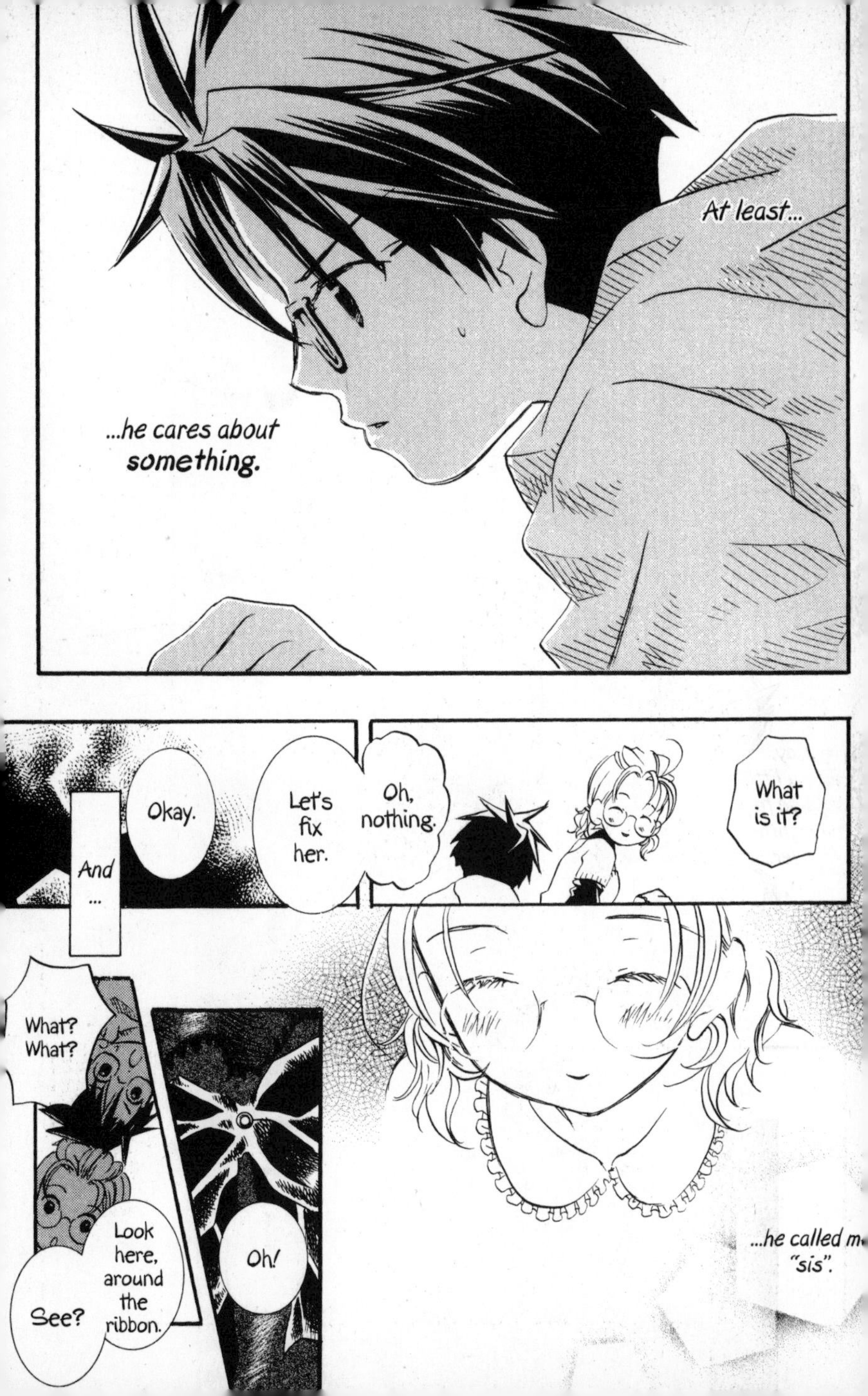

At least...
...he cares about something.
What is it?
Oh, nothing.
Let's fix her.
Okay.
And ...
...he called m
"sis".
What? What?
Look here, around the ribbon.
Oh!
See?

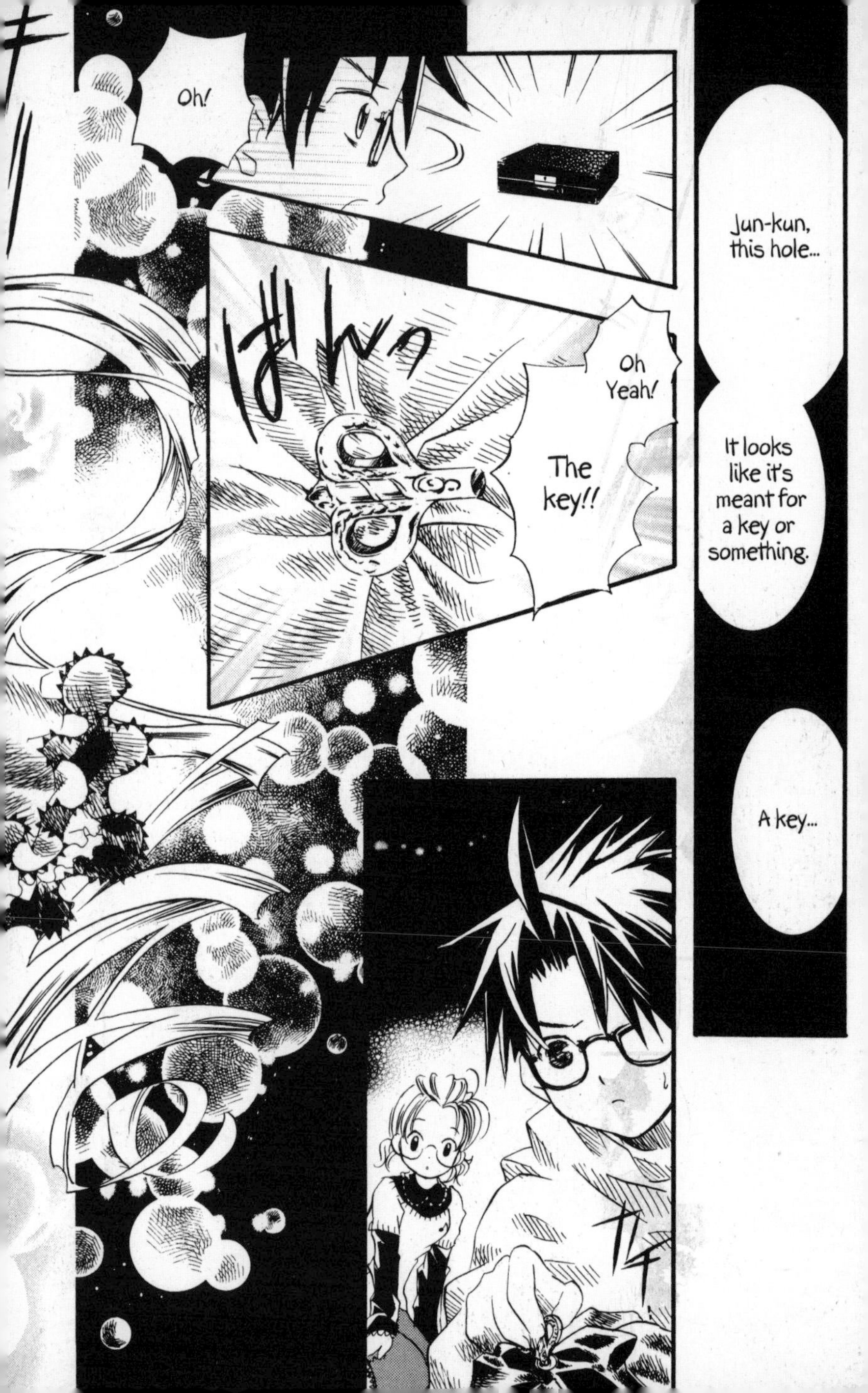
Jun-kun, this hole...
It looks like it's meant for a key or something.
A key...
Oh!
Oh Yeah!
The key!!

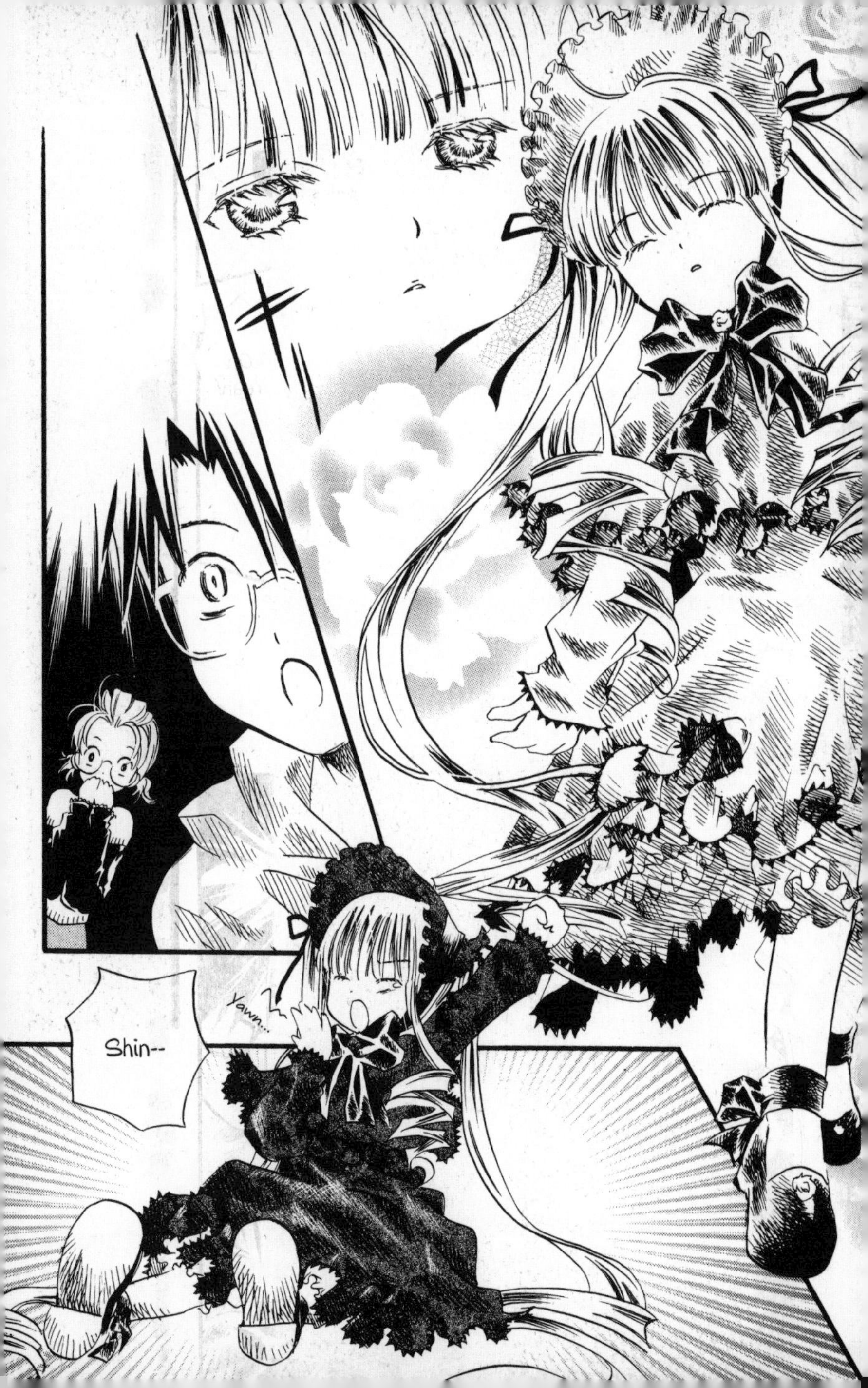
Yawn...
Shin--

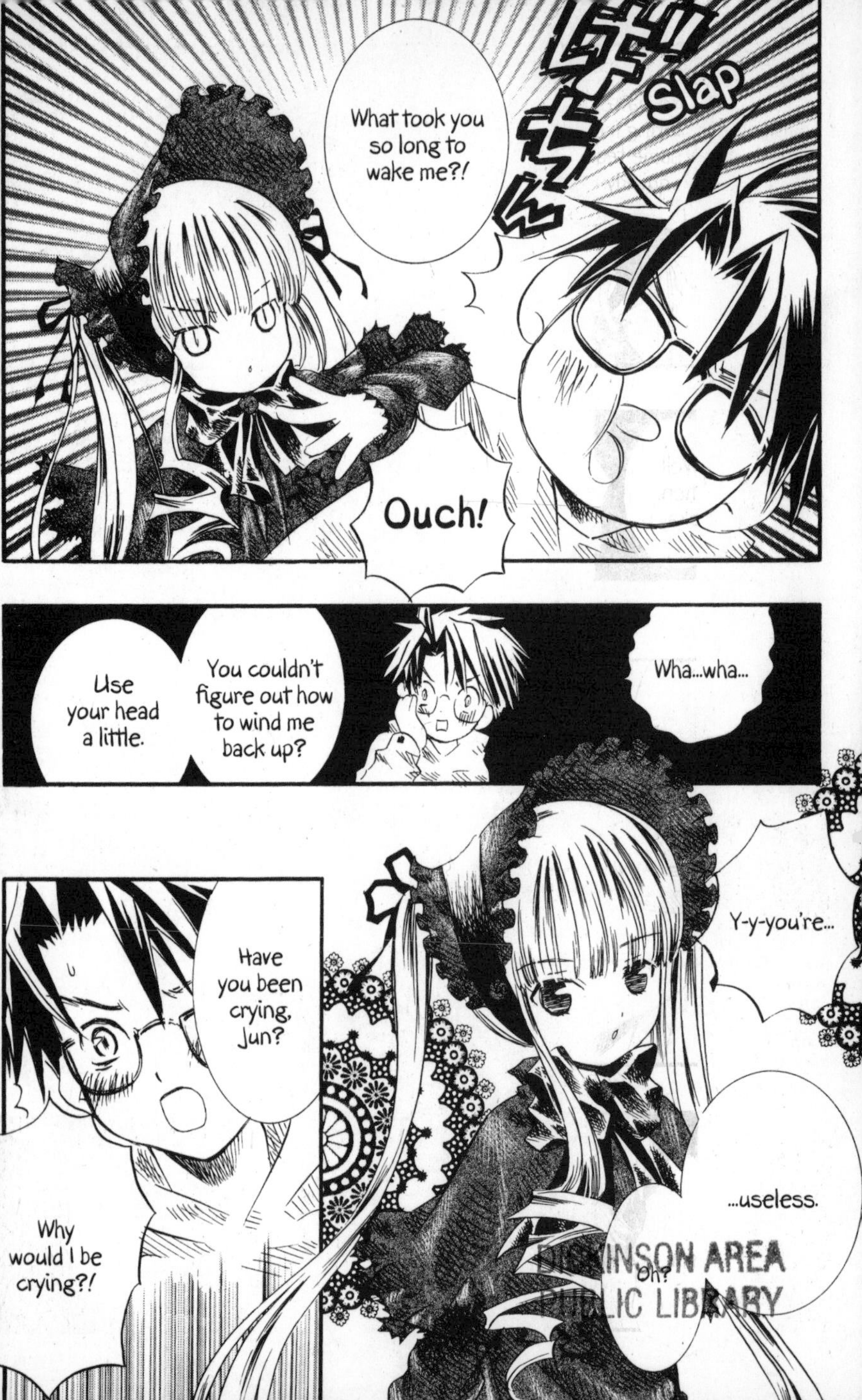
Slap
What took you so long to wake me?!
Ouch!
Wha...wha...
You couldn't figure out how to wind me back up?
Use your head a little.
Y-y-you're...
...useless.
Oh?
Have you been crying, Jun?
Why would I be crying?!

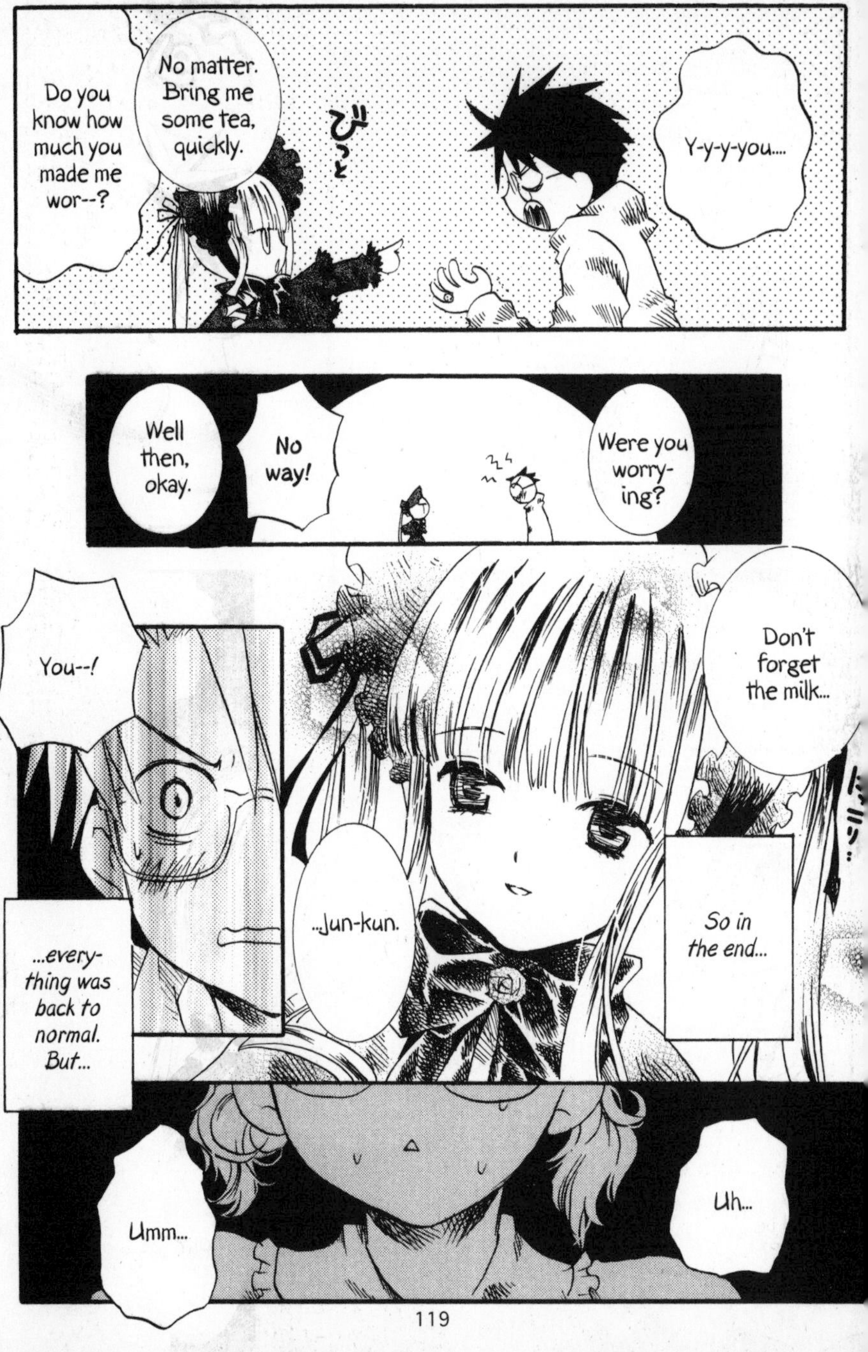

Y-y-y-you....
Do you know how much you made me wor--?
No matter. Bring me some tea, quickly.
Were you worry-ing?
No way!
Well then, okay.
Don't forget the milk...
So in the end...
...Jun-kun.
You--!
...every-thing was back to normal. But...
Uh...
Umm...

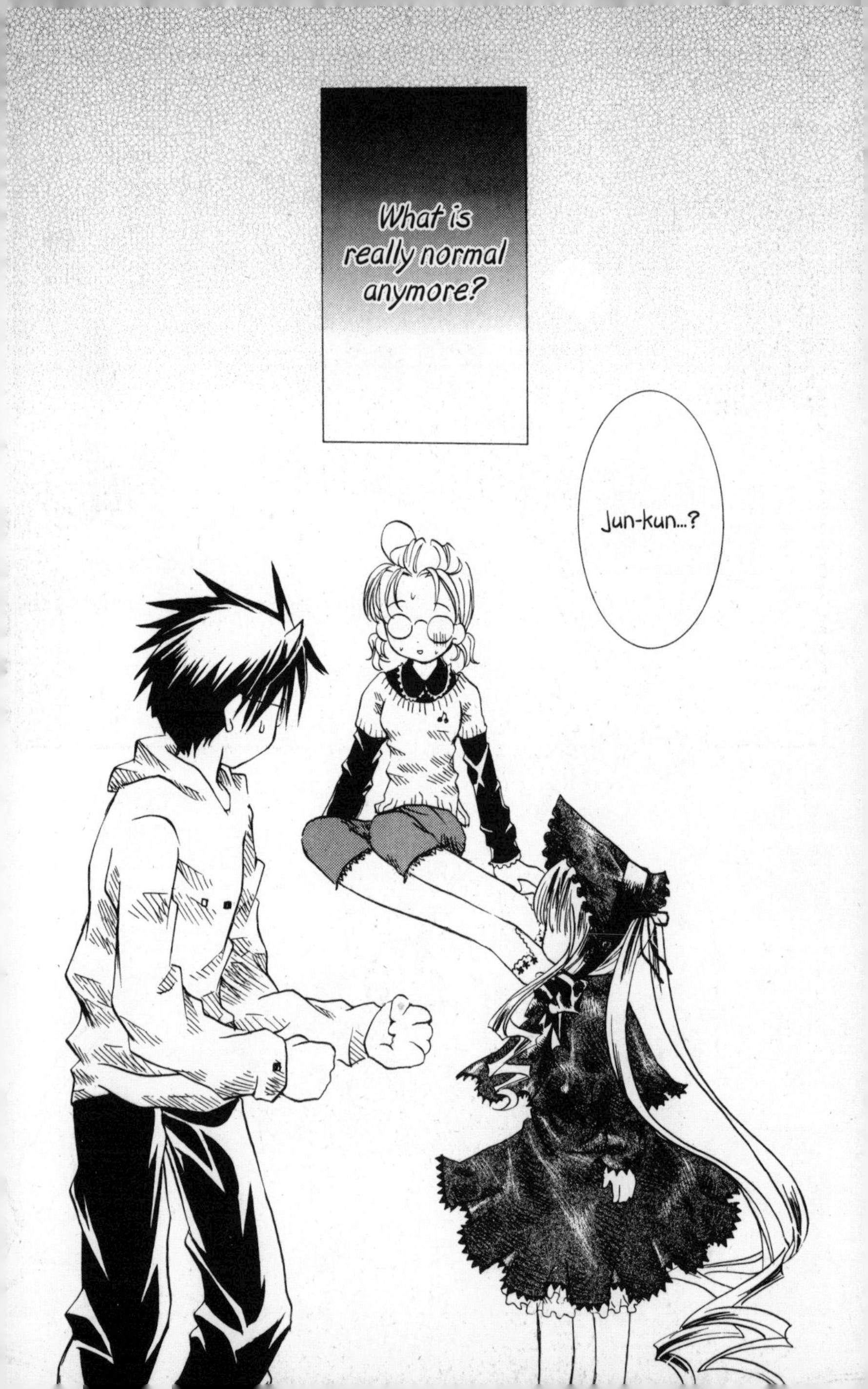
What is really normal anymore?
Jun-kun...?

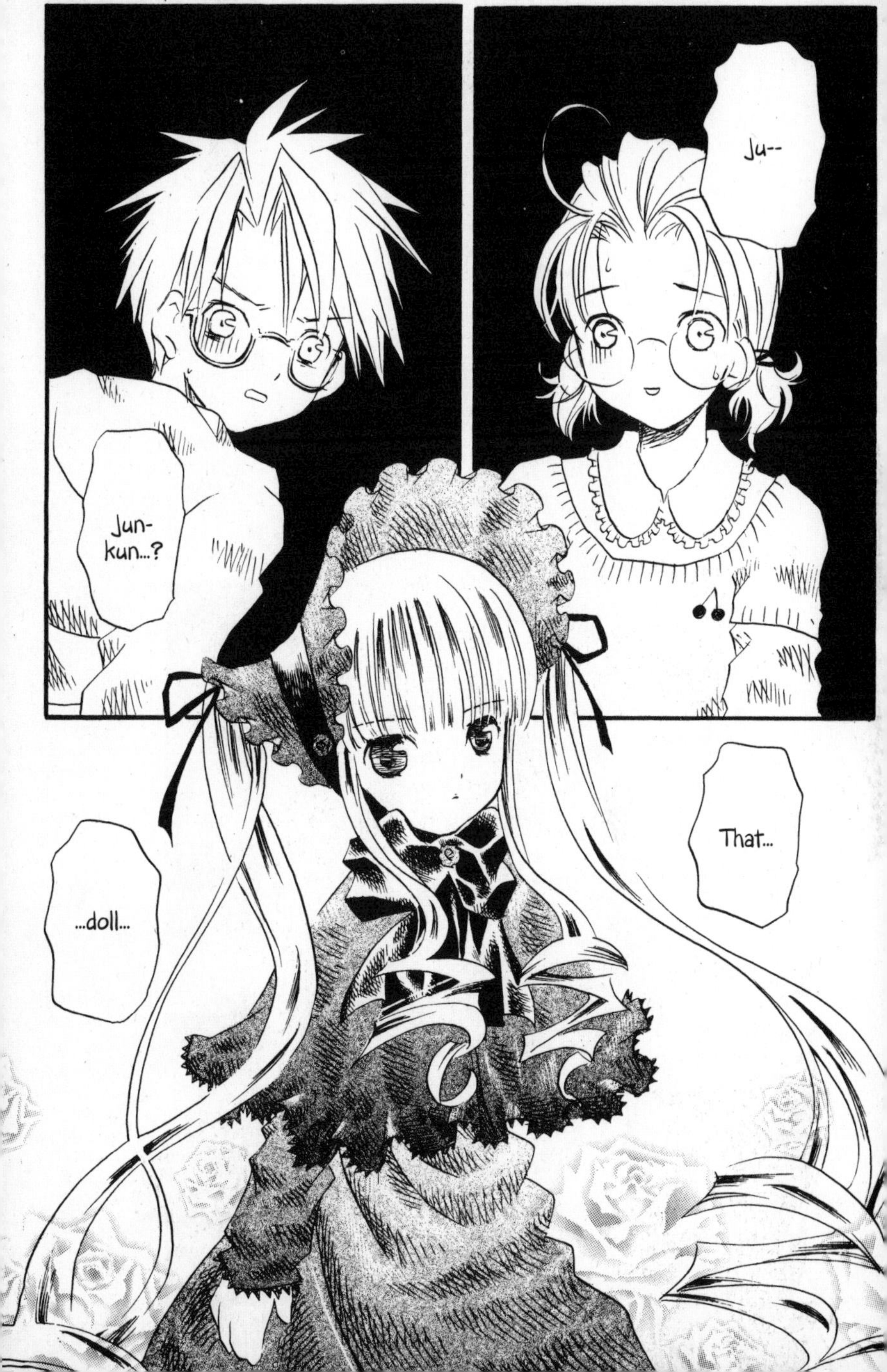
Ju--
Jun-kun...?
That...
...doll...

Phase 3

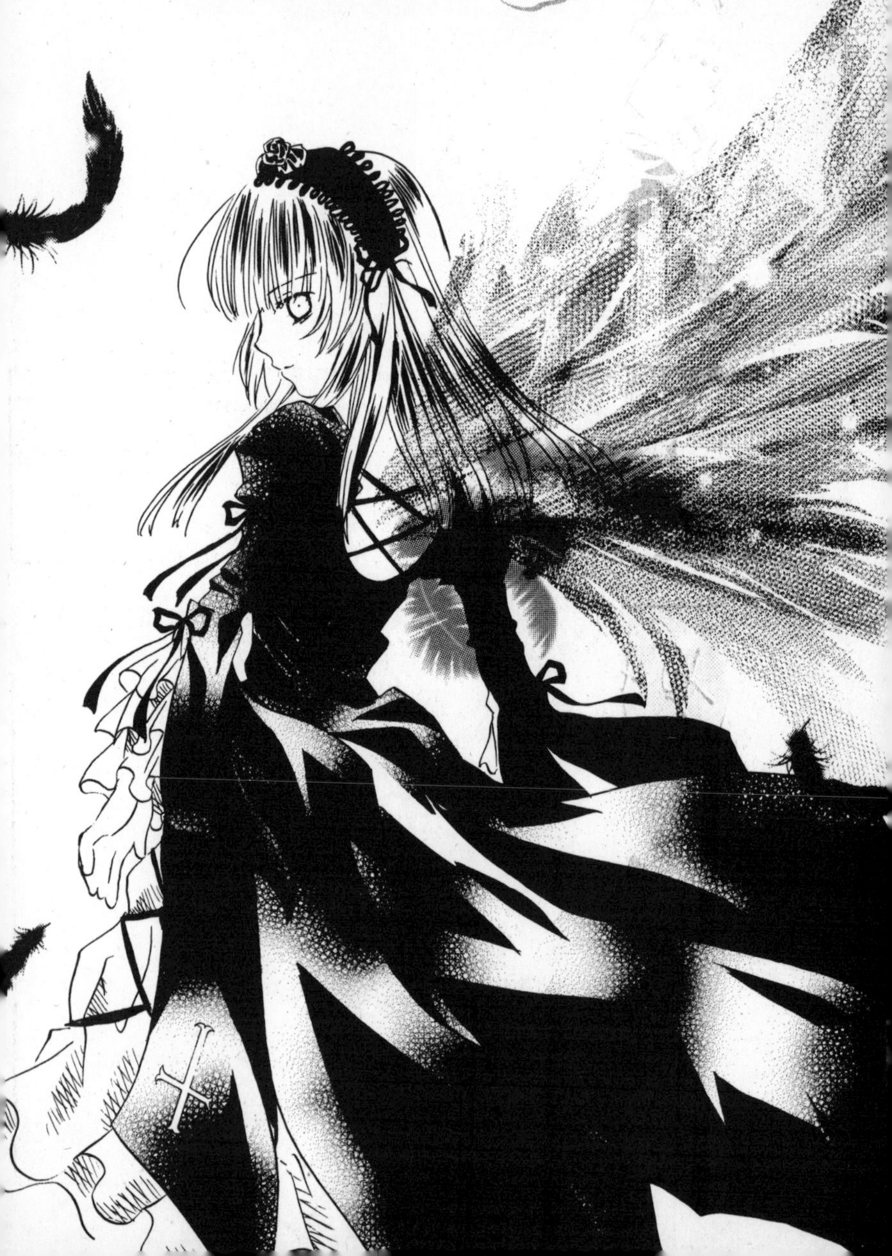

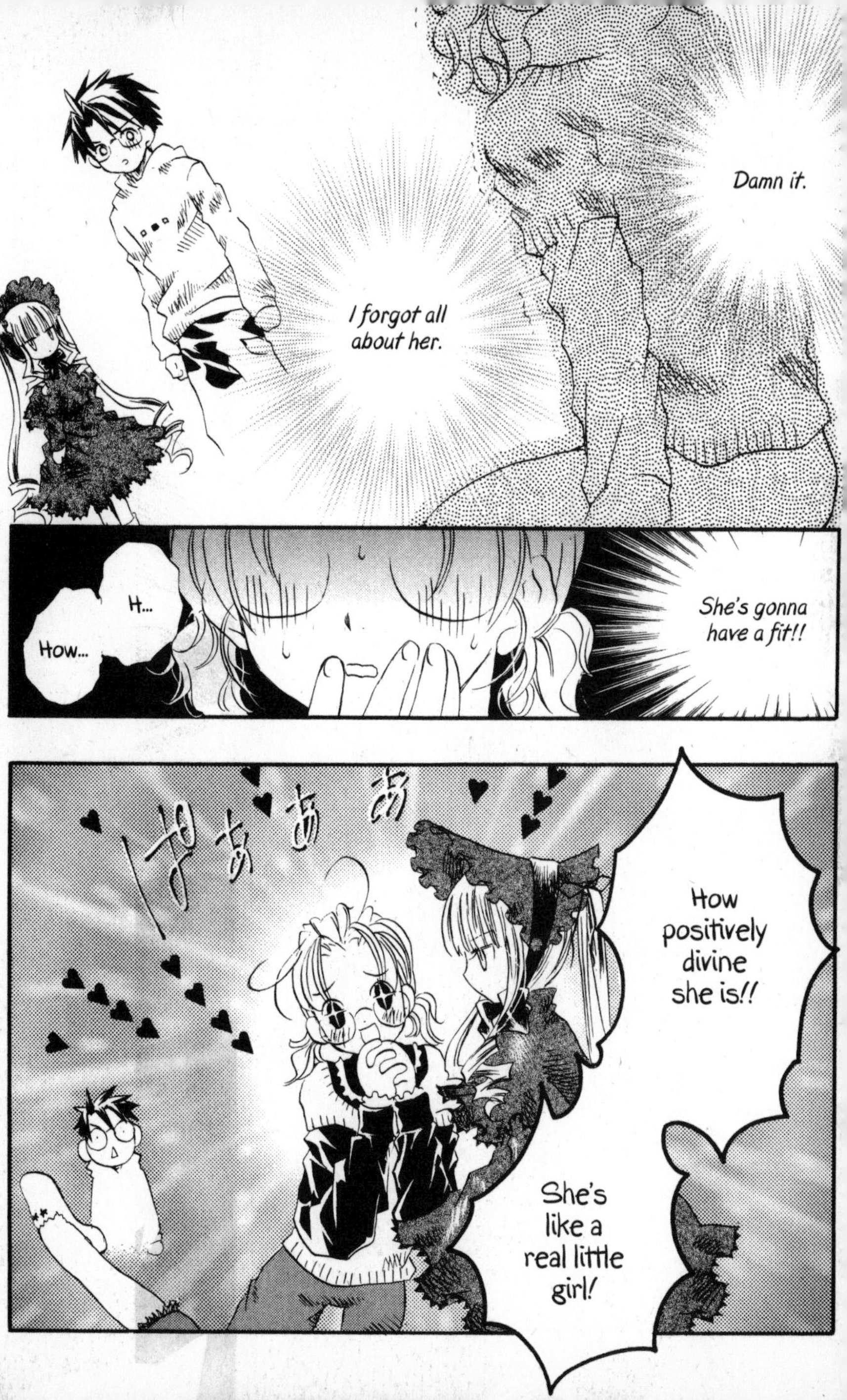
Damn it.
I forgot all about her.
She's gonna have a fit!!
H...
How...
How positively divine she is!!
She's like a real little girl!

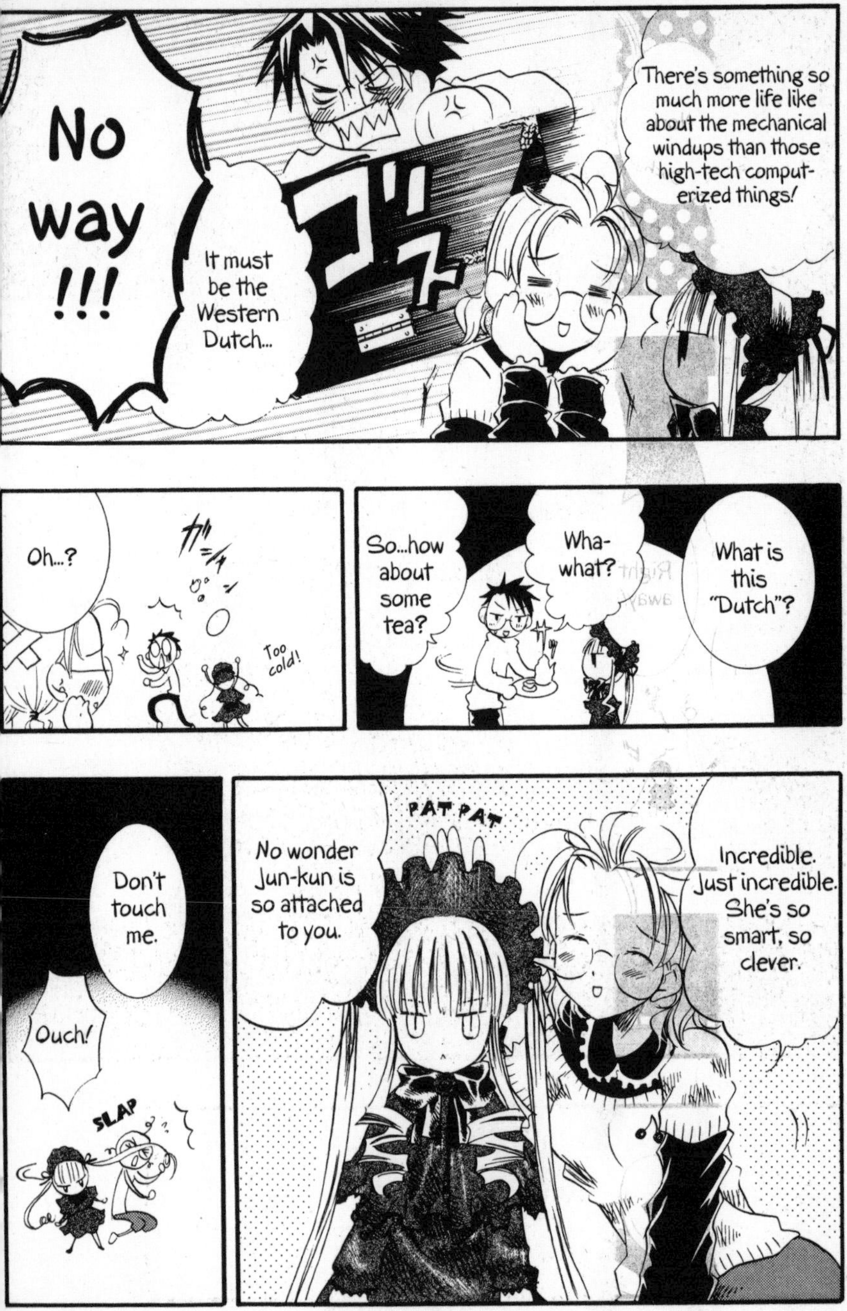
There's something so much more life like about the mechanical windups than those high-tech computerized things!
It must be the Western Dutch...
No way!!!
What is this "Dutch"?
Wha-what?
So...how about some tea?
Oh...?
Too cold!
Incredible. Just incredible. She's so smart, so clever.
PAT PAT
No wonder Jun-kun is so attached to you.
Don't touch me.
Ouch!
SLAP

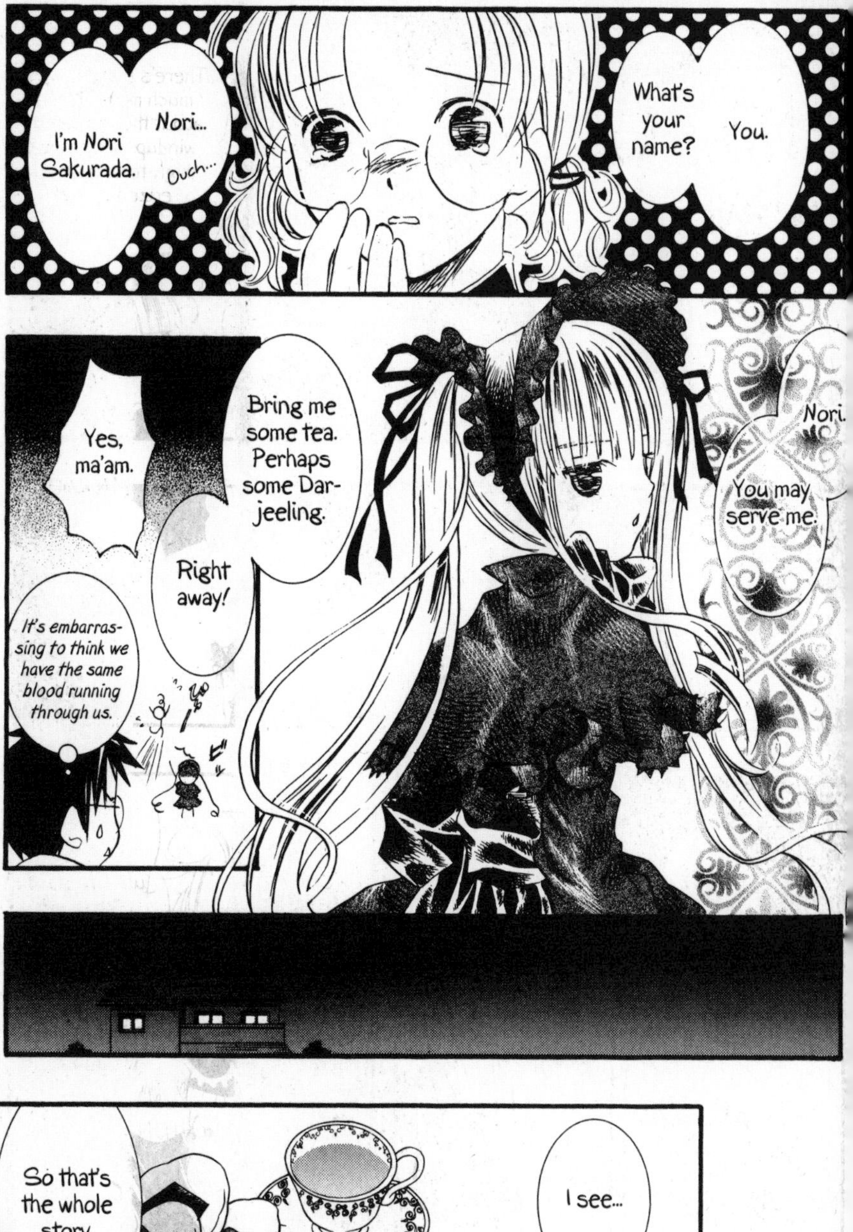
You.
What's your name?
Nori... Ouch...
I'm Nori Sakurada.
Nori.
You may serve me.
Bring me some tea. Perhaps some Dar-jeeling.
Right away!
Yes, ma'am.
It's embarras-sing to think we have the same blood running through us.
I see...
So that's the whole story.

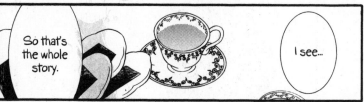

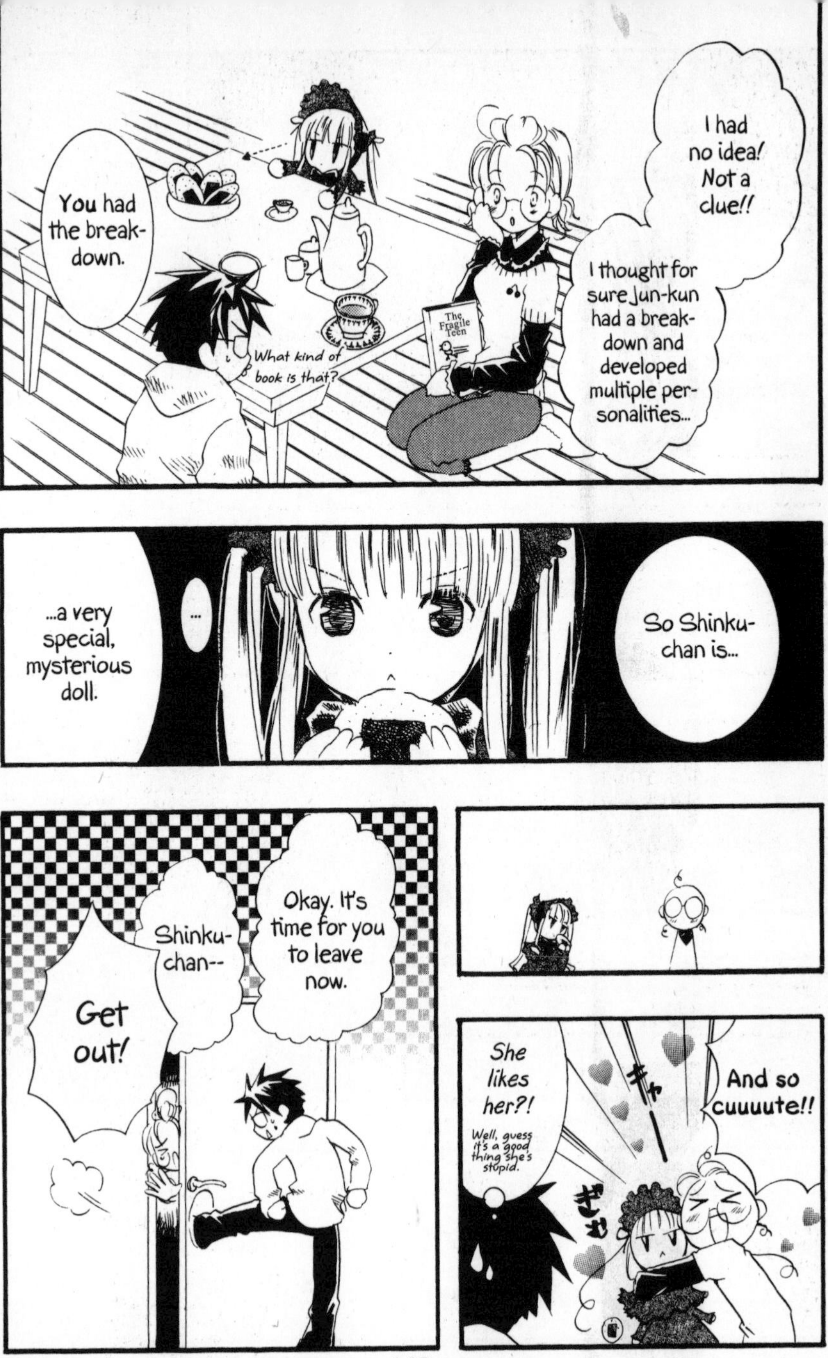

I had no idea! Not a clue!!
I thought for sure Jun-kun had a breakdown and developed multiple personalities...
The Fragile Teen
What kind of book is that?
You had the breakdown.
So Shinku-chan is...
...
...a very special, mysterious doll.
And so cuuuute!!
She likes her?!
Well, guess it's a good thing she's stupid.
Okay. It's time for you to leave now.
Shinku-chan--
Get out!

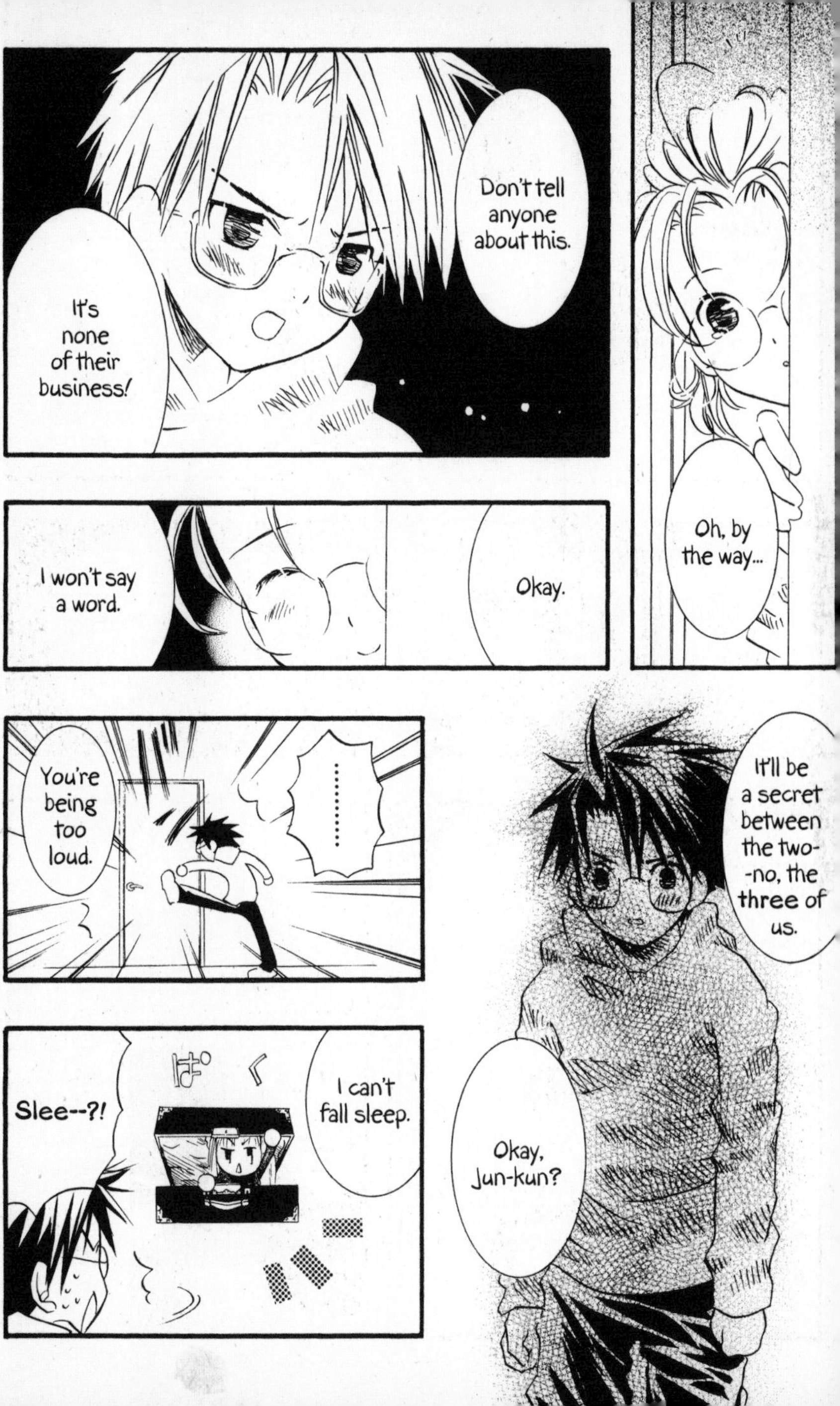

Oh, by the way...
Don't tell anyone about this.
It's none of their business!
Okay.
I won't say a word.
It'll be a secret between the two- -no, the three of us.
Okay, Jun-kun?
....
You're being too loud.
I can't fall sleep.
ぱく
Slee--?!

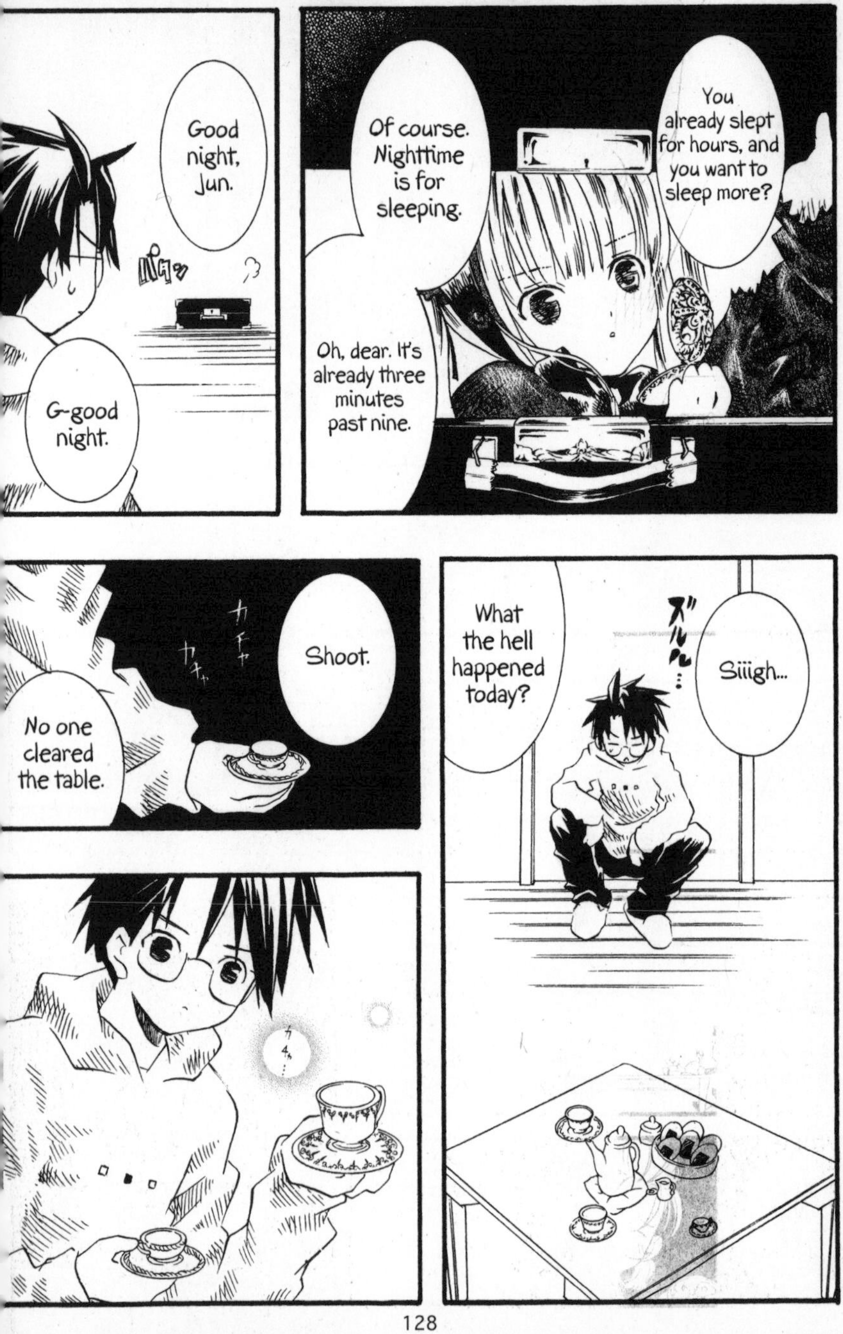
You already slept for hours, and you want to sleep more?
Of course. Nighttime is for sleeping.
Oh, dear. It's already three minutes past nine.
Good night, Jun.
G-good night.
ズルル…
Siiigh...
What the hell happened today?
Shoot.
カチャ
カチャ
No one cleared the table.

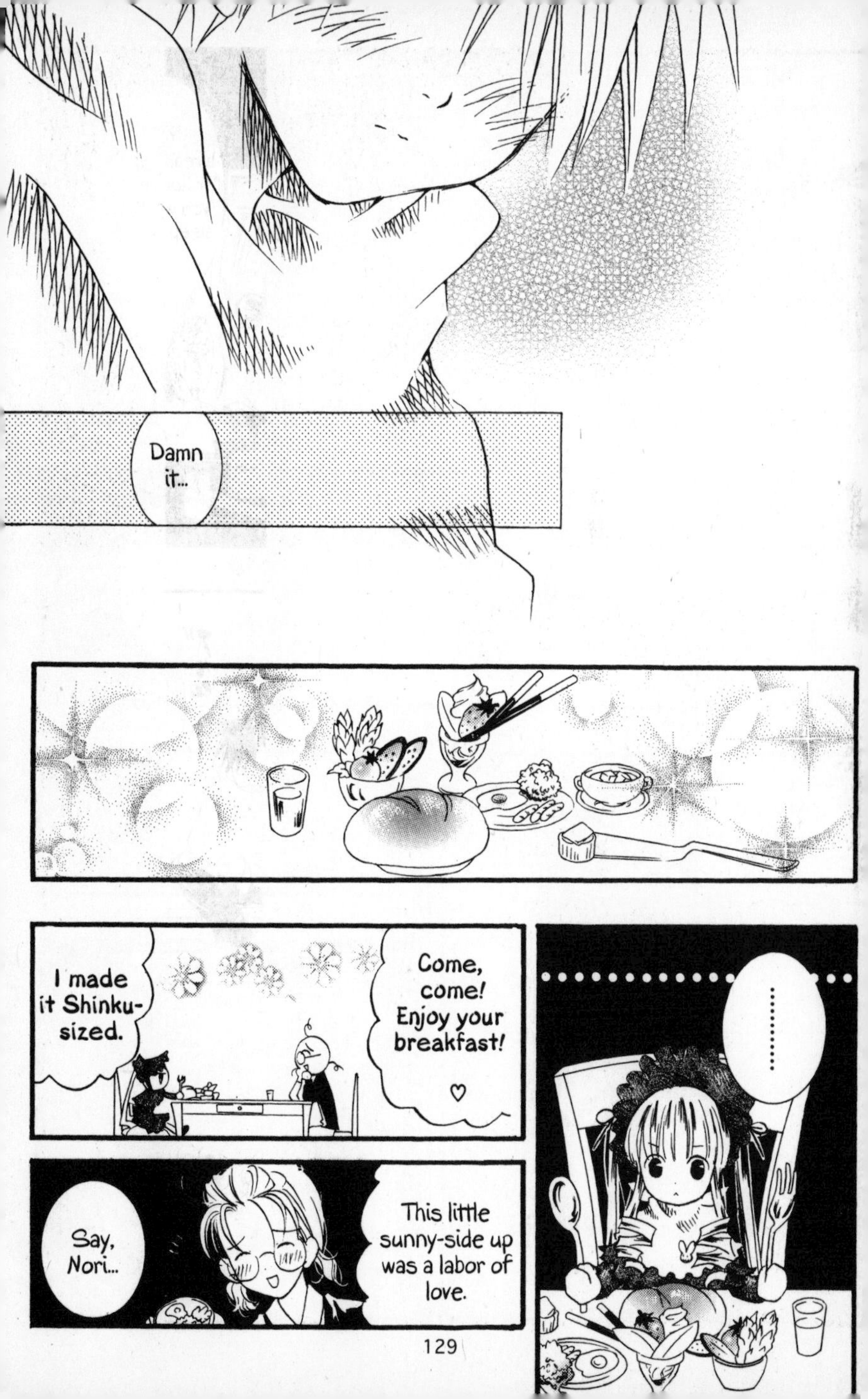
Damn it...
....
Come, come! Enjoy your breakfast! ♡
I made it Shinku-sized.
This little sunny-side up was a labor of love.
Say, Nori...

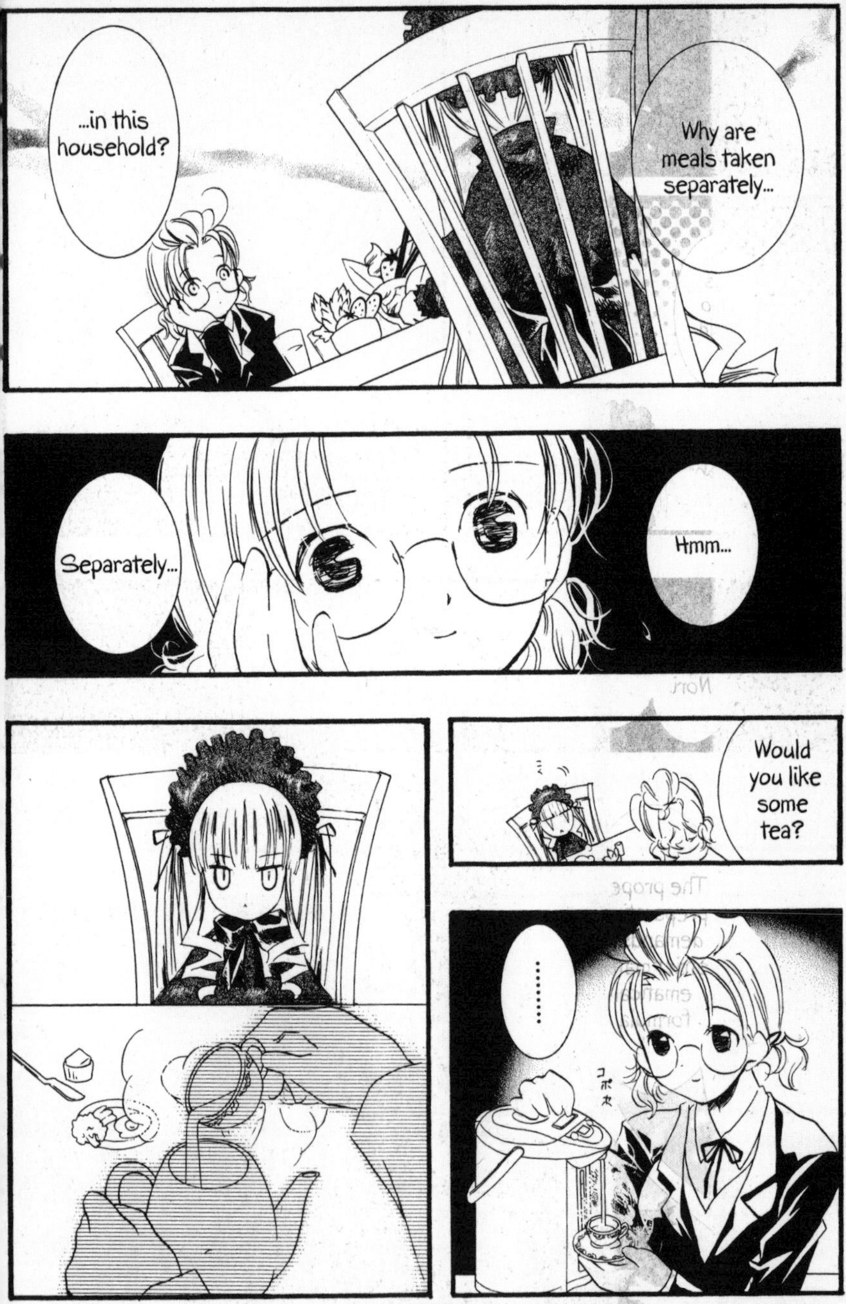

Why are meals taken separately...
...in this household?
Hmm...
Separately...
Would you like some tea?
....

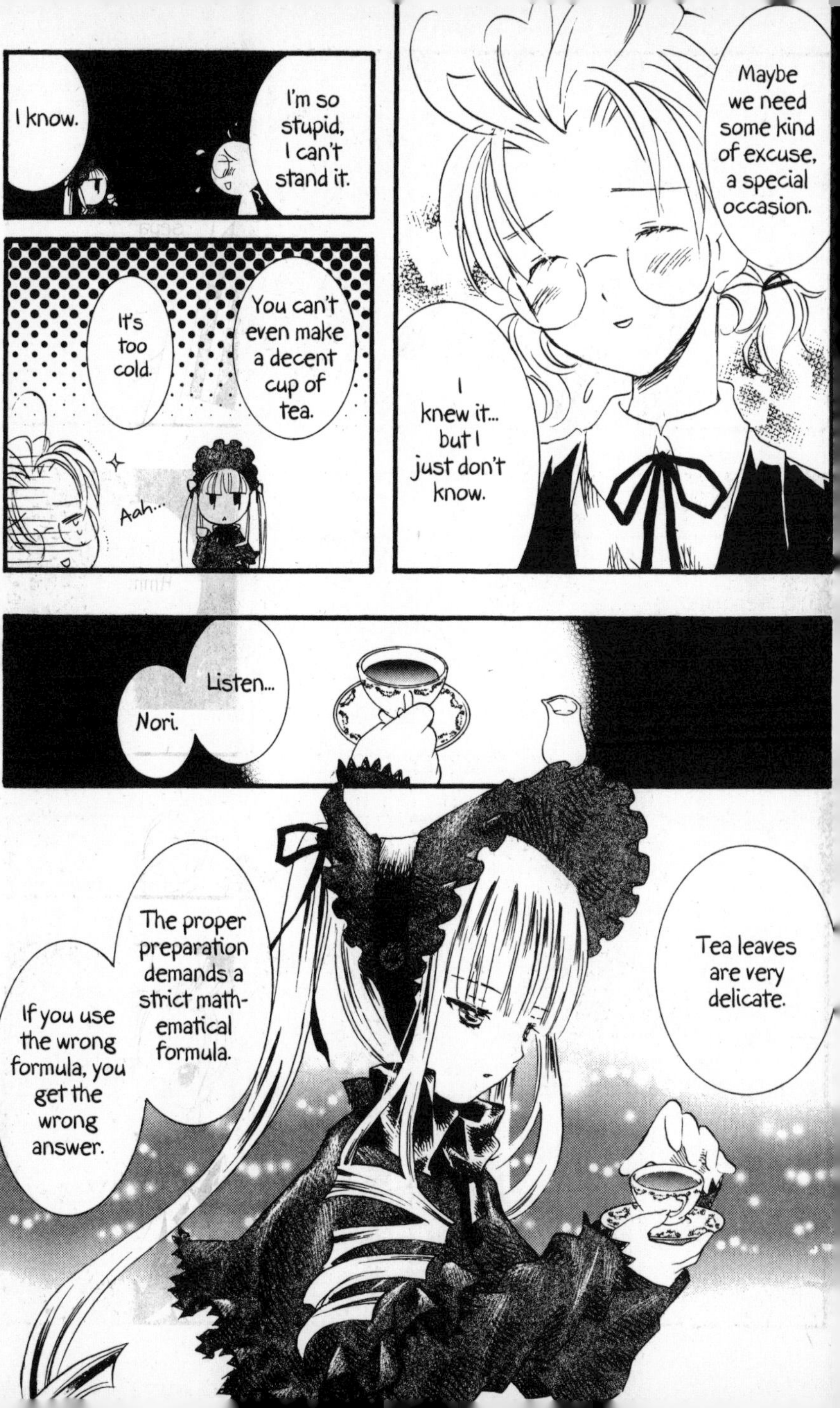
Maybe we need some kind of excuse, a special occasion.
I knew it... but I just don't know.
I'm so stupid, I can't stand it.
I know.
You can't even make a decent cup of tea.
It's too cold.
Aah...
Listen...
Nori.
Tea leaves are very delicate.
The proper preparation demands a strict math-ematical formula.
If you use the wrong formula, you get the wrong answer.

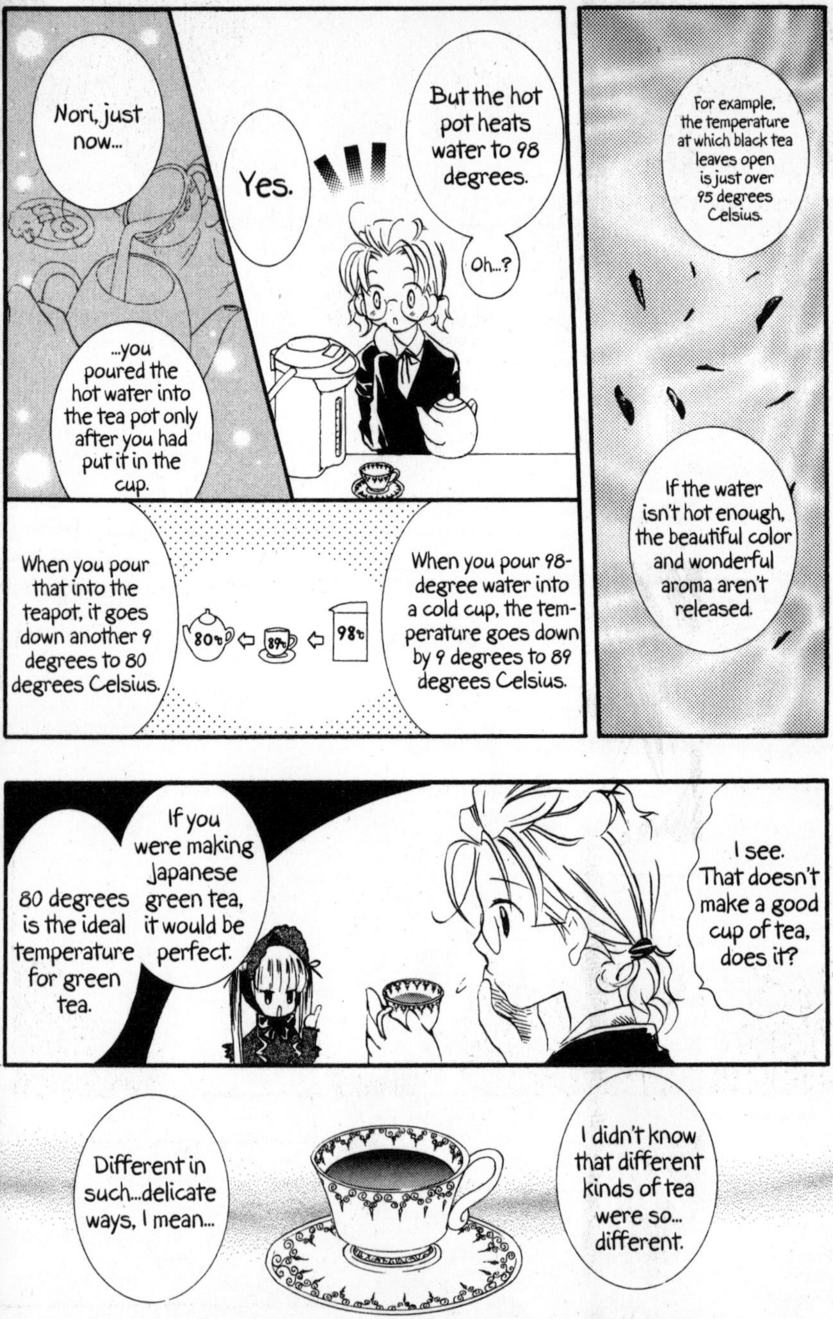
For example, the temperature at which black tea leaves open is just over 95 degrees Celsius.
If the water isn't hot enough, the beautiful color and wonderful aroma aren't released.
But the hot pot heats water to 98 degrees.
Yes.
Oh...?
Nori, just now...
...you poured the hot water into the tea pot only after you had put it in the cup.
When you pour 98-degree water into a cold cup, the temperature goes down by 9 degrees to 89 degrees Celsius.
98℃
89℃
80℃
When you pour that into the teapot, it goes down another 9 degrees to 80 degrees Celsius.
I see. That doesn't make a good cup of tea, does it?
If you were making Japanese green tea, it would be perfect.
80 degrees is the ideal temperature for green tea.
I didn't know that different kinds of tea were so... different.
Different in such...delicate ways, I mean...

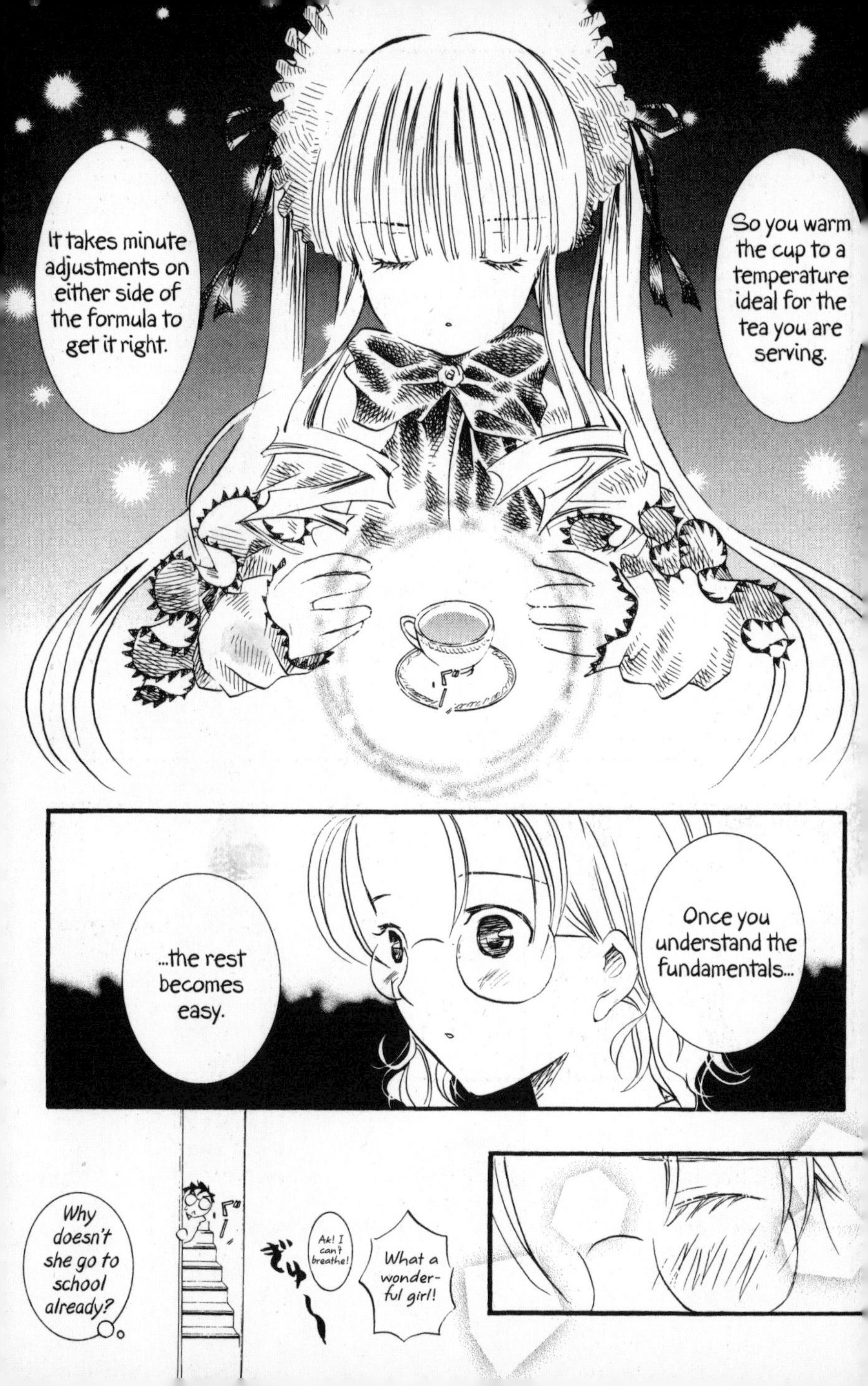
So you warm the cup to a temperature ideal for the tea you are serving.
It takes minute adjustments on either side of the formula to get it right.
Once you understand the fundamentals...
...the rest becomes easy.
What a wonder-ful girl!
Ak! I can't breathe!
Why doesn't she go to school already?

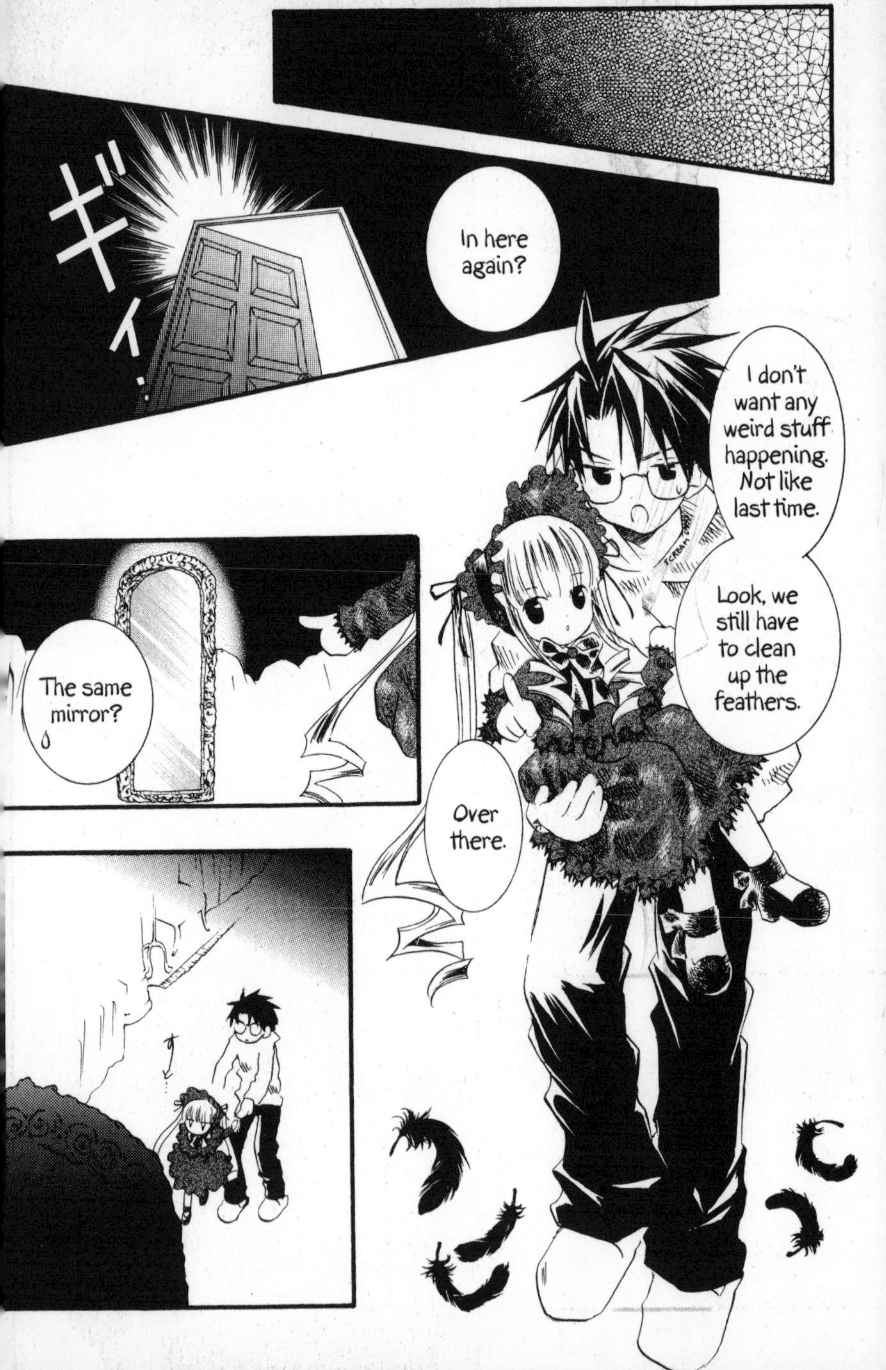
ギイ
In here again?
I don't want any weird stuff happening. Not like last time.
Look, we still have to clean up the feathers.
Over there.
The same mirror?

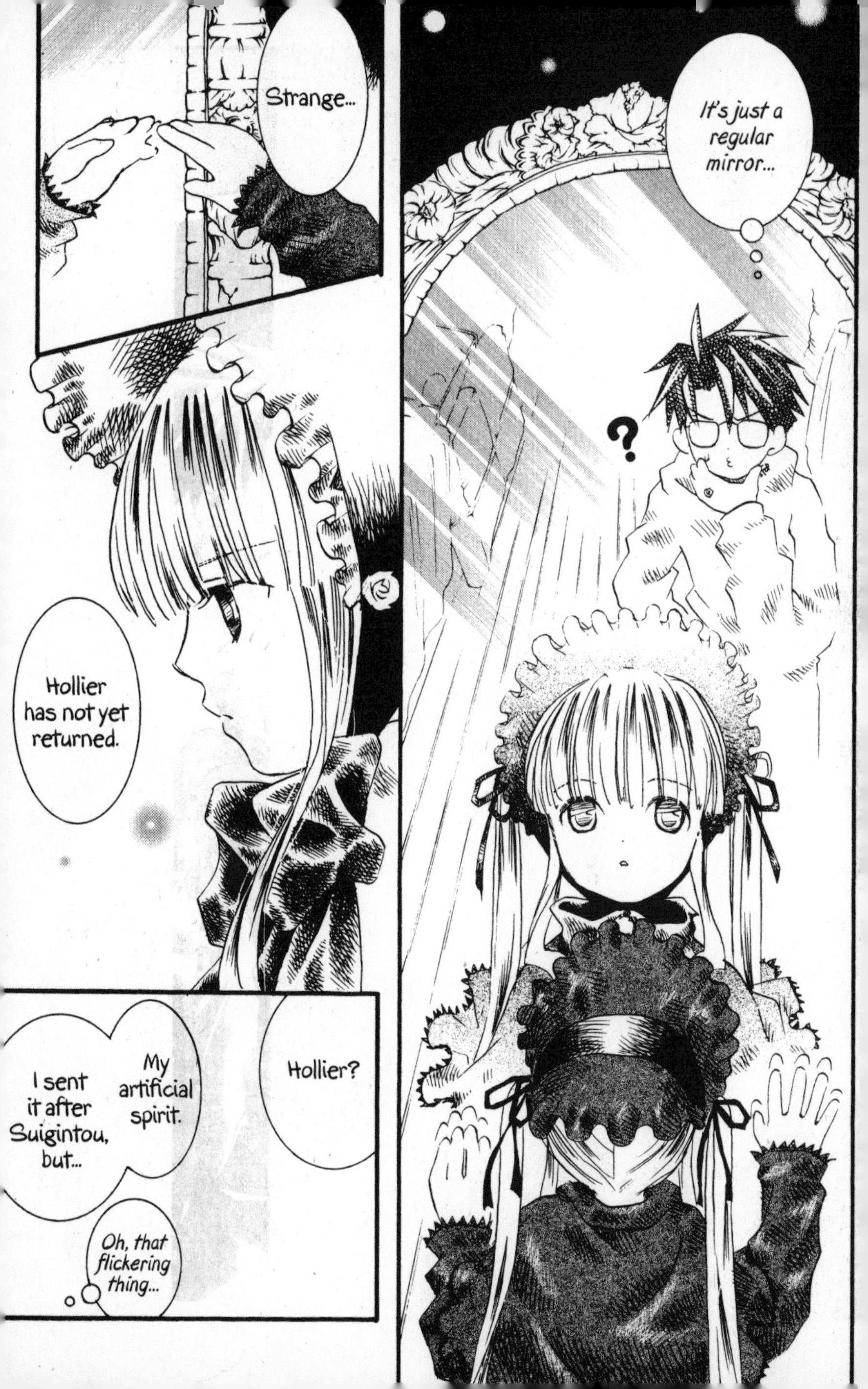
It's just a regular mirror...
?
Strange...
Hollier has not yet returned.
Hollier?
My artificial spirit.
I sent it after Suigintou, but...
Oh, that flickering thing...

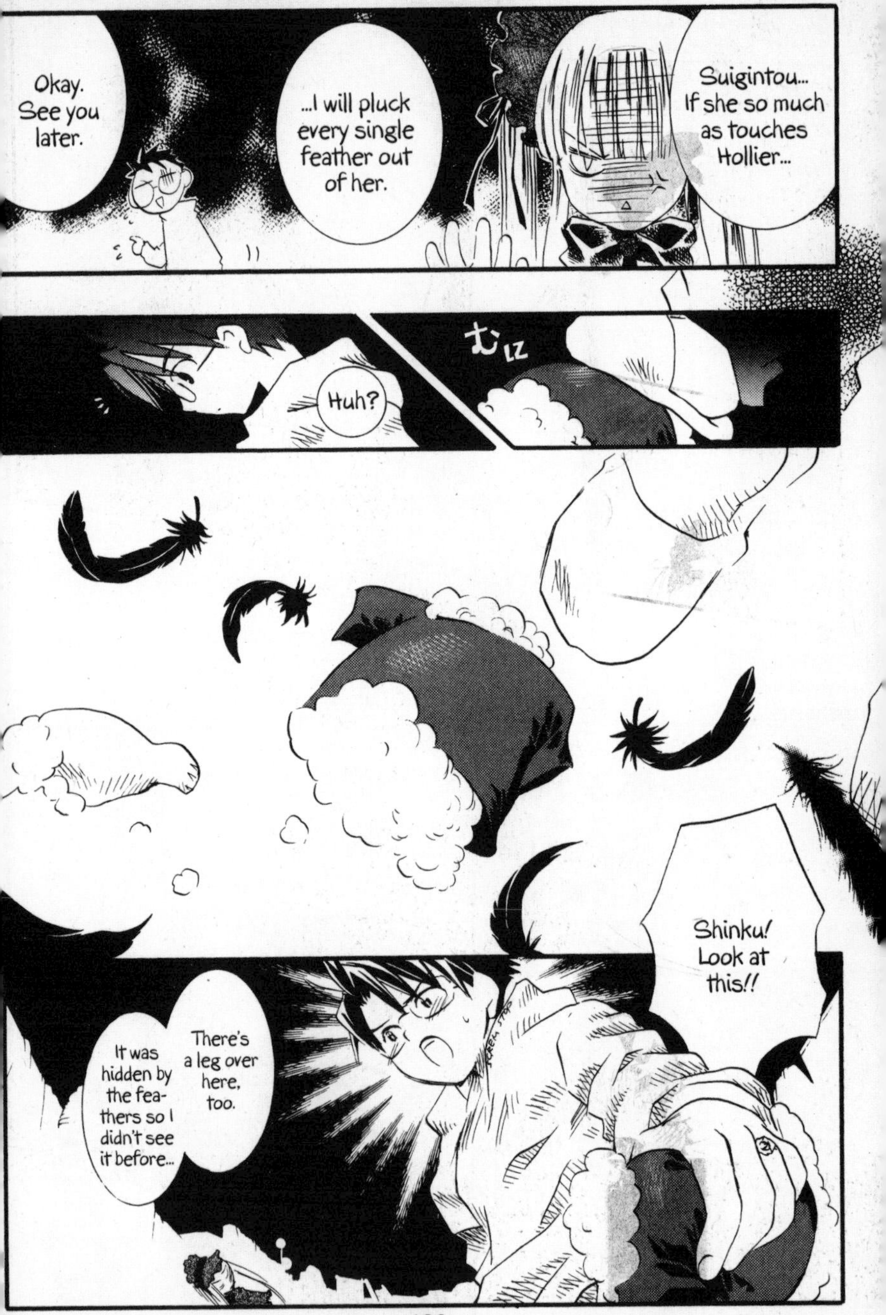
Suigintou... If she so much as touches Hollier...
...I will pluck every single feather out of her.
Okay. See you later.
むIZ
Huh?
Shinku! Look at this!!
There's a leg over here, too.
It was hidden by the feathers so I didn't see it before...

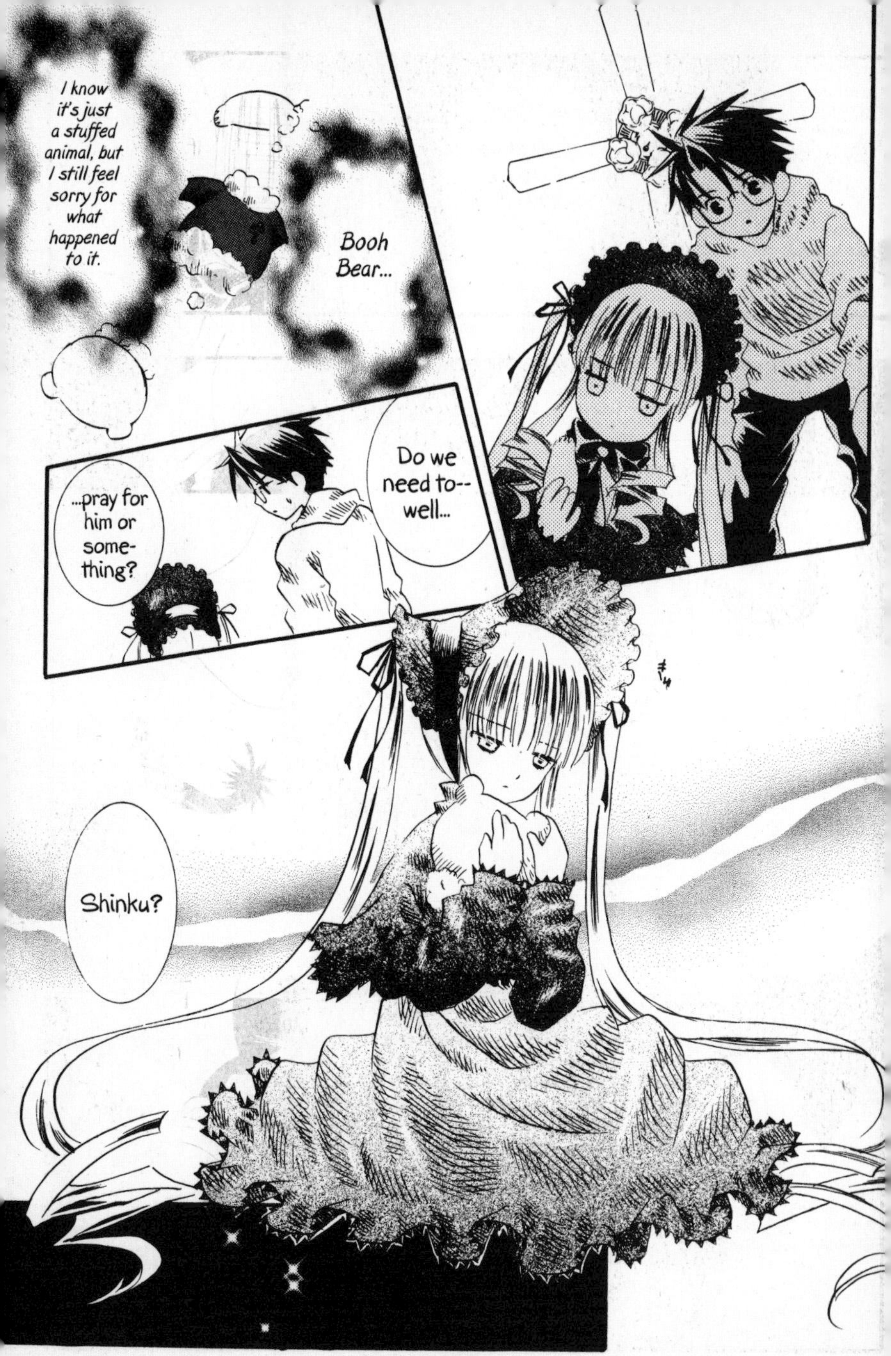
Booh Bear...
I know it's just a stuffed animal, but I still feel sorry for what happened to it.
Do we need to--well...
...pray for him or something?
Shinku?

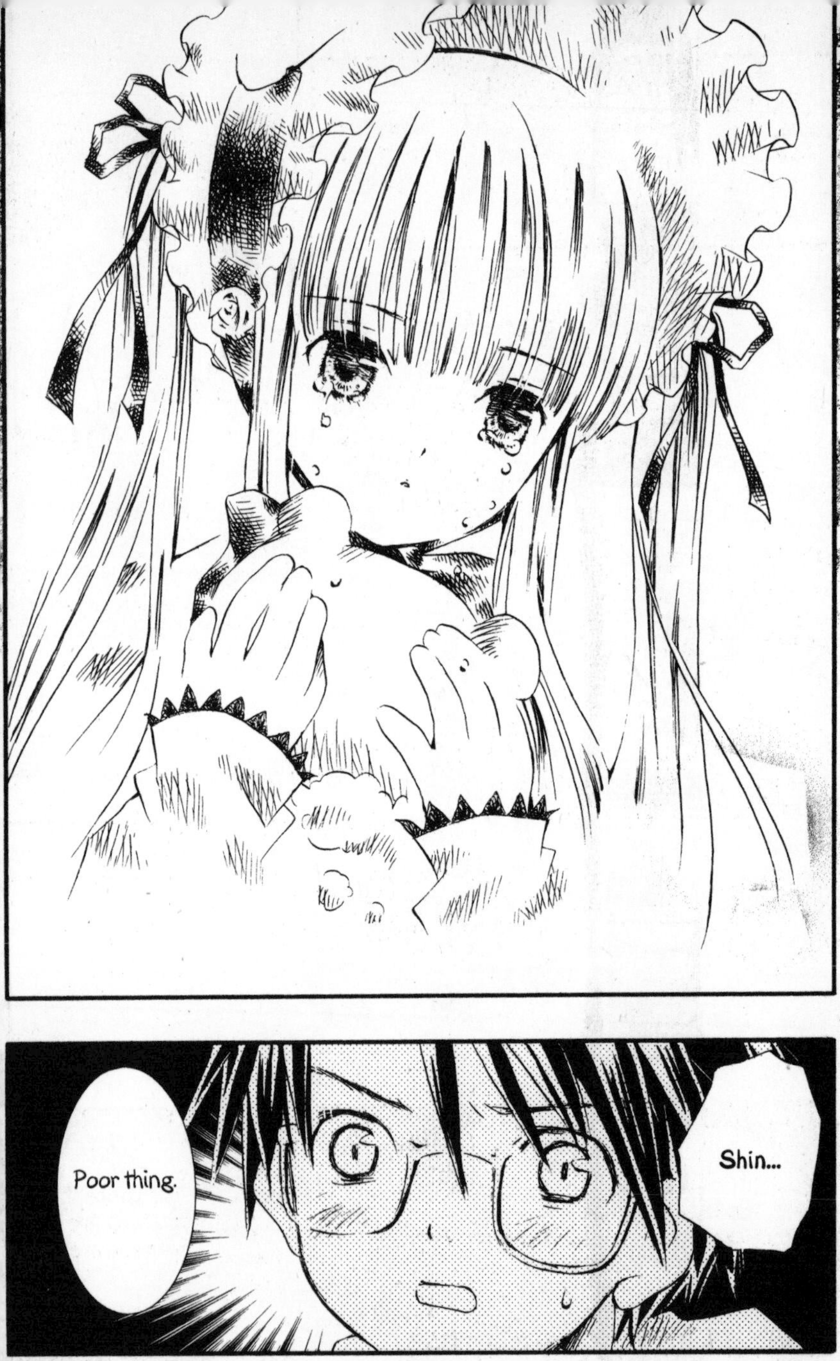
Shin...
Poor thing.

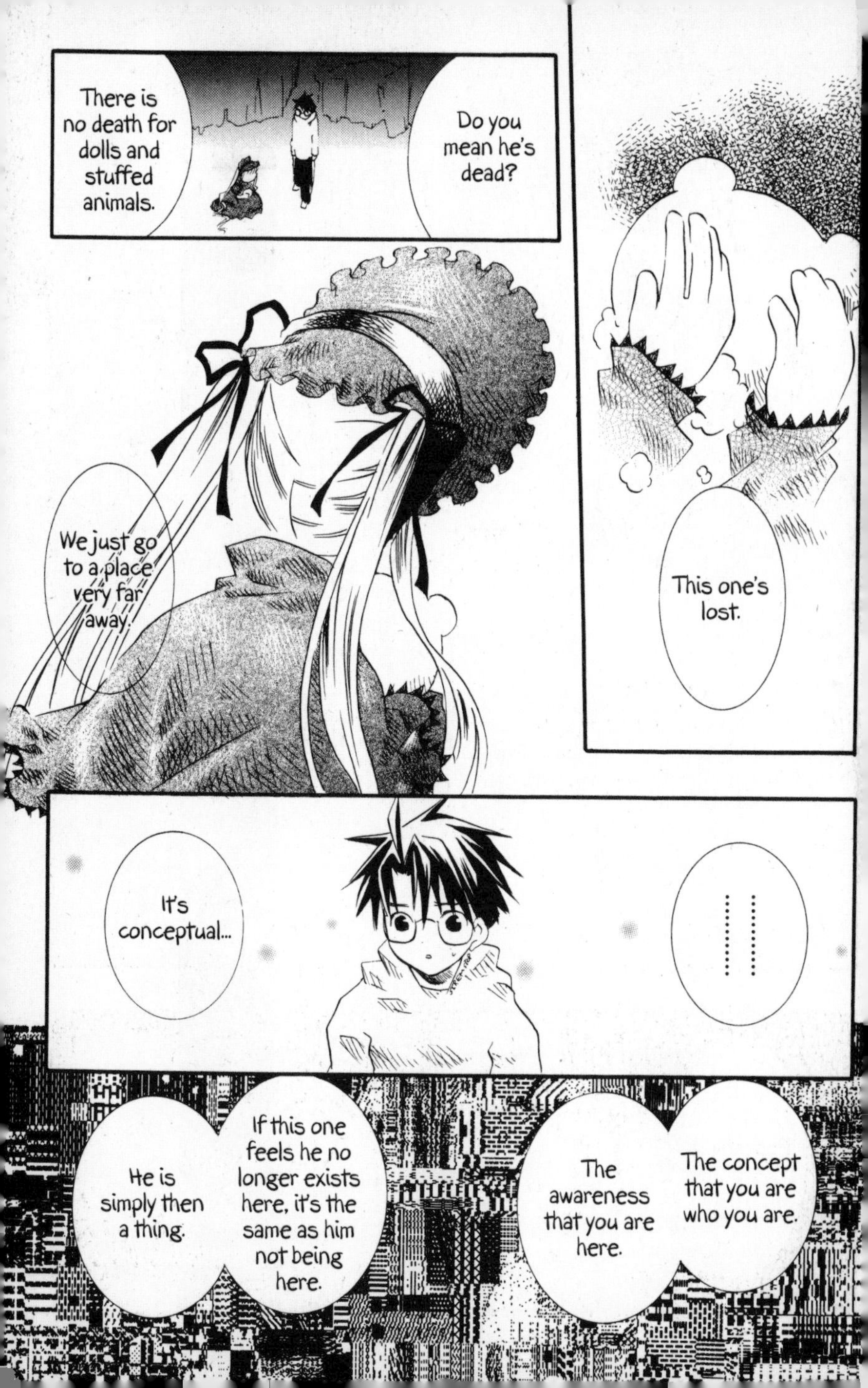
This one's lost.
Do you mean he's dead?
There is no death for dolls and stuffed animals.
We just go to a place very far away.
......
It's conceptual...
The concept that you are who you are.
The awareness that you are here.
If this one feels he no longer exists here, it's the same as him not being here.
He is simply then a thing.

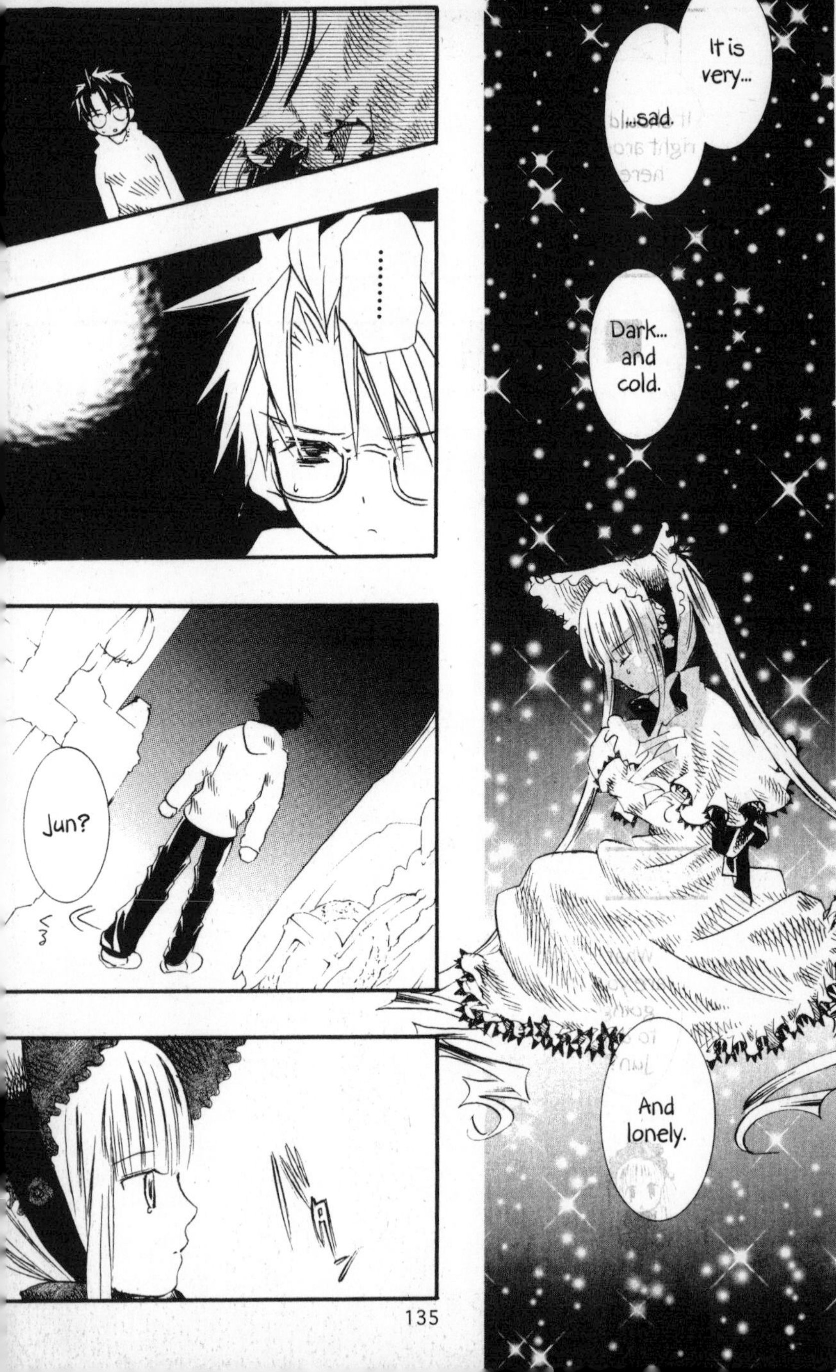
It is very...
...sad.
Dark... and cold.
And lonely.
......
Jun?

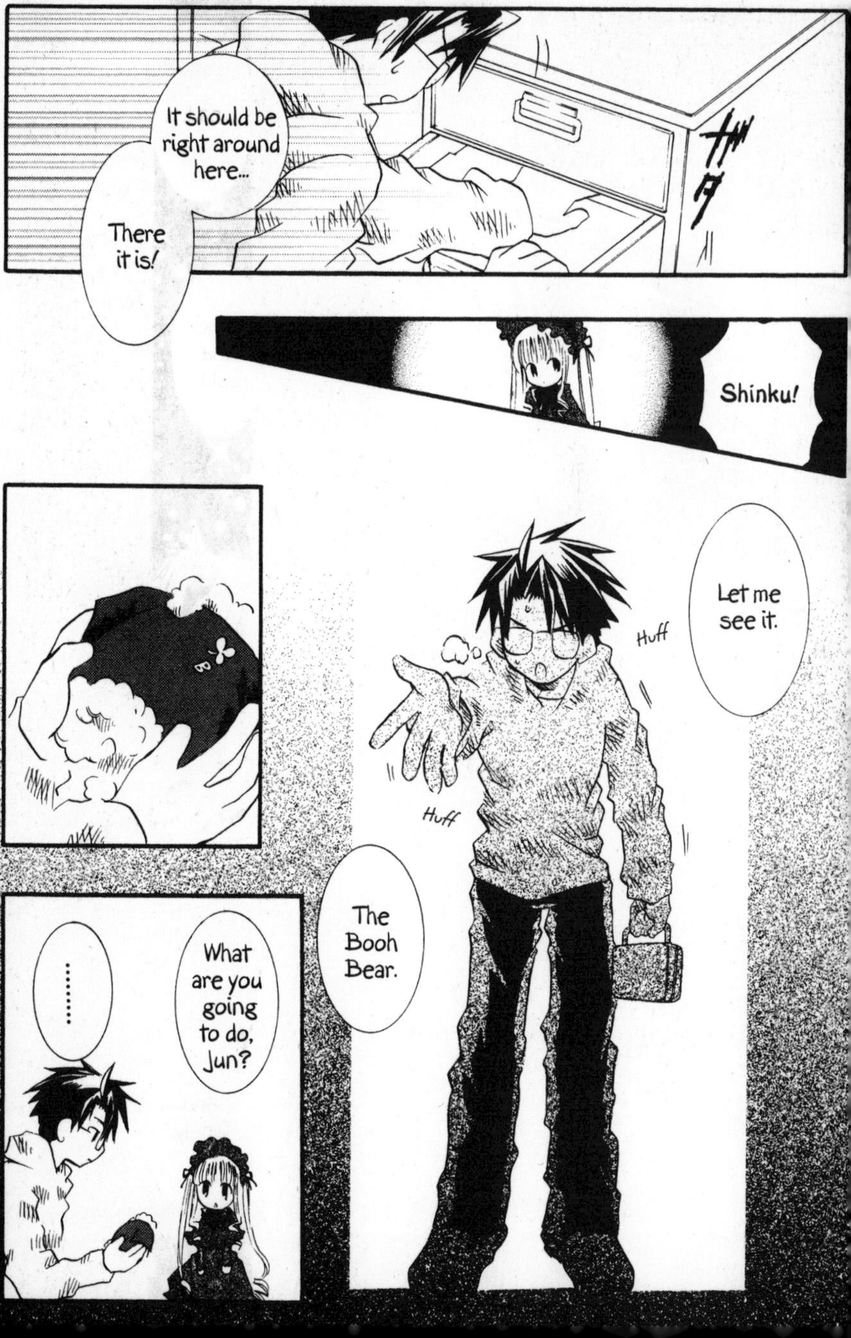
It should be right around here...
There it is!
ガタ
Shinku!
Let me see it.
Huff
Huff
The Booh Bear.
What are you going to do, Jun?
....

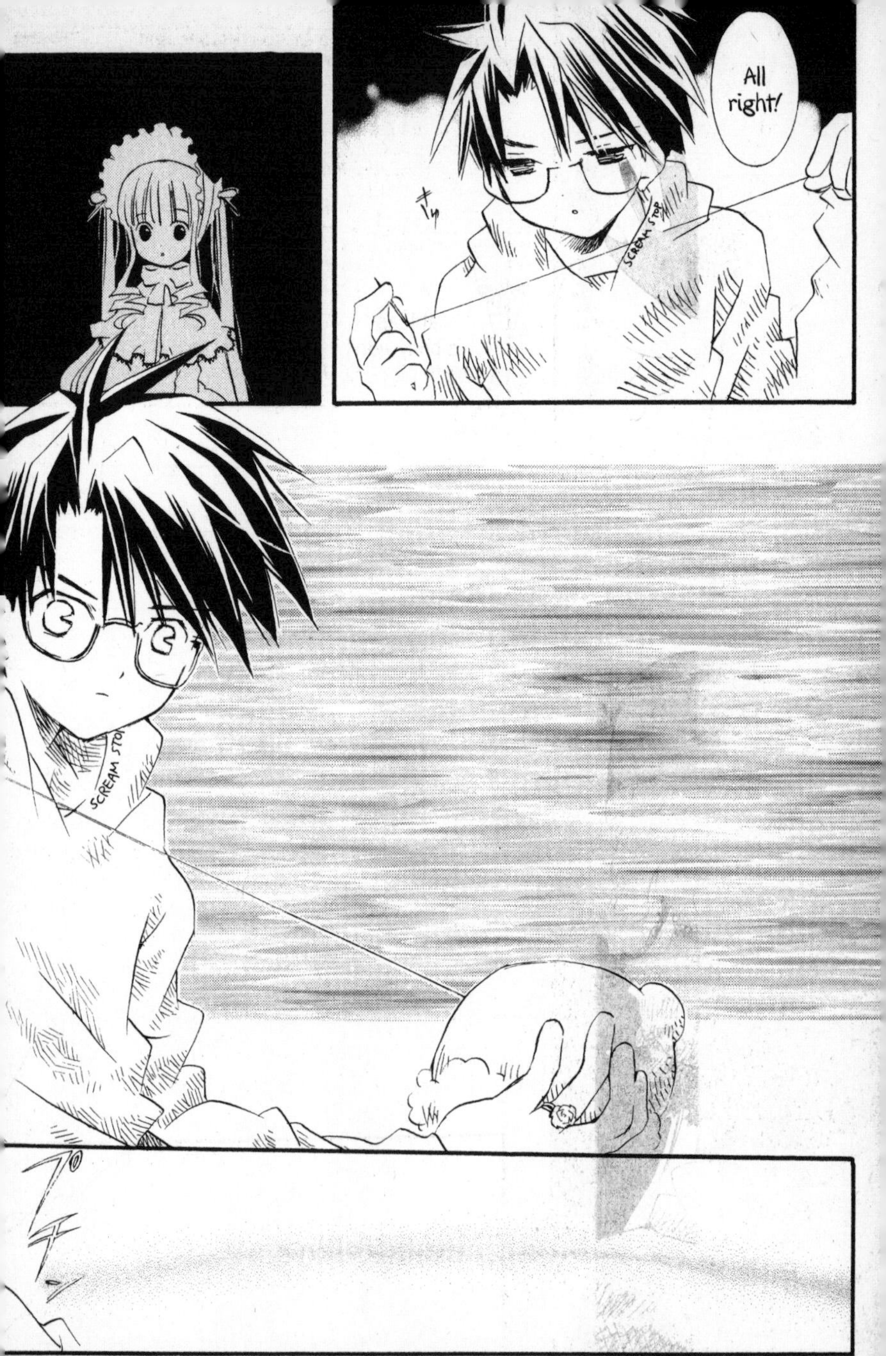
All right!
SCREAM STOP
SCREAM STOP

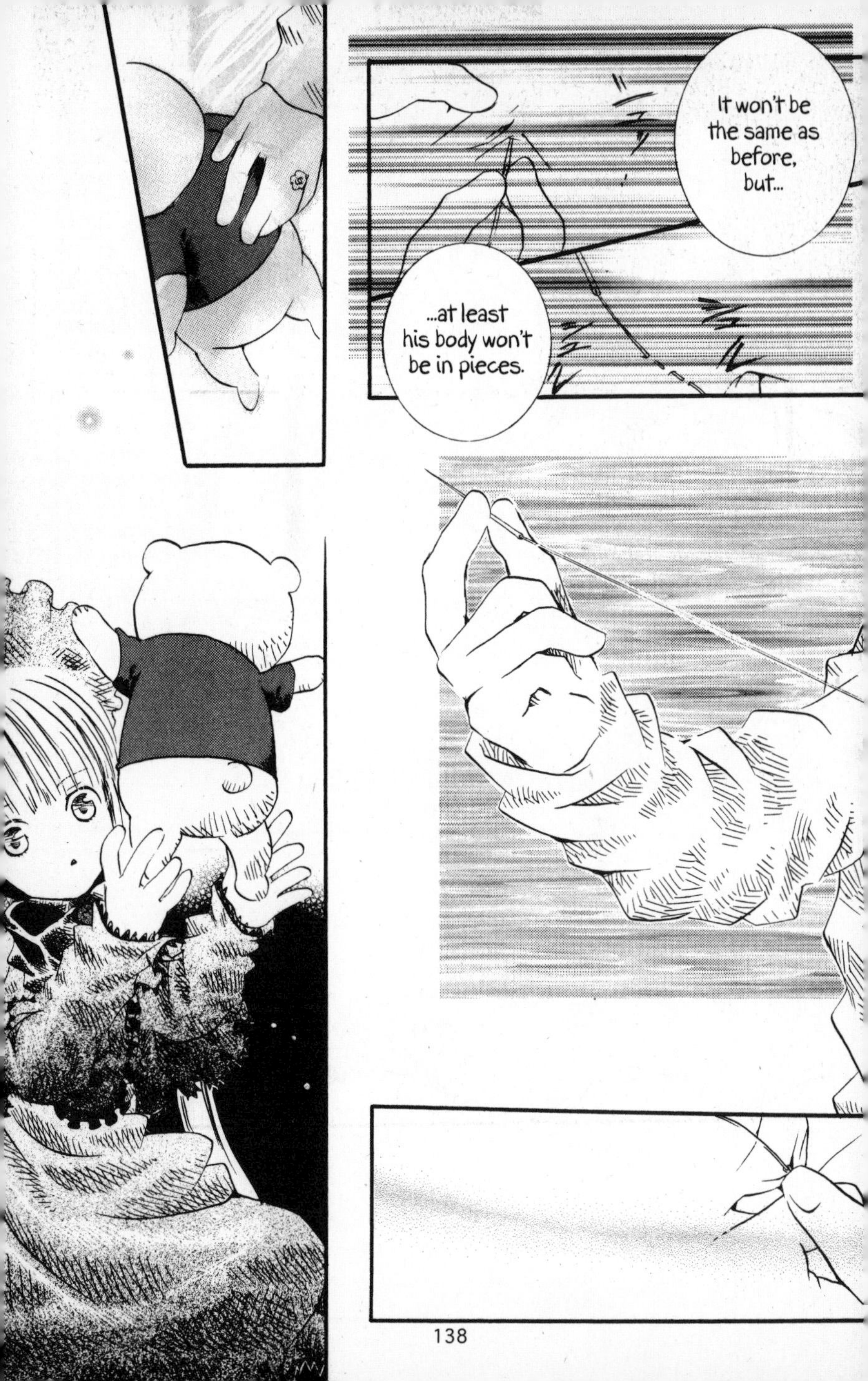
It won't be the same as before, but...
...at least his body won't be in pieces.

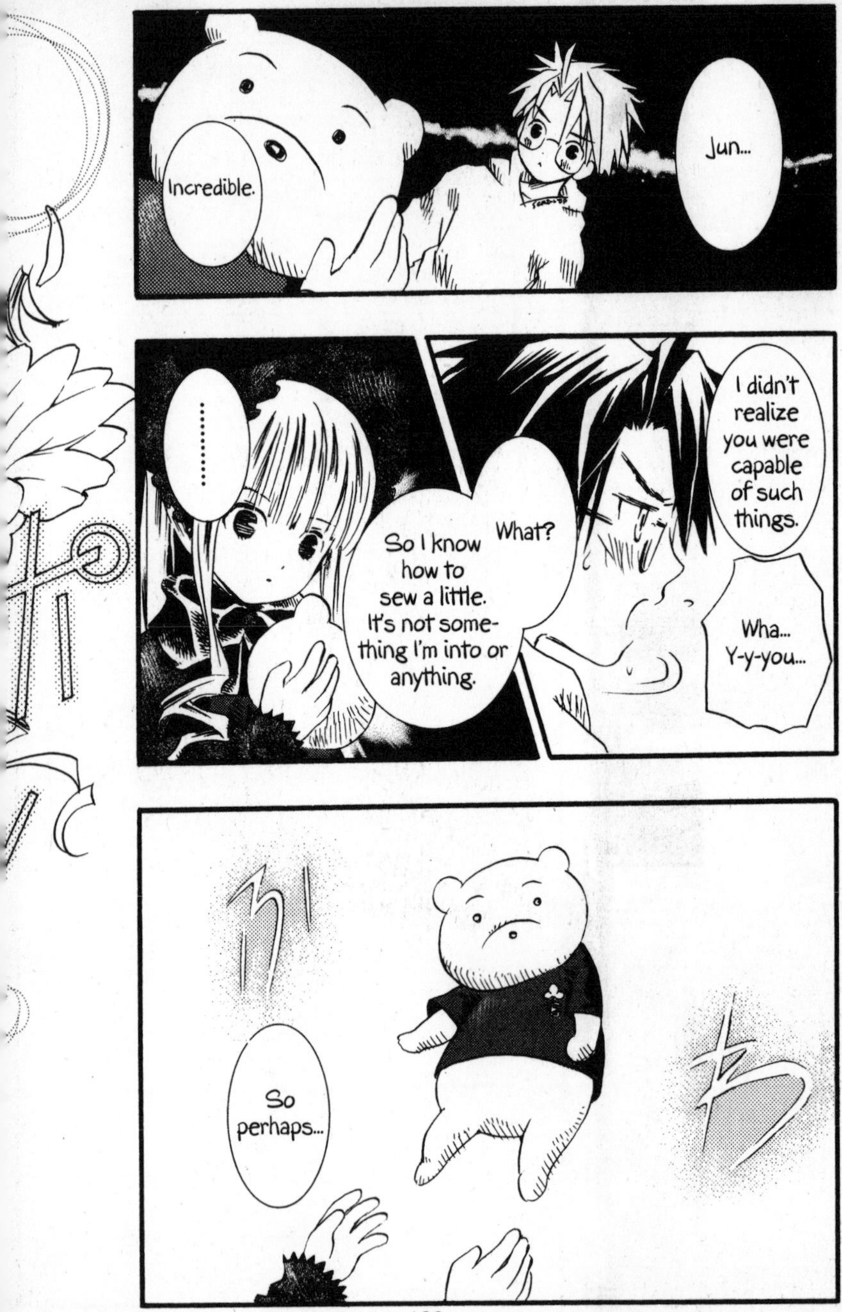
Jun...
Incredible.
I didn't realize you were capable of such things.
Wha... Y-y-you...
What?
So I know how to sew a little. It's not something I'm into or anything.
....
So perhaps...

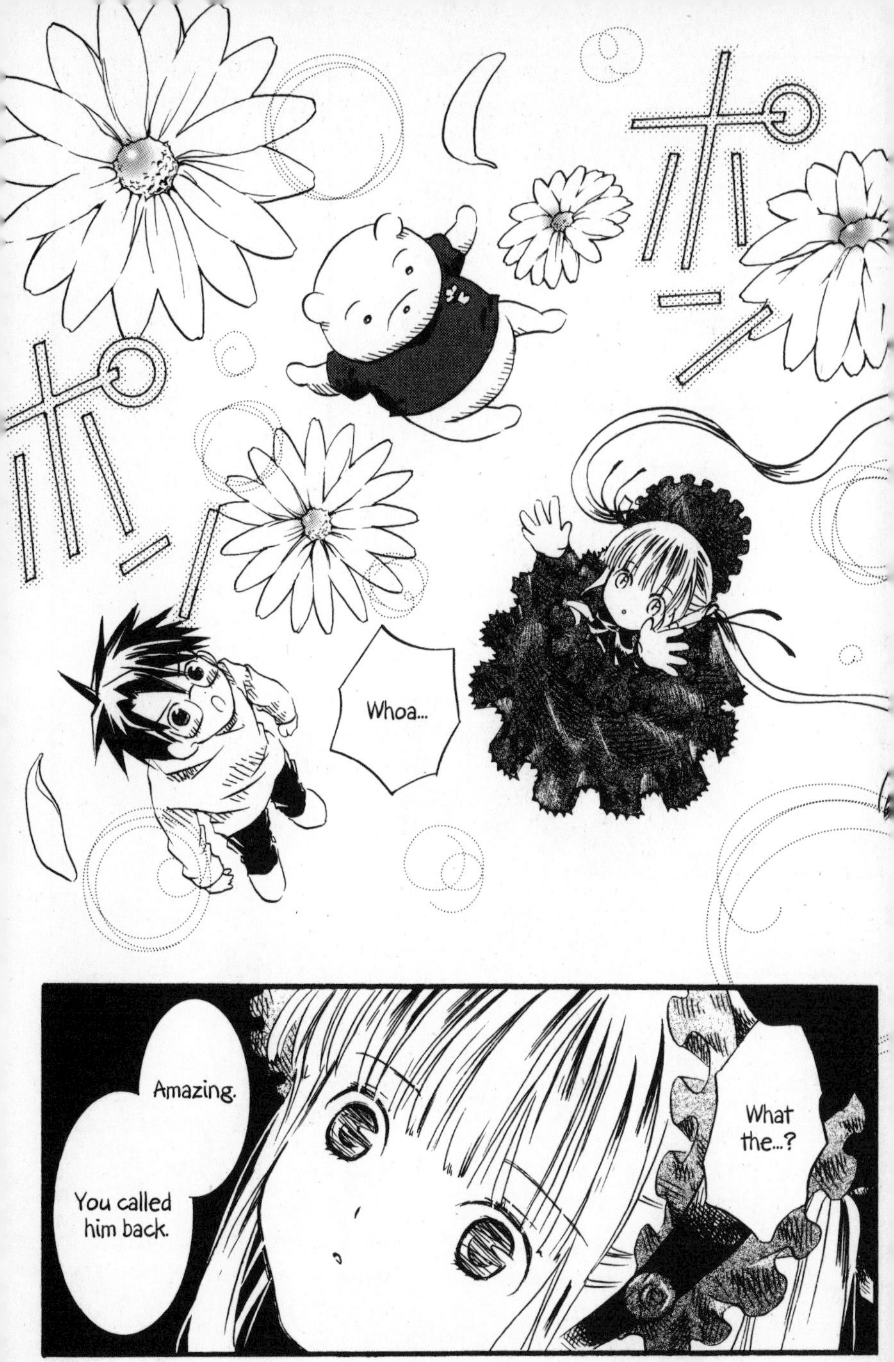
Whoa...
What the...?
Amazing.
You called him back.

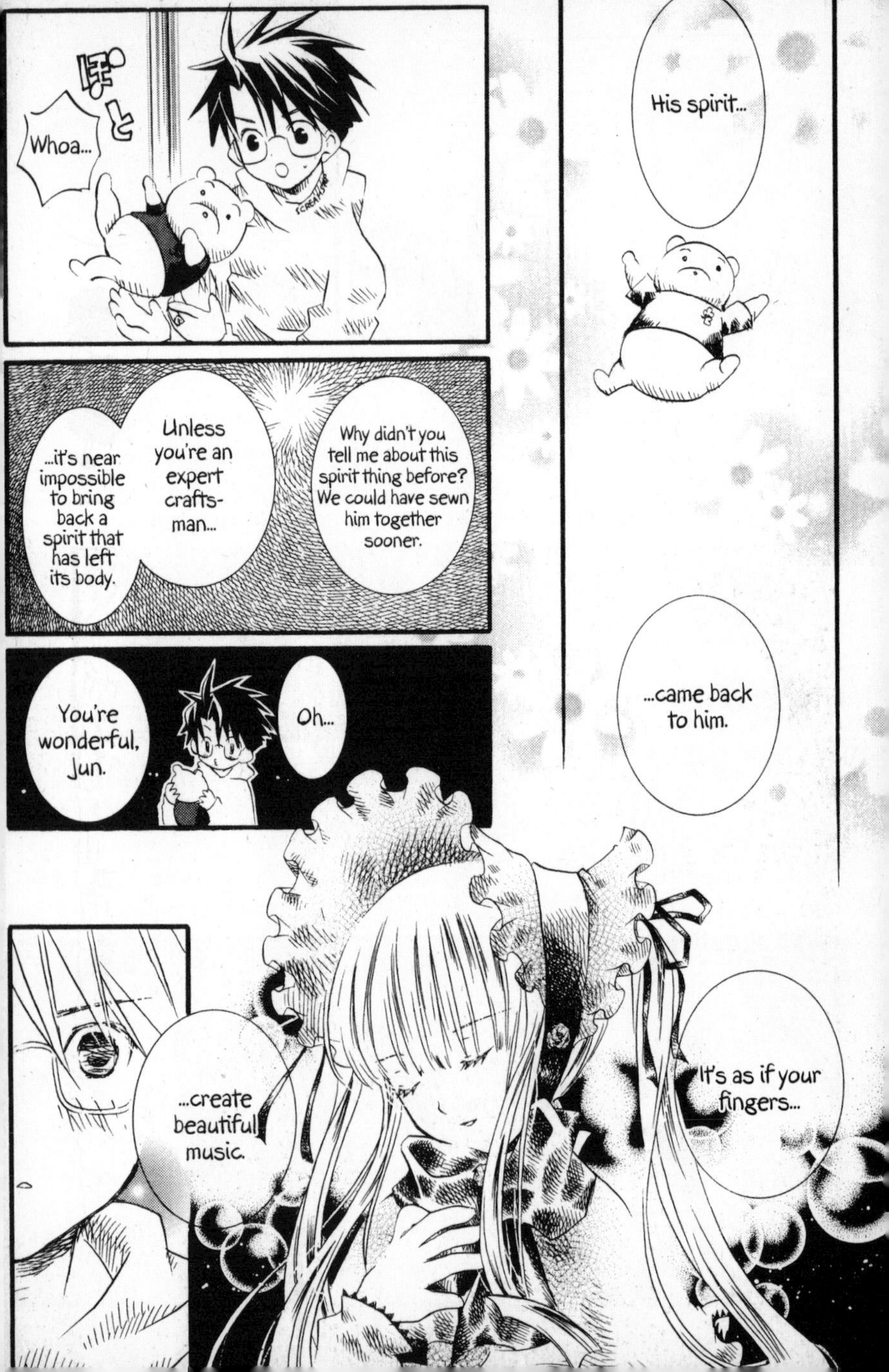
His spirit...
...came back to him.
ぽと
Whoa...
Why didn't you tell me about this spirit thing before? We could have sewn him together sooner.
Unless you're an expert crafts-man...
...it's near impossible to bring back a spirit that has left its body.
Oh...
You're wonderful, Jun.
It's as if your fingers...
...create beautiful music.

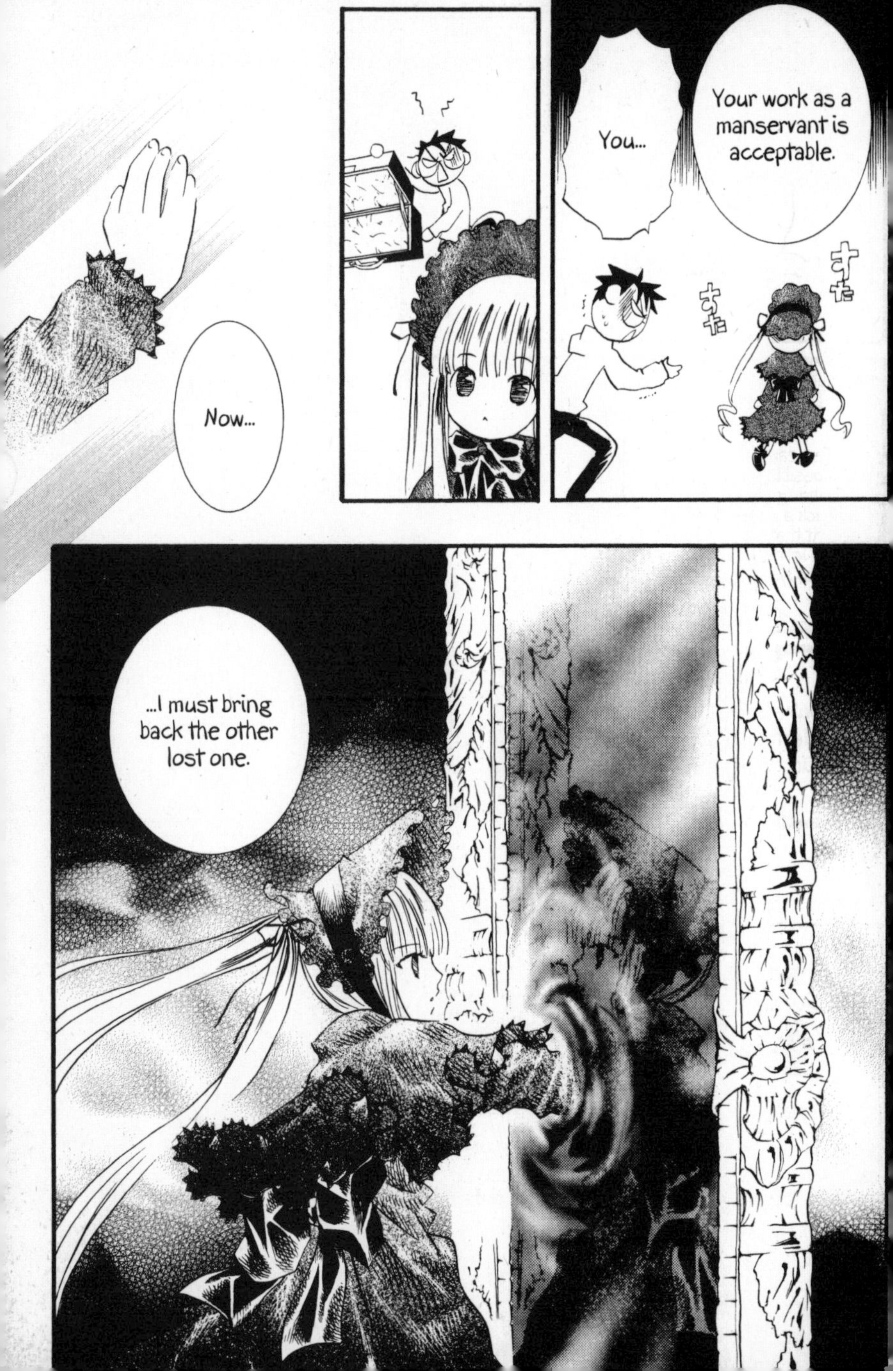
Your work as a manservant is acceptable.
You...
すた
すた
Now...
...I must bring back the other lost one.

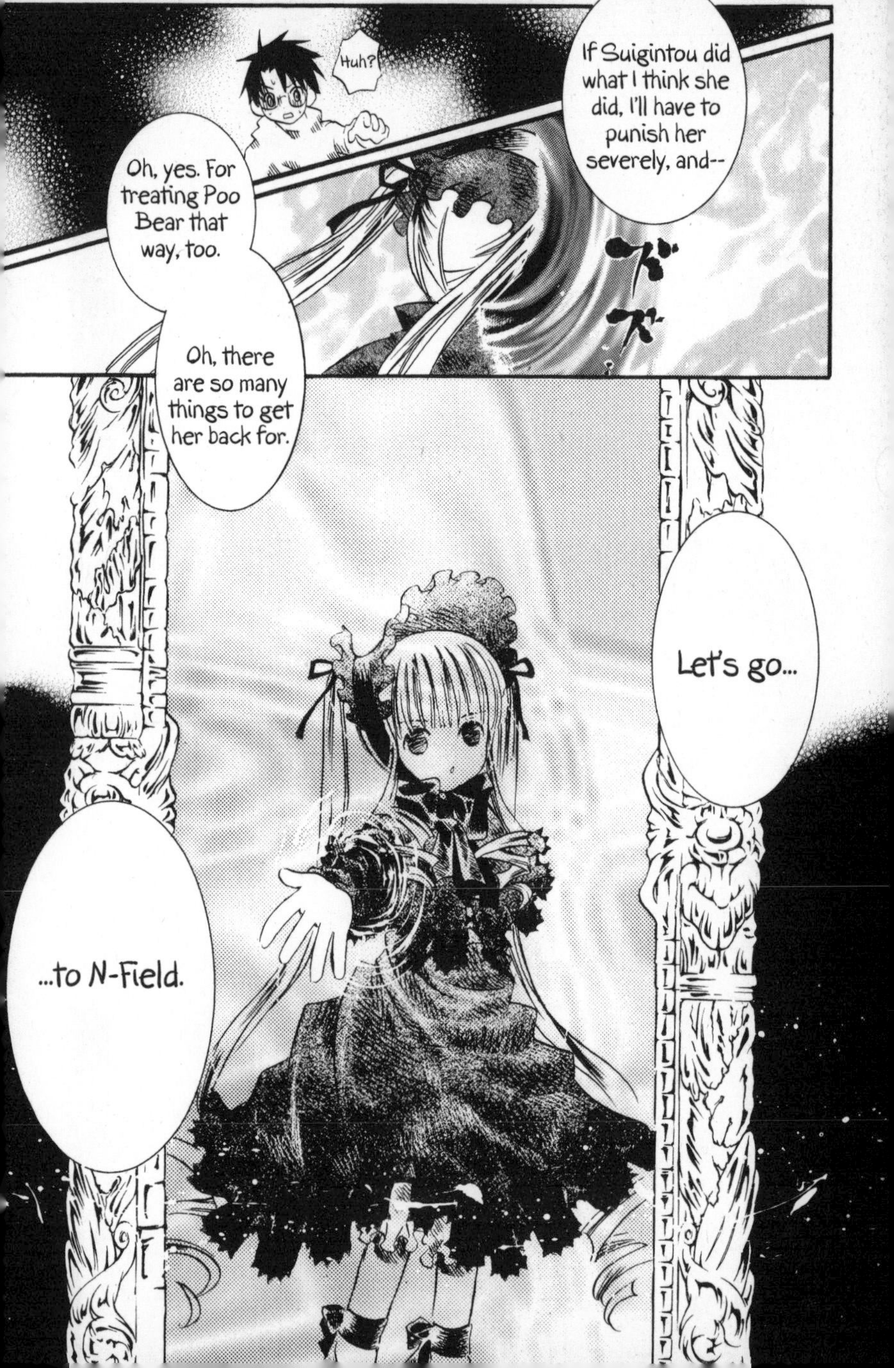

If Suigintou did what I think she did, I'll have to punish her severely, and--
Huh?
Oh, yes. For treating Poo Bear that way, too.
Oh, there are so many things to get her back for.
Let's go...
...to N-Field.

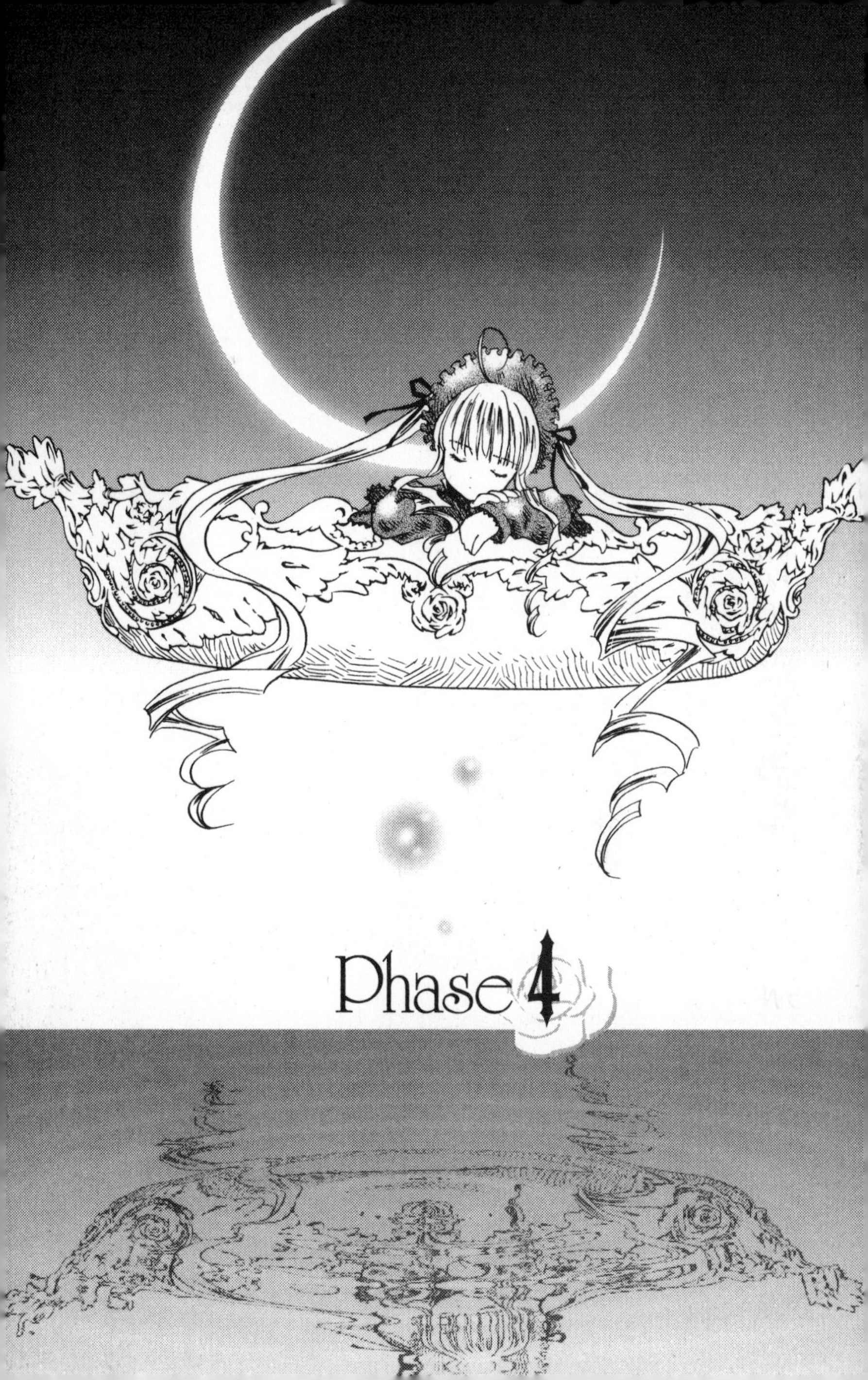
Phase 4

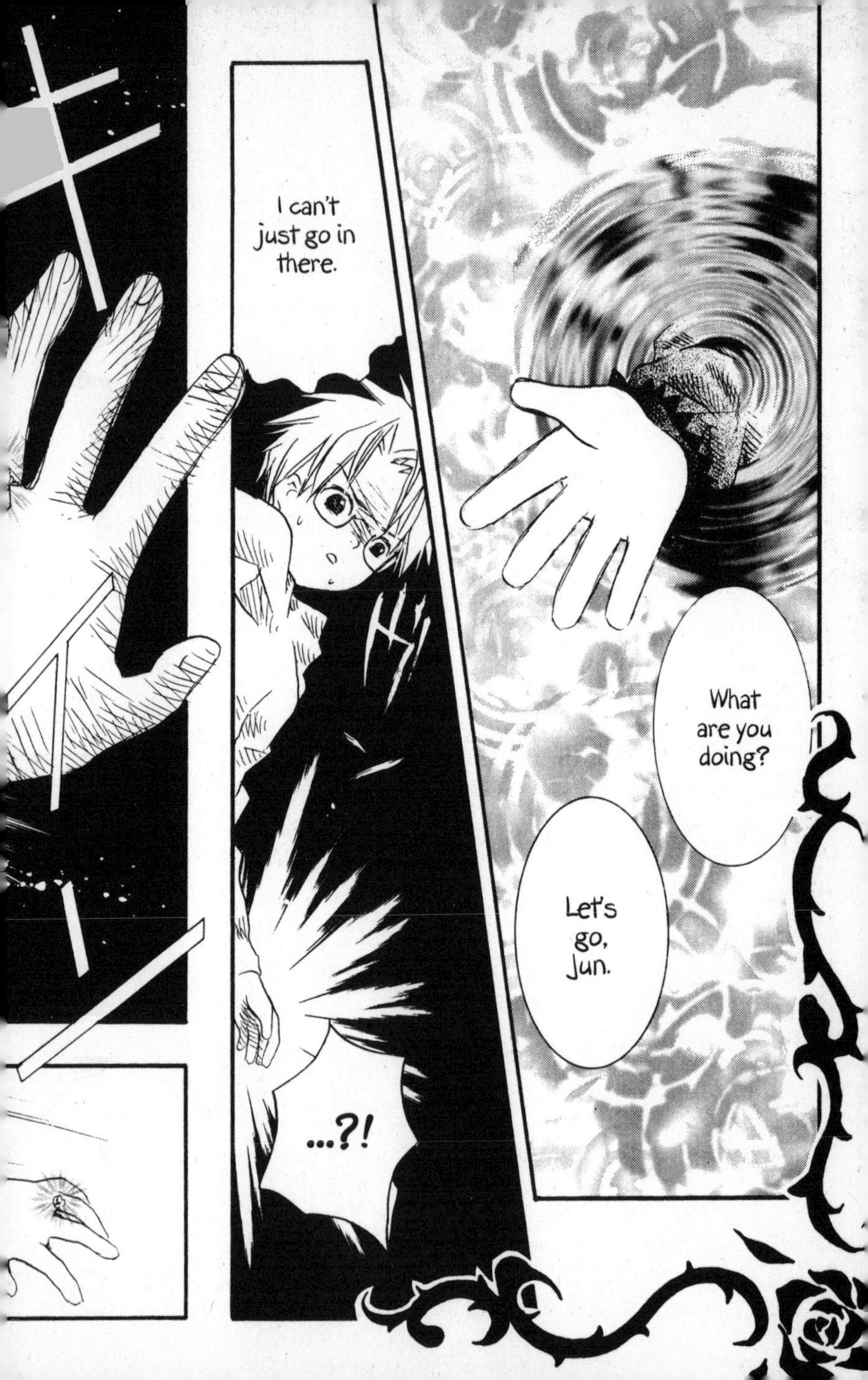
What are you doing?
Let's go, Jun.
I can't just go in there.
...?!

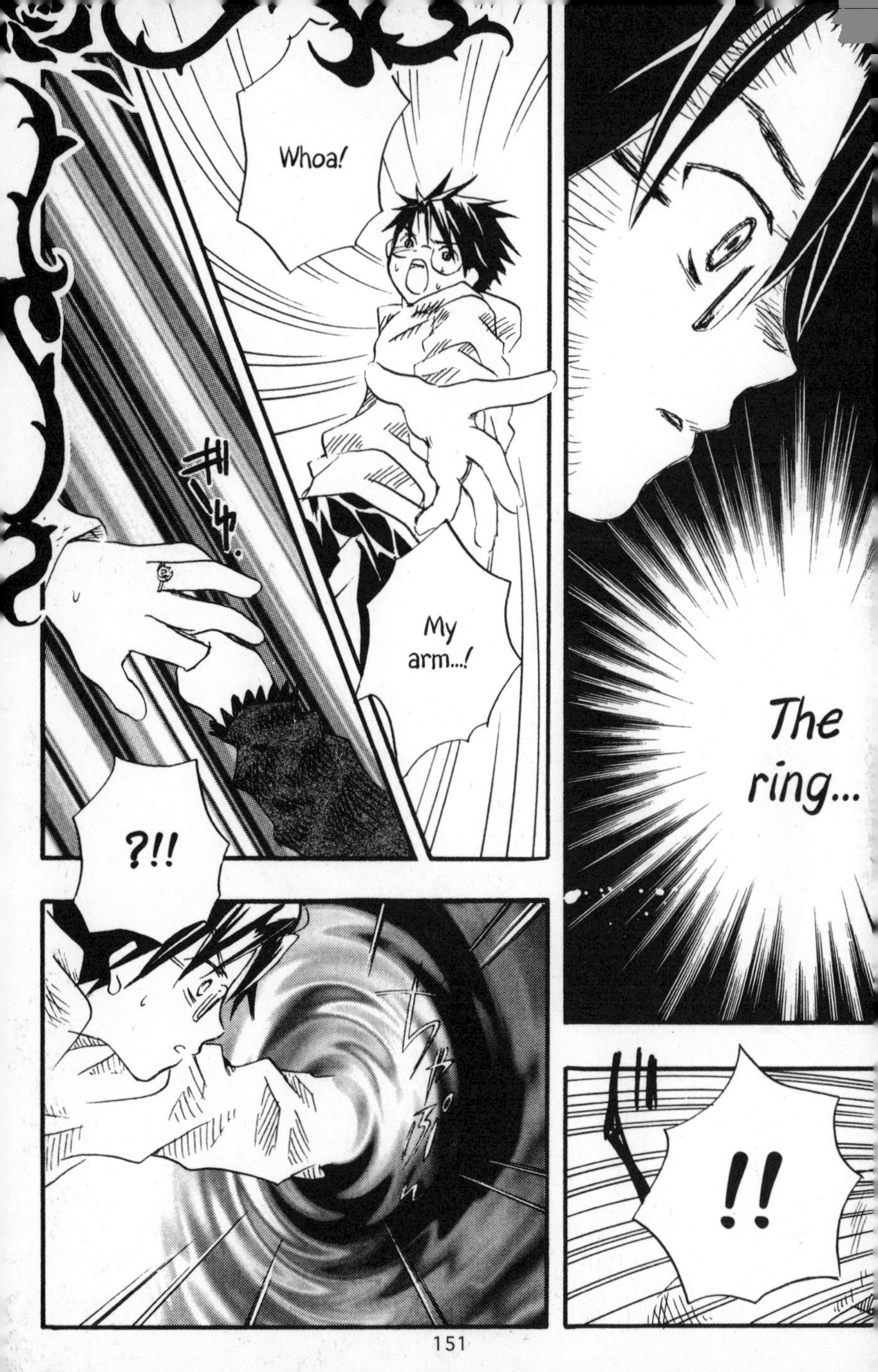
The ring...
Whoa!
My arm...!
?!!
!!

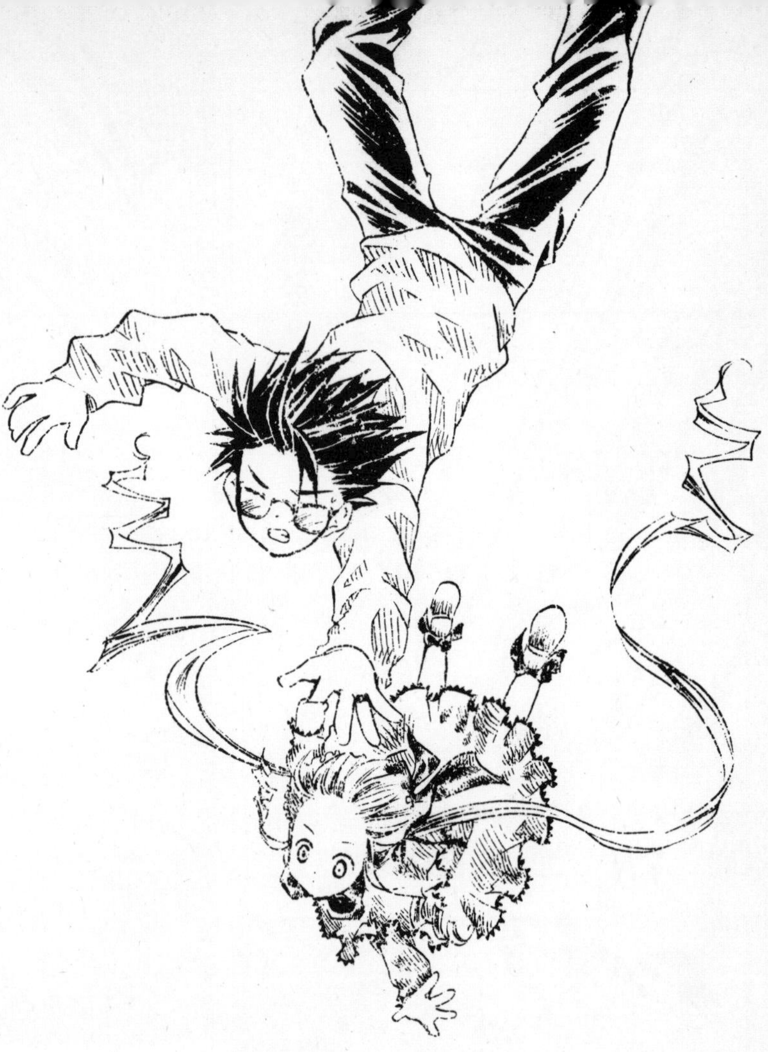

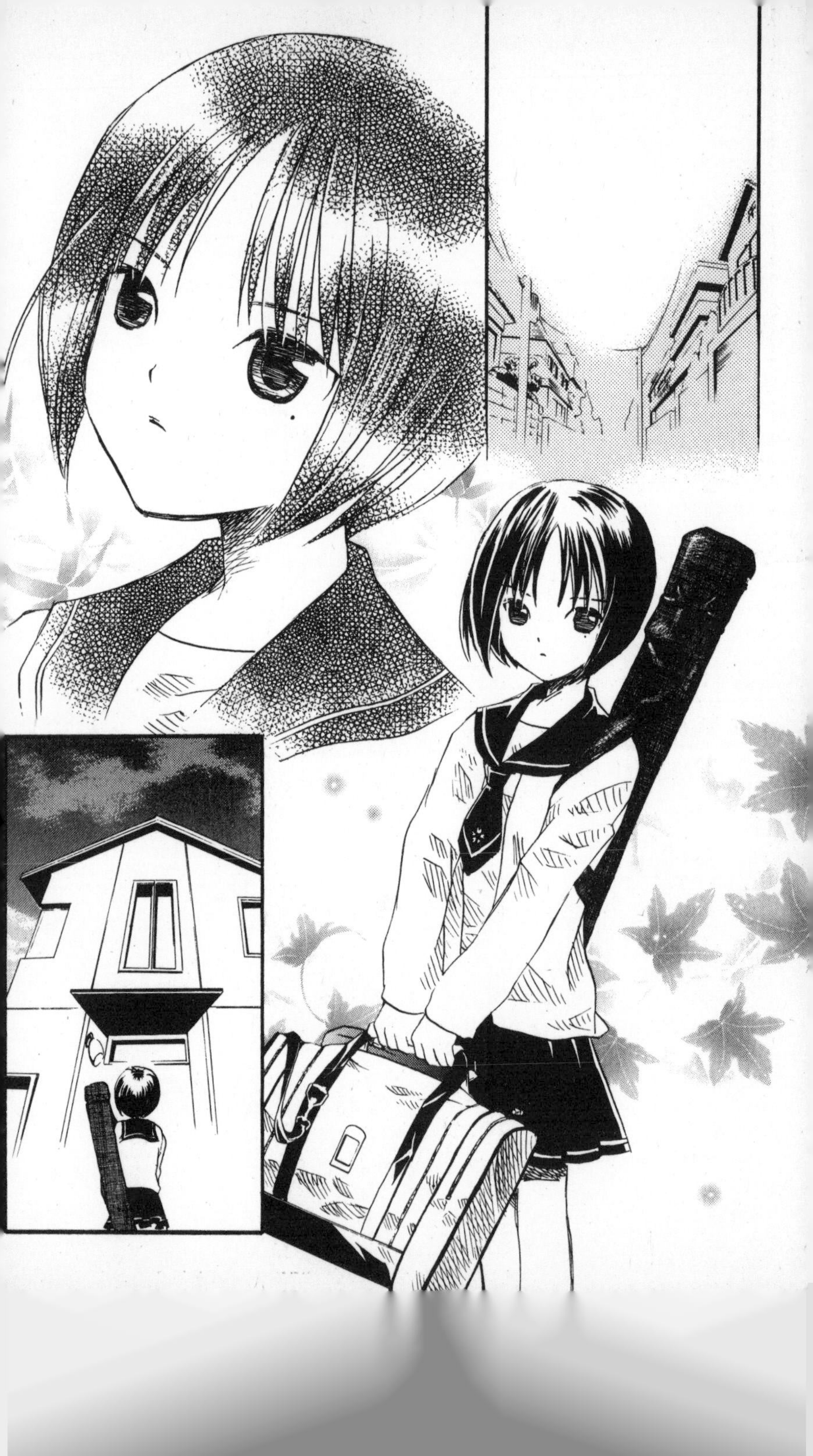

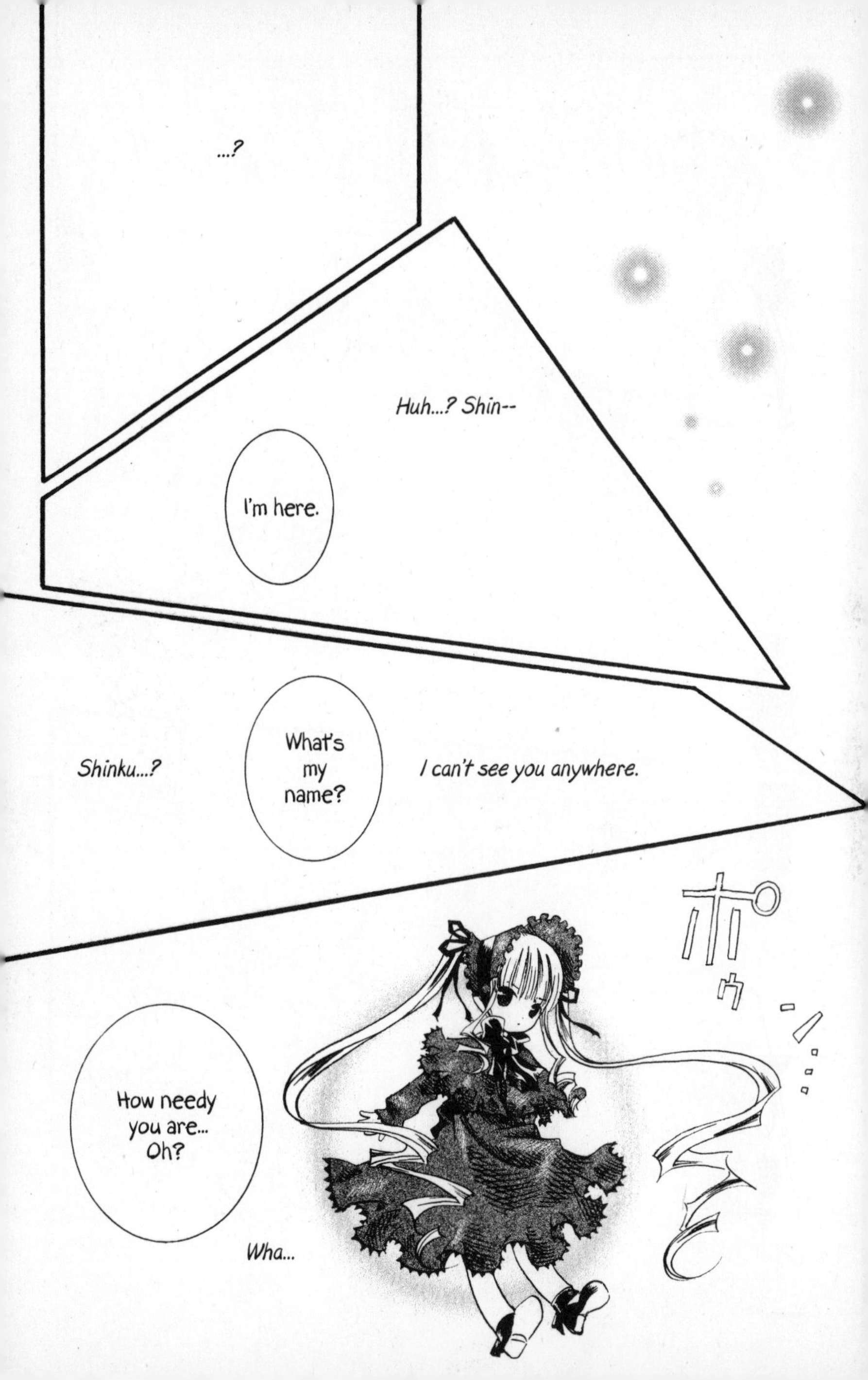

...?
Huh...? Shin--
I'm here.
I can't see you anywhere.
What's my name?
Shinku...?
ポゥ
Wha...
How needy you are... Oh?

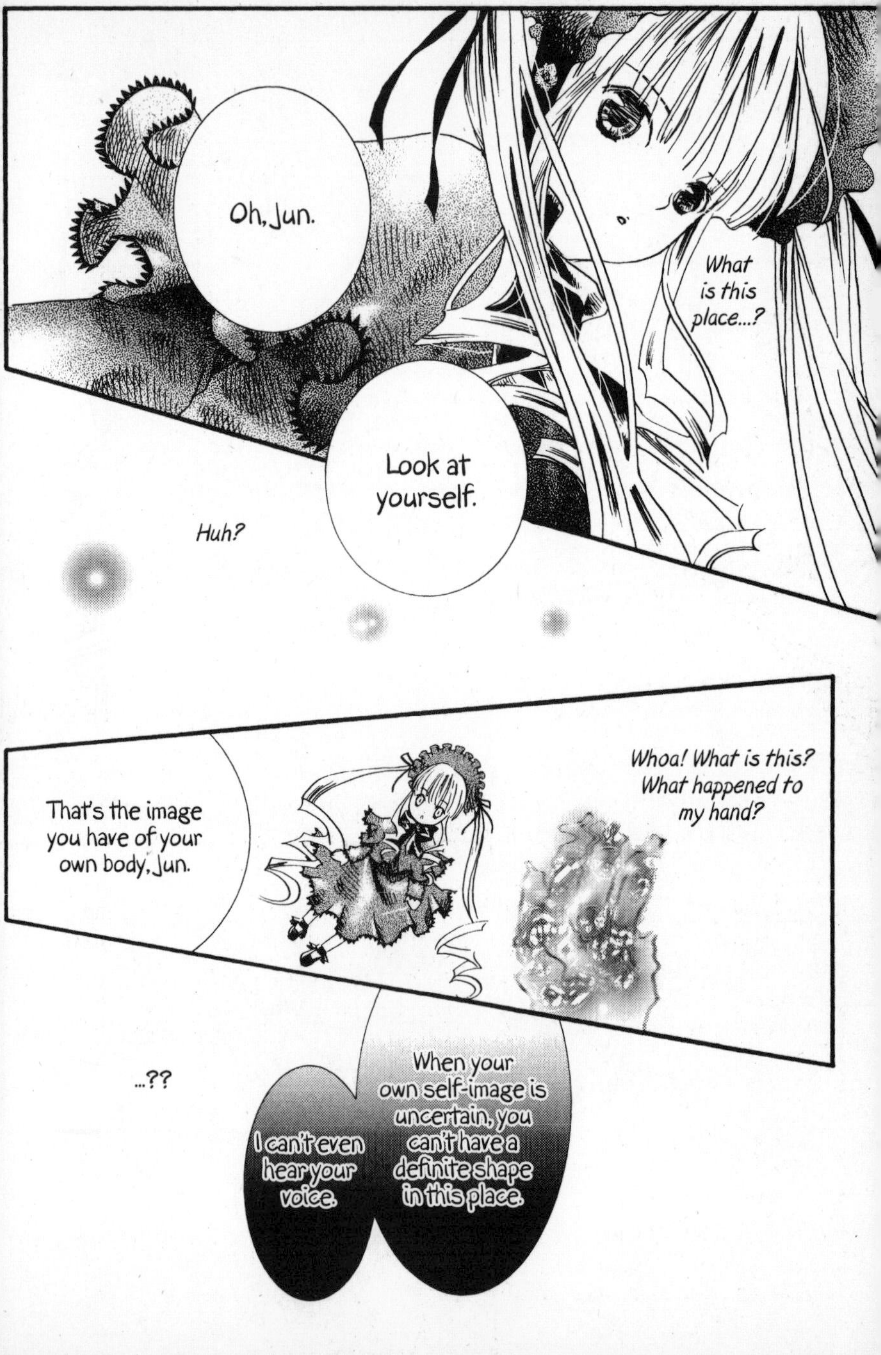
Oh, Jun.
What is this place...?
Look at yourself.
Huh?
Whoa! What is this? What happened to my hand?
That's the image you have of your own body, Jun.
When your own self-image is uncertain, you can't have a definite shape in this place.
I can't even hear your voice.
...??

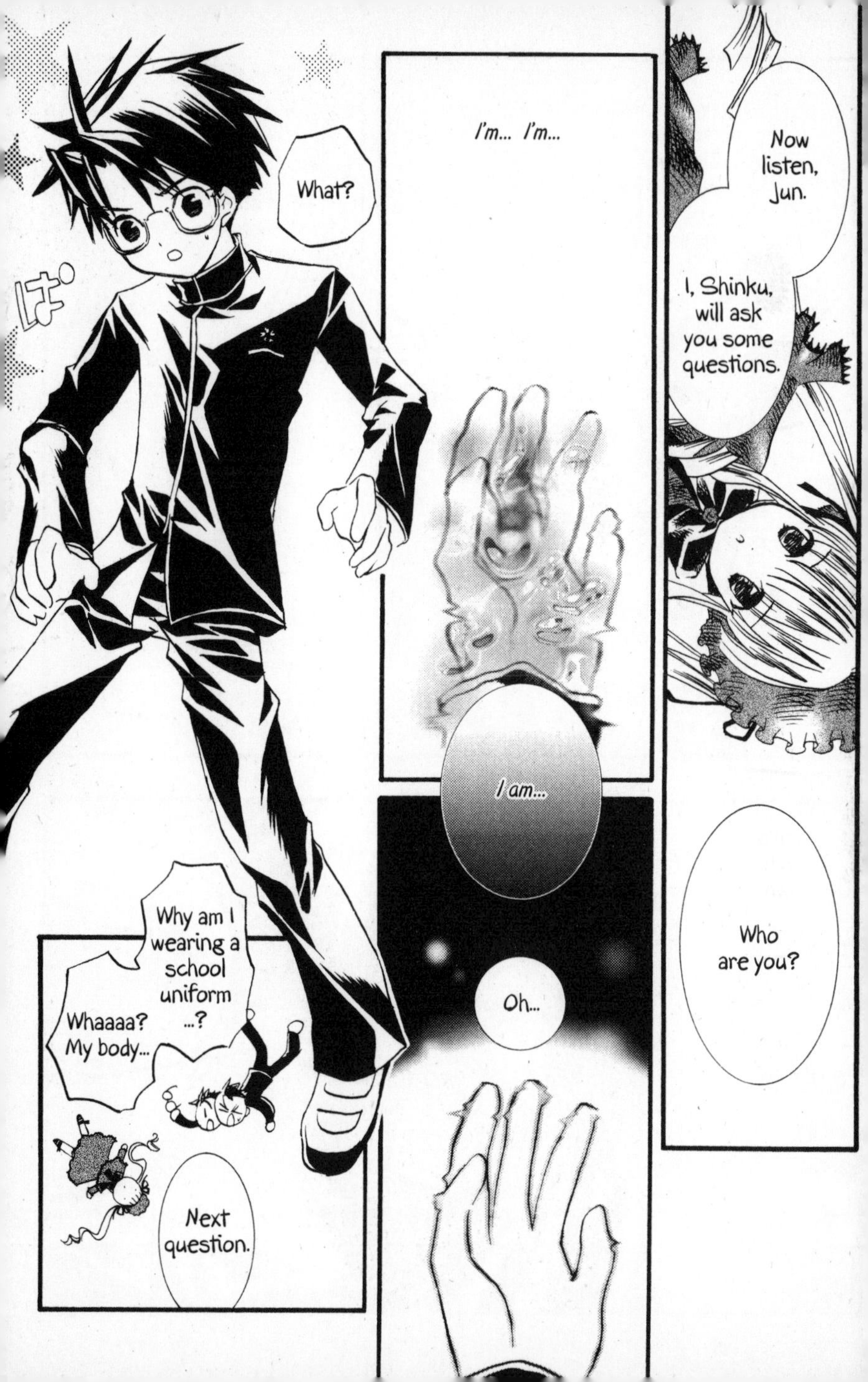

Now listen, Jun.
I, Shinku, will ask you some questions.
Who are you?
I'm... I'm...
I am...
Oh...
What?
ぱ
Why am I wearing a school uniform ...?
Whaaaa? My body...
Next question.

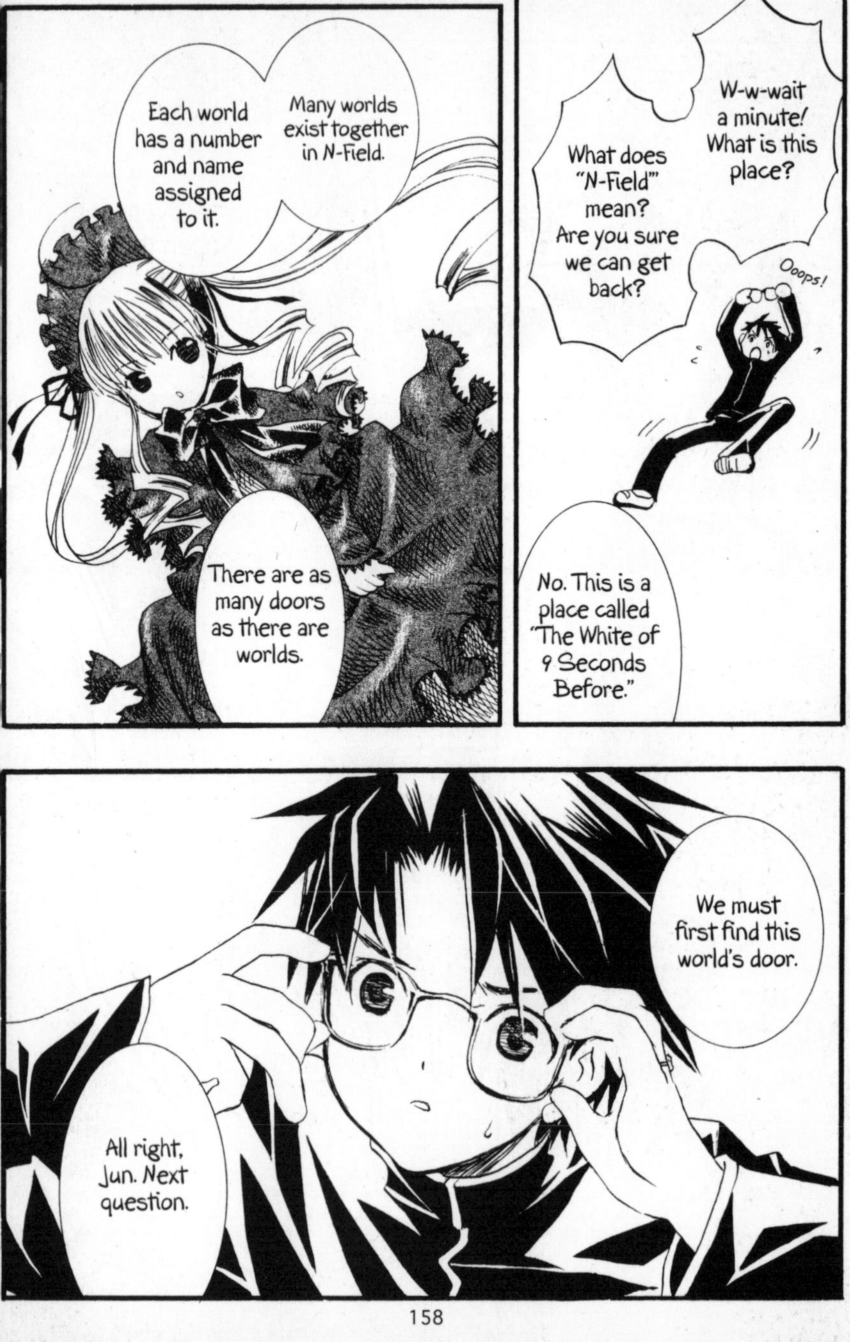
W-w-wait a minute! What is this place?
What does "N-Field" mean? Are you sure we can get back?
Ooops!
No. This is a place called "The White of 9 Seconds Before."
Many worlds exist together in N-Field.
Each world has a number and name assigned to it.
There are as many doors as there are worlds.
We must first find this world's door.
All right, Jun. Next question.

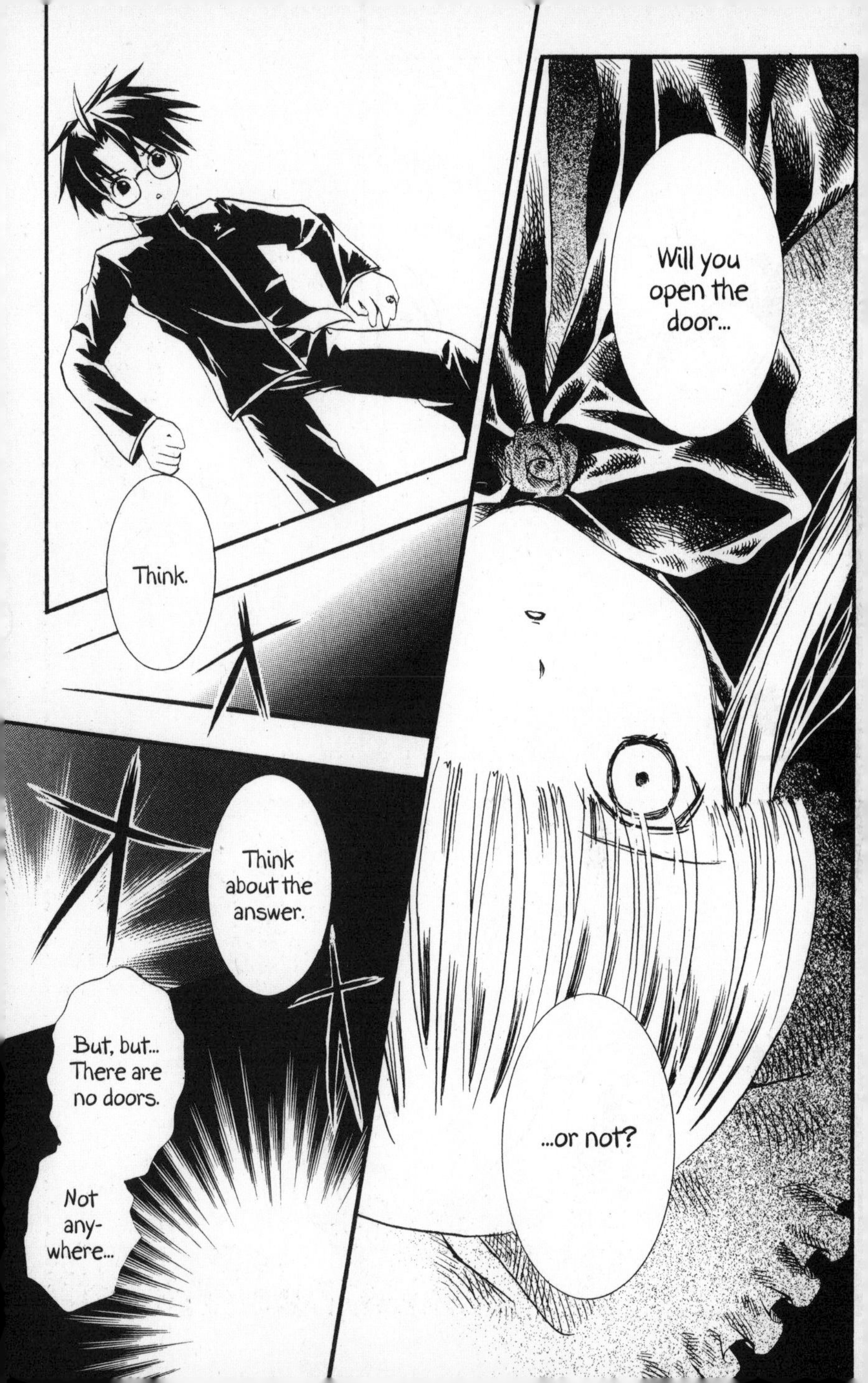
Will you open the door...
...or not?
Think.
Think about the answer.
But, but... There are no doors.
Not any-where...

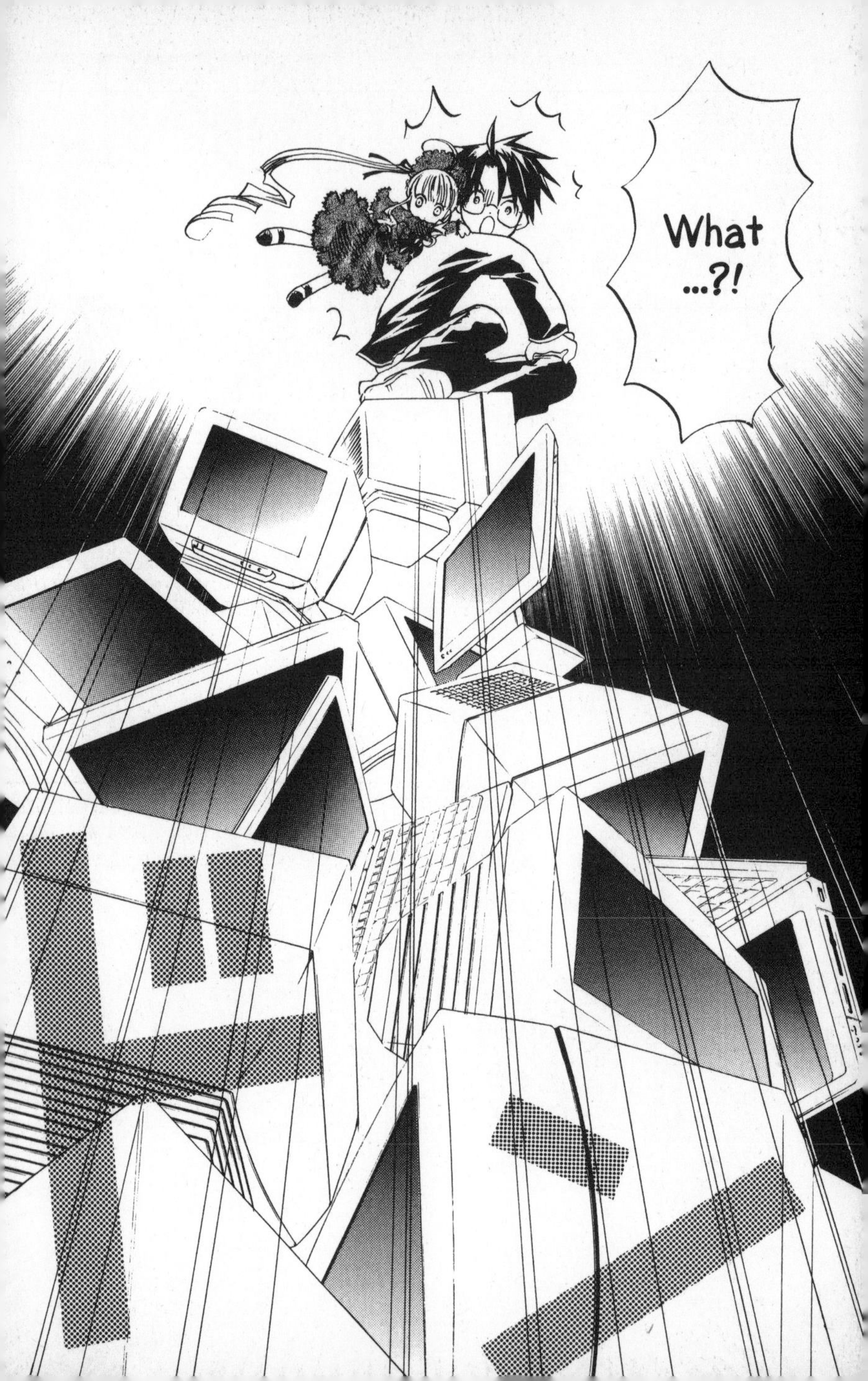
What ...?!

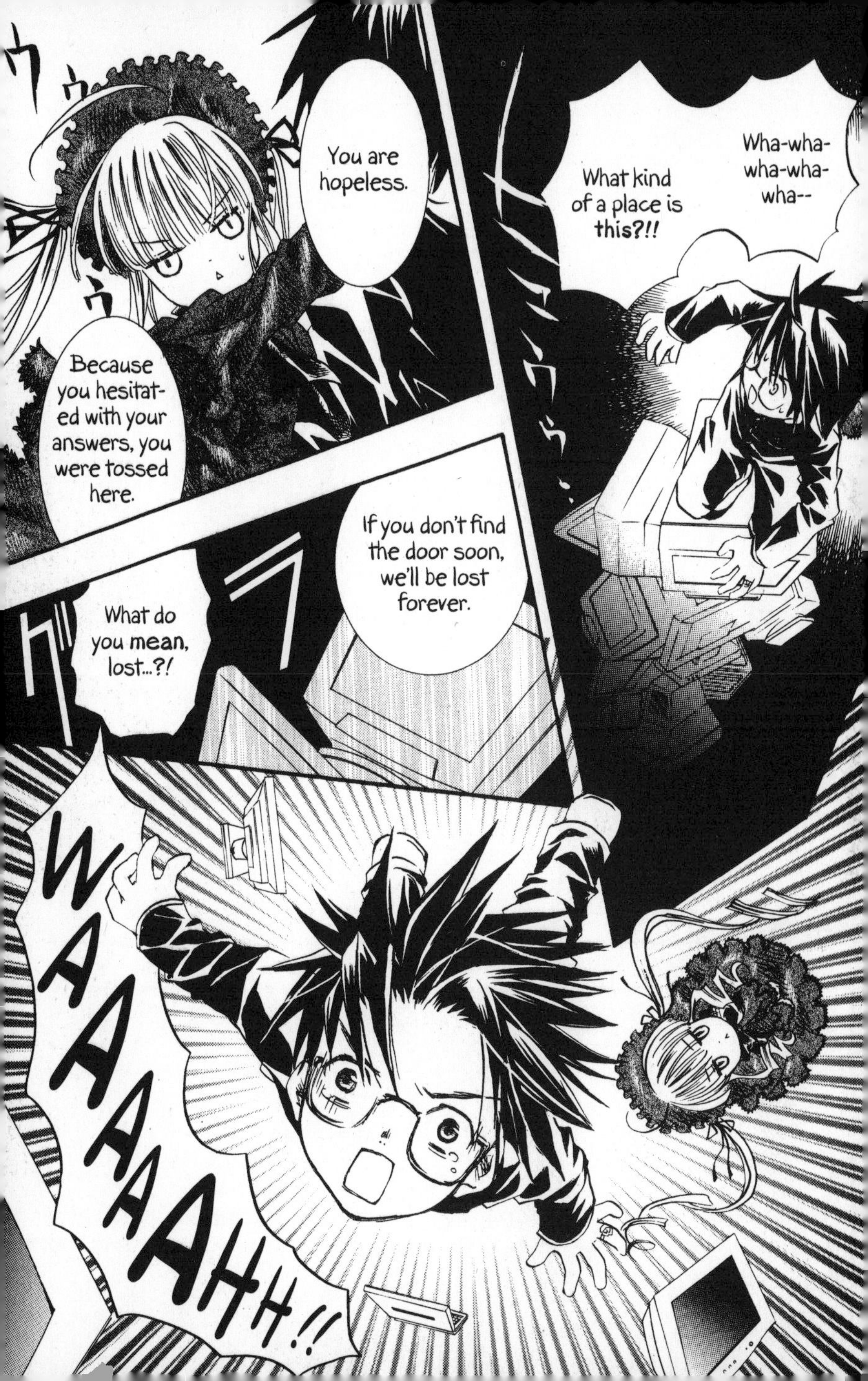
Wha-wha-wha-wha-wha--
What kind of a place is this?!!
You are hopeless.
Because you hesitated with your answers, you were tossed here.
If you don't find the door soon, we'll be lost forever.
What do you mean, lost...?!
WAAAAAHH!!

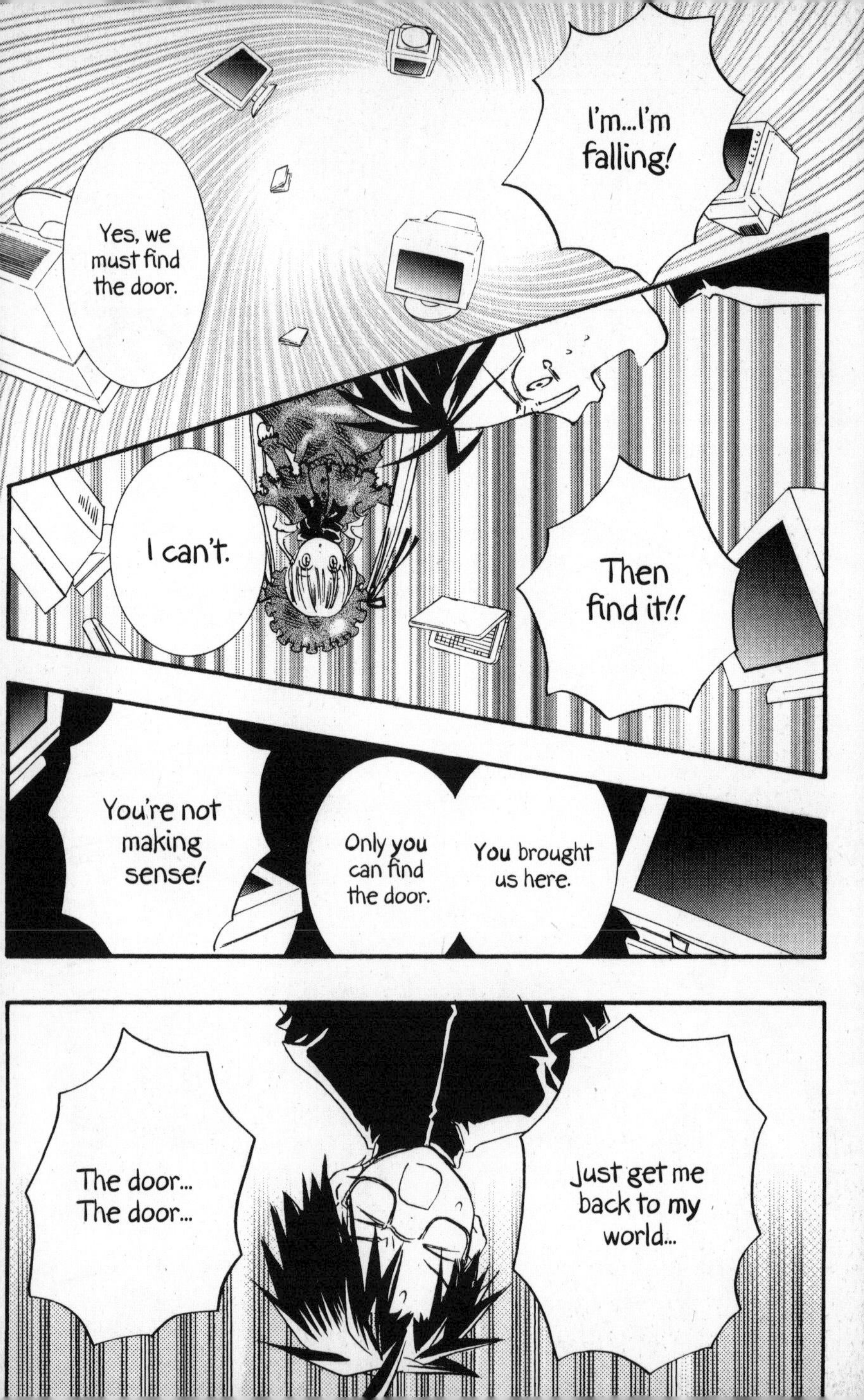
I'm...I'm falling!
Yes, we must find the door.
Then find it!!
I can't.
You brought us here.
Only you can find the door.
You're not making sense!
Just get me back to my world...
The door... The door...

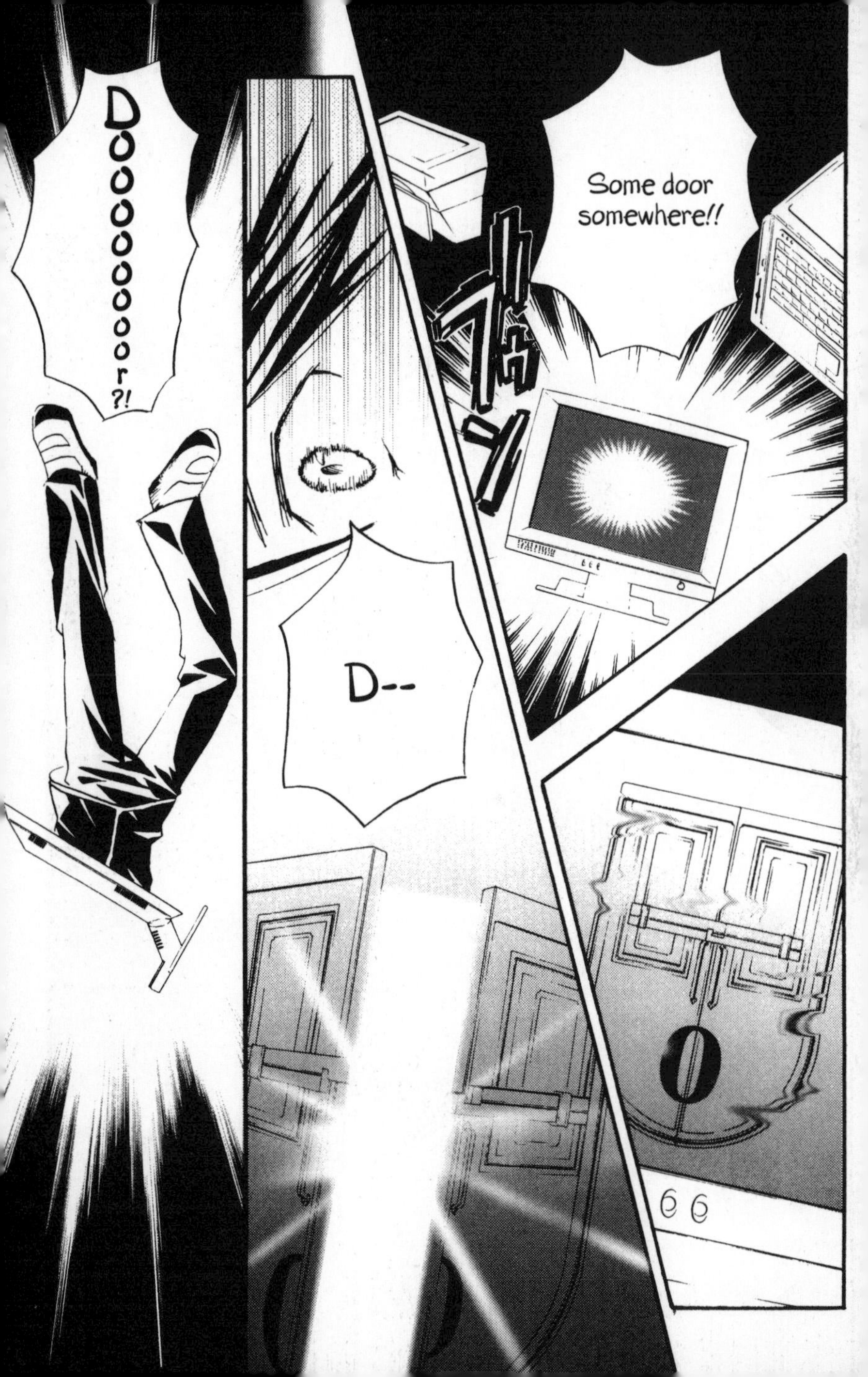
Some door somewhere!!
0
66
D--
Dooooooooooor?!

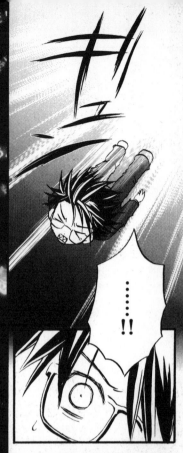

Where are we now?

No way!!

We're back in your world.

164

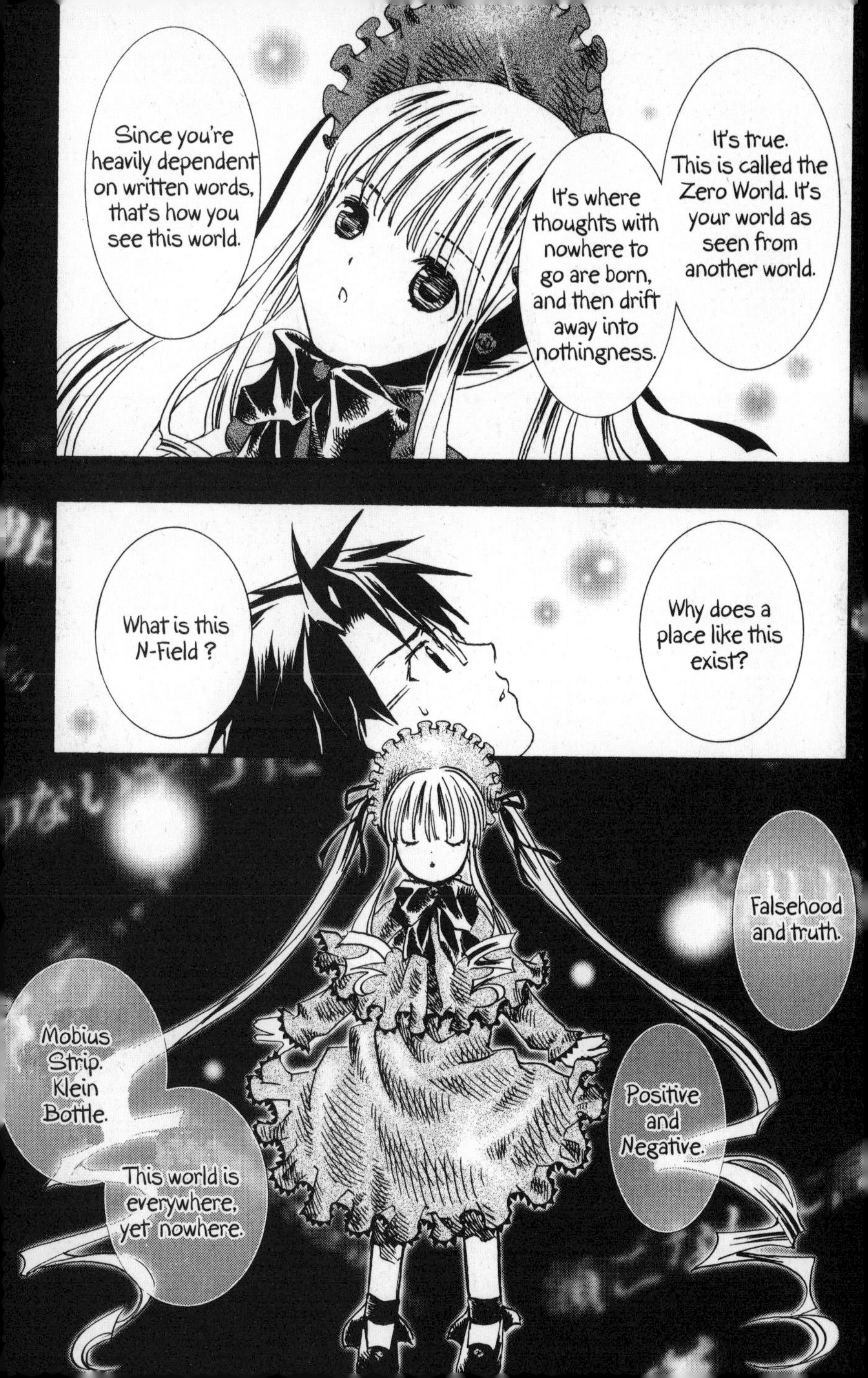
It's true. This is called the Zero World. It's your world as seen from another world.
It's where thoughts with nowhere to go are born, and then drift away into nothingness.
Since you're heavily dependent on written words, that's how you see this world.
Why does a place like this exist?
What is this N-Field ?
Falsehood and truth.
Positive and Negative.
Mobius Strip. Klein Bottle.
This world is everywhere, yet nowhere.

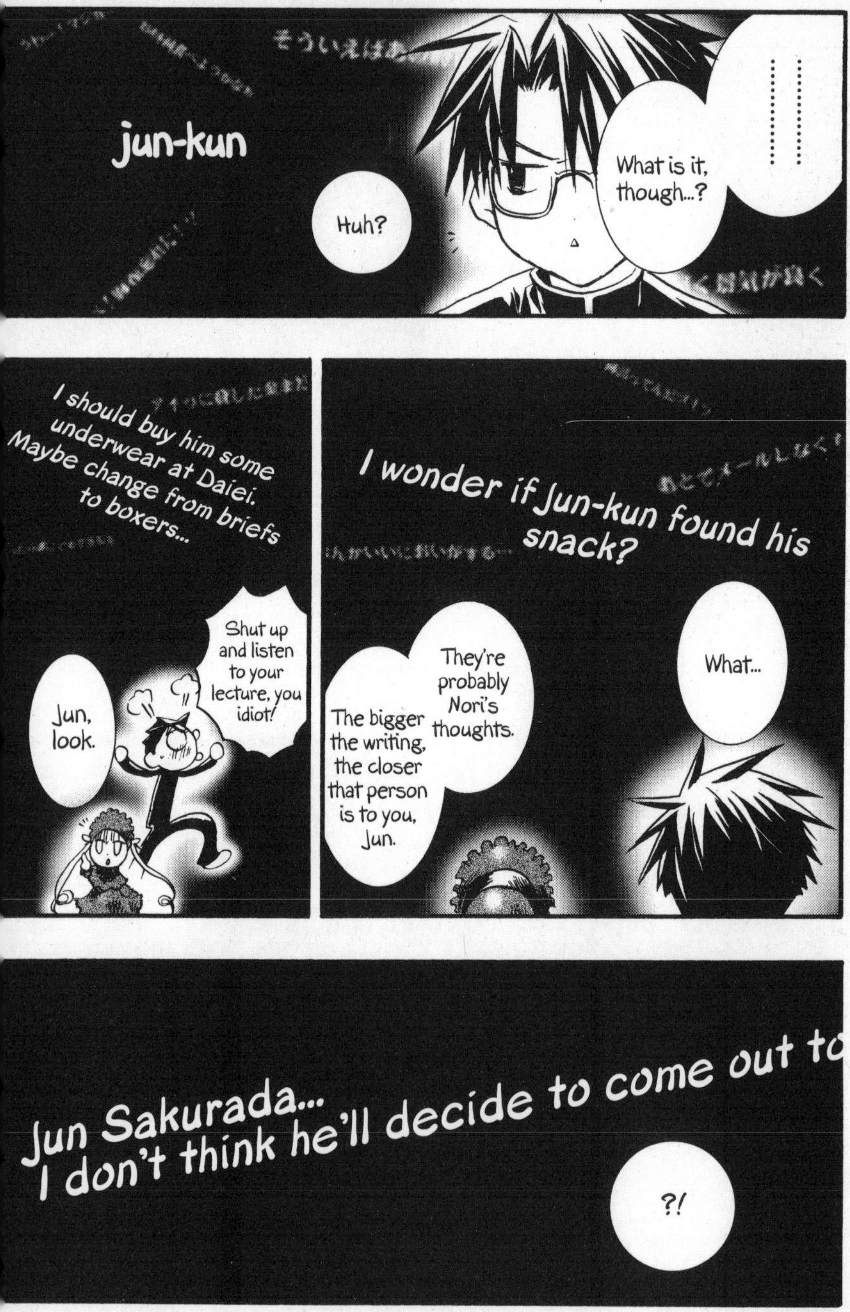
......
What is it, though...?
Huh?
jun-kun
I wonder if Jun-kun found his snack?
What...
They're probably Nori's thoughts.
The bigger the writing, the closer that person is to you, Jun.
I should buy him some underwear at Daiei. Maybe change from briefs to boxers...
Shut up and listen to your lecture, you idiot!
Jun, look.
Jun Sakurada... I don't think he'll decide to come out to
?!

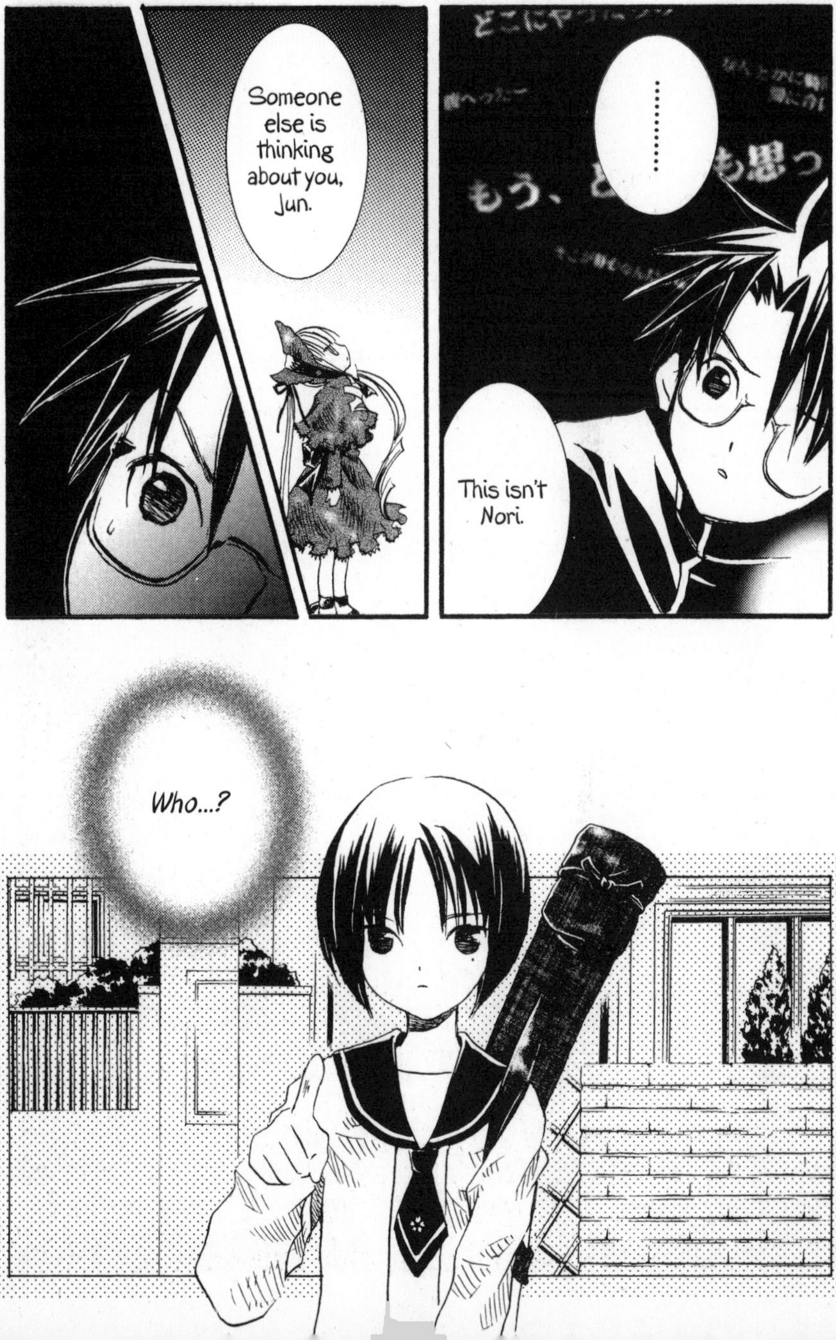
……
This isn't Nori.
Someone else is thinking about you, Jun.
Who...?

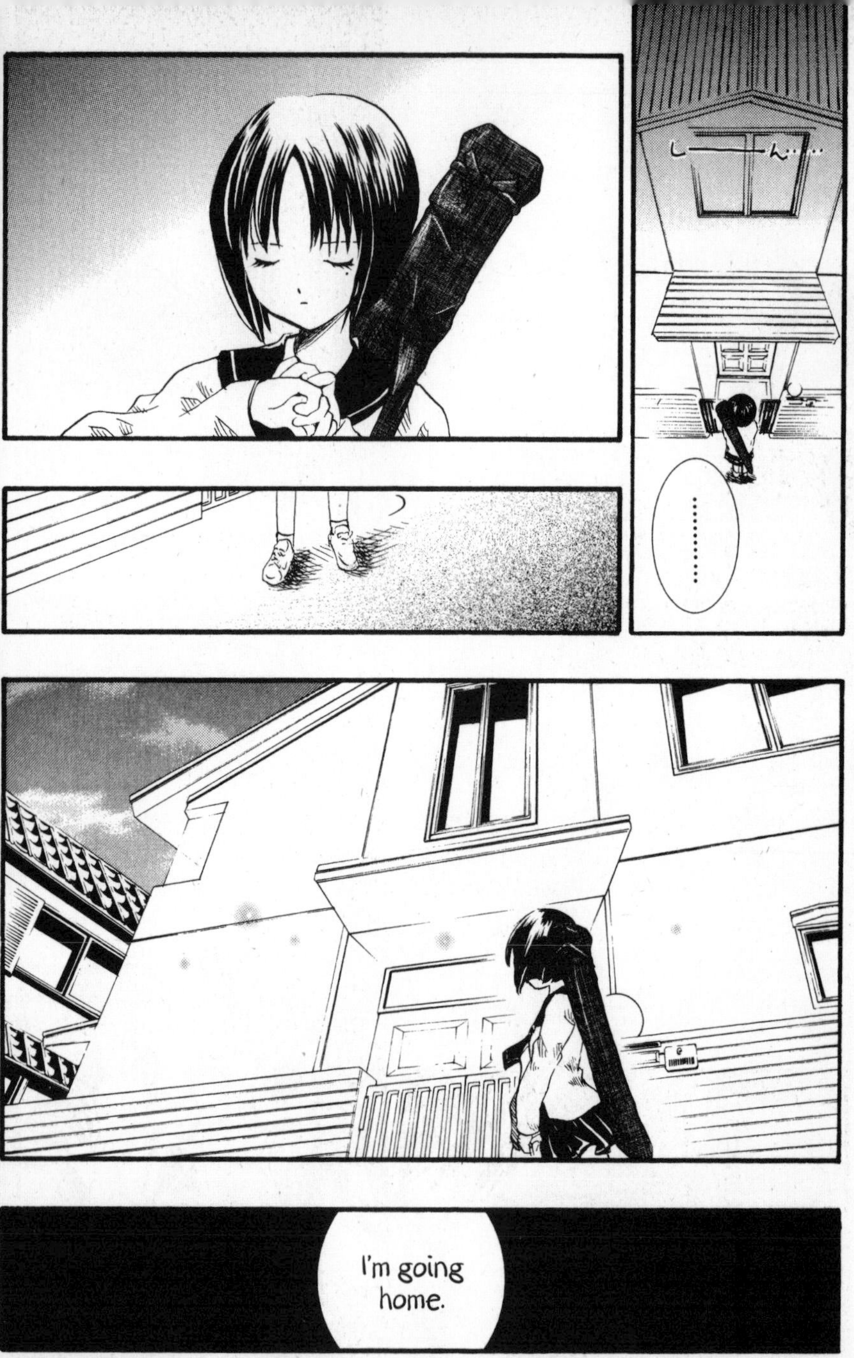
し——ん……
……
I'm going home.

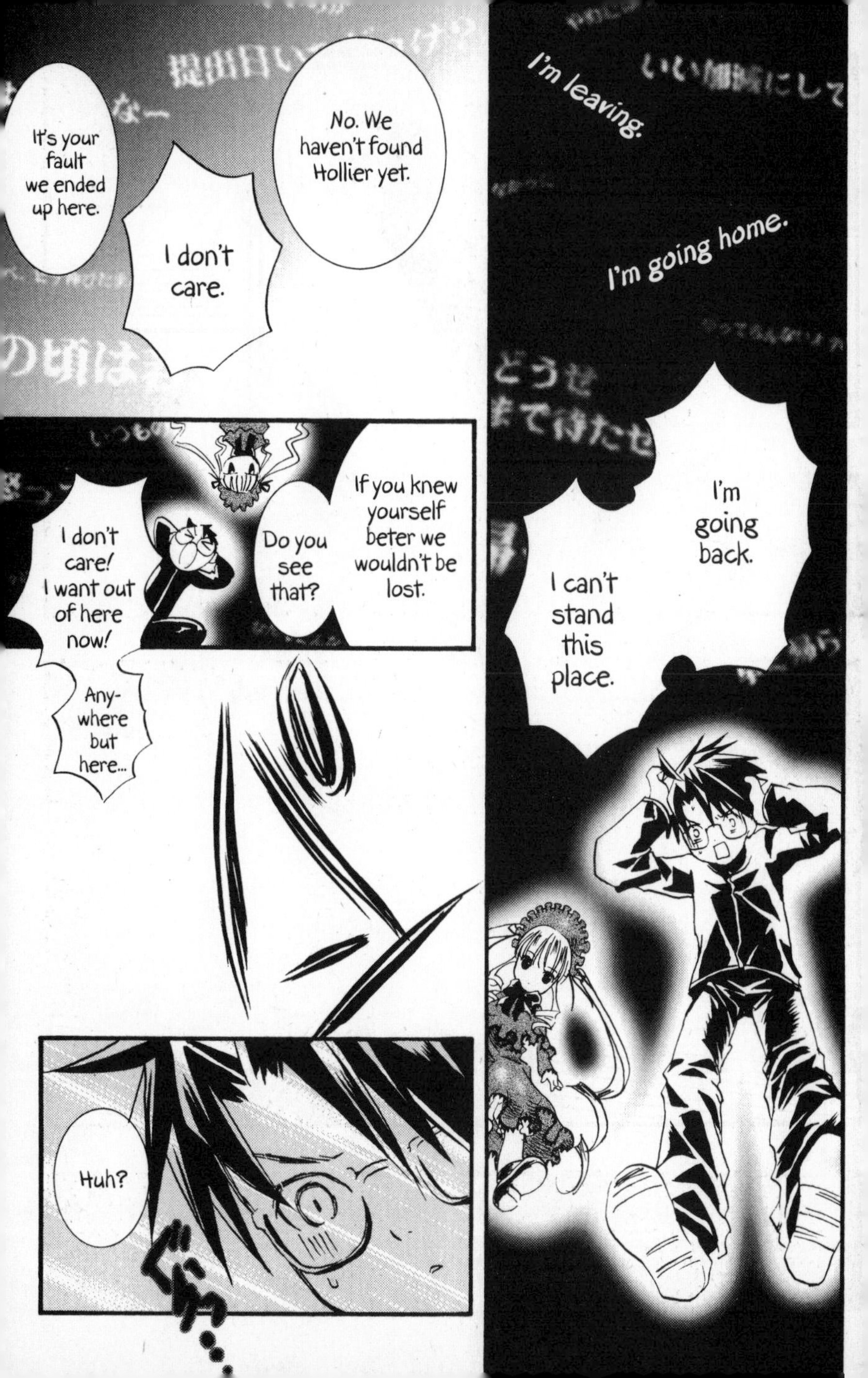
I'm leaving.
I'm going home.
I'm going back.
I can't stand this place.
No. We haven't found Hollier yet.
I don't care.
It's your fault we ended up here.
If you knew yourself beter we wouldn't be lost.
Do you see that?
I don't care! I want out of here now!
Any-where but here...
Huh?

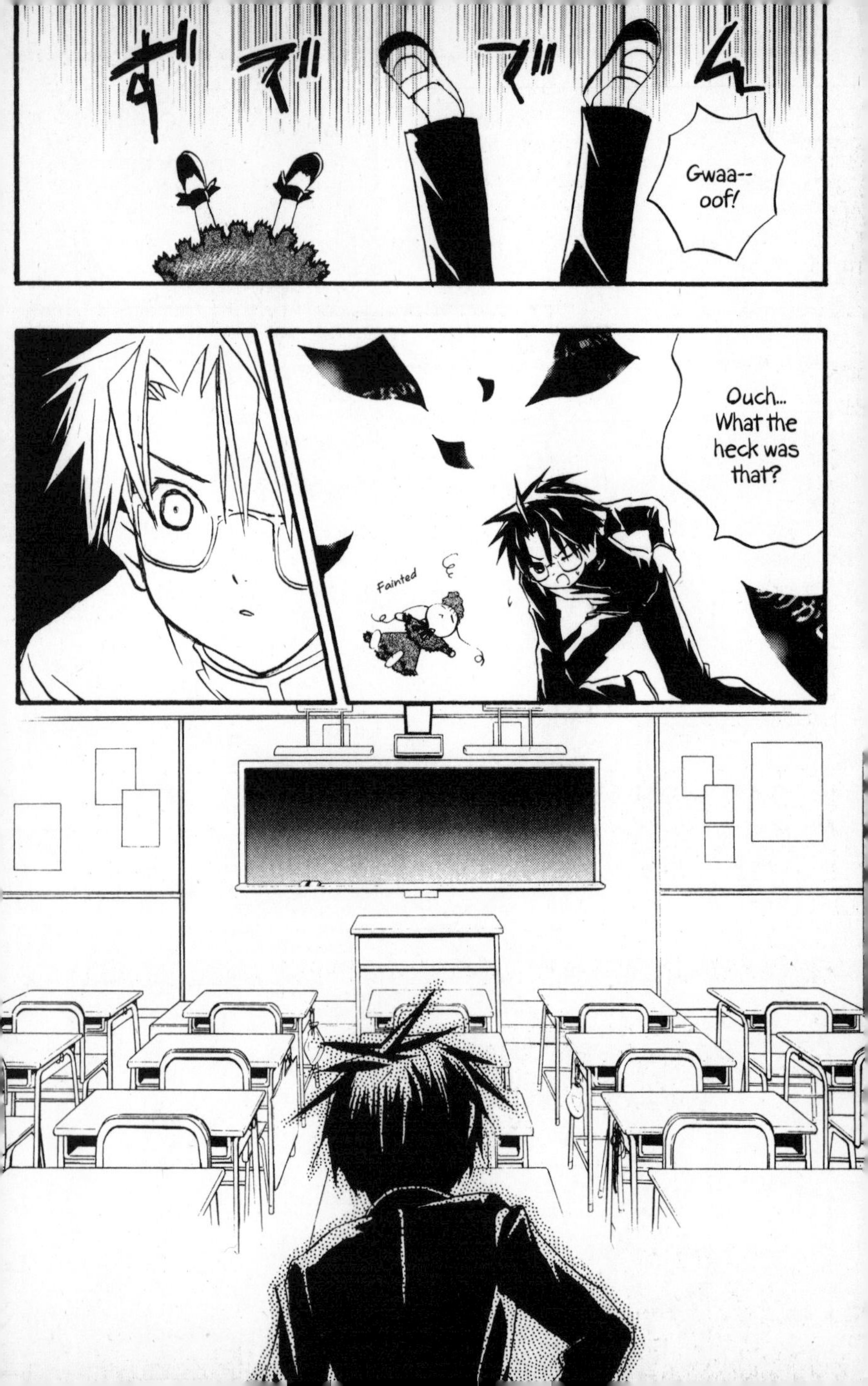
Gwaa--
oof!
Ouch... What the heck was that?
Fainted

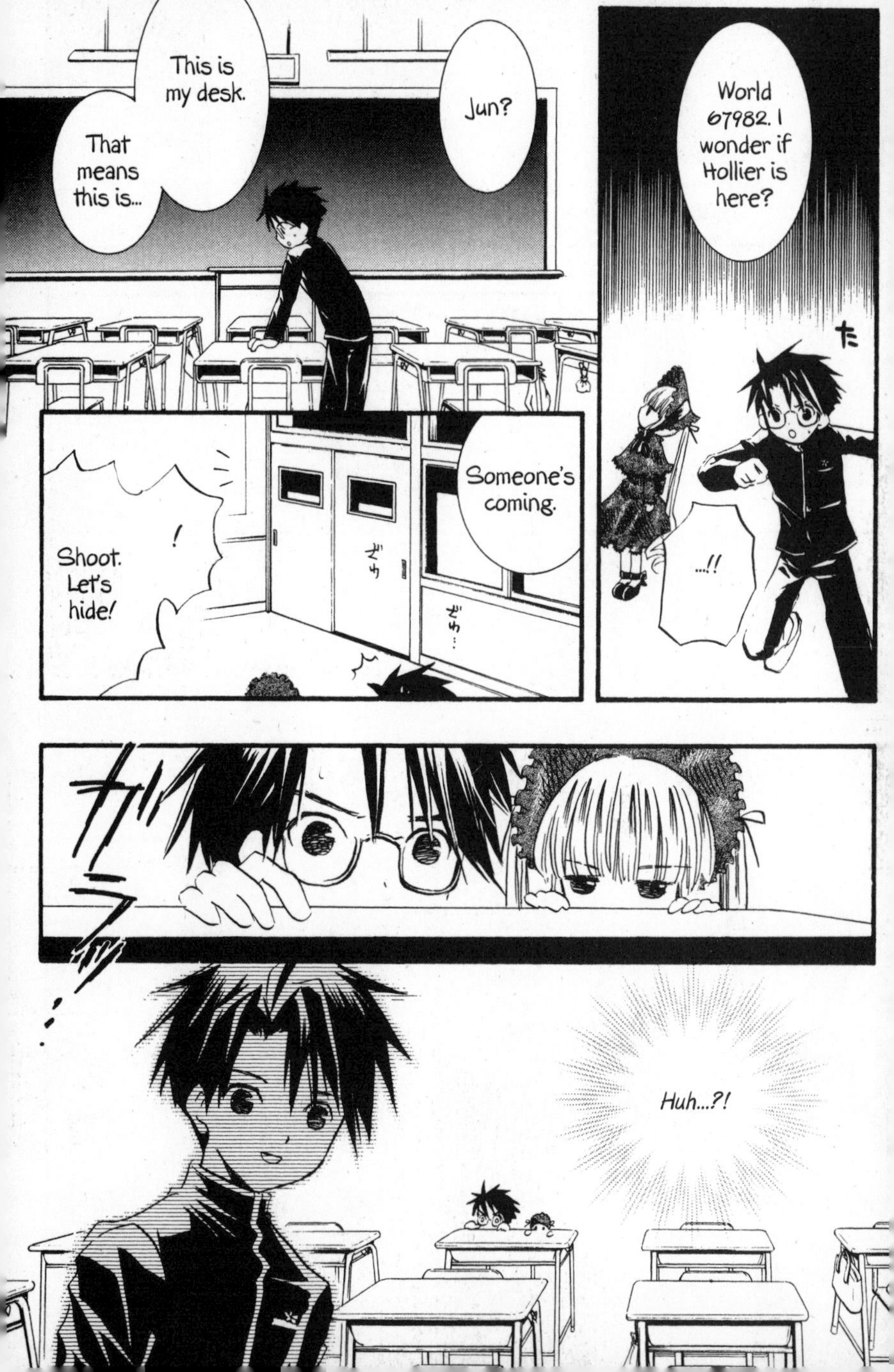
World 67982. I wonder if Hollier is here?
...!!
Jun?
This is my desk.
That means this is...
Someone's coming.
ざわ
ざわ…
!
Shoot. Let's hide!
Huh...?!

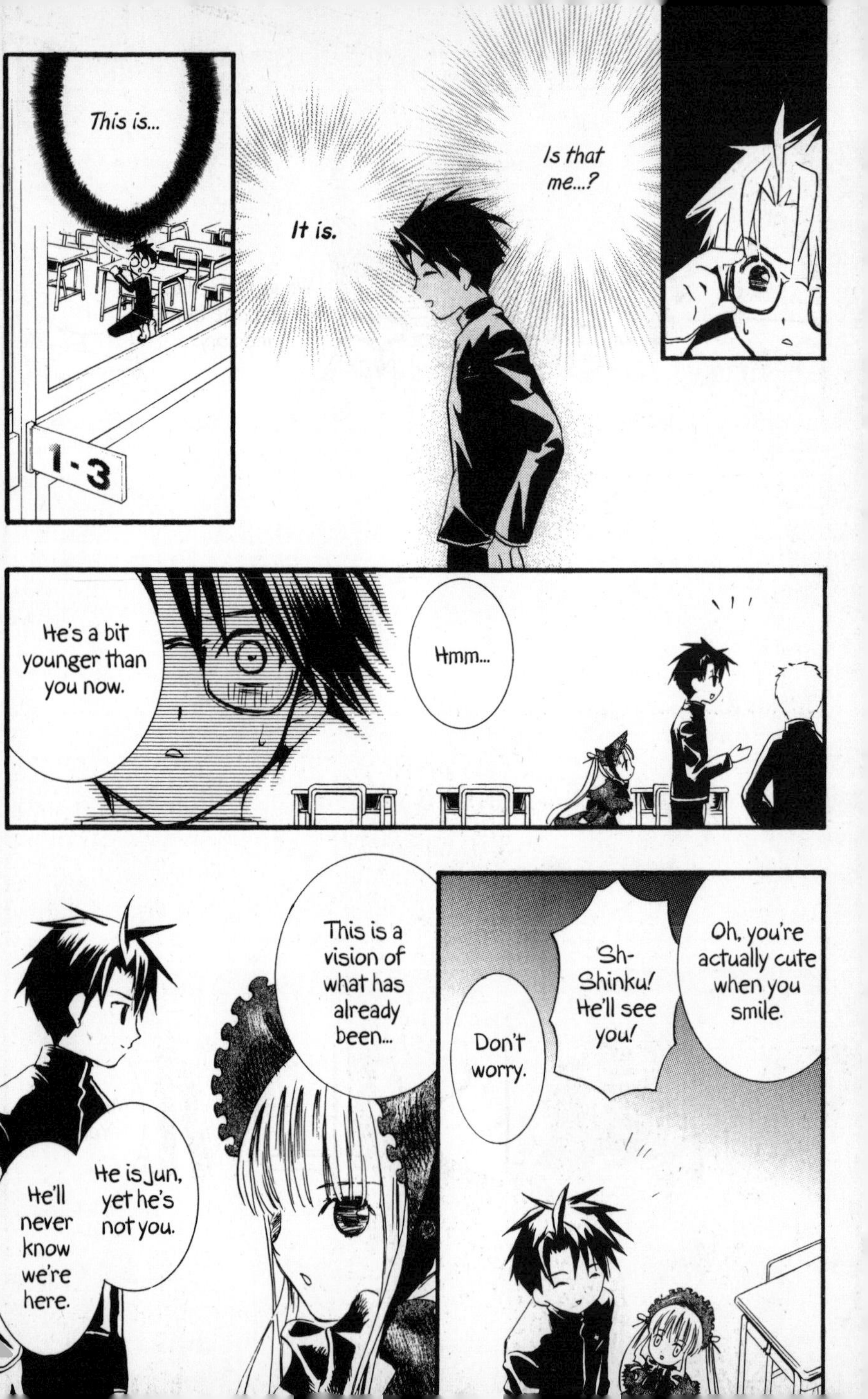
Is that me...?
It is.
This is...
1-3
Hmm...
He's a bit younger than you now.
Oh, you're actually cute when you smile.
Sh- Shinku! He'll see you!
Don't worry.
This is a vision of what has already been...
He is Jun, yet he's not you.
He'll never know we're here.

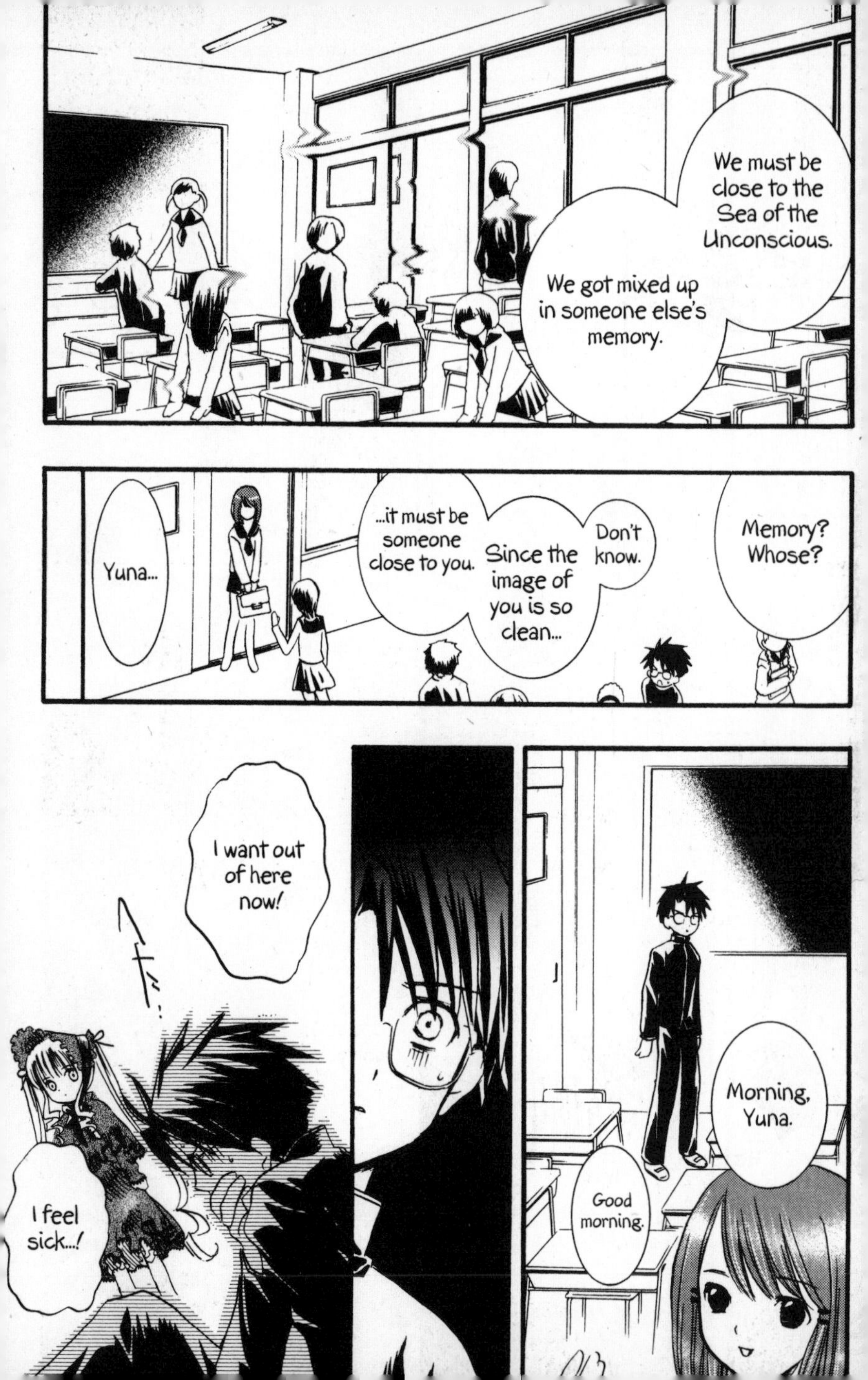
We must be close to the Sea of the Unconscious.
We got mixed up in someone else's memory.
Memory? Whose?
Don't know.
Since the image of you is so clean...
...it must be someone close to you.
Yuna...
Morning, Yuna.
Good morning.
I want out of here now!
I feel sick...!

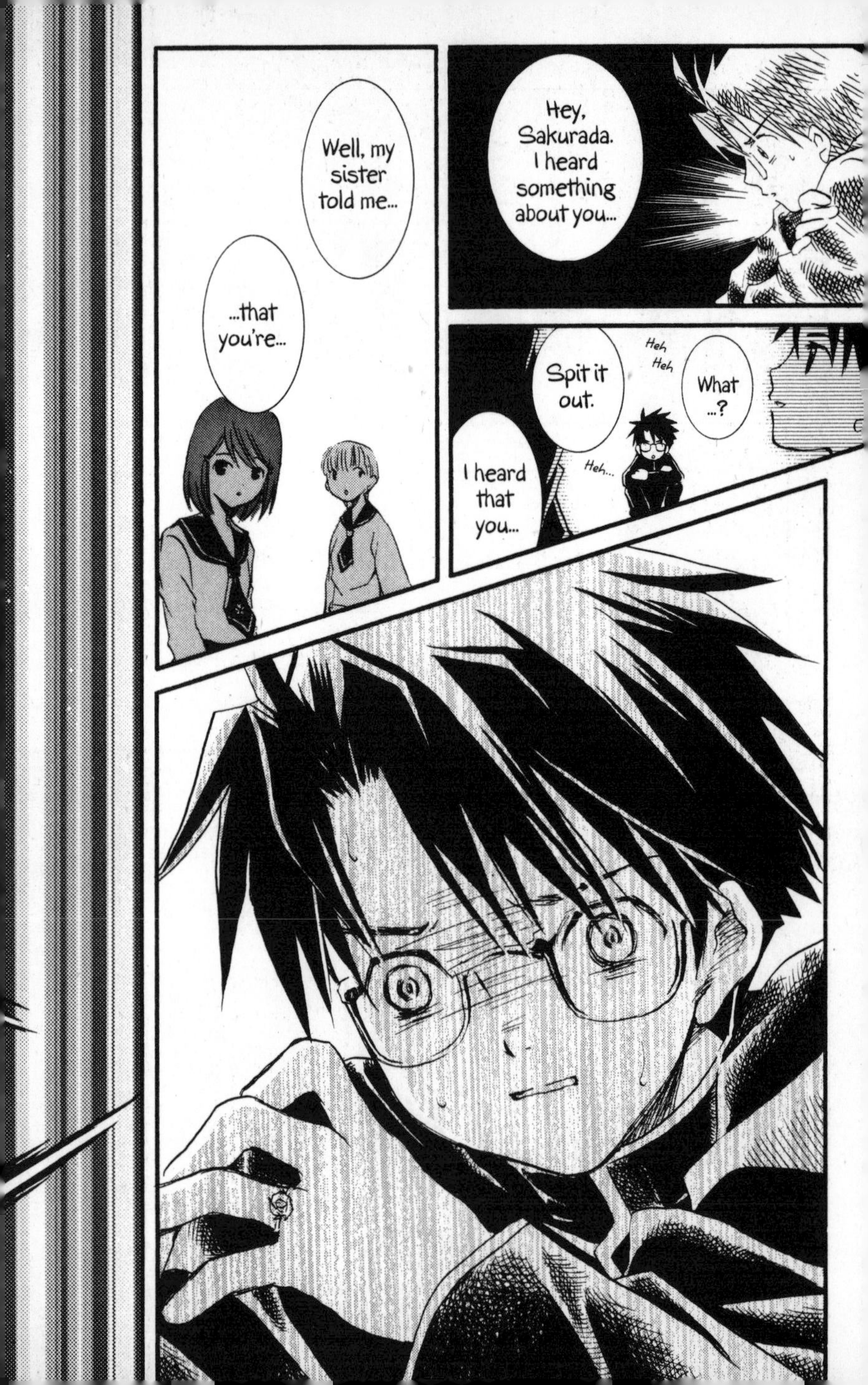
Hey, Sakurada. I heard something about you...
What ...?
Heh Heh
Spit it out.
Heh...
I heard that you...
Well, my sister told me...
...that you're...

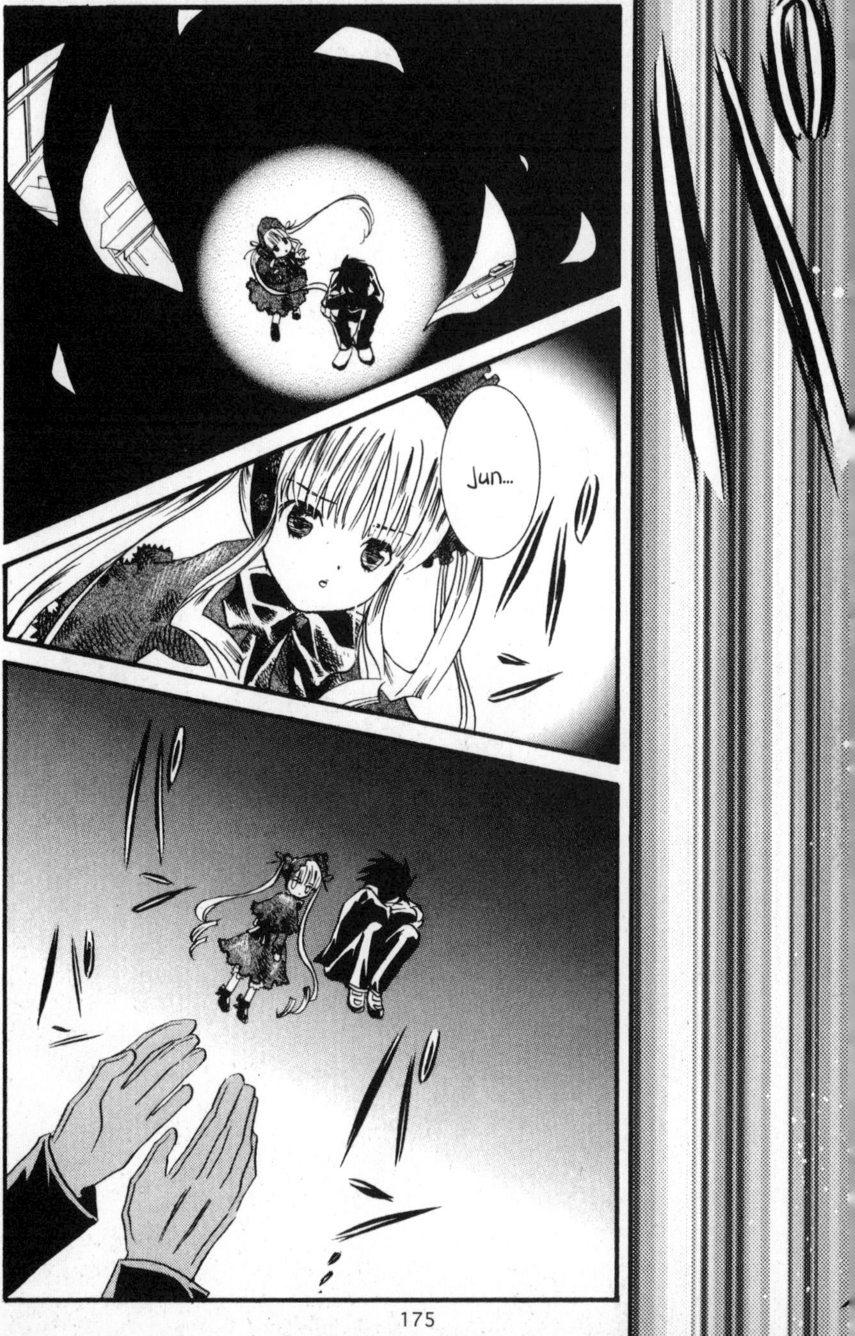
Jun...

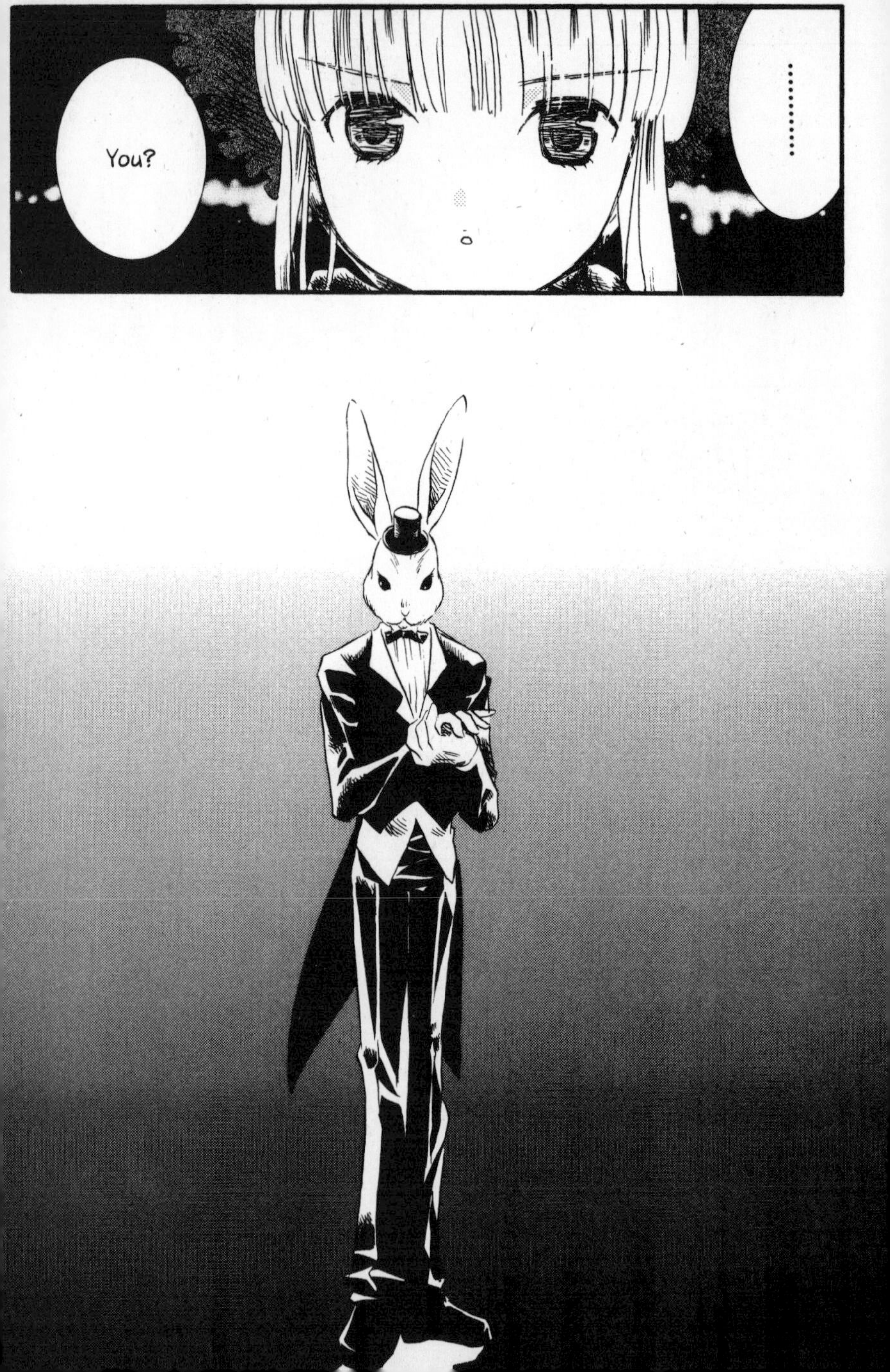
......
You?

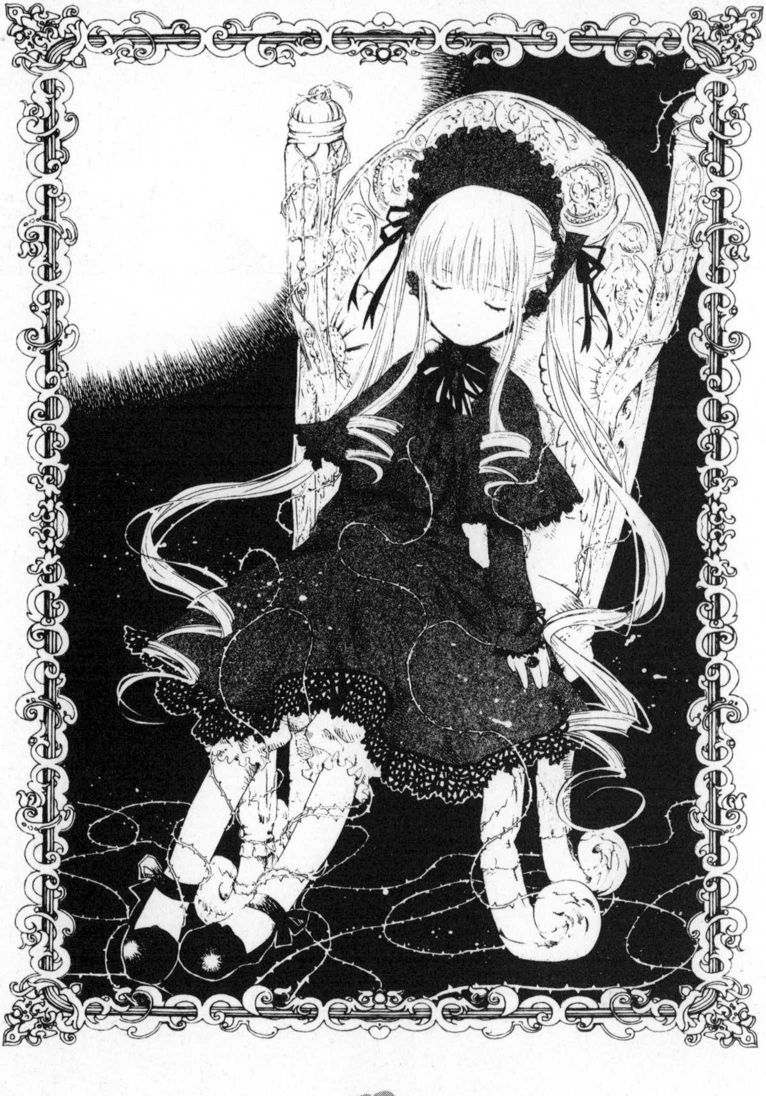

To be continued, see you next phase.

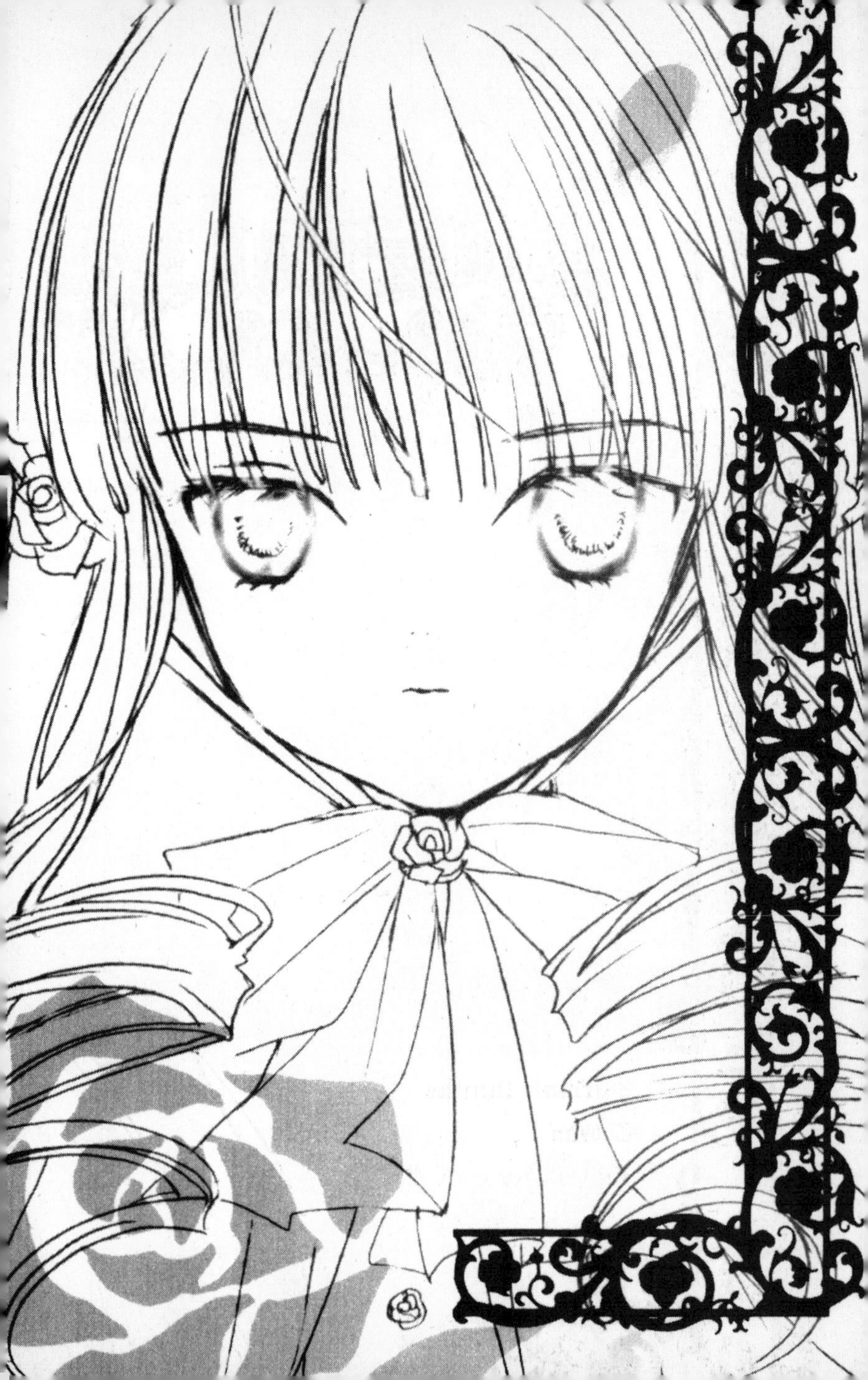

ローゼン メイデン

Rozen Maiden

all produced by

PEACH-PIT

Shibuko Ebara***Banri Sendou

MAIN STAFF
Nao
Zaki
Momiji
Kinomin
Bunbun

Special thanks
T.Oda
Kai Takako A.Minami
...and your reading

Preview for Volume 2

Shinku gets a new servant in Hinaichigo,
who it turns out belongs to Tomoe, Jun's
childhood friend. However, Hinaichigo's
insatiable need for companionship might
prove harmful to the new doll owner.
And when another Rosen Maiden,
Suiseiseki, shows up exclaiming
that her twin, Soseiseki, has been
taken hostage by a bad human,
its time for Shinku and Jun to find
the missing doll.

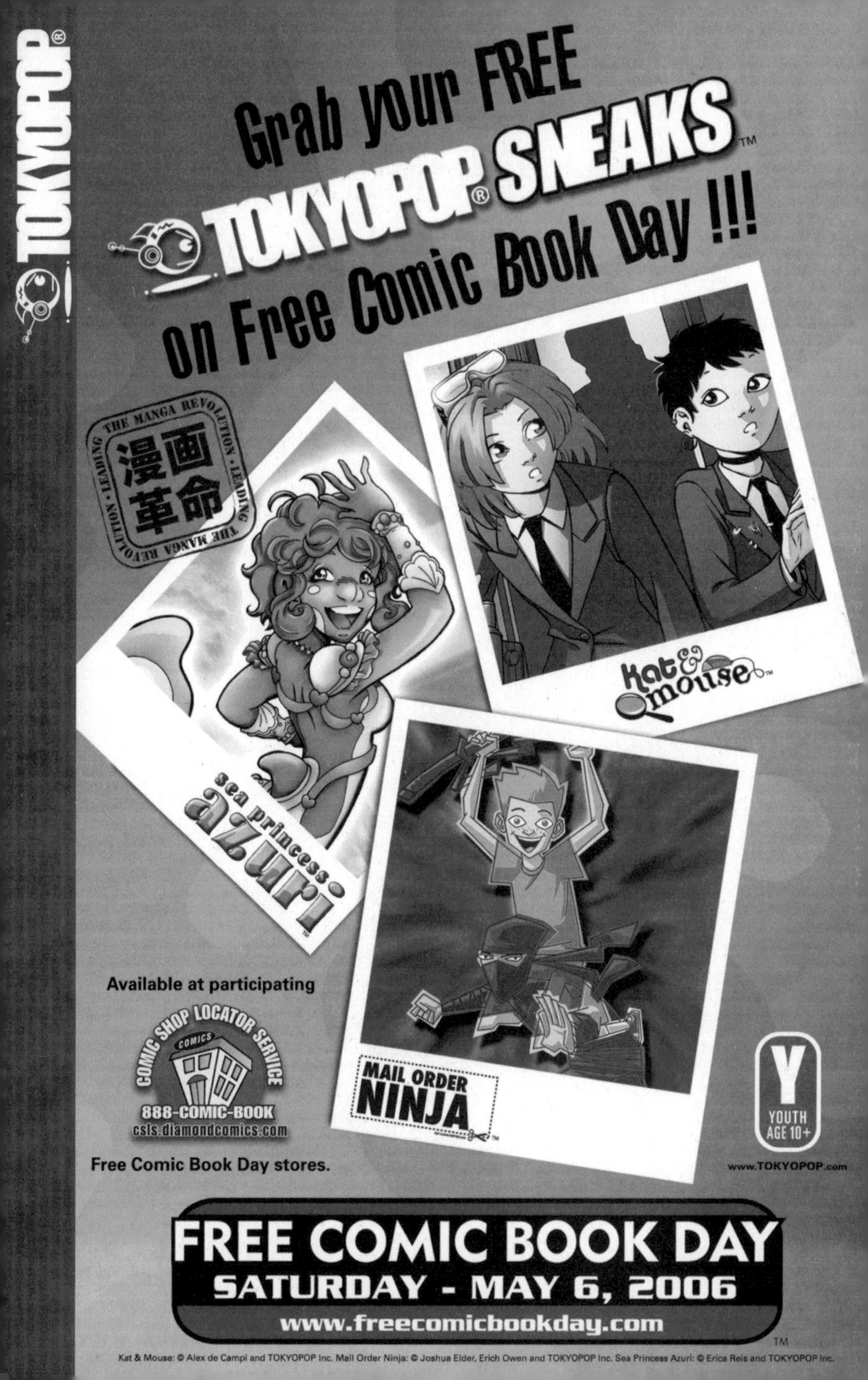
TOKYOPOP®
Grab your FREE
TOKYOPOP® SNEAKS™
on Free Comic Book Day !!!
THE MANGA REVOLUTION · LEADING
漫画革命
THE MANGA REVOLUTION · LEADING
sea princess: azuri™
kat & mouse™
MAIL ORDER NINJA™
Available at participating
COMIC SHOP LOCATOR SERVICE
COMICS
888-COMIC-BOOK
csls.diamondcomics.com
Free Comic Book Day stores.
Y
YOUTH
AGE 10+
www.TOKYOPOP.com
FREE COMIC BOOK DAY
SATURDAY - MAY 6, 2006
www.freecomicbookday.com
TM
Kat & Mouse: © Alex de Campi and TOKYOPOP Inc. Mail Order Ninja: © Joshua Elder, Erich Owen and TOKYOPOP Inc. Sea Princess Azuri: © Erica Reis and TOKYOPOP Inc.

TOKYOPOP SHOP

WWW.TOKYOPOP.COM/SHOP

HOT NEWS!

Check out the **TOKYOPOP SHOP!** The world's best collection of manga in English is now available online in one place!

SOKORA REFUGEES T-SHIRT

LOVE HINA NOVEL

WWW.TOKYOPOP.COM/SHOP

+ANIMA

- LOOK FOR SPECIAL OFFERS
- PRE-ORDER UPCOMING RELEASES
- COMPLETE YOUR COLLECTIONS

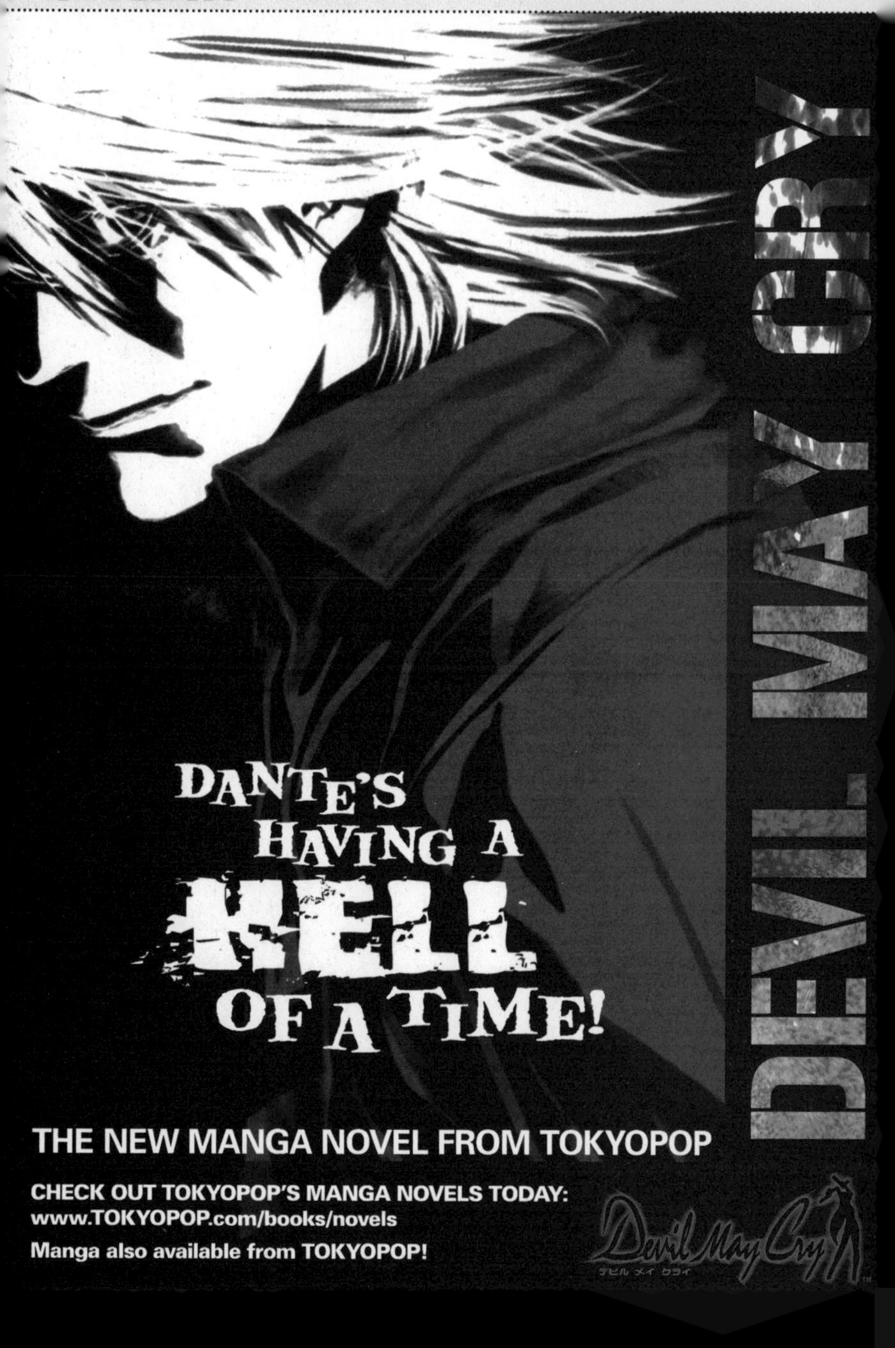
DEVIL MAY CRY
DANTE'S HAVING A HELL OF A TIME!
THE NEW MANGA NOVEL FROM TOKYOPOP
CHECK OUT TOKYOPOP'S MANGA NOVELS TODAY:
www.TOKYOPOP.com/books/novels
Manga also available from TOKYOPOP!
Devil May Cry
デビル メイ クライ

THIS FALL, TOKYOPOP CREATES A FRESH, NEW CHAPTER IN TEEN NOVELS...

For Adventurers...
Witches' Forest:
The Adventures of Duan Surk

By Mishio Fukazawa
Duan Surk is a 16-year-old Level 2 fighter who embarks on the quest of a lifetime—battling mythical creatures and outwitting evil sorceresses, all in an impossible rescue mission in the spooky Witches' Forest!

BASED ON THE FAMOUS
FORTUNE QUEST **WORLD**

For Dreamers...
Magic Moon

By Wolfgang and Heike Hohlbein
Kim enters the enigmatic realm of Magic Moon, where he battles unthinkable monsters and fantastical creatures—in order to unravel the secret that keeps his sister locked in a coma.

THE WORLDWIDE BESTSELLING FANTASY
*THRILL*OGY **ARRIVES IN THE U.S.!**

TOKYOPOP PRESENTS

POP FICTION

For Believers...

Scrapped Princess:
A Tale of Destiny

By Ichiro Sakaki
A dark prophecy reveals that the queen will give birth to a daughter who will usher in the Apocalypse. But despite all attempts to destroy the baby, the myth of the "Scrapped Princess" lingers on...

THE INSPIRATION FOR THE HIT ANIME AND MANGA SERIES!

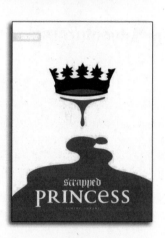

For Thinkers...

Kino no Tabi:
Book One of The Beautiful World

By Keiichi Sigsawa
Kino roams the world on the back of Hermes, her unusual motorcycle, in a journey filled with happiness and pain, decadence and violence, and magic and loss.

THE SENSATIONAL BESTSELLER IN JAPAN HAS FINALLY ARRIVED!

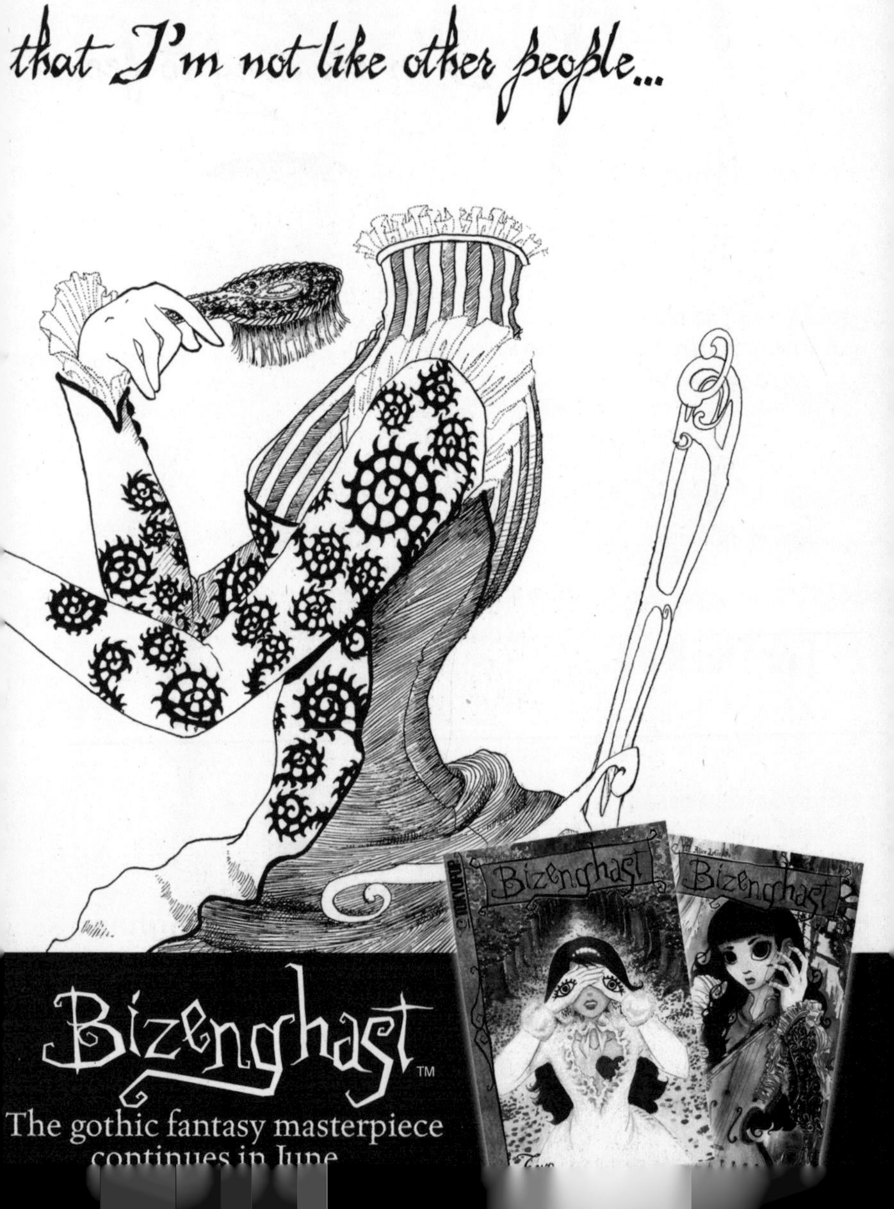
that I'm not like other people...
Bizenghast
Bizenghast
Bizenghast™
The gothic fantasy masterpiece continues in June

Dear Diary,
I'm starting to feel

When a young girl moves to the forgotten town of Bizenghast, she uncovers a terrifying collection of lost souls that leads her to the brink of insanity. One thing becomes painfully clear: The residents of Bizenghast are just dying to come home.

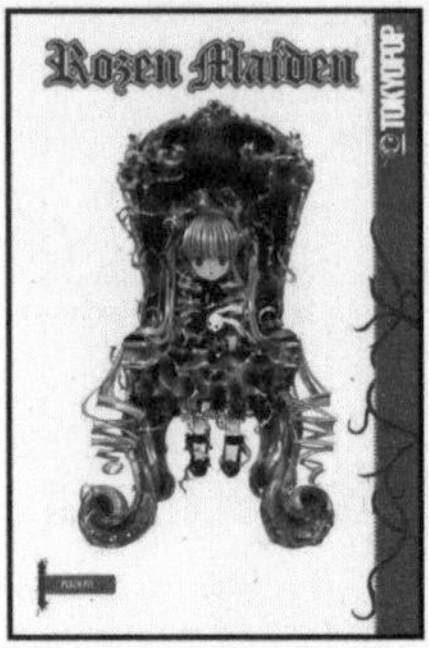
Rozen Maiden
TOKYOPOP

ROZEN MAIDEN

BY PEACH-PIT

Welcome to the world of *Rozen Maiden* where a boy must enter an all-new reality to protect and serve a living doll!

FANTASY

T TEEN AGE 13+

From the creators of *DearS*!

BOYS OF SUMMER

BY CHUCK AUSTEN AND HIROKI OTSUKA

Just because you strike out on your first attempt at scoring with a girl doesn't mean you won't end up hitting a home run!

COMEDY

OT OLDER TEEN AGE 16+

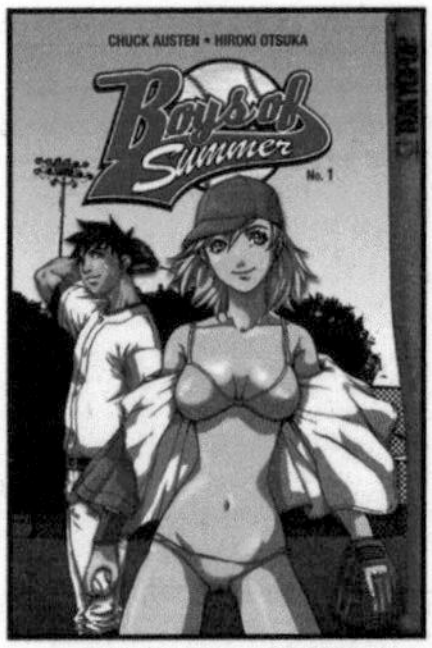
CHUCK AUSTEN • HIROKI OTSUKA
Boys of Summer
No. 1
TOKYOPOP

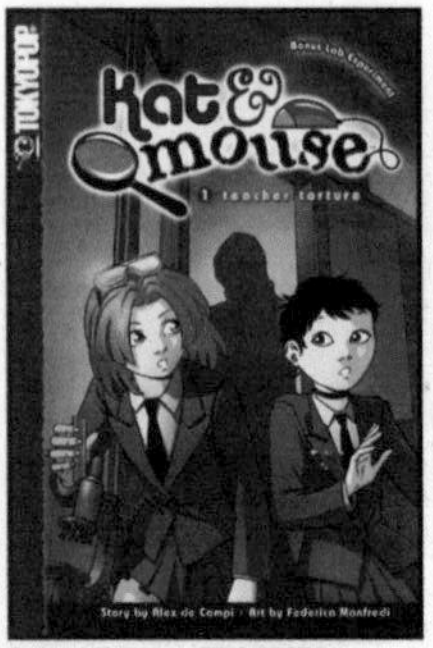
TOKYOPOP
Kat & Mouse
1 teacher torture
Story by Alex de Campi / Art by Federica Manfredi

KAT & MOUSE

BY ALEX DE CAMPI AND FEDERICA MANFREDI

When science whiz Kat teams up with computer nerd Mouse, bullies and blackmailers don't stand a chance!

MYSTERY

A ALL AGES

SHRINE OF THE MORNING MIST

BY HIROKI UGAWA

When the spirit world suddenly shifts out of balance, it's up to sisters Kurako, Yuzu and Tama to save us—but first they must get through their family drama.

FANTASY

T TEEN AGE 13+

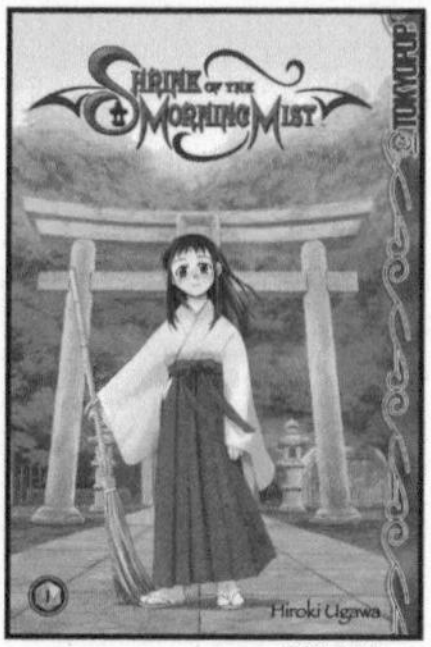
SHRINE OF THE MORNING MIST
TOKYOPOP
Hiroki Ugawa
1

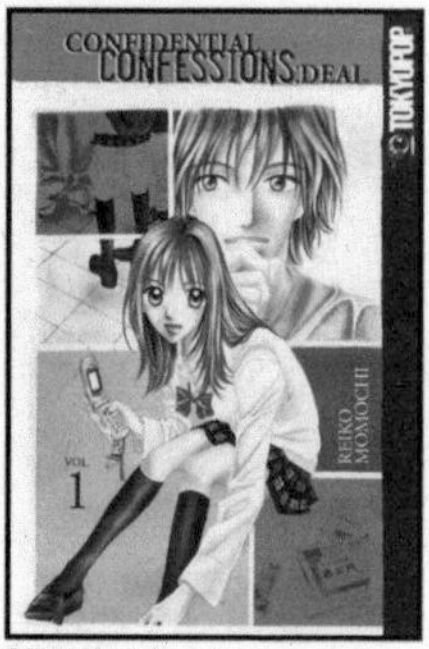
CONFIDENTIAL CONFESSIONS DEAI
TOKYOPOP
REIKO MOMOCHI
VOL. 1

CONFIDENTIAL CONFESSIONS -DEAI-

BY REIKO MOMOCHI

In this unflinching portrayal of teens in crisis, silence isn't always golden...

DRAMA

OT OLDER TEEN AGE 16+

DEATH JAM

BY JEON SANG YOUNG

Muchaca Smooth is an assassin with just one shot to make it big!

ACTION

OT OLDER TEEN AGE 16+

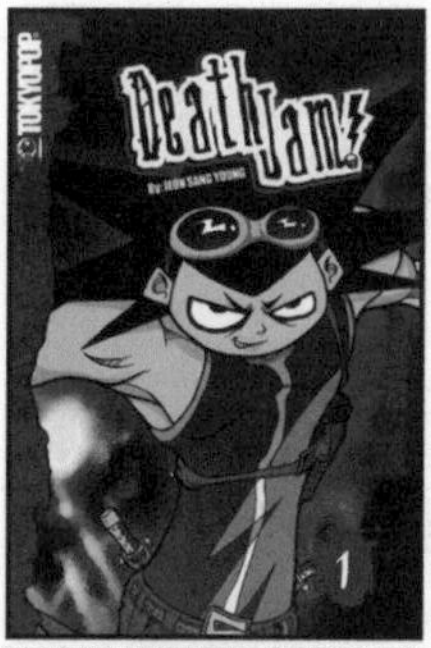
TOKYOPOP
Death Jam
1